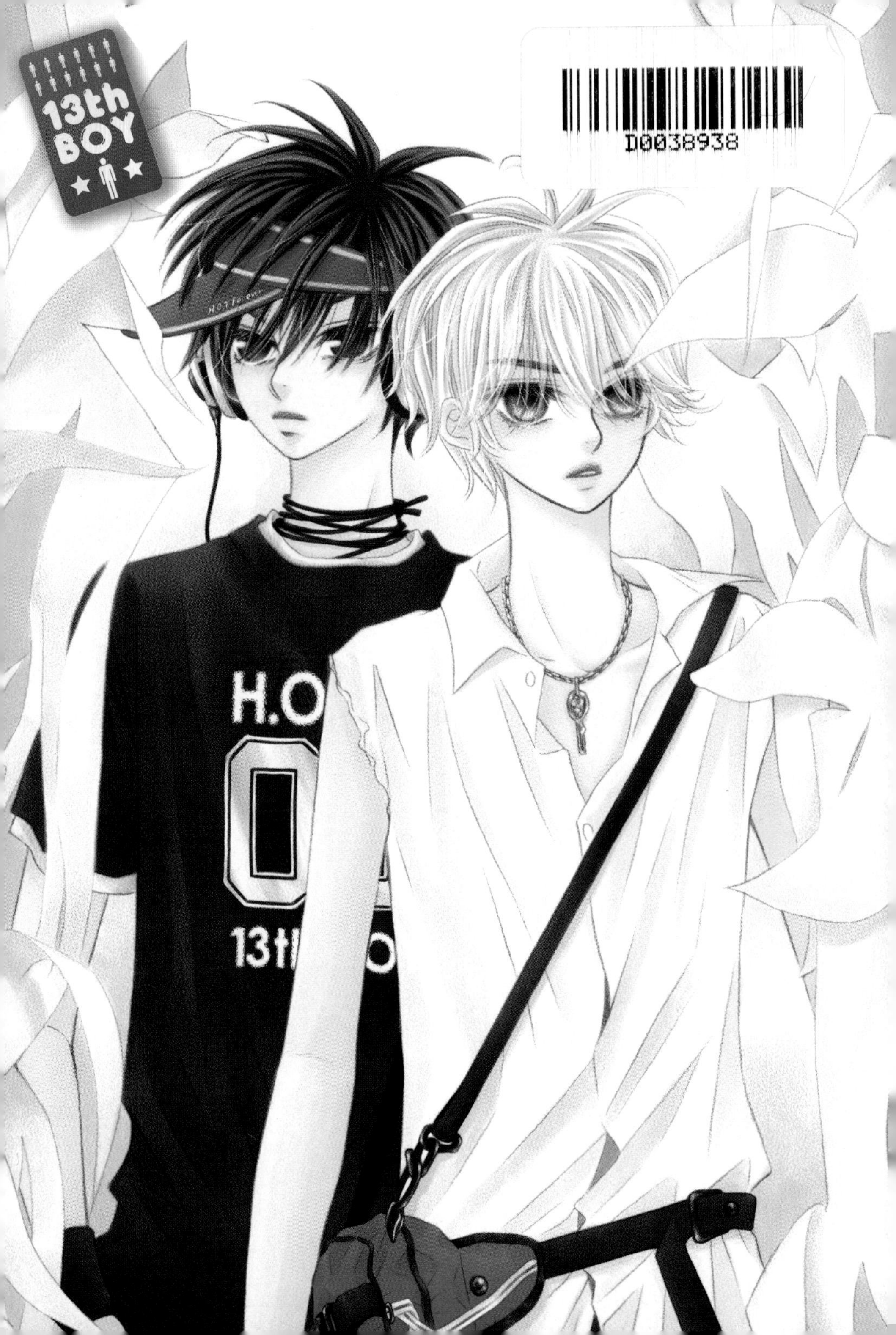
13th BOY
H.O

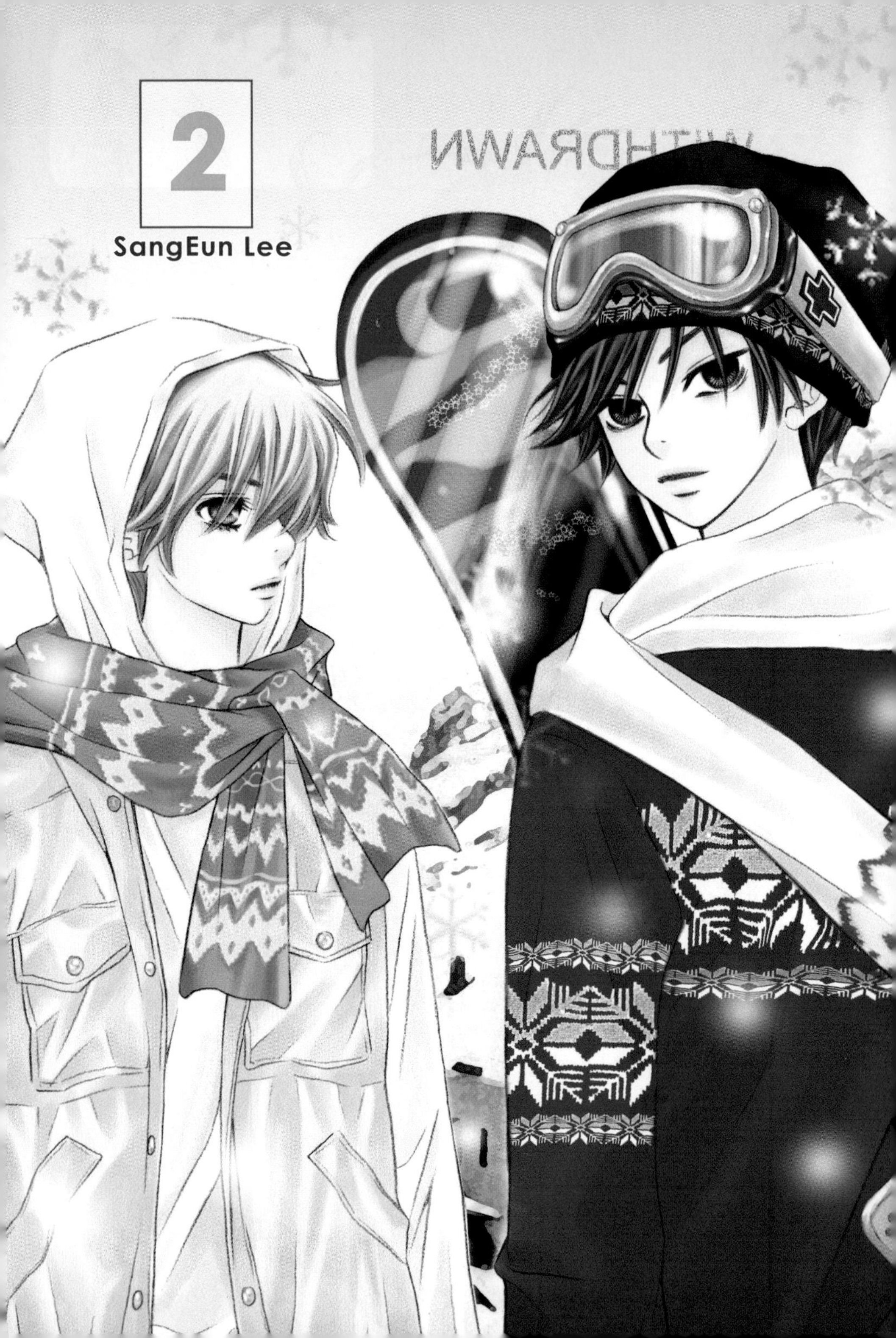
2
SangEun Lee

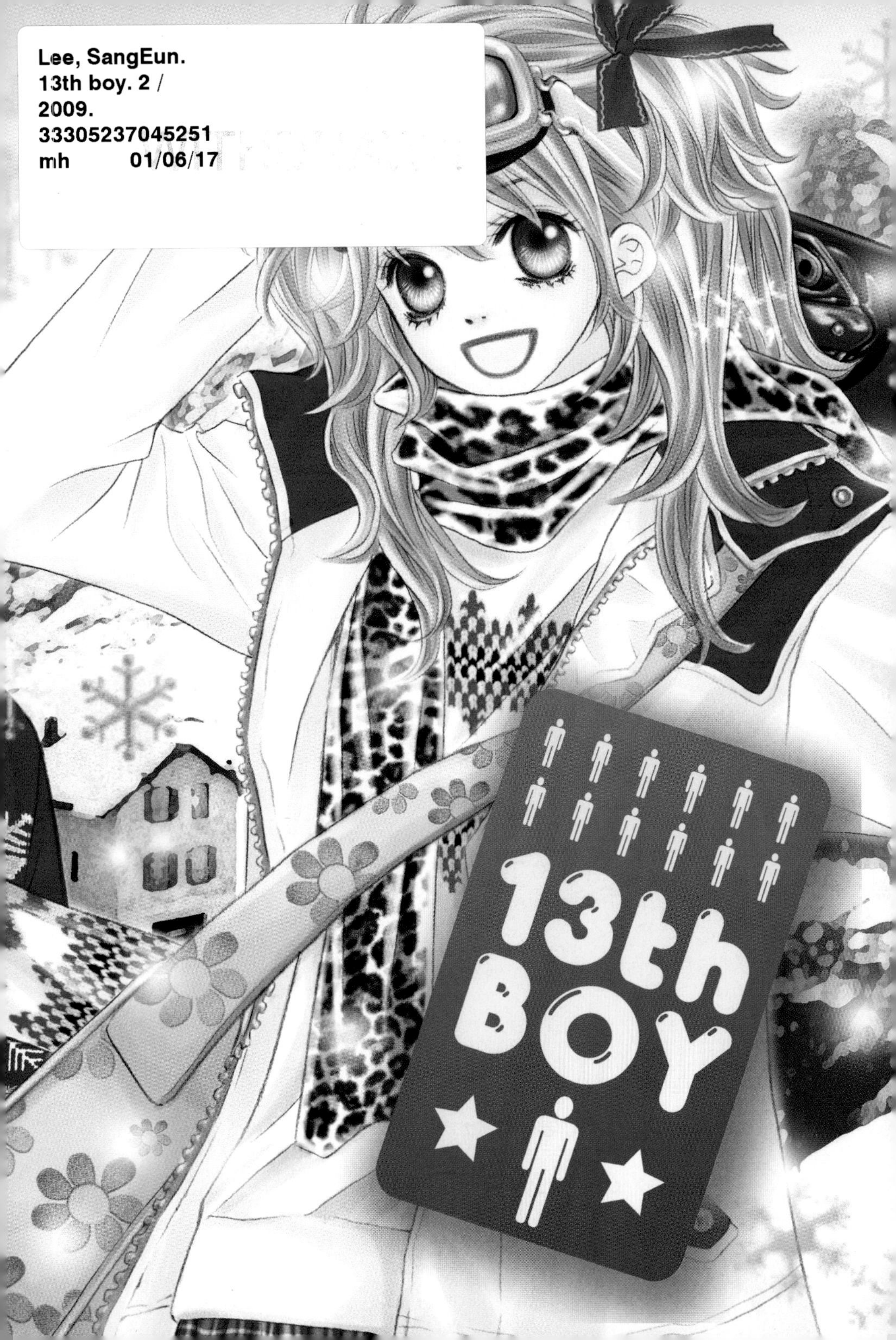
13th
BOY

13th BOY♥ CONTENTS

STEP 6. LET'S BE A GIRL SCOUT!   5

STEP 7. HEE-SO'S STORMY CAMPOUT   60

STEP 8. WHIE-YOUNG JANG,
         YOU'RE SO MYSTERIOUS!   175

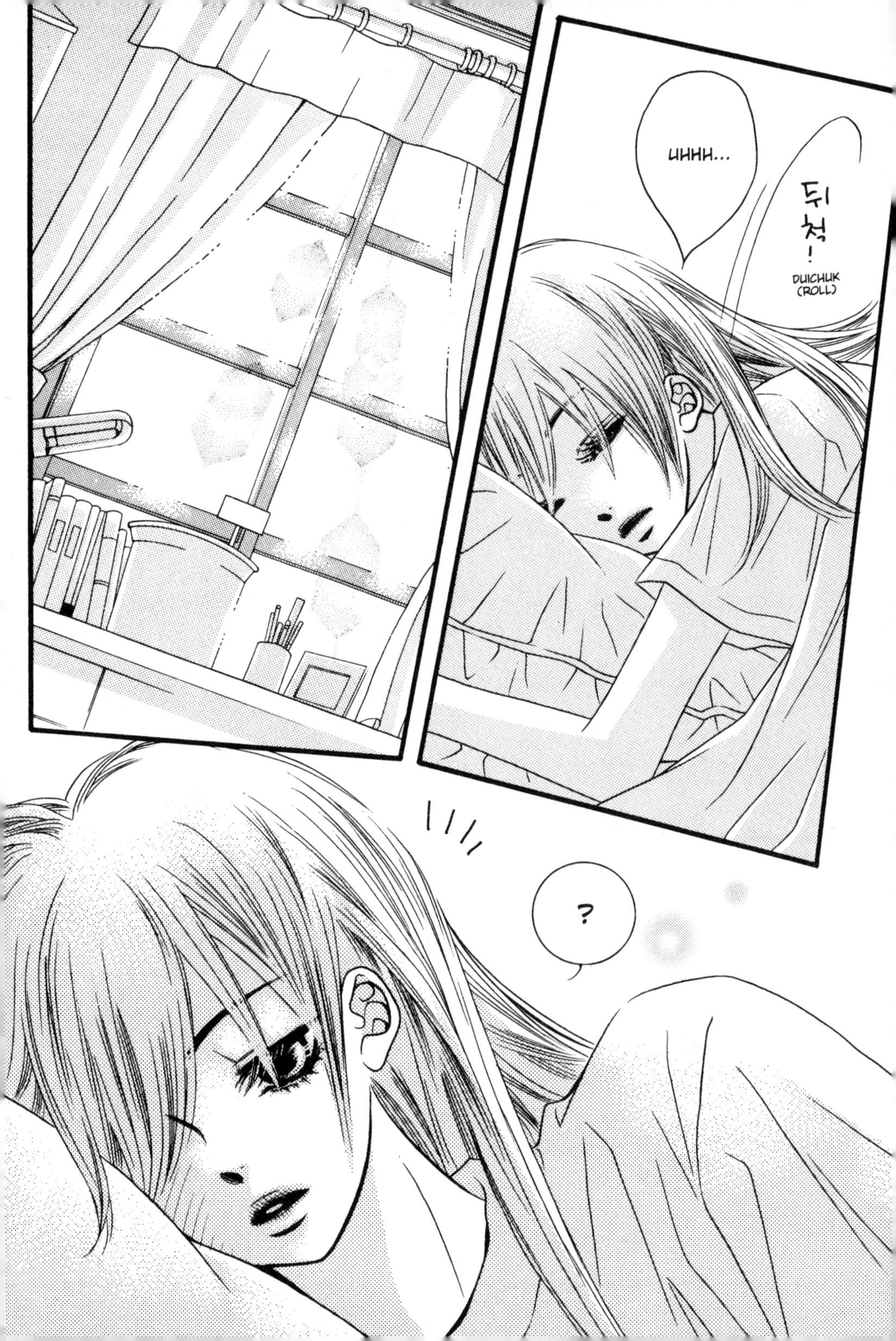
UHHH...
뒤척!
DUICHUK (ROLL)
?

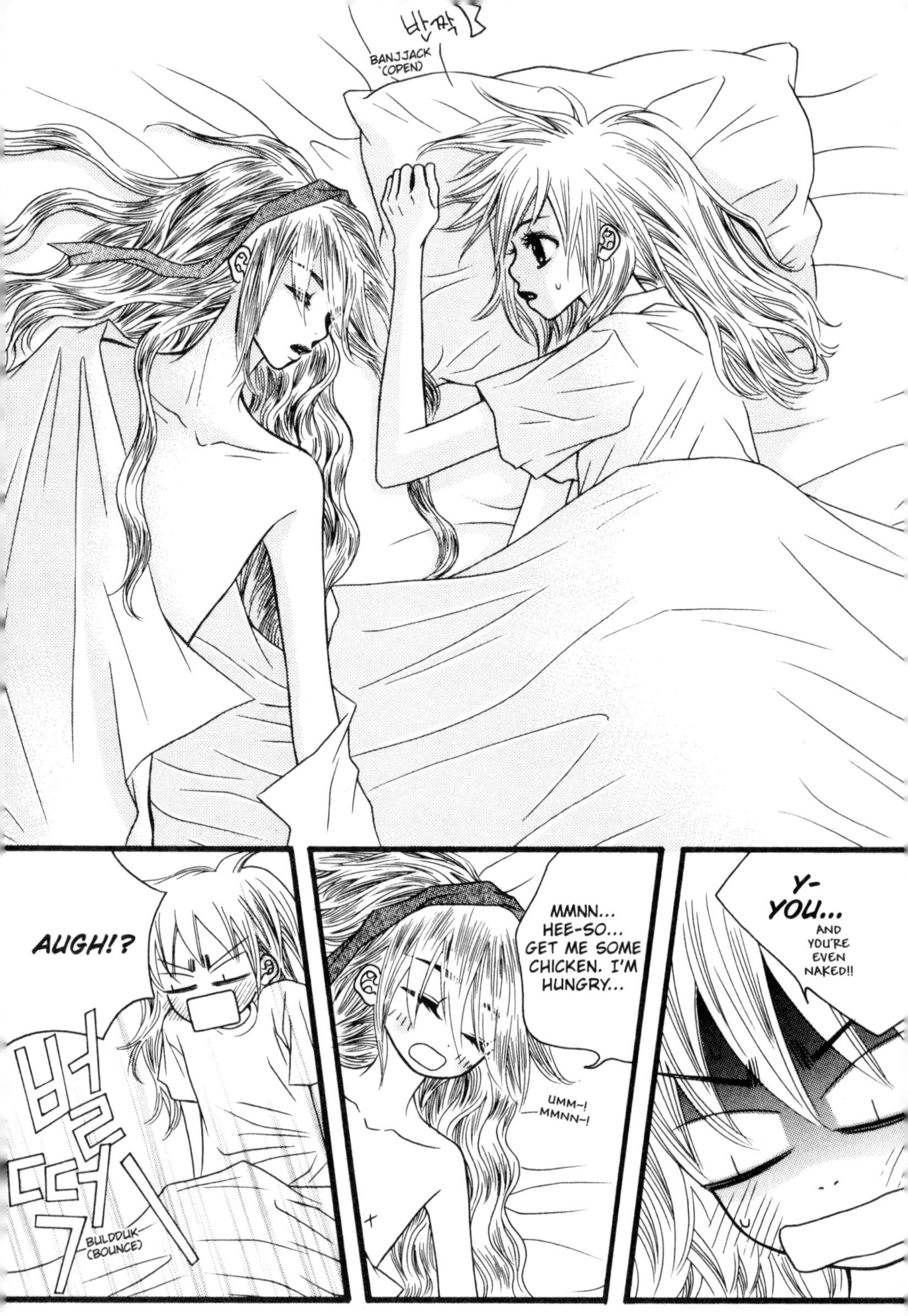
반짝
BANJJACK (OPEN)
AUGH!?
벌떡
BULDDUK (BOUNCE)
MMNN... HEE-SO... GET ME SOME CHICKEN. I'M HUNGRY...
UMM~! MMNN~!
Y-YOU...
AND YOU'RE EVEN NAKED!!

STEP 6. LET'S BE A GIRL SCOUT!

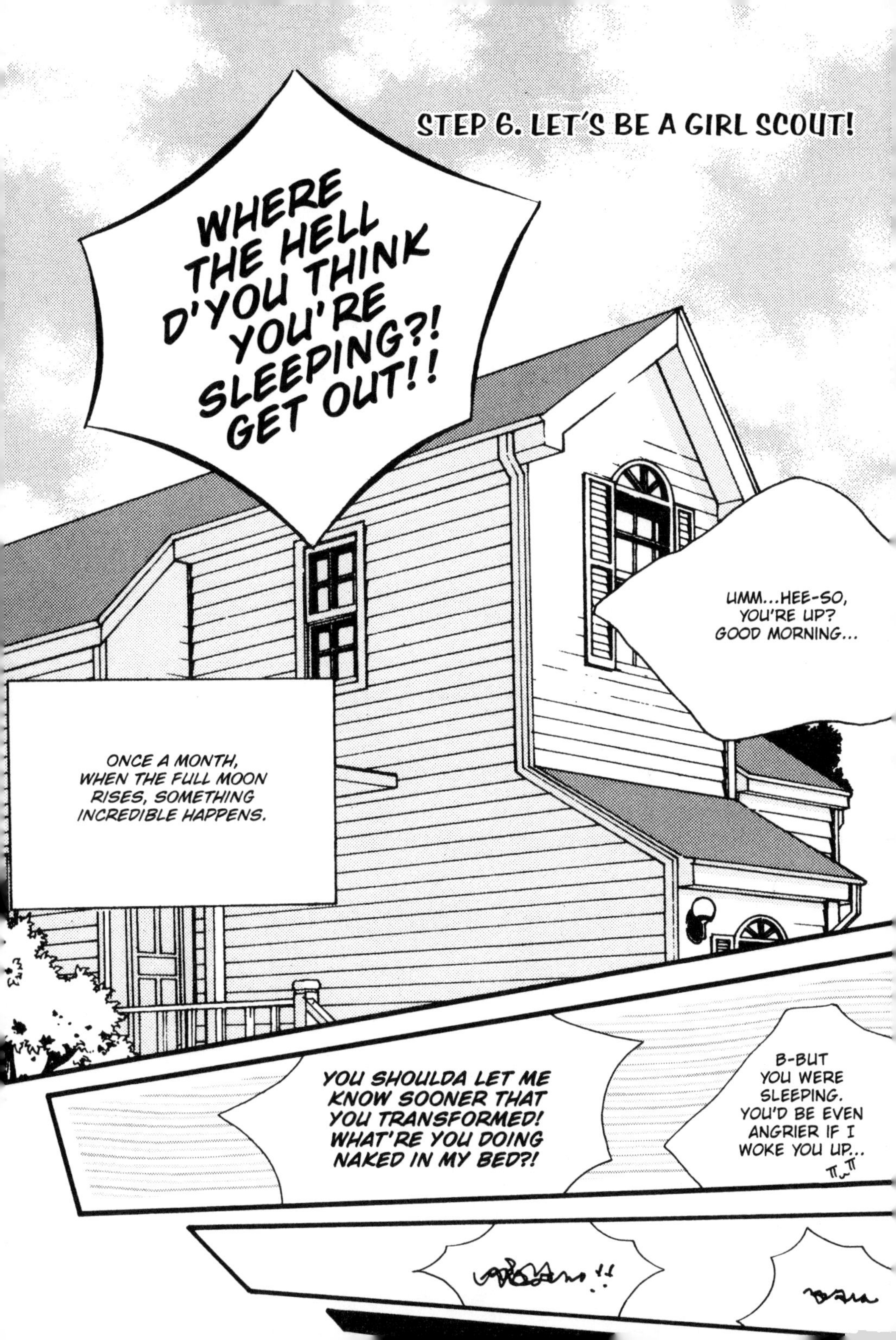
WHERE THE HELL D'YOU THINK YOU'RE SLEEPING?! GET OUT!!
ONCE A MONTH, WHEN THE FULL MOON RISES, SOMETHING INCREDIBLE HAPPENS.
UMM...HEE-SO, YOU'RE UP? GOOD MORNING...
YOU SHOULDA LET ME KNOW SOONER THAT YOU TRANSFORMED! WHAT'RE YOU DOING NAKED IN MY BED?!
B-BUT YOU WERE SLEEPING. YOU'D BE EVEN ANGRIER IF I WOKE YOU UP...

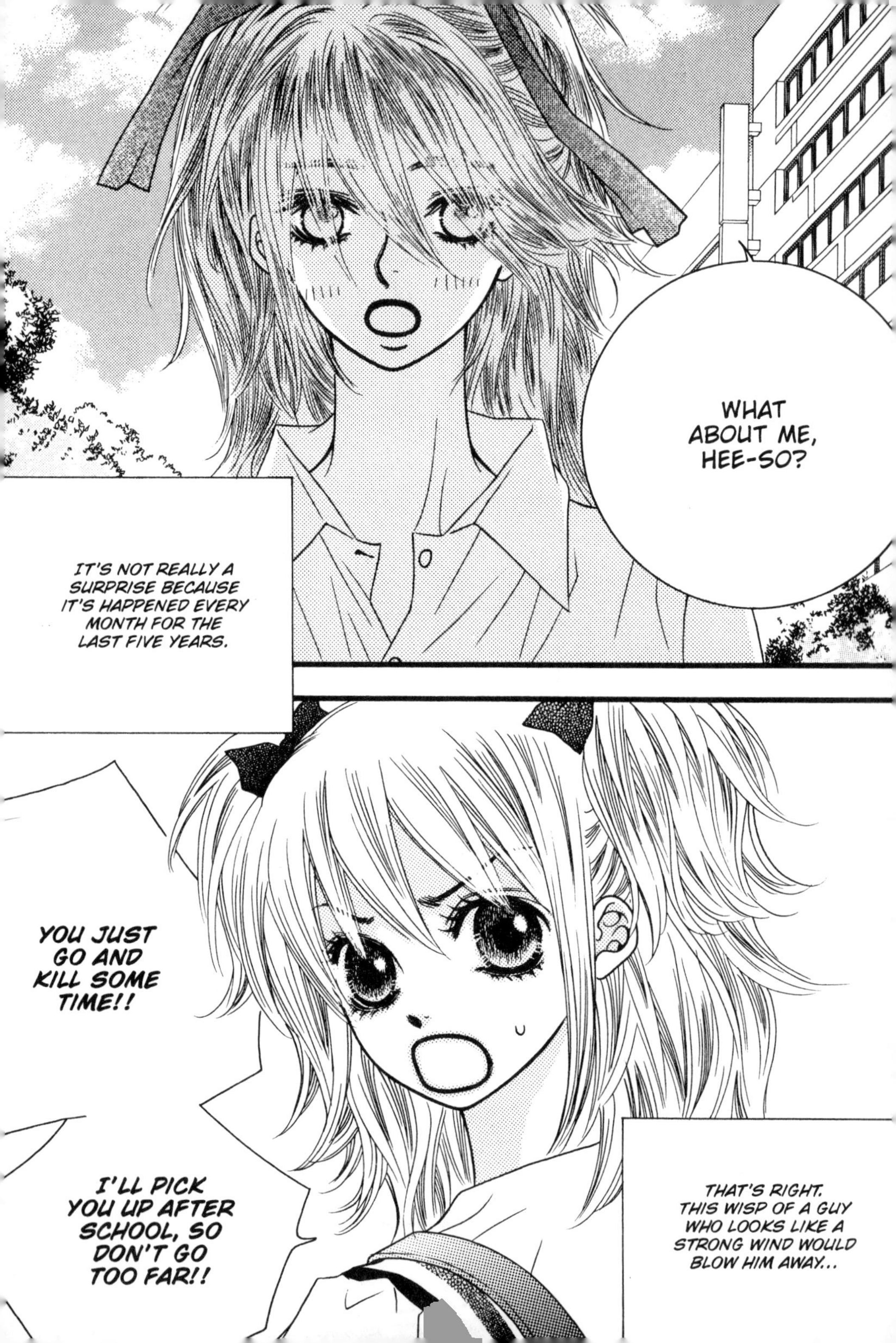
WHAT ABOUT ME, HEE-SO?
IT'S NOT REALLY A SURPRISE BECAUSE IT'S HAPPENED EVERY MONTH FOR THE LAST FIVE YEARS.
YOU JUST GO AND KILL SOME TIME!!
I'LL PICK YOU UP AFTER SCHOOL, SO DON'T GO TOO FAR!!
THAT'S RIGHT. THIS WISP OF A GUY WHO LOOKS LIKE A STRONG WIND WOULD BLOW HIM AWAY...

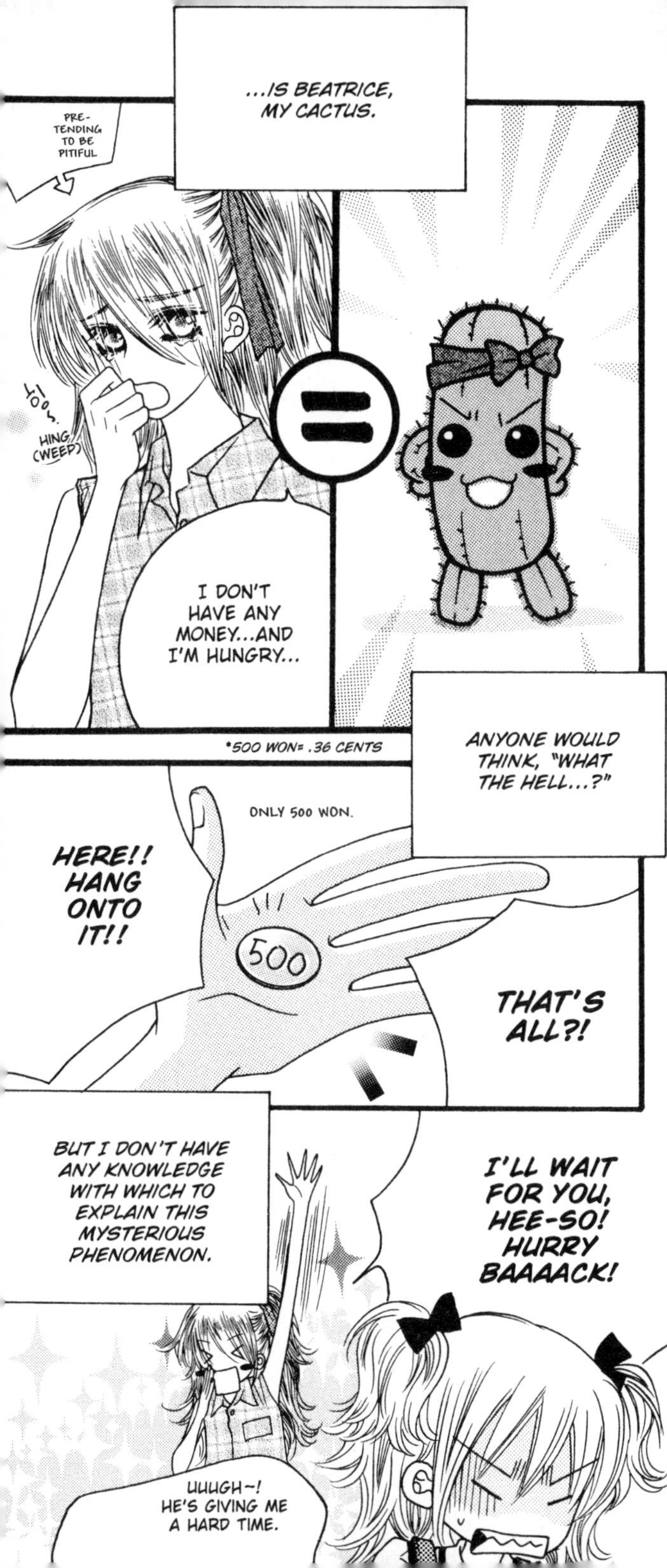
PRE-TENDING TO BE PITIFUL
...IS BEATRICE, MY CACTUS.
HING (WEEP)
I DON'T HAVE ANY MONEY...AND I'M HUNGRY...
*500 WON= .36 CENTS
HERE!! HANG ONTO IT!!
ONLY 500 WON.
500
ANYONE WOULD THINK, "WHAT THE HELL...?"
THAT'S ALL?!
BUT I DON'T HAVE ANY KNOWLEDGE WITH WHICH TO EXPLAIN THIS MYSTERIOUS PHENOMENON.
I'LL WAIT FOR YOU, HEE-SO! HURRY BAAAACK!
UUUGH~! HE'S GIVING ME A HARD TIME.

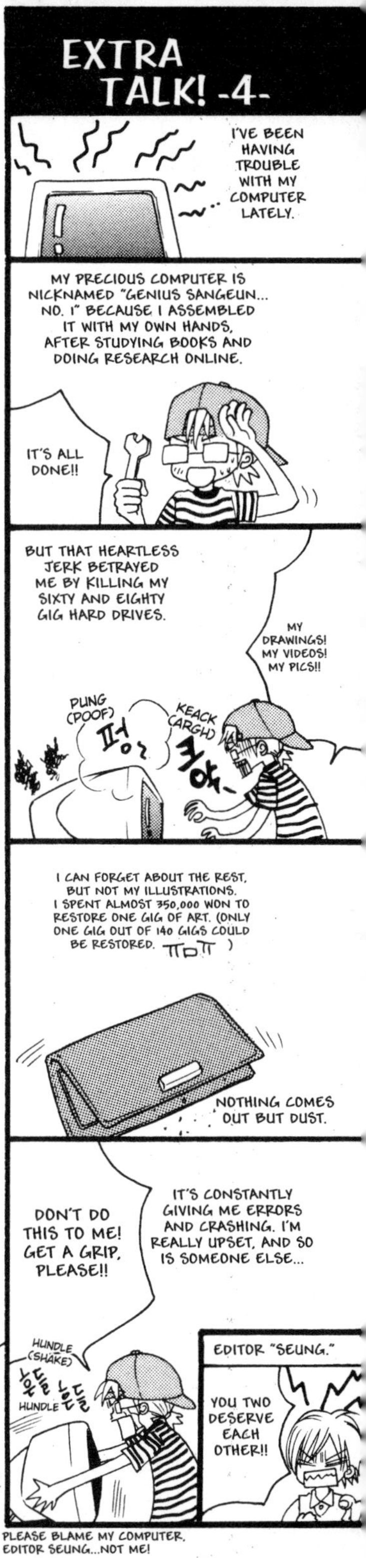
EXTRA TALK! -4-
I'VE BEEN HAVING TROUBLE WITH MY COMPUTER LATELY.
MY PRECIOUS COMPUTER IS NICKNAMED "GENIUS SANGEUN... NO. 1" BECAUSE I ASSEMBLED IT WITH MY OWN HANDS, AFTER STUDYING BOOKS AND DOING RESEARCH ONLINE.
IT'S ALL DONE!!
BUT THAT HEARTLESS JERK BETRAYED ME BY KILLING MY SIXTY AND EIGHTY GIG HARD DRIVES.
MY DRAWINGS! MY VIDEOS! MY PICS!!
PUNG (POOF)
KEACK (ARGH)
I CAN FORGET ABOUT THE REST, BUT NOT MY ILLUSTRATIONS. I SPENT ALMOST 350,000 WON TO RESTORE ONE GIG OF ART. (ONLY ONE GIG OUT OF 140 GIGS COULD BE RESTORED. TTㅁTT)
NOTHING COMES OUT BUT DUST.
DON'T DO THIS TO ME! GET A GRIP, PLEASE!!
IT'S CONSTANTLY GIVING ME ERRORS AND CRASHING. I'M REALLY UPSET, AND SO IS SOMEONE ELSE...
HUNDLE (SHAKE)
HUNDLE
EDITOR "SEUNG."
YOU TWO DESERVE EACH OTHER!!
PLEASE BLAME MY COMPUTER, EDITOR SEUNG...NOT ME!

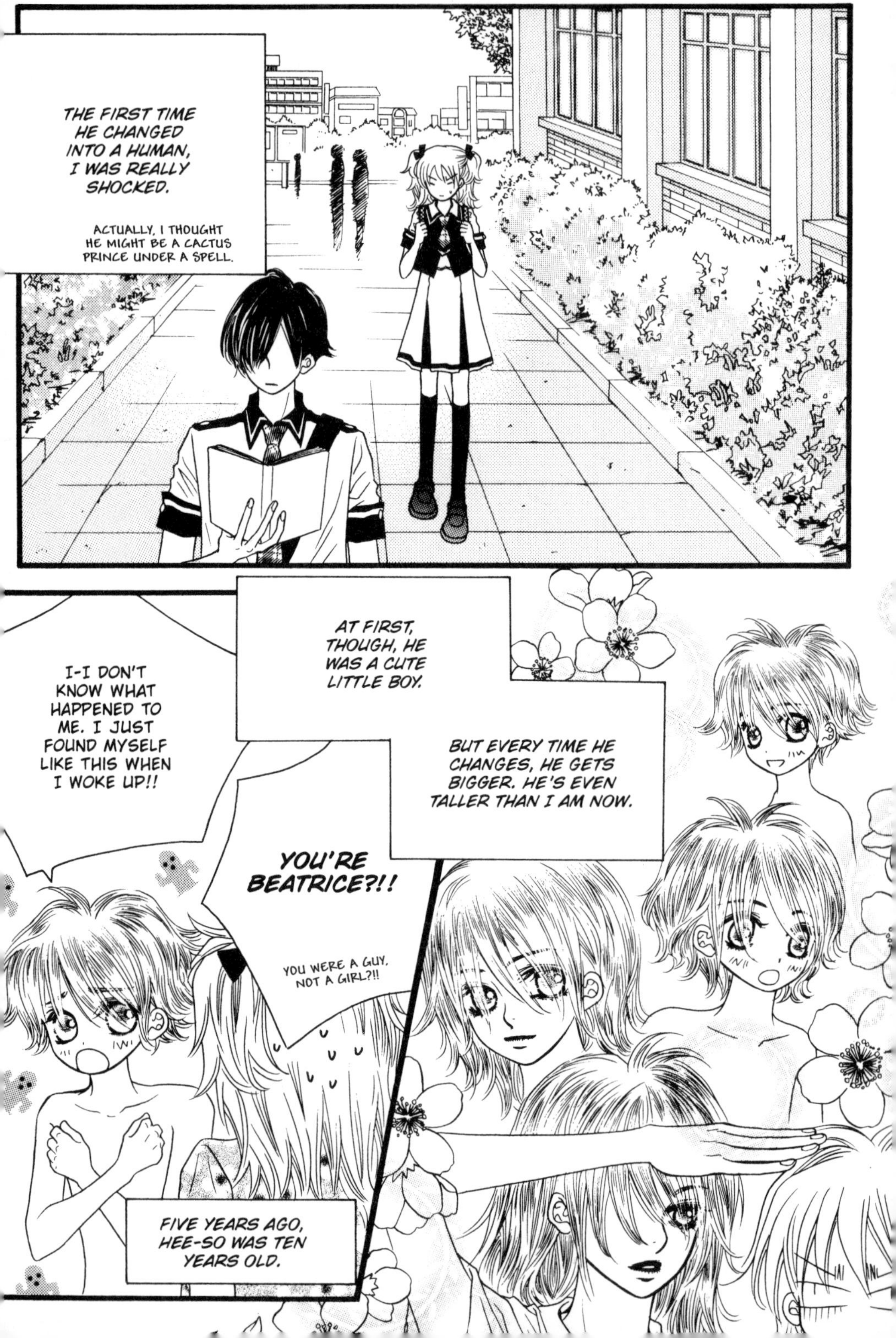
THE FIRST TIME HE CHANGED INTO A HUMAN, I WAS REALLY SHOCKED.
ACTUALLY, I THOUGHT HE MIGHT BE A CACTUS PRINCE UNDER A SPELL.
I-I DON'T KNOW WHAT HAPPENED TO ME. I JUST FOUND MYSELF LIKE THIS WHEN I WOKE UP!!
YOU'RE BEATRICE?!!
YOU WERE A GUY, NOT A GIRL?!!
FIVE YEARS AGO, HEE-SO WAS TEN YEARS OLD.
AT FIRST, THOUGH, HE WAS A CUTE LITTLE BOY.
BUT EVERY TIME HE CHANGES, HE GETS BIGGER. HE'S EVEN TALLER THAN I AM NOW.

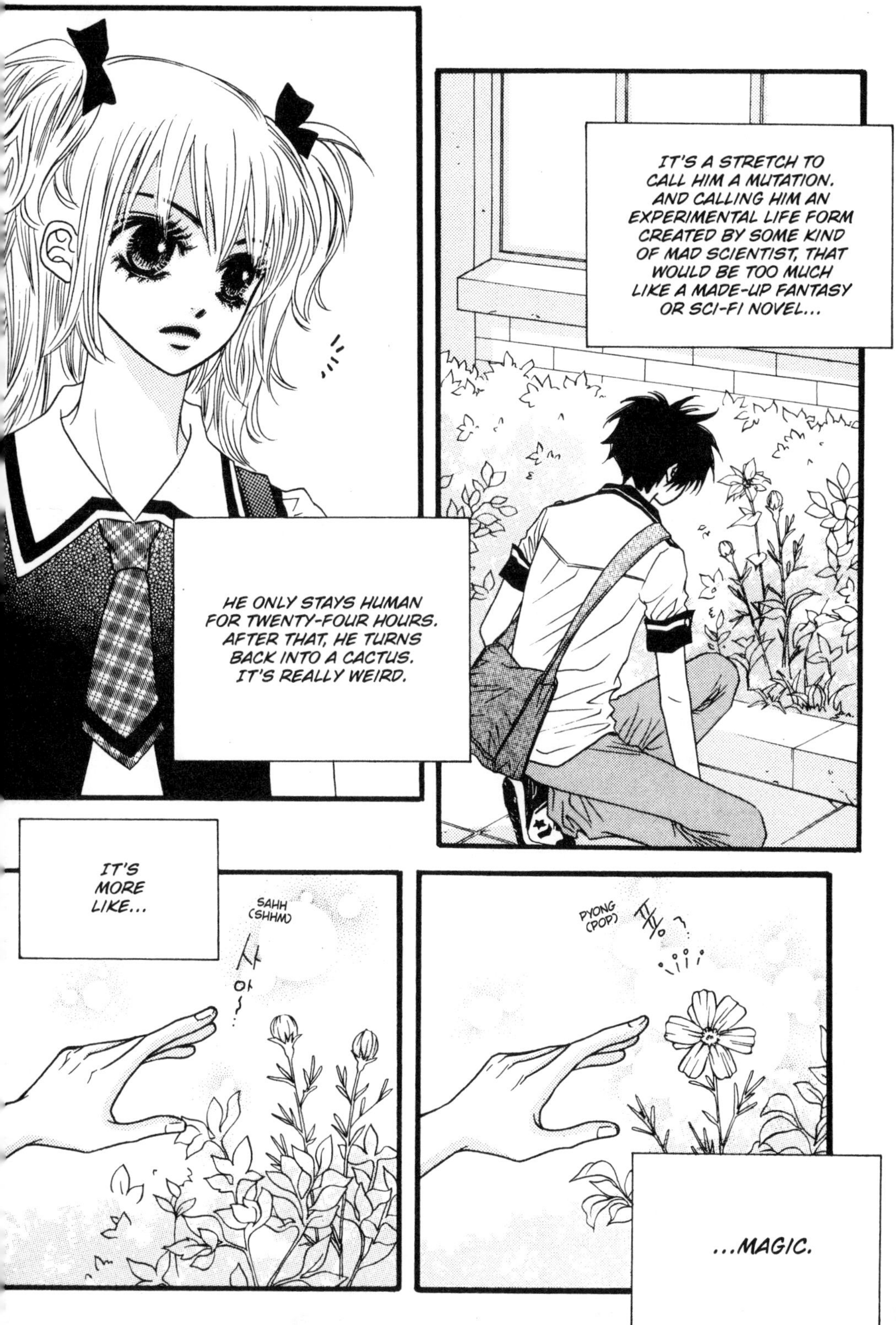
HE ONLY STAYS HUMAN FOR TWENTY-FOUR HOURS. AFTER THAT, HE TURNS BACK INTO A CACTUS. IT'S REALLY WEIRD.
IT'S A STRETCH TO CALL HIM A MUTATION. AND CALLING HIM AN EXPERIMENTAL LIFE FORM CREATED BY SOME KIND OF MAD SCIENTIST, THAT WOULD BE TOO MUCH LIKE A MADE-UP FANTASY OR SCI-FI NOVEL...
IT'S MORE LIKE...
SAHH (SHHM)
PYONG (POP)
...MAGIC.

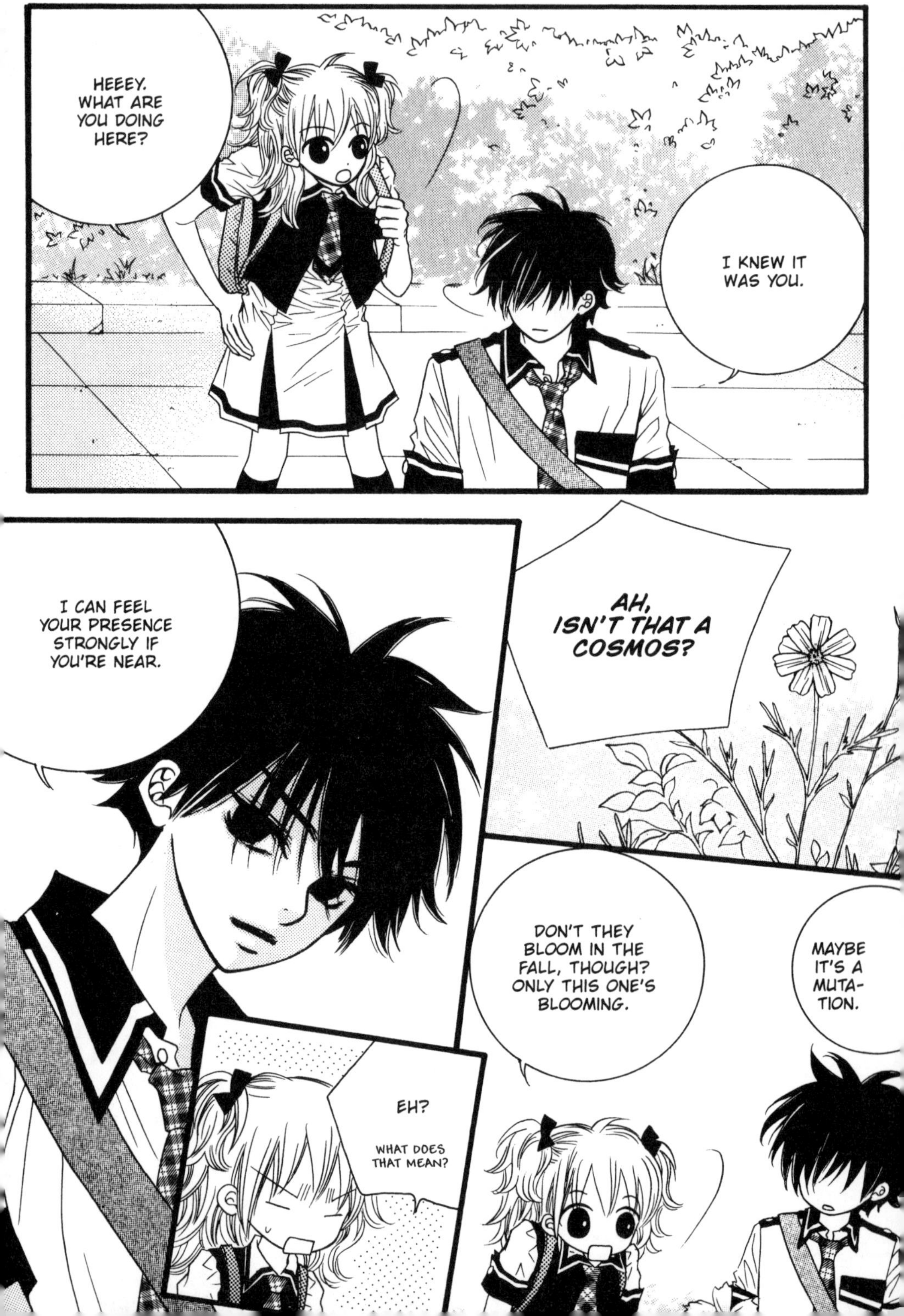
HEEEY. WHAT ARE YOU DOING HERE?
I KNEW IT WAS YOU.
I CAN FEEL YOUR PRESENCE STRONGLY IF YOU'RE NEAR.
EH?
WHAT DOES THAT MEAN?
AH, ISN'T THAT A COSMOS?
DON'T THEY BLOOM IN THE FALL, THOUGH? ONLY THIS ONE'S BLOOMING.
MAYBE IT'S A MUTA-TION.

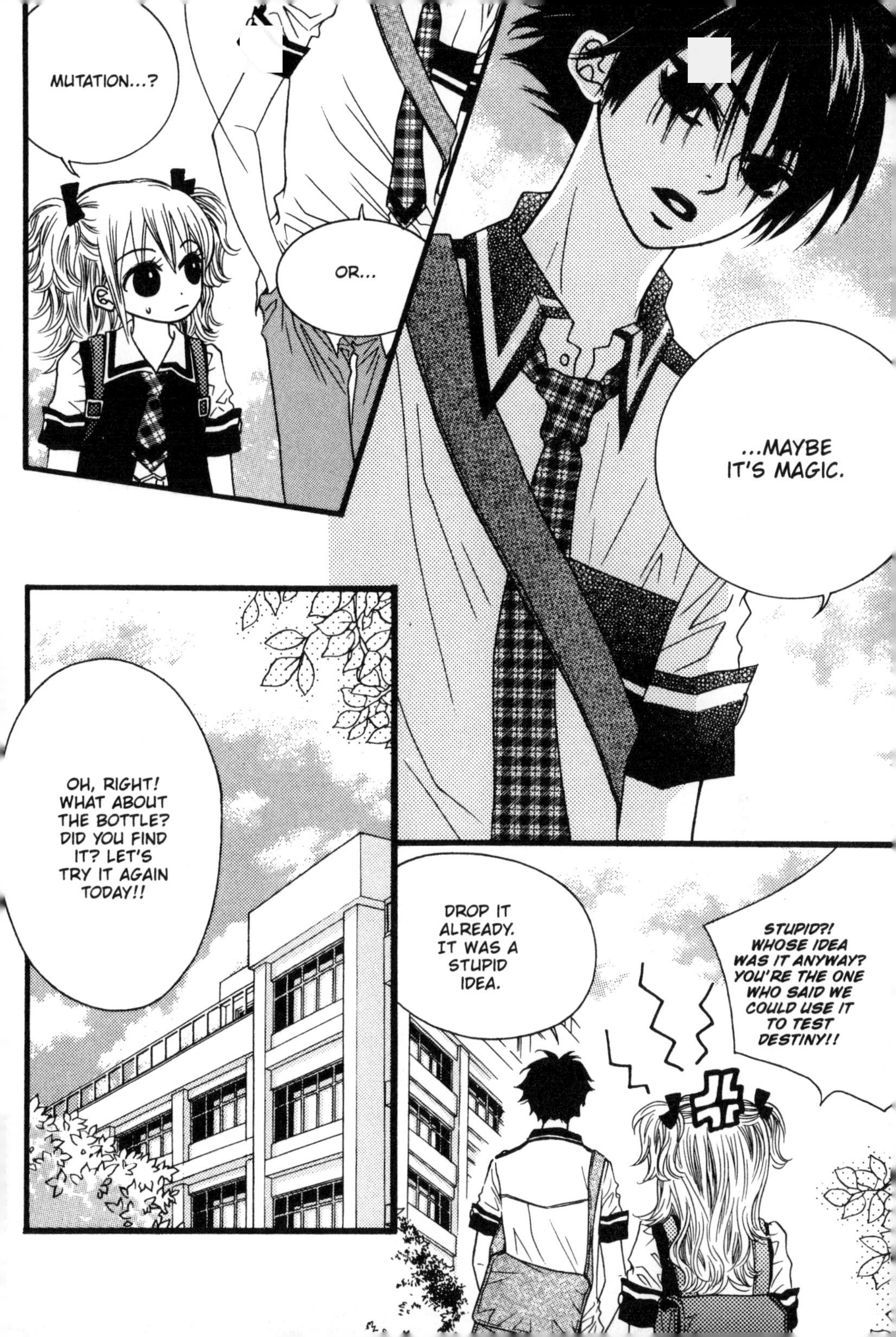
MUTATION...?
OR...
...MAYBE IT'S MAGIC.
OH, RIGHT! WHAT ABOUT THE BOTTLE? DID YOU FIND IT? LET'S TRY IT AGAIN TODAY!!
DROP IT ALREADY. IT WAS A STUPID IDEA.
STUPID?! WHOSE IDEA WAS IT ANYWAY? YOU'RE THE ONE WHO SAID WE COULD USE IT TO TEST DESTINY!!

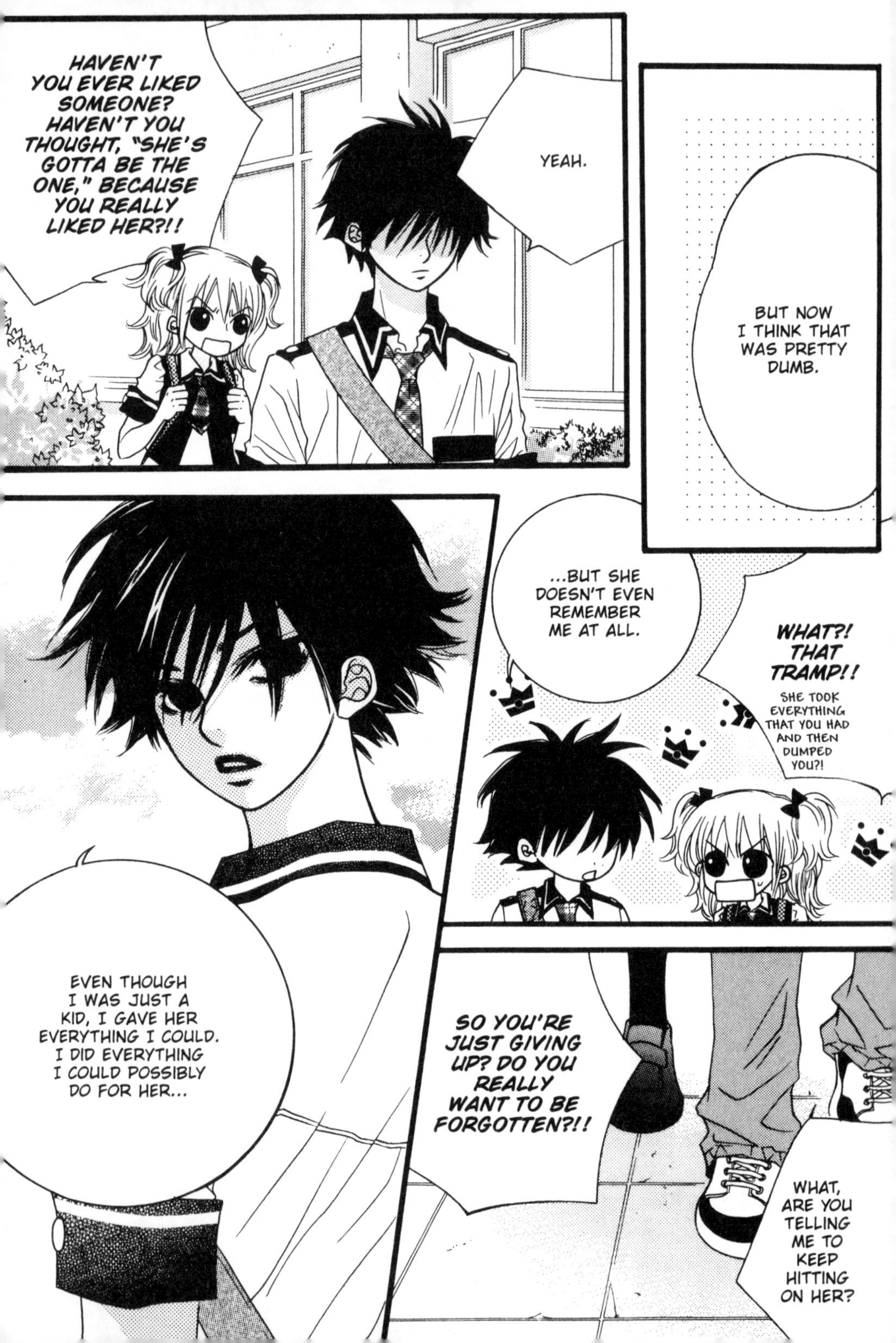
HAVEN'T YOU EVER LIKED SOMEONE? HAVEN'T YOU THOUGHT, "SHE'S GOTTA BE THE ONE," BECAUSE YOU REALLY LIKED HER?!!
YEAH.
BUT NOW I THINK THAT WAS PRETTY DUMB.
EVEN THOUGH I WAS JUST A KID, I GAVE HER EVERYTHING I COULD. I DID EVERYTHING I COULD POSSIBLY DO FOR HER...
...BUT SHE DOESN'T EVEN REMEMBER ME AT ALL.
WHAT?! THAT TRAMP!!
SHE TOOK EVERYTHING THAT YOU HAD AND THEN DUMPED YOU?!
SO YOU'RE JUST GIVING UP? DO YOU REALLY WANT TO BE FORGOTTEN?!!
WHAT, ARE YOU TELLING ME TO KEEP HITTING ON HER?

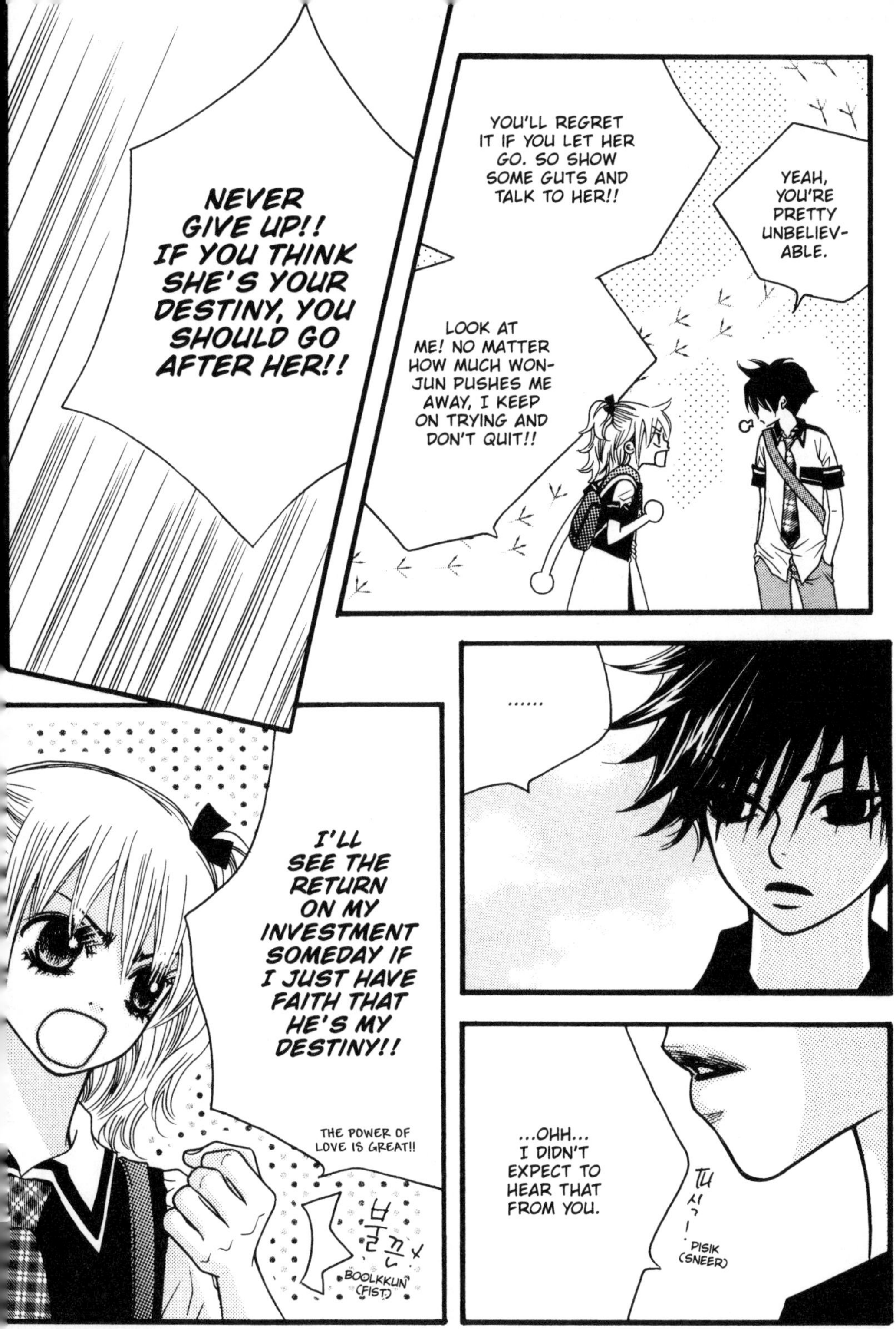
NEVER GIVE UP!! IF YOU THINK SHE'S YOUR DESTINY, YOU SHOULD GO AFTER HER!!
YOU'LL REGRET IT IF YOU LET HER GO. SO SHOW SOME GUTS AND TALK TO HER!!
YEAH, YOU'RE PRETTY UNBELIEV-ABLE.
LOOK AT ME! NO MATTER HOW MUCH WON-JUN PUSHES ME AWAY, I KEEP ON TRYING AND DON'T QUIT!!
I'LL SEE THE RETURN ON MY INVESTMENT SOMEDAY IF I JUST HAVE FAITH THAT HE'S MY DESTINY!!
THE POWER OF LOVE IS GREAT!!
불끈
BOOLKKUN (FIST)
......
...OHH... I DIDN'T EXPECT TO HEAR THAT FROM YOU.
피식!
PISIK (SNEER)

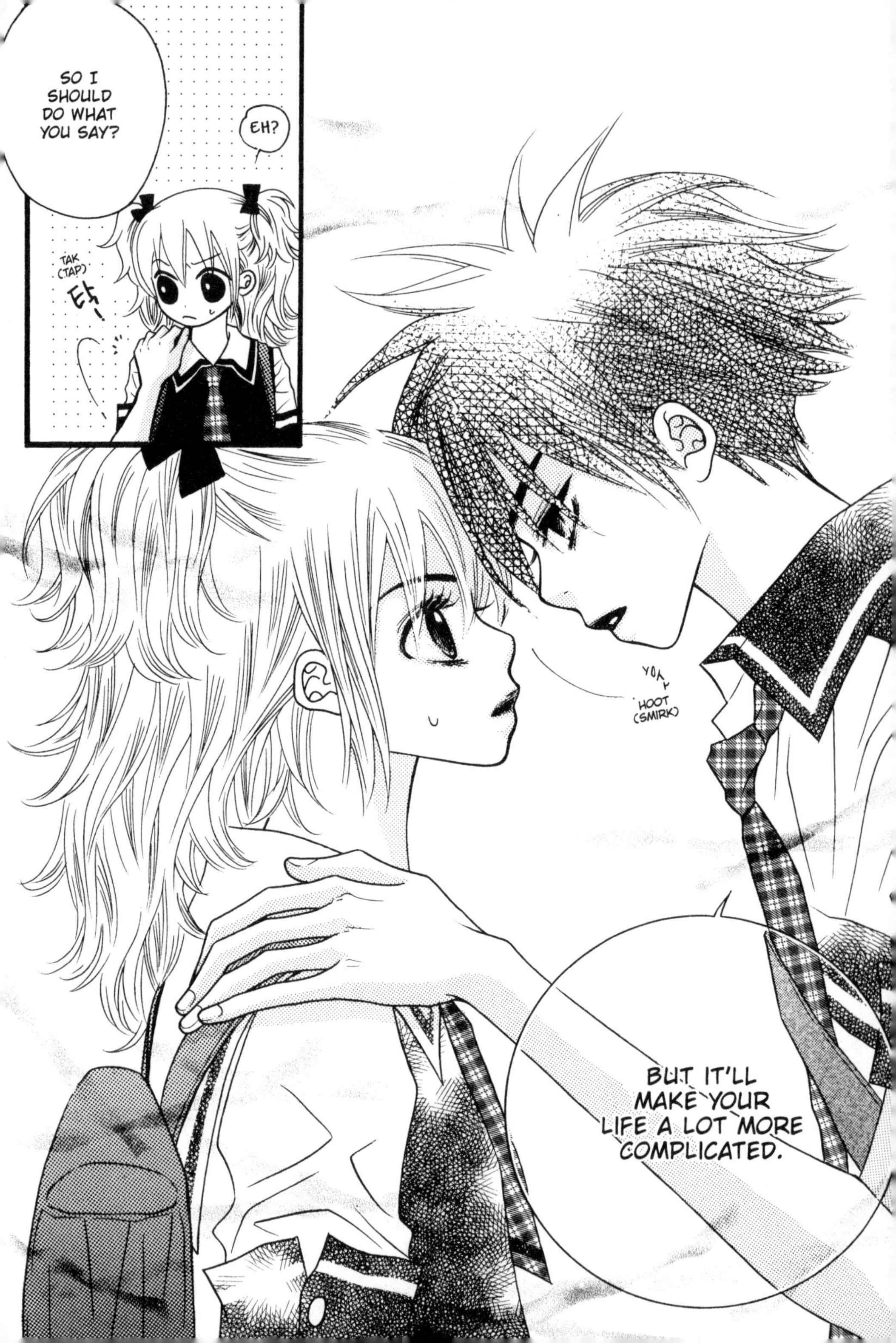

SO I SHOULD DO WHAT YOU SAY?
EH?
TAK (TAP)
탁!
YOㅅ
HOOT (SMIRK)
BUT IT'LL MAKE YOUR LIFE A LOT MORE COMPLICATED.

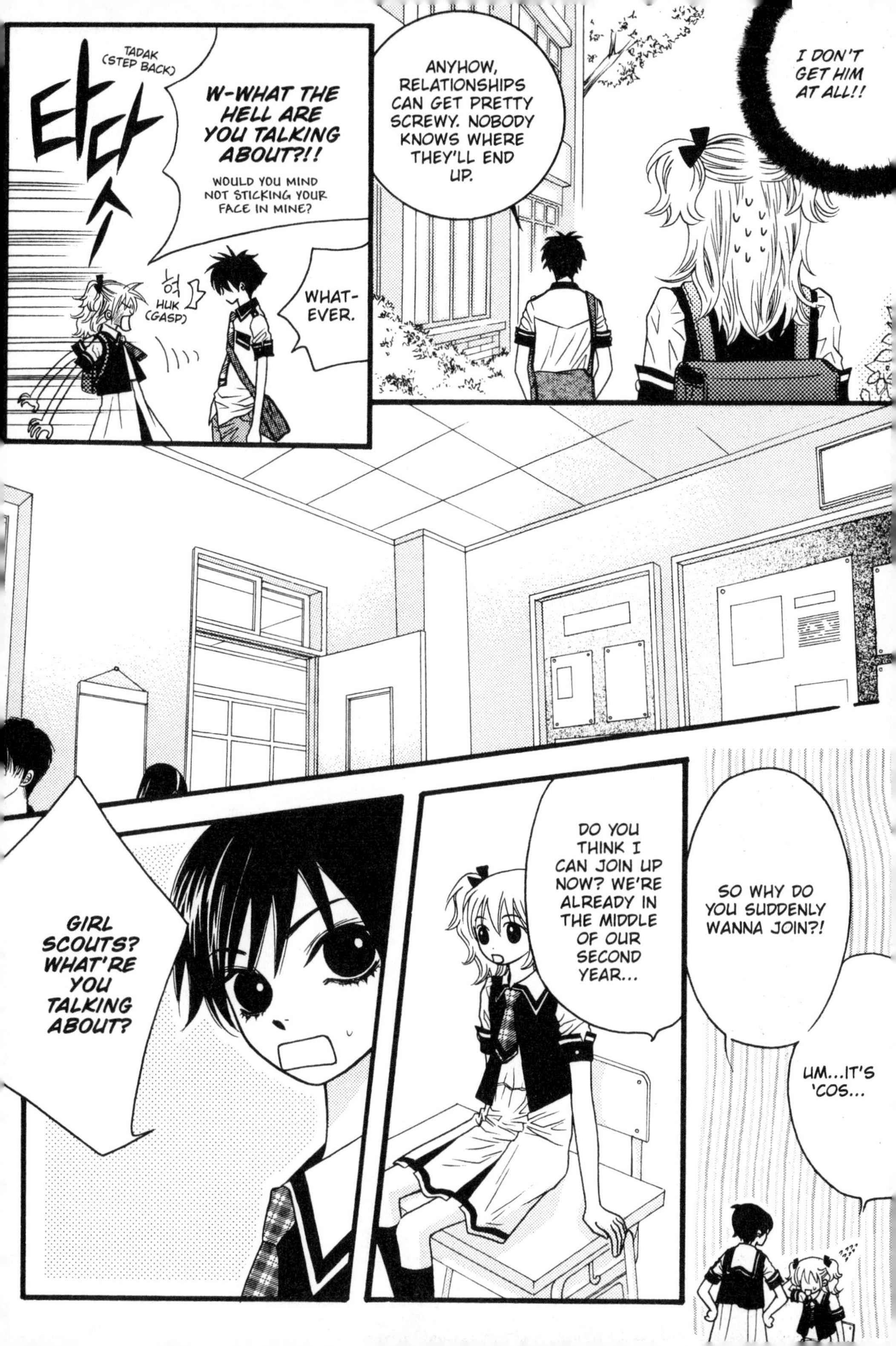
TADAK (STEP BACK)
W-WHAT THE HELL ARE YOU TALKING ABOUT?!!
WOULD YOU MIND NOT STICKING YOUR FACE IN MINE?
헉 HUK (GASP)
WHAT-EVER.
ANYHOW, RELATIONSHIPS CAN GET PRETTY SCREWY. NOBODY KNOWS WHERE THEY'LL END UP.
I DON'T GET HIM AT ALL!!
GIRL SCOUTS? WHAT'RE YOU TALKING ABOUT?
DO YOU THINK I CAN JOIN UP NOW? WE'RE ALREADY IN THE MIDDLE OF OUR SECOND YEAR...
SO WHY DO YOU SUDDENLY WANNA JOIN?!
UM...IT'S 'COS...

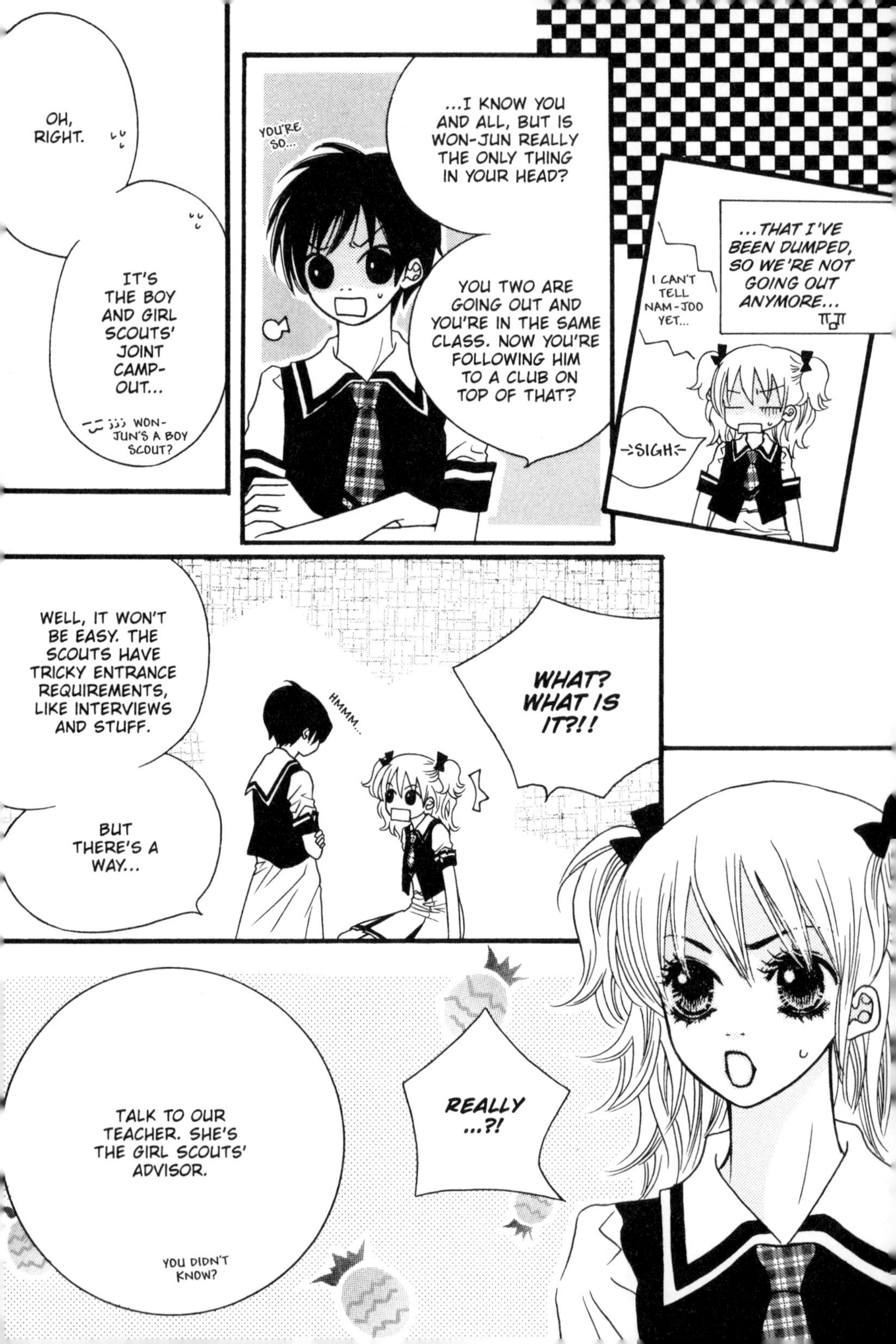
OH, RIGHT.
IT'S THE BOY AND GIRL SCOUTS' JOINT CAMP-OUT...
WON-JUN'S A BOY SCOUT?
YOU'RE SO...
...I KNOW YOU AND ALL, BUT IS WON-JUN REALLY THE ONLY THING IN YOUR HEAD?
YOU TWO ARE GOING OUT AND YOU'RE IN THE SAME CLASS. NOW YOU'RE FOLLOWING HIM TO A CLUB ON TOP OF THAT?
I CAN'T TELL NAM-JOO YET...
...THAT I'VE BEEN DUMPED, SO WE'RE NOT GOING OUT ANYMORE...
SIGH
WELL, IT WON'T BE EASY. THE SCOUTS HAVE TRICKY ENTRANCE REQUIREMENTS, LIKE INTERVIEWS AND STUFF.
BUT THERE'S A WAY...
HMMM...
WHAT? WHAT IS IT?!!
TALK TO OUR TEACHER. SHE'S THE GIRL SCOUTS' ADVISOR.
YOU DIDN'T KNOW?
REALLY ...?!

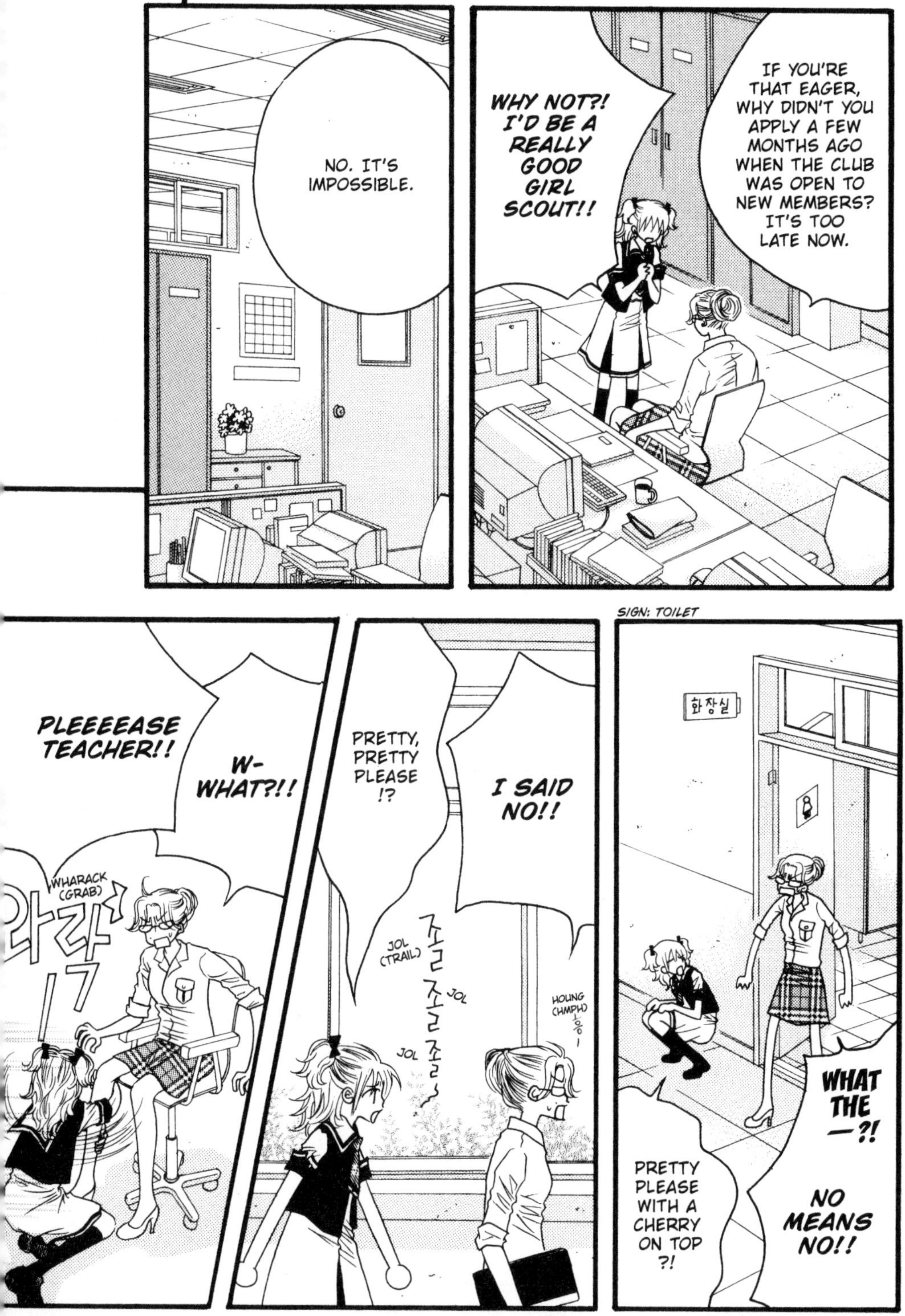
NO. IT'S IMPOSSIBLE.
WHY NOT?! I'D BE A REALLY GOOD GIRL SCOUT!!
IF YOU'RE THAT EAGER, WHY DIDN'T YOU APPLY A FEW MONTHS AGO WHEN THE CLUB WAS OPEN TO NEW MEMBERS? IT'S TOO LATE NOW.
PLEEEEASE TEACHER!!
W-WHAT?!!
WHARACK (GRAB)
와락
PRETTY, PRETTY PLEASE !?
I SAID NO!!
JOL (TRAIL)
졸졸졸졸
JOL
JOL
HOUNG (HMPH)
흥
SIGN: TOILET
화장실
WHAT THE—?!
PRETTY PLEASE WITH A CHERRY ON TOP ?!
NO MEANS NO!!

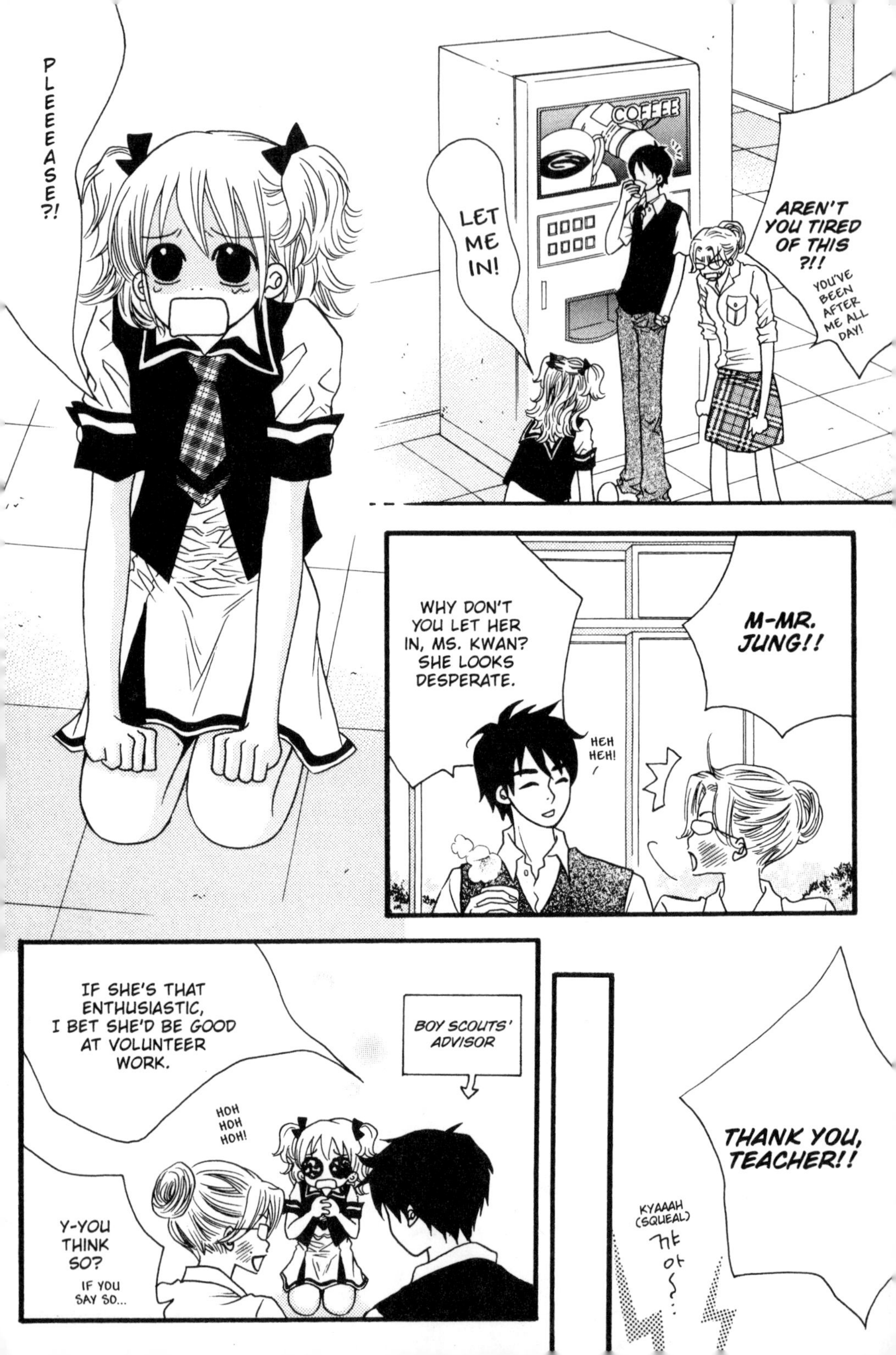
PLEEEASE?!
LET ME IN!
COFFEE
AREN'T YOU TIRED OF THIS ?!!
YOU'VE BEEN AFTER ME ALL DAY!
WHY DON'T YOU LET HER IN, MS. KWAN? SHE LOOKS DESPERATE.
HEH HEH!
M-MR. JUNG!!
IF SHE'S THAT ENTHUSIASTIC, I BET SHE'D BE GOOD AT VOLUNTEER WORK.
BOY SCOUTS' ADVISOR
HOH HOH HOH!
Y-YOU THINK SO?
IF YOU SAY SO...
THANK YOU, TEACHER!!
KYAAAH (SQUEAL)
꺄아~

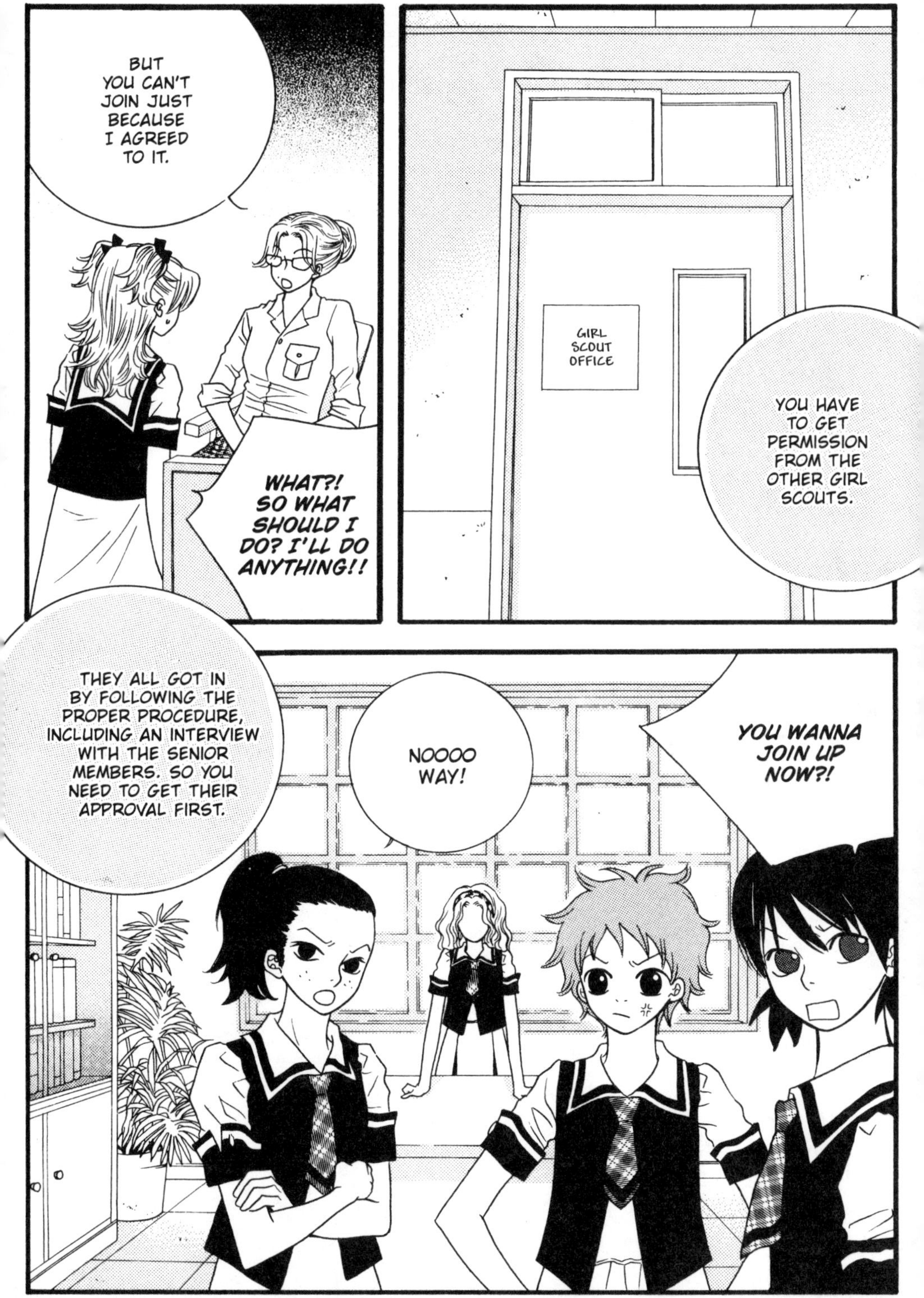

BUT YOU CAN'T JOIN JUST BECAUSE I AGREED TO IT.
WHAT?! SO WHAT SHOULD I DO? I'LL DO ANYTHING!!
GIRL SCOUT OFFICE
YOU HAVE TO GET PERMISSION FROM THE OTHER GIRL SCOUTS.
THEY ALL GOT IN BY FOLLOWING THE PROPER PROCEDURE, INCLUDING AN INTERVIEW WITH THE SENIOR MEMBERS. SO YOU NEED TO GET THEIR APPROVAL FIRST.
NOOOO WAY!
YOU WANNA JOIN UP NOW?!

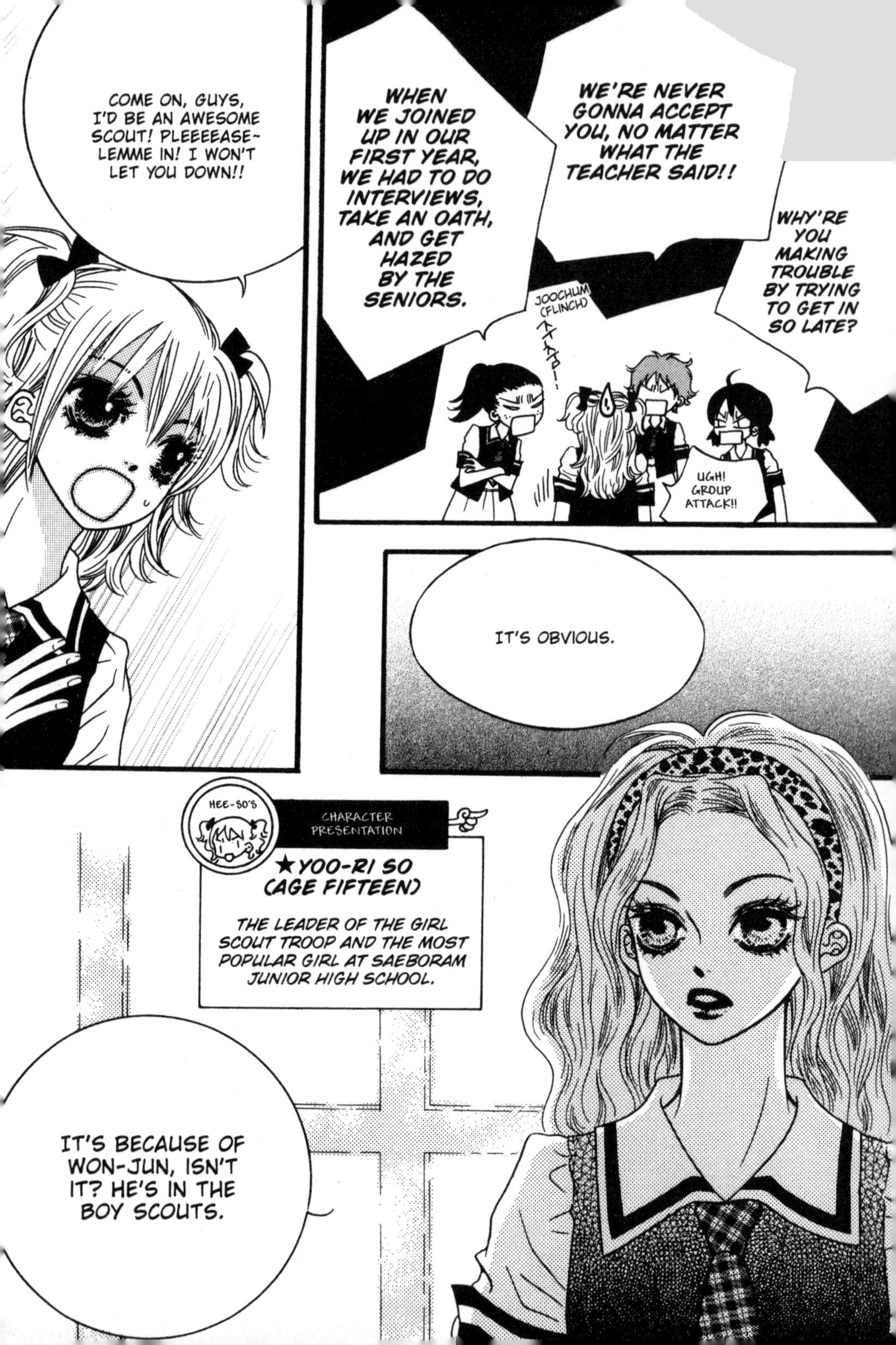
COME ON, GUYS, I'D BE AN AWESOME SCOUT! PLEEEEASE~ LEMME IN! I WON'T LET YOU DOWN!!
WHEN WE JOINED UP IN OUR FIRST YEAR, WE HAD TO DO INTERVIEWS, TAKE AN OATH, AND GET HAZED BY THE SENIORS.
WE'RE NEVER GONNA ACCEPT YOU, NO MATTER WHAT THE TEACHER SAID!!
WHY'RE YOU MAKING TROUBLE BY TRYING TO GET IN SO LATE?
JOOCHUM (FLINCH)
UGH! GROUP ATTACK!!
IT'S OBVIOUS.
HEE-SO'S
CHARACTER PRESENTATION
★YOO-RI SO (AGE FIFTEEN)
THE LEADER OF THE GIRL SCOUT TROOP AND THE MOST POPULAR GIRL AT SAEBORAM JUNIOR HIGH SCHOOL.
IT'S BECAUSE OF WON-JUN, ISN'T IT? HE'S IN THE BOY SCOUTS.

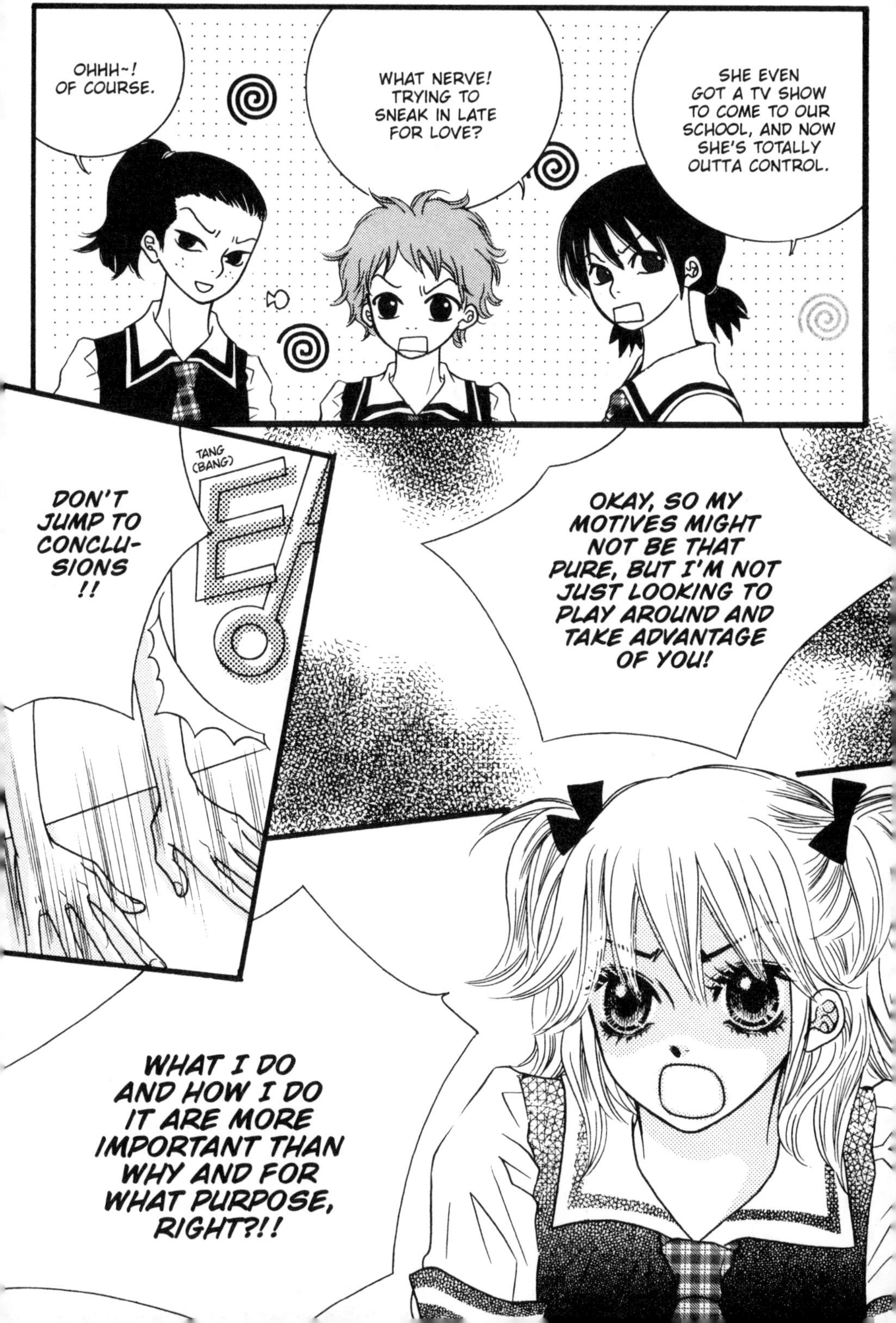
OHHH~! OF COURSE.
WHAT NERVE! TRYING TO SNEAK IN LATE FOR LOVE?
SHE EVEN GOT A TV SHOW TO COME TO OUR SCHOOL, AND NOW SHE'S TOTALLY OUTTA CONTROL.
TANG (BANG)
DON'T JUMP TO CONCLU-SIONS !!
OKAY, SO MY MOTIVES MIGHT NOT BE THAT PURE, BUT I'M NOT JUST LOOKING TO PLAY AROUND AND TAKE ADVANTAGE OF YOU!
WHAT I DO AND HOW I DO IT ARE MORE IMPORTANT THAN WHY AND FOR WHAT PURPOSE, RIGHT?!!

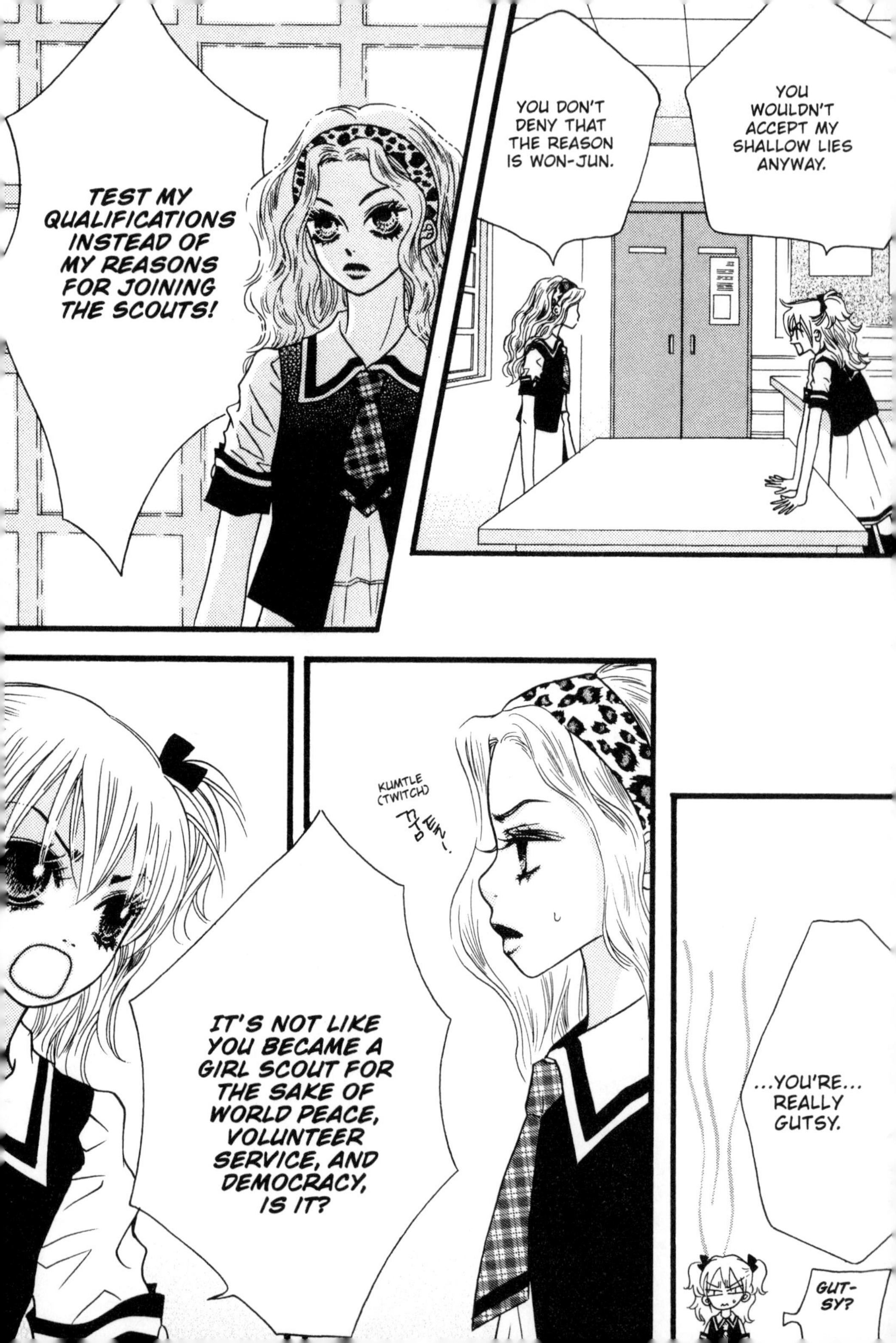
TEST MY QUALIFICATIONS INSTEAD OF MY REASONS FOR JOINING THE SCOUTS!
YOU DON'T DENY THAT THE REASON IS WON-JUN.
YOU WOULDN'T ACCEPT MY SHALLOW LIES ANYWAY.
IT'S NOT LIKE YOU BECAME A GIRL SCOUT FOR THE SAKE OF WORLD PEACE, VOLUNTEER SERVICE, AND DEMOCRACY, IS IT?
KUMTLE (TWITCH)
...YOU'RE... REALLY GUTSY.
GUT-SY?

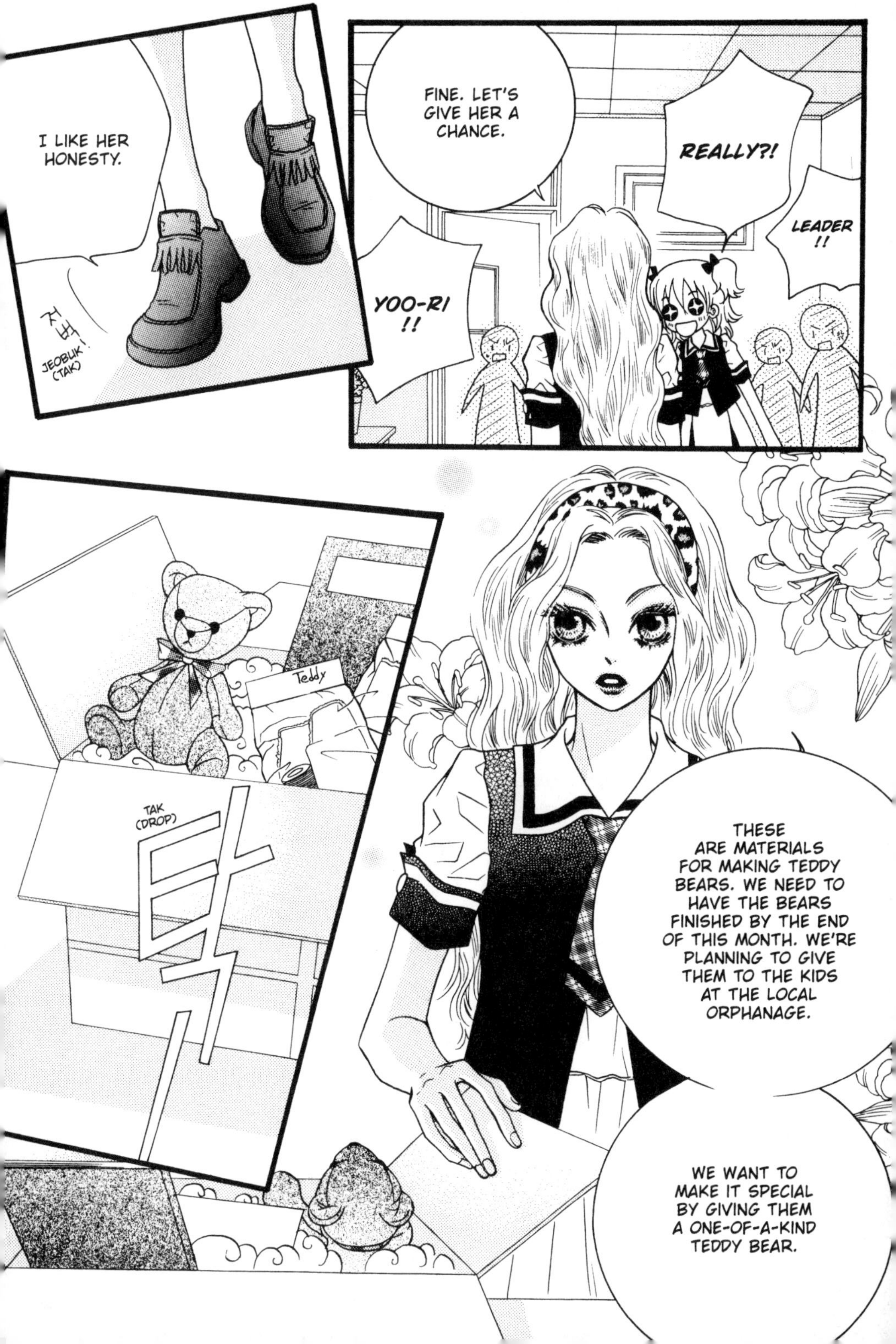

I LIKE HER HONESTY.
저벅
JEOBUK (TAK)
FINE. LET'S GIVE HER A CHANCE.
REALLY?!
YOO-RI !!
LEADER !!
TAK (DROP)
탁
THESE ARE MATERIALS FOR MAKING TEDDY BEARS. WE NEED TO HAVE THE BEARS FINISHED BY THE END OF THIS MONTH. WE'RE PLANNING TO GIVE THEM TO THE KIDS AT THE LOCAL ORPHANAGE.
WE WANT TO MAKE IT SPECIAL BY GIVING THEM A ONE-OF-A-KIND TEDDY BEAR.

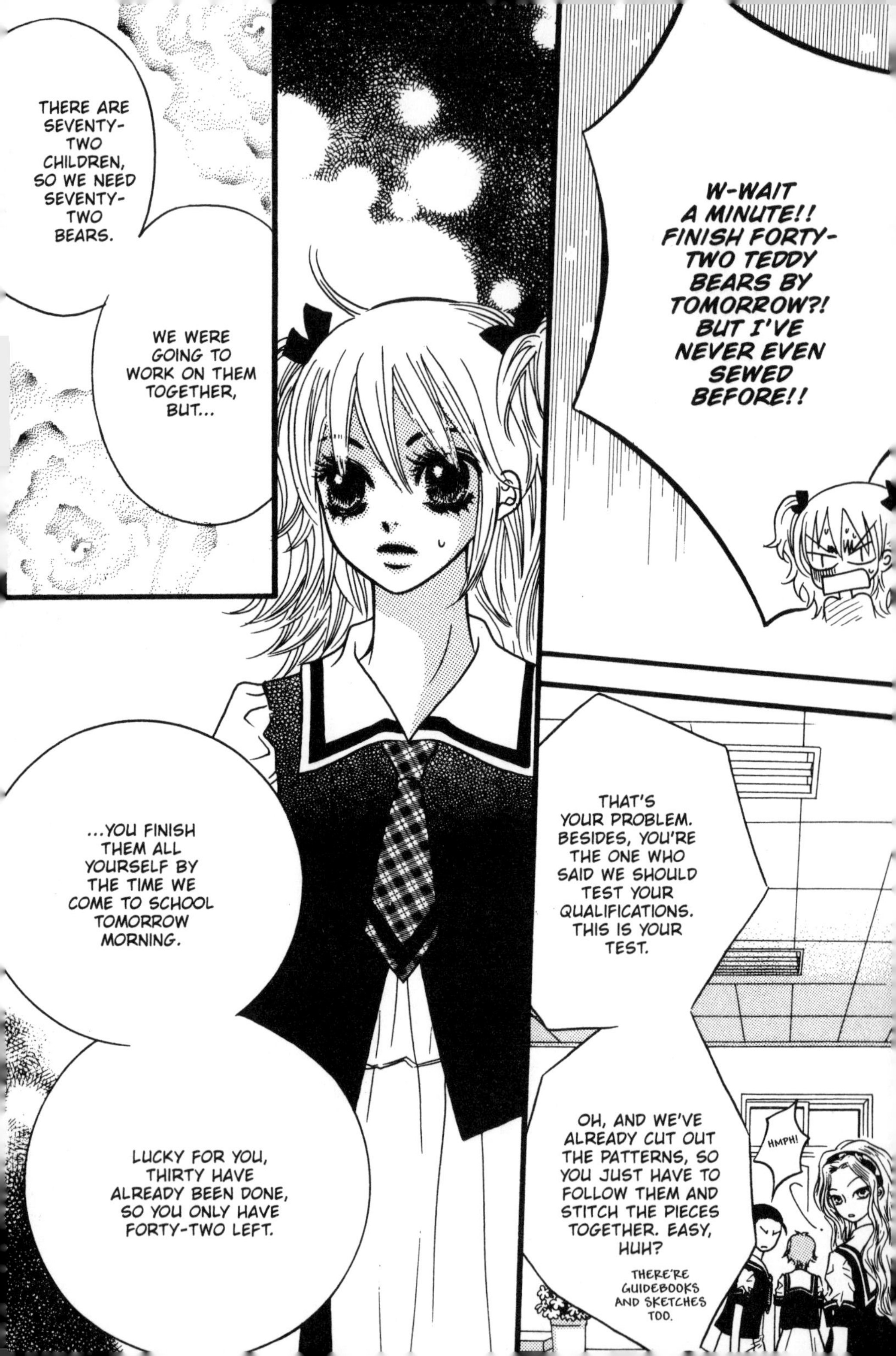
THERE ARE SEVENTY-TWO CHILDREN, SO WE NEED SEVENTY-TWO BEARS.
WE WERE GOING TO WORK ON THEM TOGETHER, BUT...
...YOU FINISH THEM ALL YOURSELF BY THE TIME WE COME TO SCHOOL TOMORROW MORNING.
LUCKY FOR YOU, THIRTY HAVE ALREADY BEEN DONE, SO YOU ONLY HAVE FORTY-TWO LEFT.
W-WAIT A MINUTE!! FINISH FORTY-TWO TEDDY BEARS BY TOMORROW?! BUT I'VE NEVER EVEN SEWED BEFORE!!
THAT'S YOUR PROBLEM. BESIDES, YOU'RE THE ONE WHO SAID WE SHOULD TEST YOUR QUALIFICATIONS. THIS IS YOUR TEST.
OH, AND WE'VE ALREADY CUT OUT THE PATTERNS, SO YOU JUST HAVE TO FOLLOW THEM AND STITCH THE PIECES TOGETHER. EASY, HUH?
HMPH!
THERE'RE GUIDEBOOKS AND SKETCHES TOO.

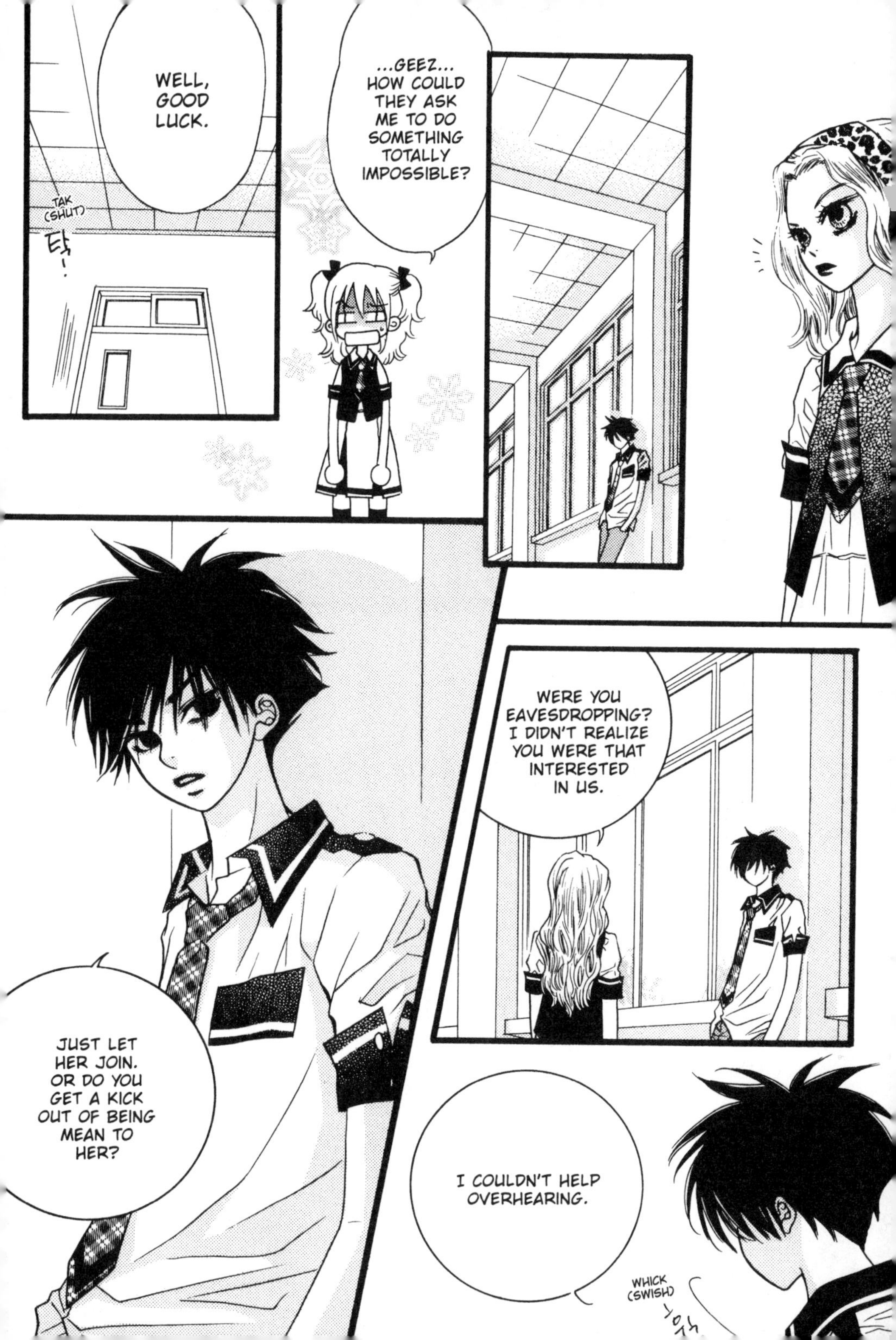
WELL, GOOD LUCK.
TAK (SHUT)
탁!
...GEEZ... HOW COULD THEY ASK ME TO DO SOMETHING TOTALLY IMPOSSIBLE?
JUST LET HER JOIN. OR DO YOU GET A KICK OUT OF BEING MEAN TO HER?
WERE YOU EAVESDROPPING? I DIDN'T REALIZE YOU WERE THAT INTERESTED IN US.
I COULDN'T HELP OVERHEARING.
WHICK (SWISH)

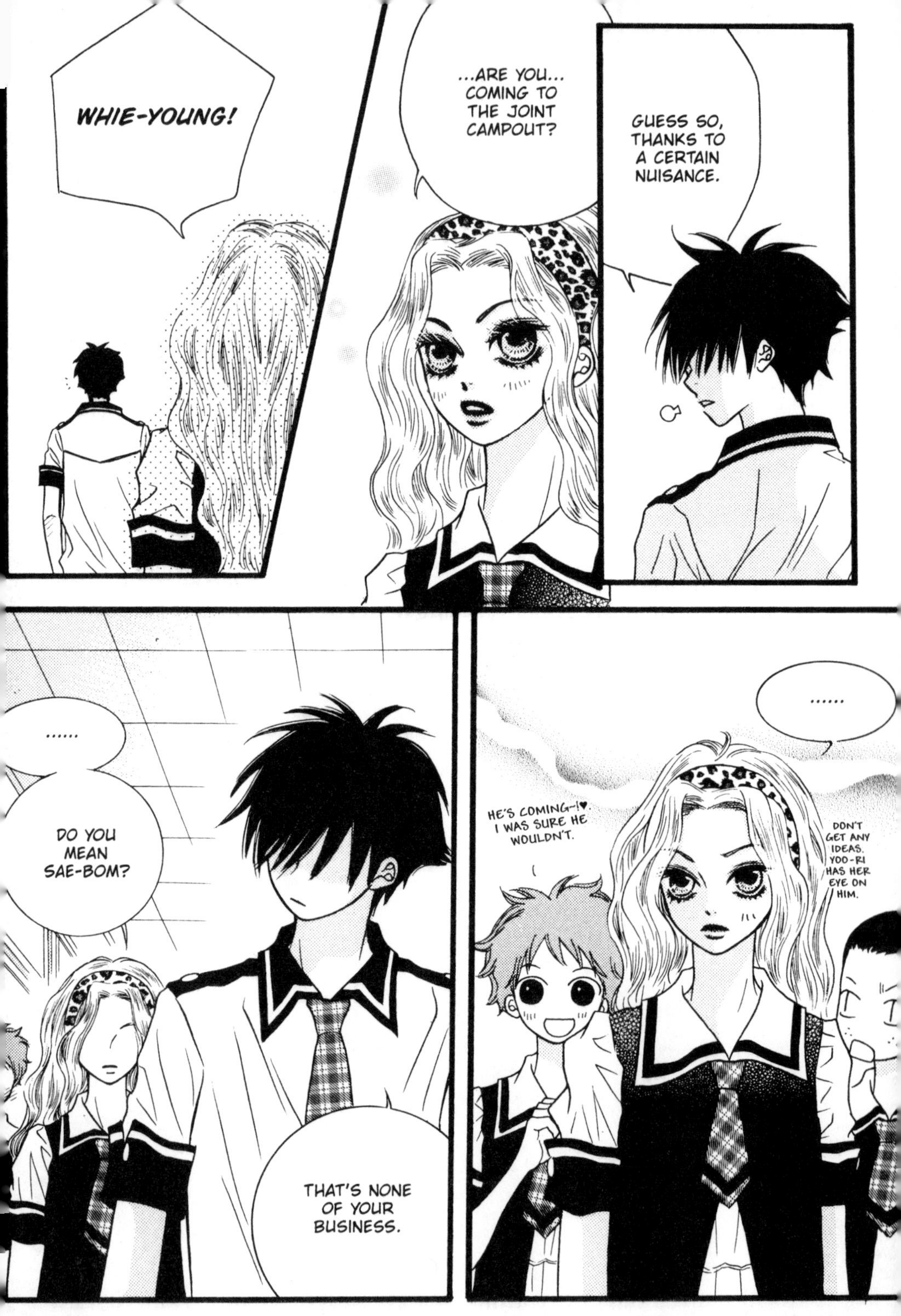
WHIE-YOUNG!
...ARE YOU... COMING TO THE JOINT CAMPOUT?
GUESS SO, THANKS TO A CERTAIN NUISANCE.
......
DO YOU MEAN SAE-BOM?
THAT'S NONE OF YOUR BUSINESS.
......
HE'S COMING-!♥. I WAS SURE HE WOULDN'T.
DON'T GET ANY IDEAS. YOO-RI HAS HER EYE ON HIM.

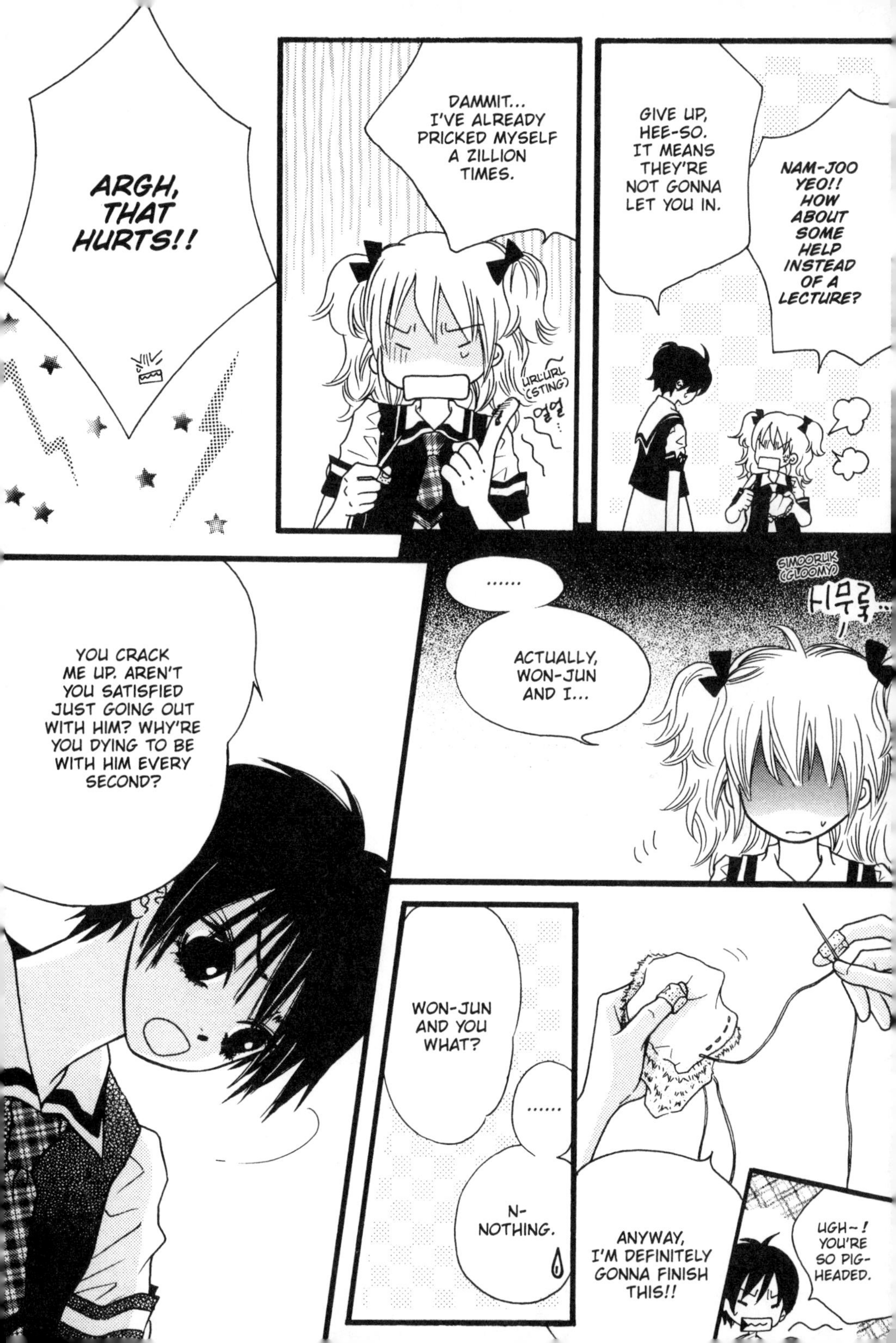
ARGH, THAT HURTS!!
DAMMIT... I'VE ALREADY PRICKED MYSELF A ZILLION TIMES.
URL-URL (STING)
얼얼...
GIVE UP, HEE-SO. IT MEANS THEY'RE NOT GONNA LET YOU IN.
NAM-JOO YEO!! HOW ABOUT SOME HELP INSTEAD OF A LECTURE?
YOU CRACK ME UP. AREN'T YOU SATISFIED JUST GOING OUT WITH HIM? WHY'RE YOU DYING TO BE WITH HIM EVERY SECOND?
......
SIMOORUK (GLOOMY)
시무룩...
ACTUALLY, WON-JUN AND I...
WON-JUN AND YOU WHAT?
......
N-NOTHING.
ANYWAY, I'M DEFINITELY GONNA FINISH THIS!!
UGH~! YOU'RE SO PIG-HEADED.

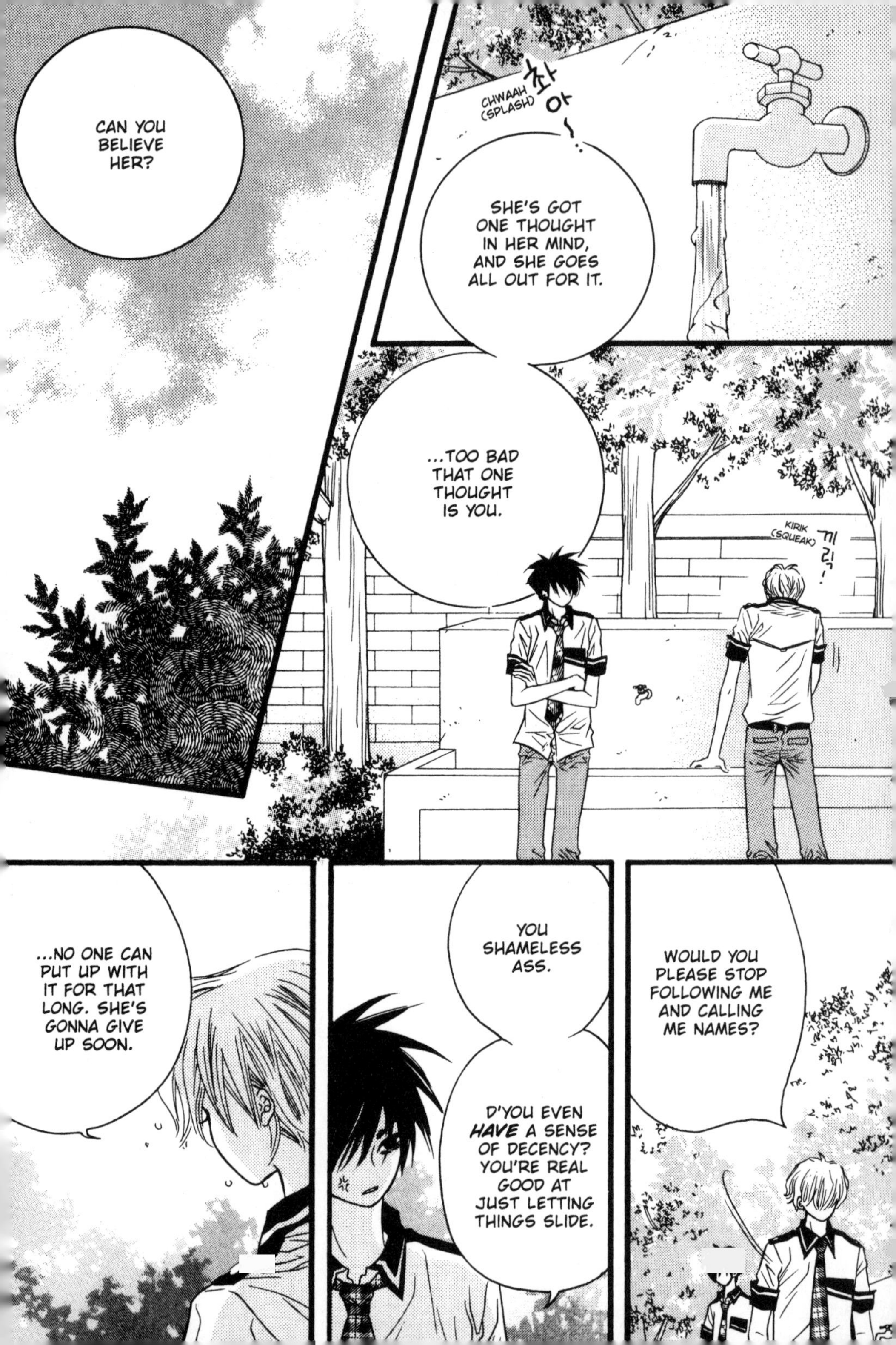
CAN YOU BELIEVE HER?
CHWAAH (SPLASH)
촤아~
SHE'S GOT ONE THOUGHT IN HER MIND, AND SHE GOES ALL OUT FOR IT.
...TOO BAD THAT ONE THOUGHT IS YOU.
KIRIK (SQUEAK)
끼릭
...NO ONE CAN PUT UP WITH IT FOR THAT LONG. SHE'S GONNA GIVE UP SOON.
YOU SHAMELESS ASS.
D'YOU EVEN *HAVE* A SENSE OF DECENCY? YOU'RE REAL GOOD AT JUST LETTING THINGS SLIDE.
WOULD YOU PLEASE STOP FOLLOWING ME AND CALLING ME NAMES?

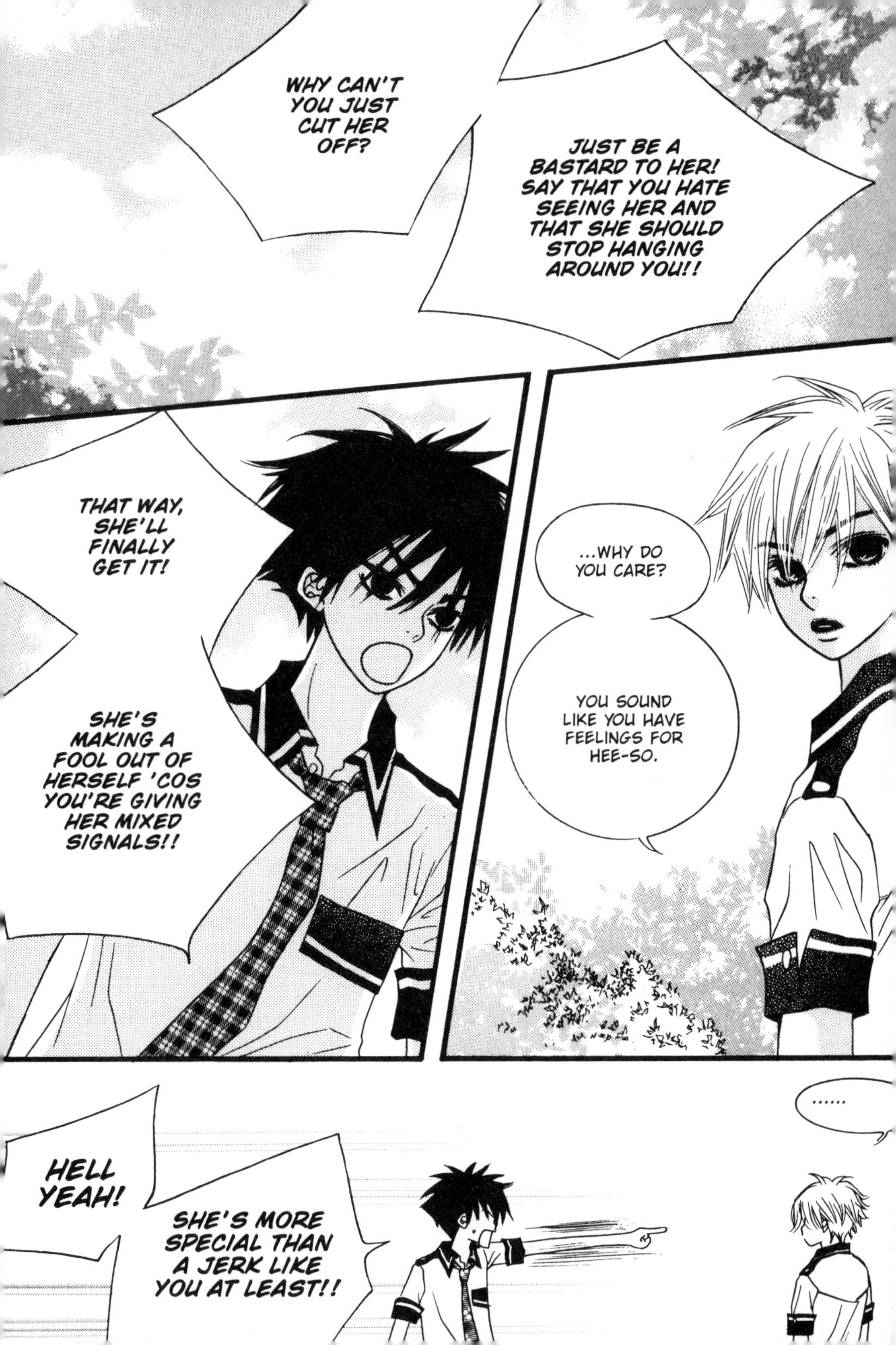
WHY CAN'T YOU JUST CUT HER OFF?
JUST BE A BASTARD TO HER! SAY THAT YOU HATE SEEING HER AND THAT SHE SHOULD STOP HANGING AROUND YOU!!
THAT WAY, SHE'LL FINALLY GET IT!
SHE'S MAKING A FOOL OUT OF HERSELF 'COS YOU'RE GIVING HER MIXED SIGNALS!!
...WHY DO YOU CARE?
YOU SOUND LIKE YOU HAVE FEELINGS FOR HEE-SO.
HELL YEAH!
SHE'S MORE SPECIAL THAN A JERK LIKE YOU AT LEAST!!
......

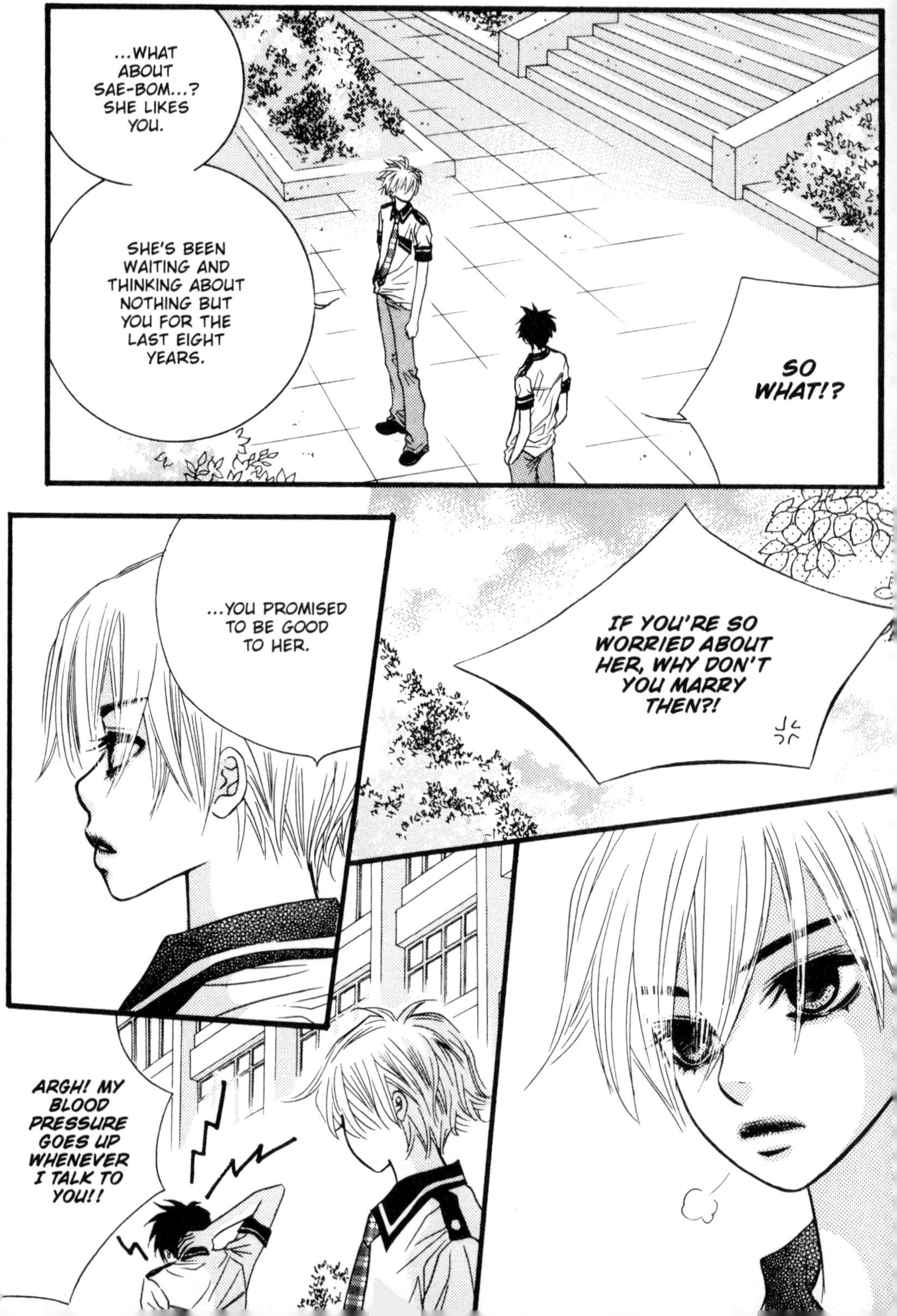
...WHAT ABOUT SAE-BOM...? SHE LIKES YOU.
SHE'S BEEN WAITING AND THINKING ABOUT NOTHING BUT YOU FOR THE LAST EIGHT YEARS.
SO WHAT!?
...YOU PROMISED TO BE GOOD TO HER.
IF YOU'RE SO WORRIED ABOUT HER, WHY DON'T YOU MARRY THEN?!
ARGH! MY BLOOD PRESSURE GOES UP WHENEVER I TALK TO YOU!!

HEE-SO MADE THIS ONE.

I MADE THAT ONE!!

SHABANG (GLITTER)

SHABANG

KOOJIL (UGLY)

KOOJIL

...YOU'RE... REALLY TERRIBLE AT THIS, HEE-SO.

SHUT UP!!

CHUKEUN (PITIFUL)

DON'T POUR OIL ON THE FIRE!!

IT'S ALMOST MIDNIGHT. HAVE YOU CALLED HOME?

TO SAY THAT YOU'RE STAYING AT SCHOOL?

H.O.T

I SAID I WAS STAYING AT NAM-JOO'S HOUSE.

THEY'LL KILL ME IF I TELL THEM THE TRUTH.

YOU NEED FORTY-TWO BEARS, BUT WE'VE ONLY MADE TWO.

YOU MADE ONE, AND I MADE ONE.

SHE HAS NO ONE TO HELP HER BUT BEATRICE IN HUMAN FORM.

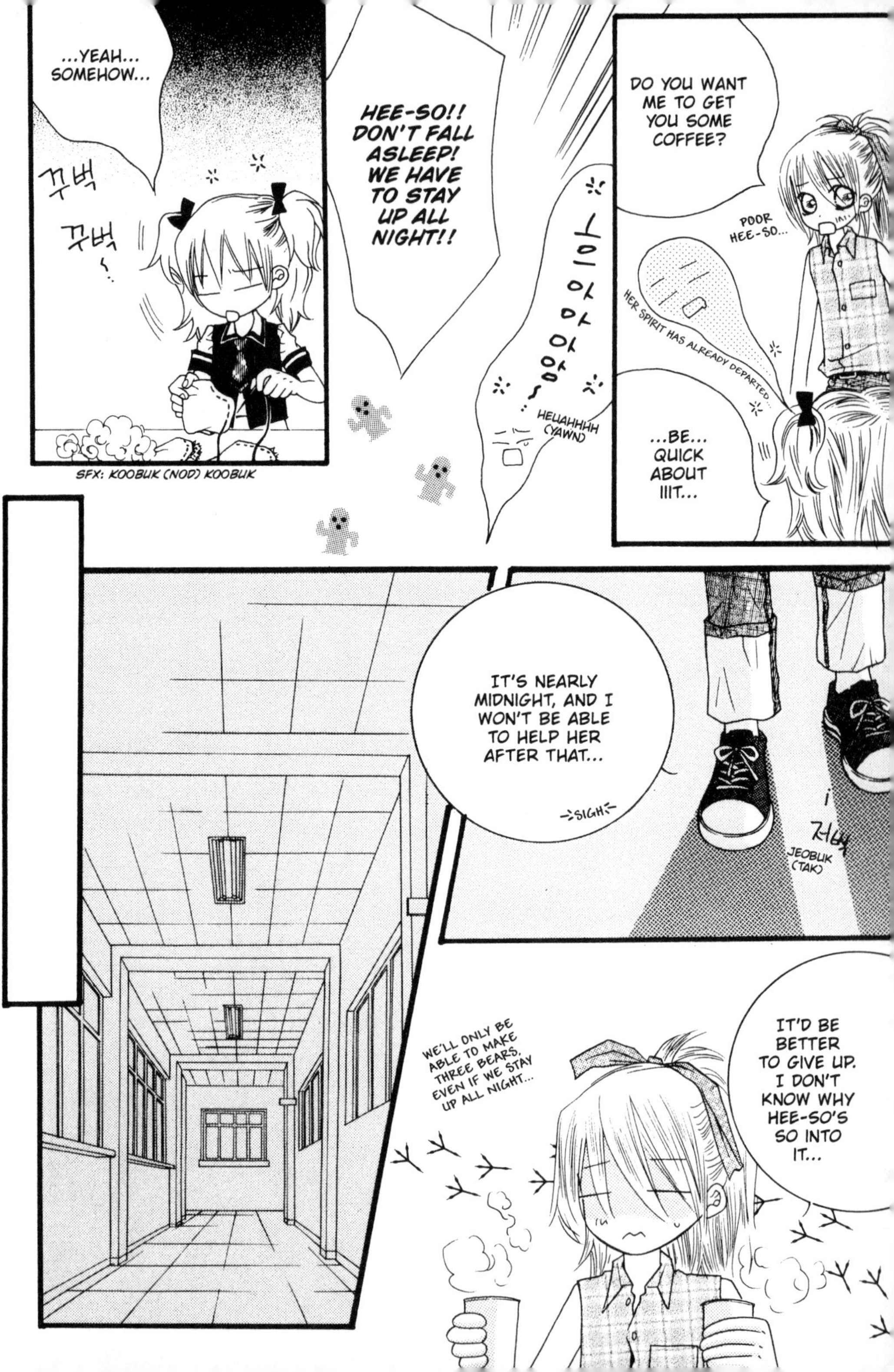
...YEAH... SOMEHOW...
꾸벅 꾸벅~...
SFX: KOOBUK (NOD) KOOBUK
HEE-SO!! DON'T FALL ASLEEP! WE HAVE TO STAY UP ALL NIGHT!!
흐아아아앙~...
HEUAHHHH (YAWN)
DO YOU WANT ME TO GET YOU SOME COFFEE?
POOR HEE-SO...
HER SPIRIT HAS ALREADY DEPARTED...
...BE... QUICK ABOUT IIIT...
IT'S NEARLY MIDNIGHT, AND I WON'T BE ABLE TO HELP HER AFTER THAT...
SIGH
저벅
JEOBUK (TAK)
WE'LL ONLY BE ABLE TO MAKE THREE BEARS, EVEN IF WE STAY UP ALL NIGHT...
IT'D BE BETTER TO GIVE UP. I DON'T KNOW WHY HEE-SO'S SO INTO IT...

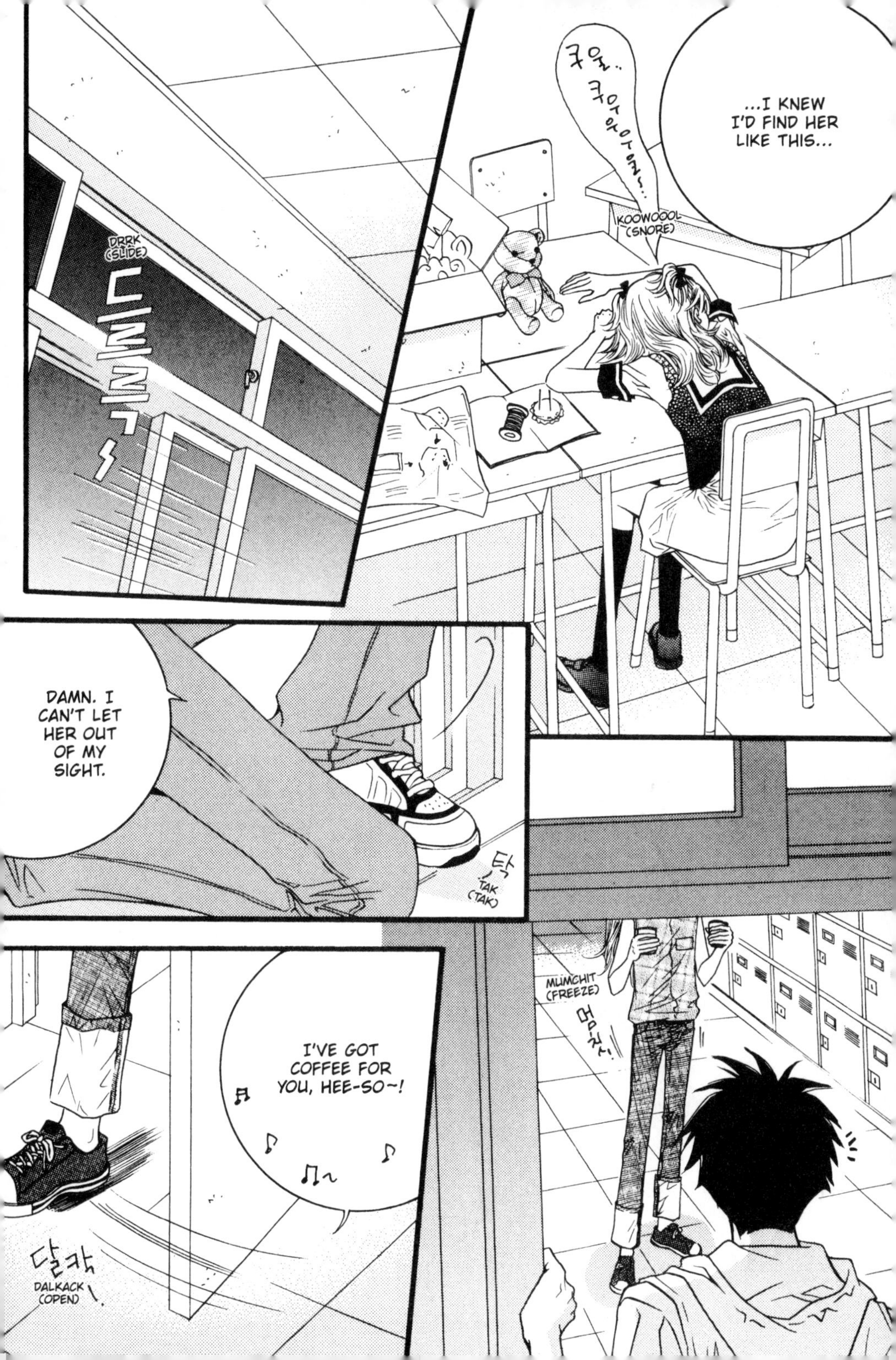
DRRK (SLIDE)
KOOWOOL (SNORE)
...I KNEW I'D FIND HER LIKE THIS...
DAMN. I CAN'T LET HER OUT OF MY SIGHT.
탁
TAK (TAK)
I'VE GOT COFFEE FOR YOU, HEE-SO~!
달칵
DALKACK (OPEN)
MUMCHIT (FREEZE)
멈칫!

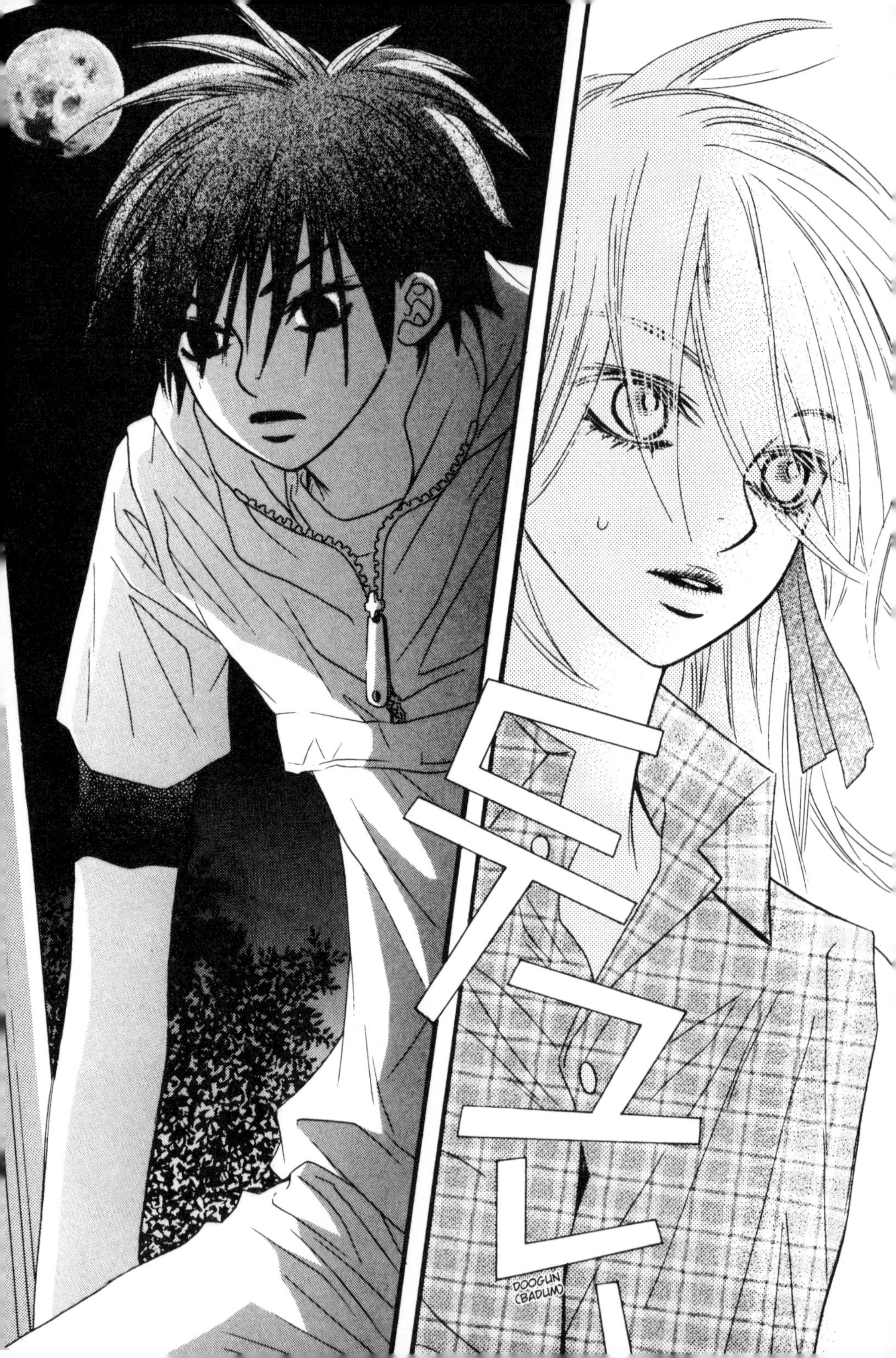
DOOGUN
(BADUM)

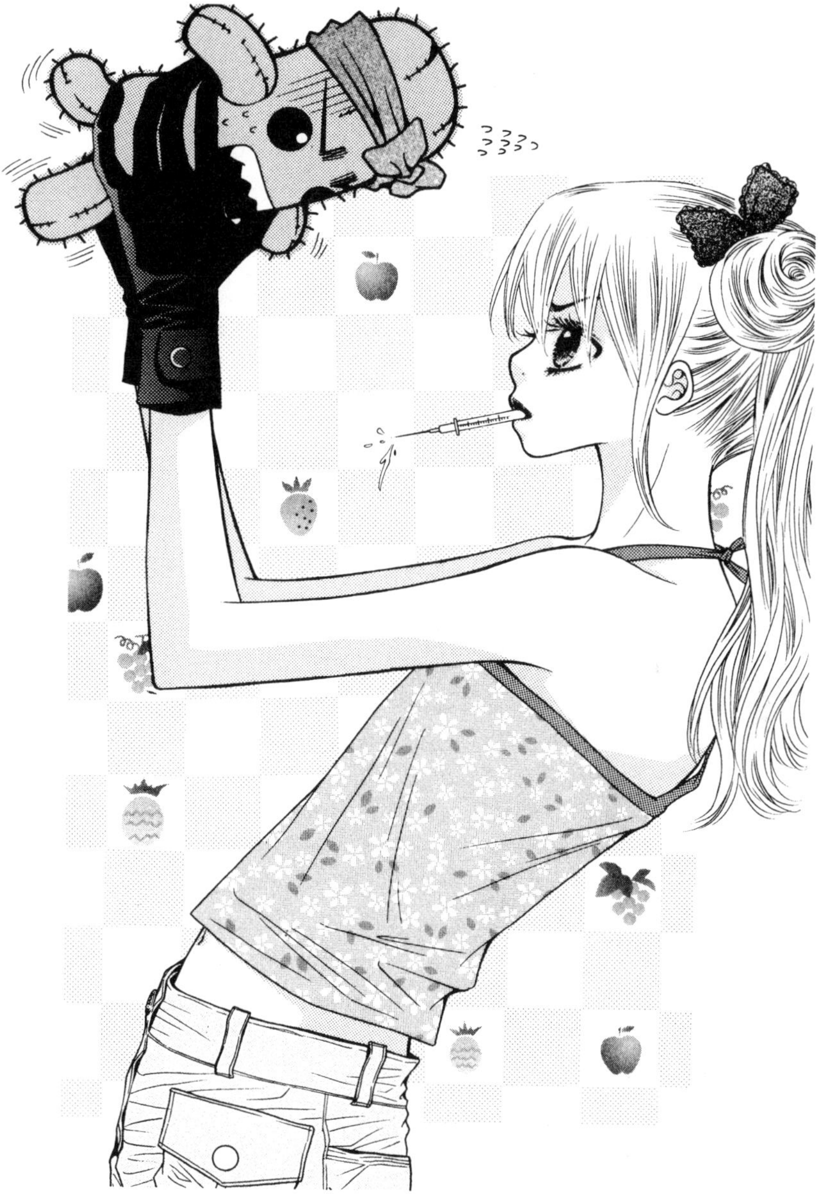

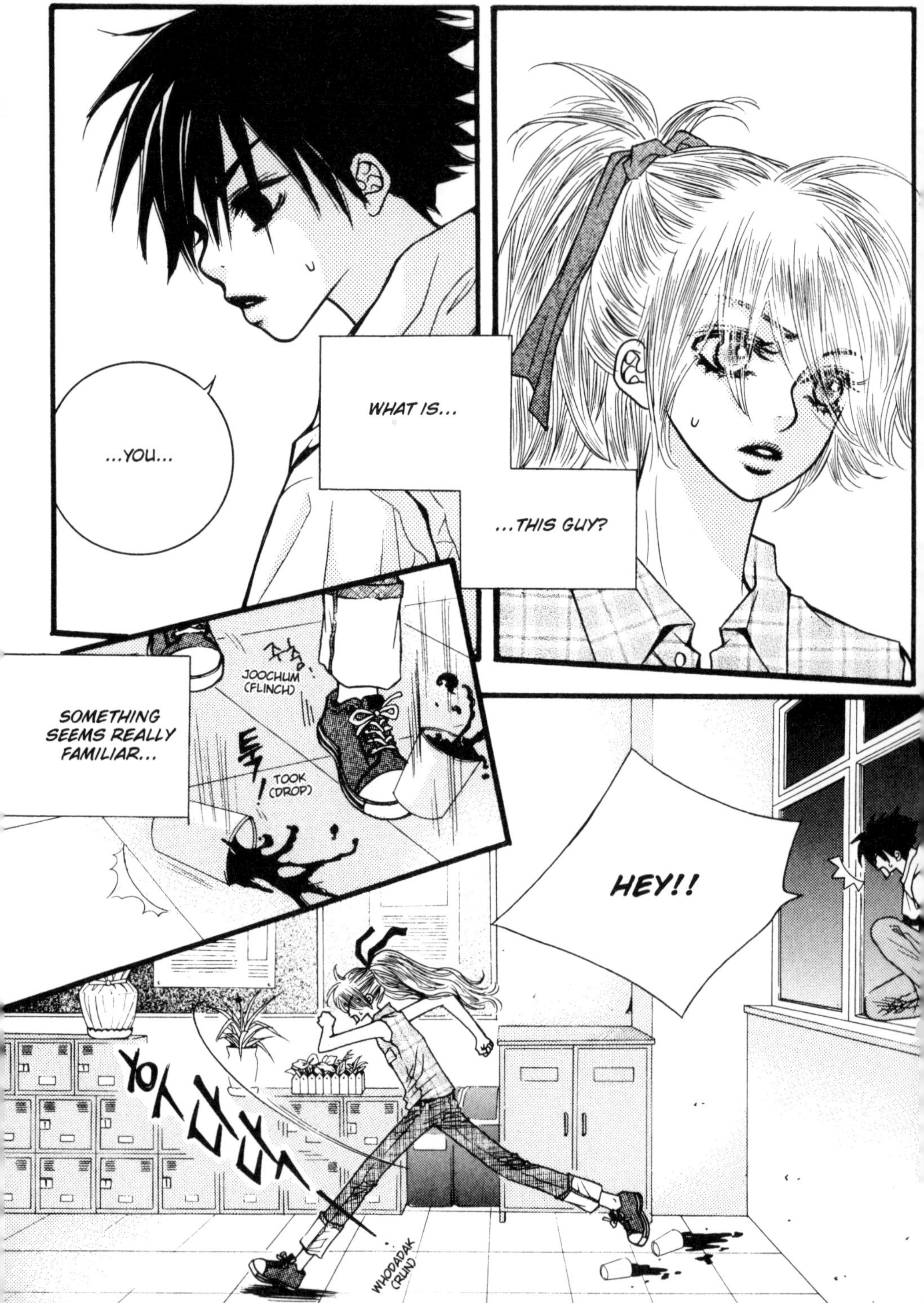
...YOU...
WHAT IS...
...THIS GUY?
SOMETHING SEEMS REALLY FAMILIAR...
JOOCHUM (FLINCH)
TOOK (DROP)
HEY!!
WHODADAK (RUN)

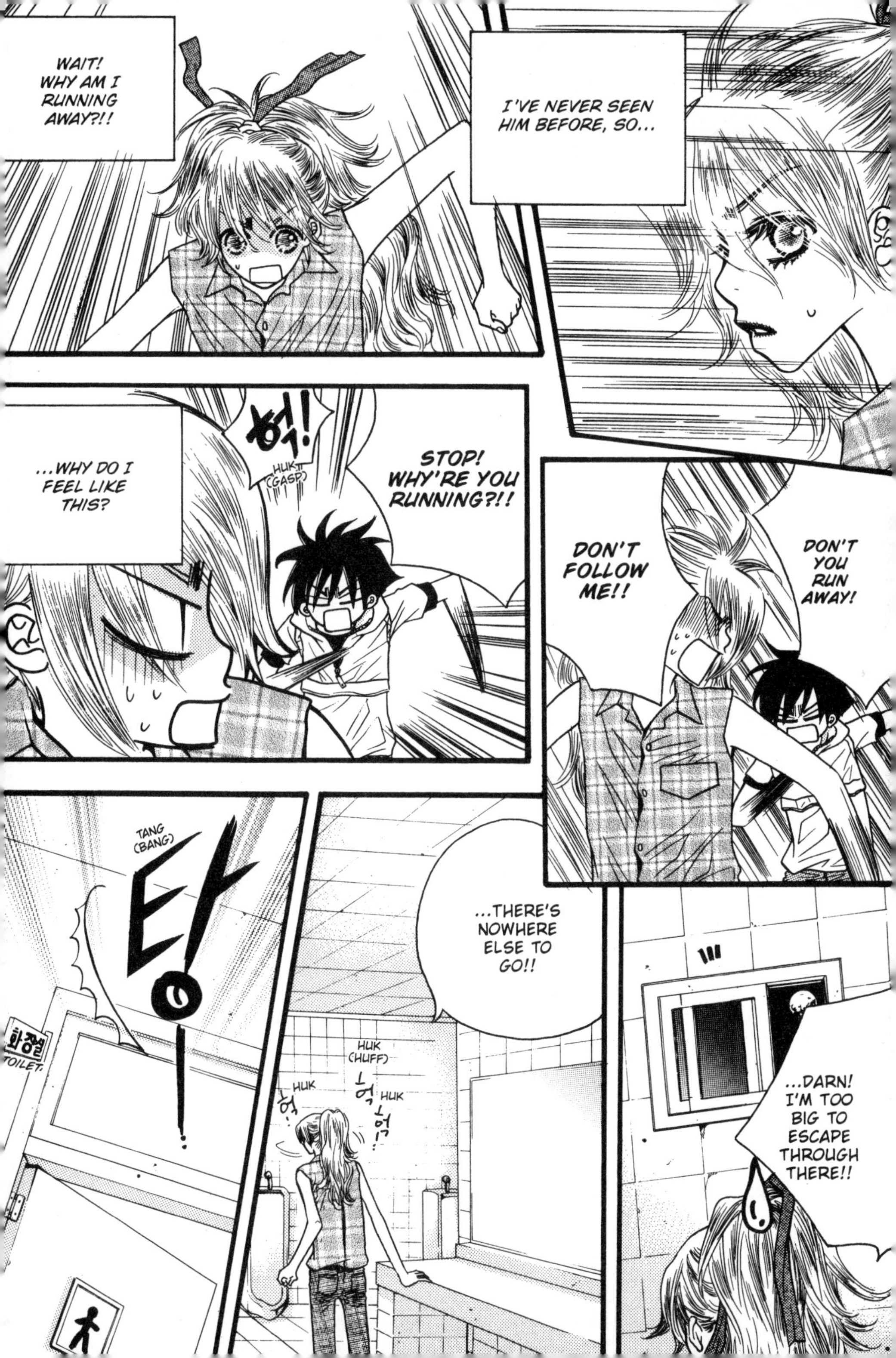
WAIT! WHY AM I RUNNING AWAY?!!
I'VE NEVER SEEN HIM BEFORE, SO...
...WHY DO I FEEL LIKE THIS?
헉!
HUK (GASP)
STOP! WHY'RE YOU RUNNING?!!
DON'T FOLLOW ME!!
DON'T YOU RUN AWAY!
TANG (BANG)
탕!
화장실
TOILET
...THERE'S NOWHERE ELSE TO GO!!
HUK
헉
HUK (HUFF)
헉
HUK
헉!
...DARN! I'M TOO BIG TO ESCAPE THROUGH THERE!!

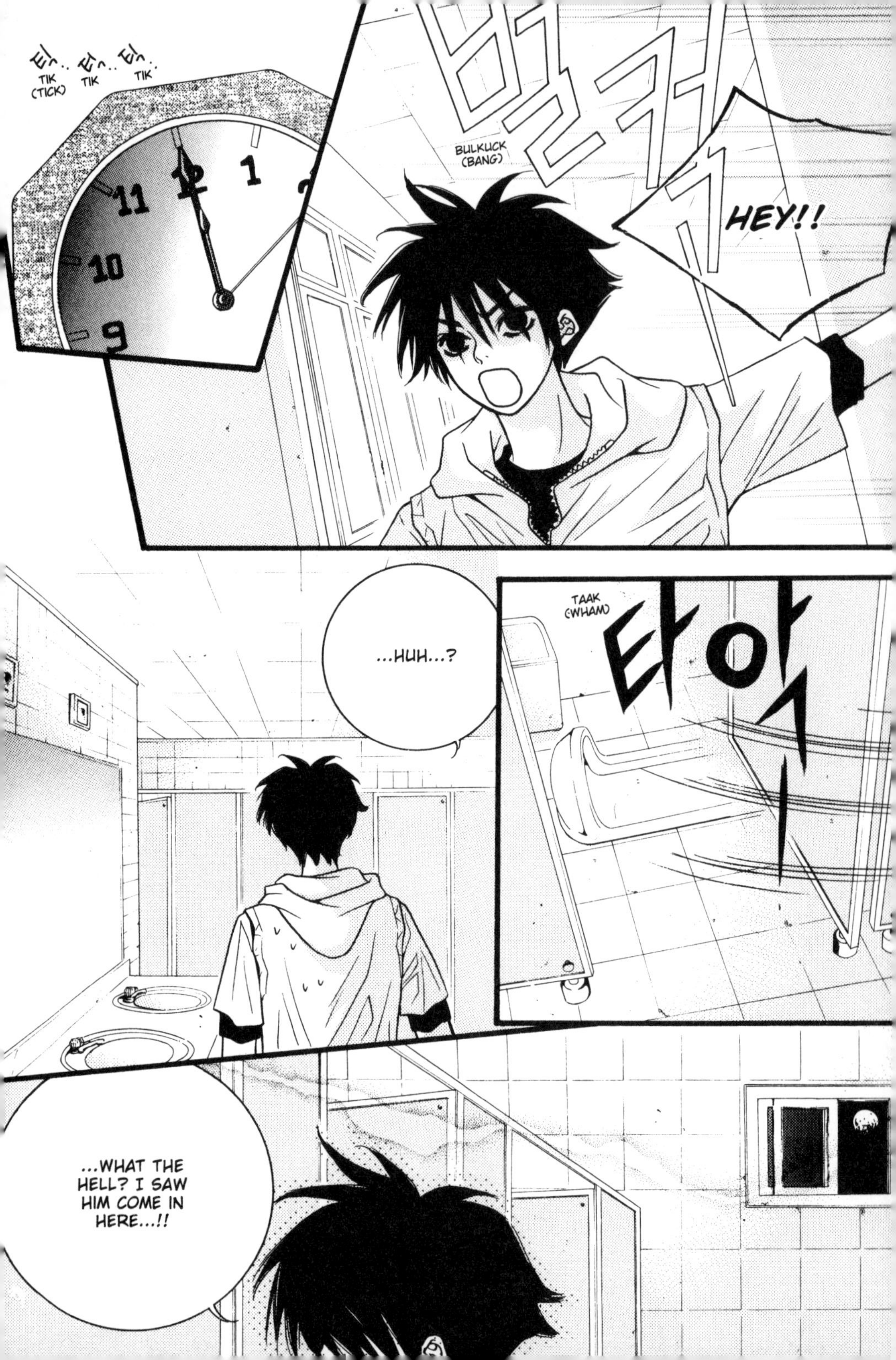
틱.. 틱.. 틱..
TIK (TICK) TIK TIK
벌컥
BULKUCK (BANG)
HEY!!
...HUH...?
탁
TAAK (WHAM)
...WHAT THE HELL? I SAW HIM COME IN HERE...!!

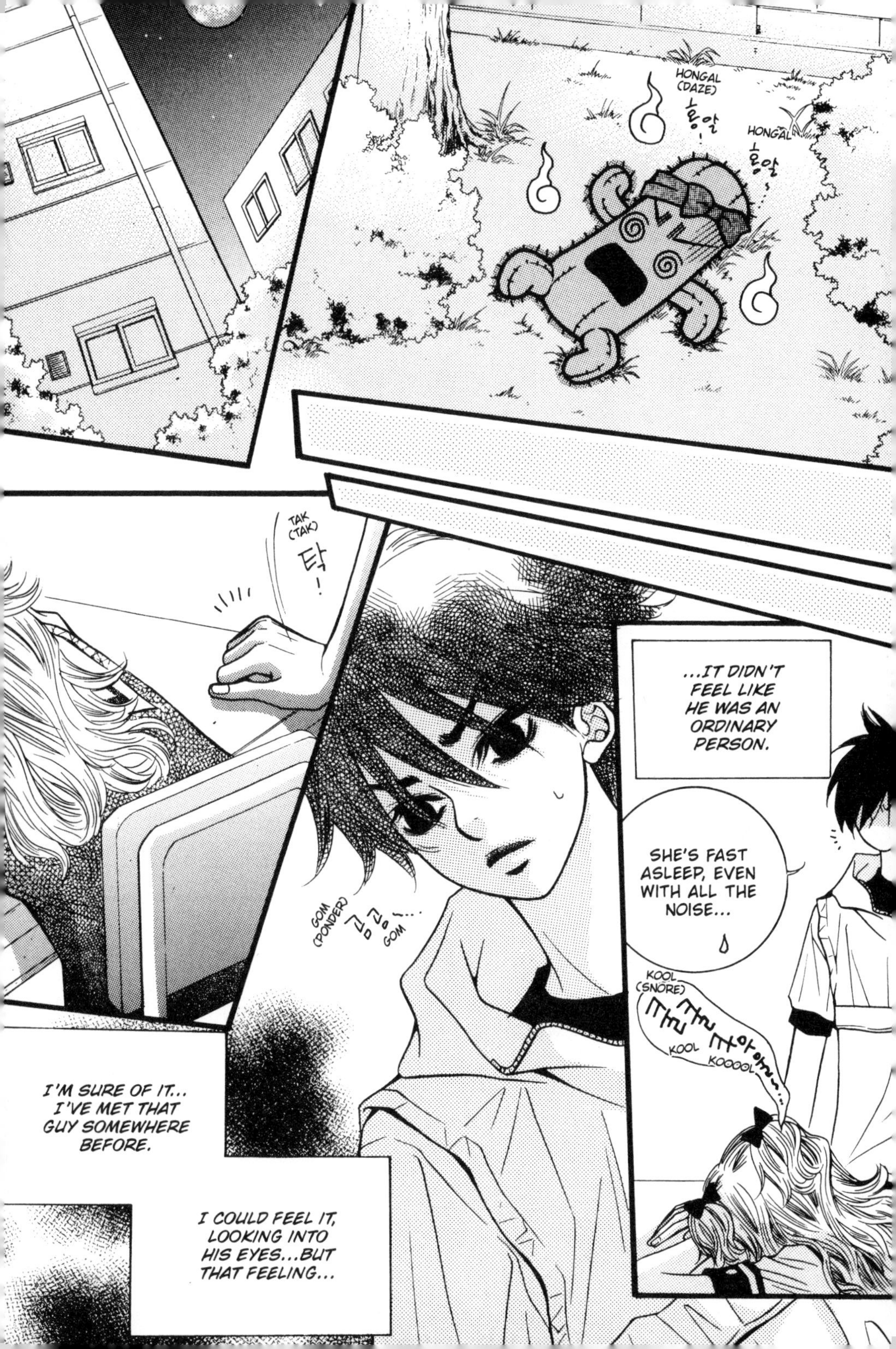
HONGAL (DAZE)
홍알!
HONGAL
홍알
TAK (TAK)
탁!
I'M SURE OF IT... I'VE MET THAT GUY SOMEWHERE BEFORE.
GOM (PONDER)
곰곰...
GOM
I COULD FEEL IT, LOOKING INTO HIS EYES...BUT THAT FEELING...
...IT DIDN'T FEEL LIKE HE WAS AN ORDINARY PERSON.
SHE'S FAST ASLEEP, EVEN WITH ALL THE NOISE...
KOOL (SNORE)
KOOL
KOOOOL

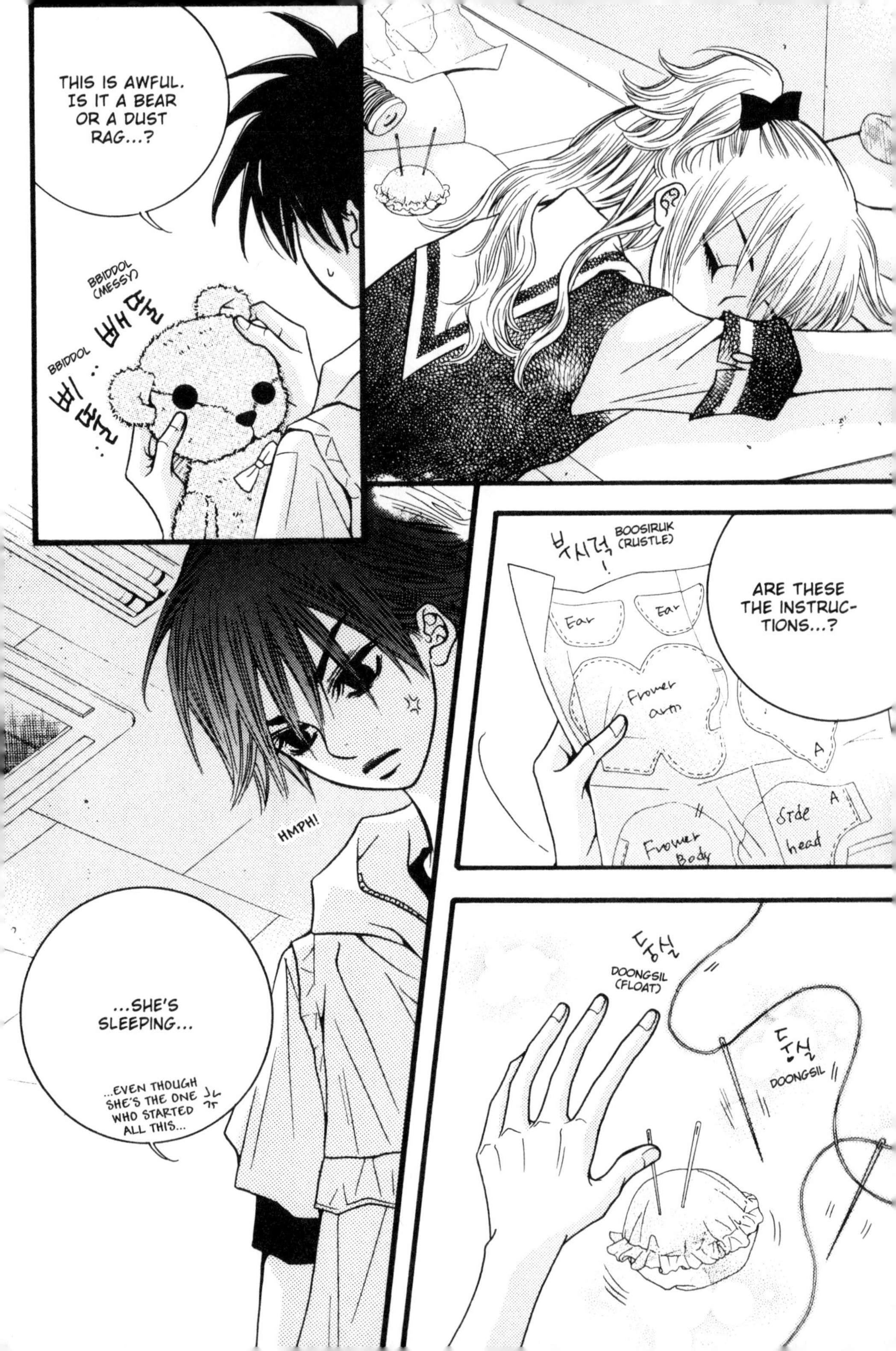
THIS IS AWFUL. IS IT A BEAR OR A DUST RAG...?
삐뚤.. 삐뚤..
BBIDDOL BBIDDOL (MESSY)
HMPH!
...SHE'S SLEEPING...
...EVEN THOUGH SHE'S THE ONE WHO STARTED ALL THIS...
부시럭
BOOSIRUK (RUSTLE)
ARE THESE THE INSTRUCTIONS...?
Ear
Ear
Frower arm
A
Side head
Frower Body
둥실
DOONGSIL (FLOAT)
둥실
DOONGSIL

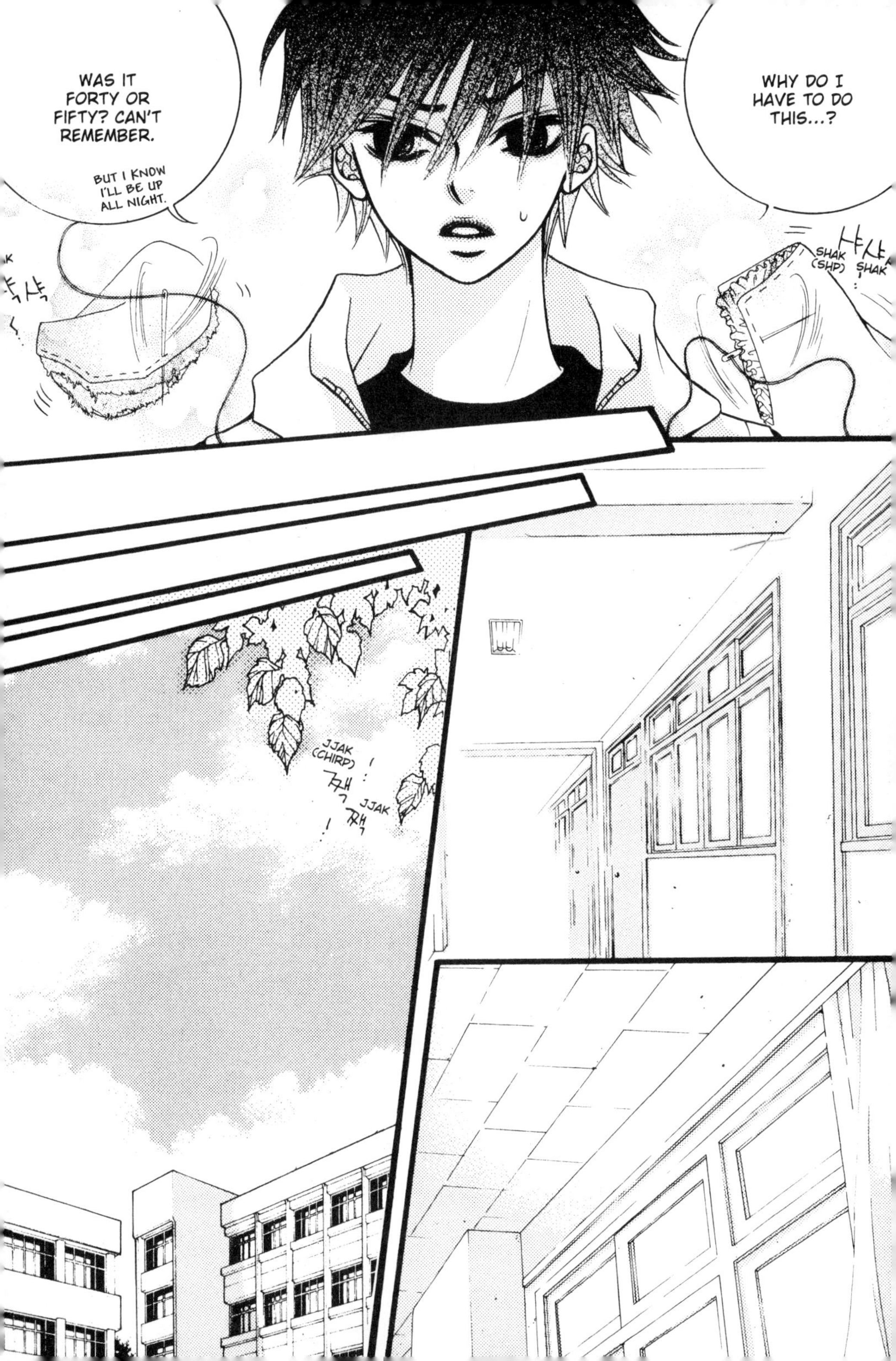
WAS IT FORTY OR FIFTY? CAN'T REMEMBER.
BUT I KNOW I'LL BE UP ALL NIGHT.
WHY DO I HAVE TO DO THIS...?
SHAK (SHP)
SHAK
JJAK (CHIRP)
짹
JJAK
짹

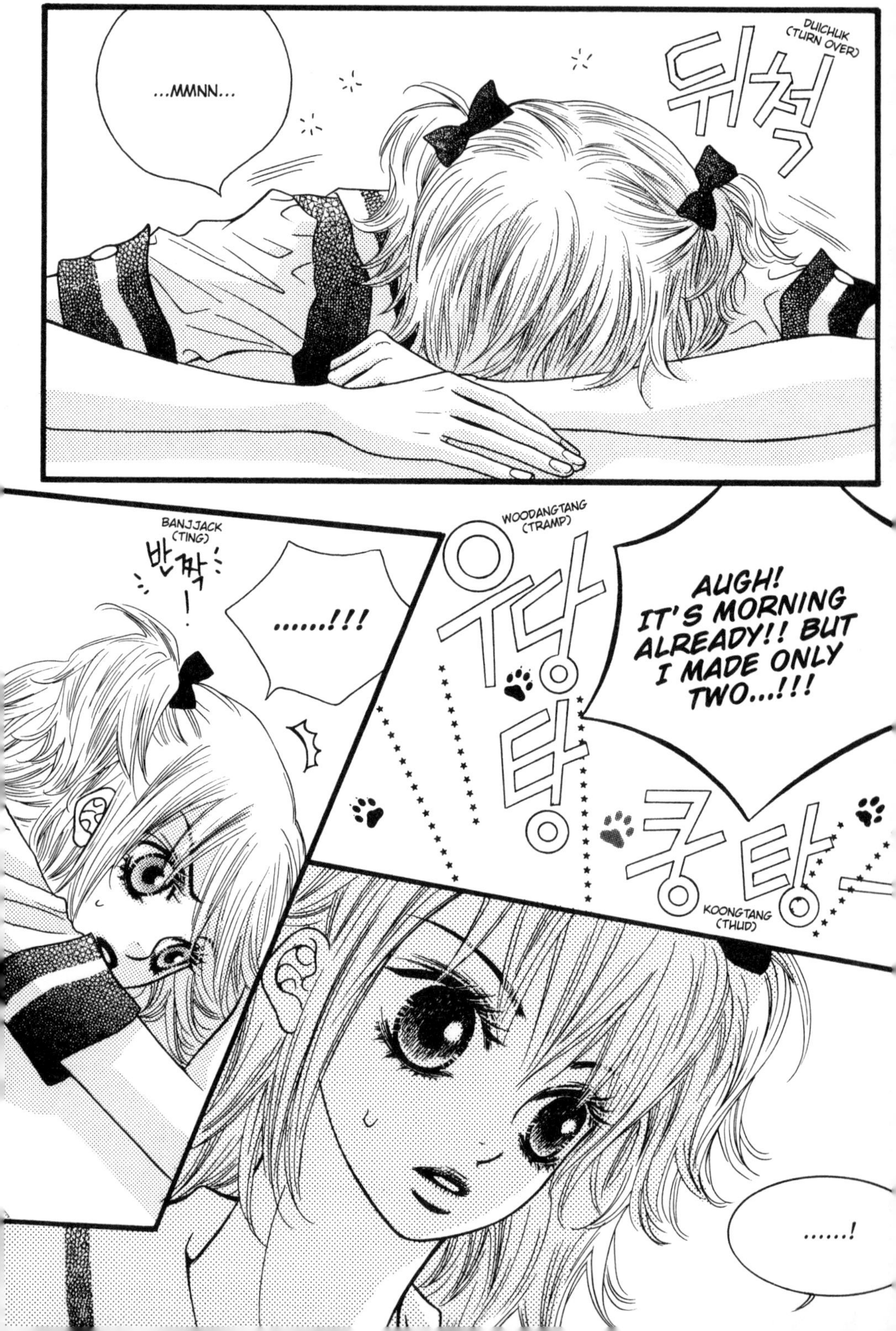
...MMNN...
DUICHUK
(TURN OVER)
뒤척
BANJJACK
(TING)
반짝
......!!!
WOODANGTANG
(TRAMP)
우당탕
AUGH! IT'S MORNING ALREADY!! BUT I MADE ONLY TWO...!!!
쿵탕
KOONGTANG
(THUD)
......!

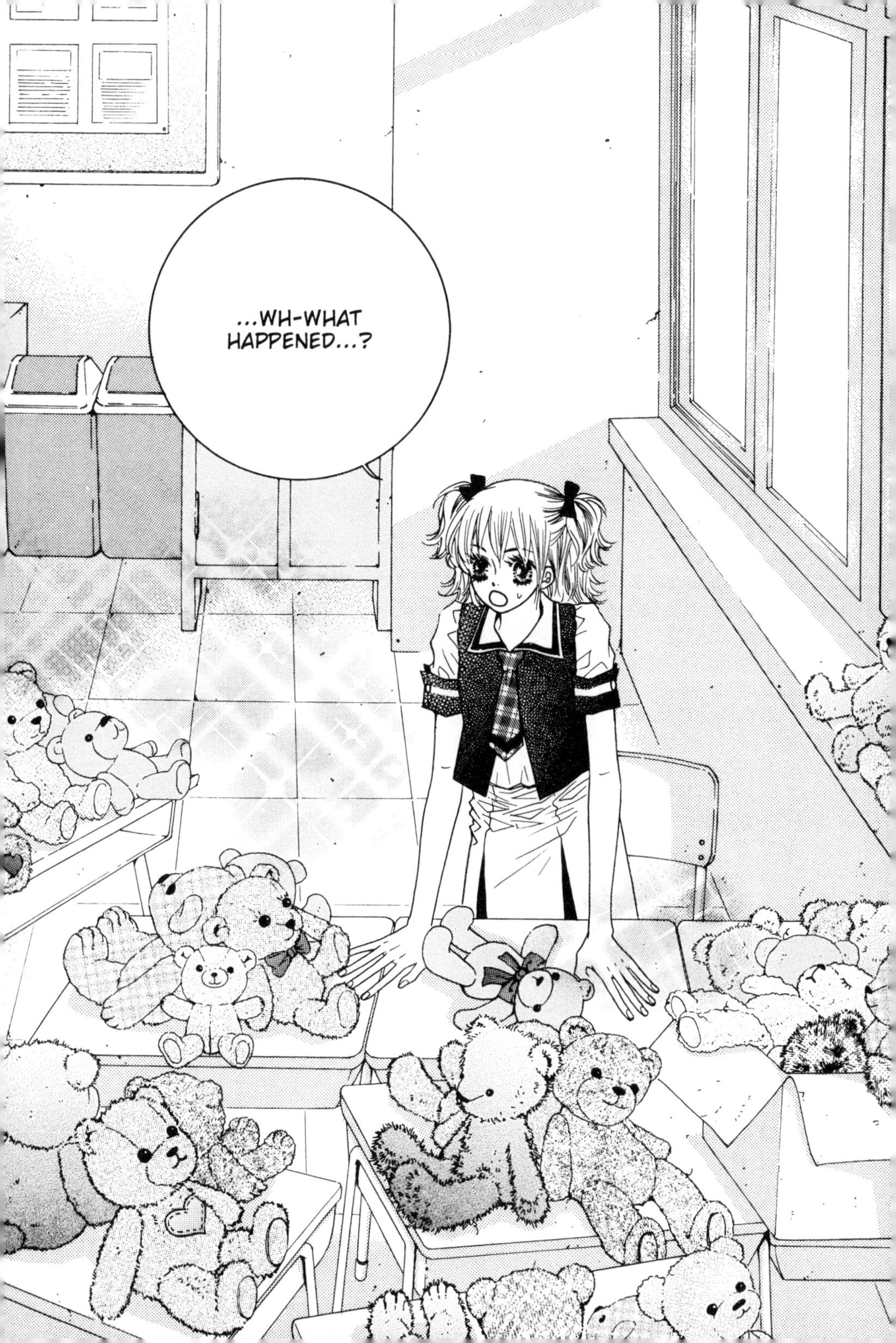
...WH-WHAT HAPPENED...?

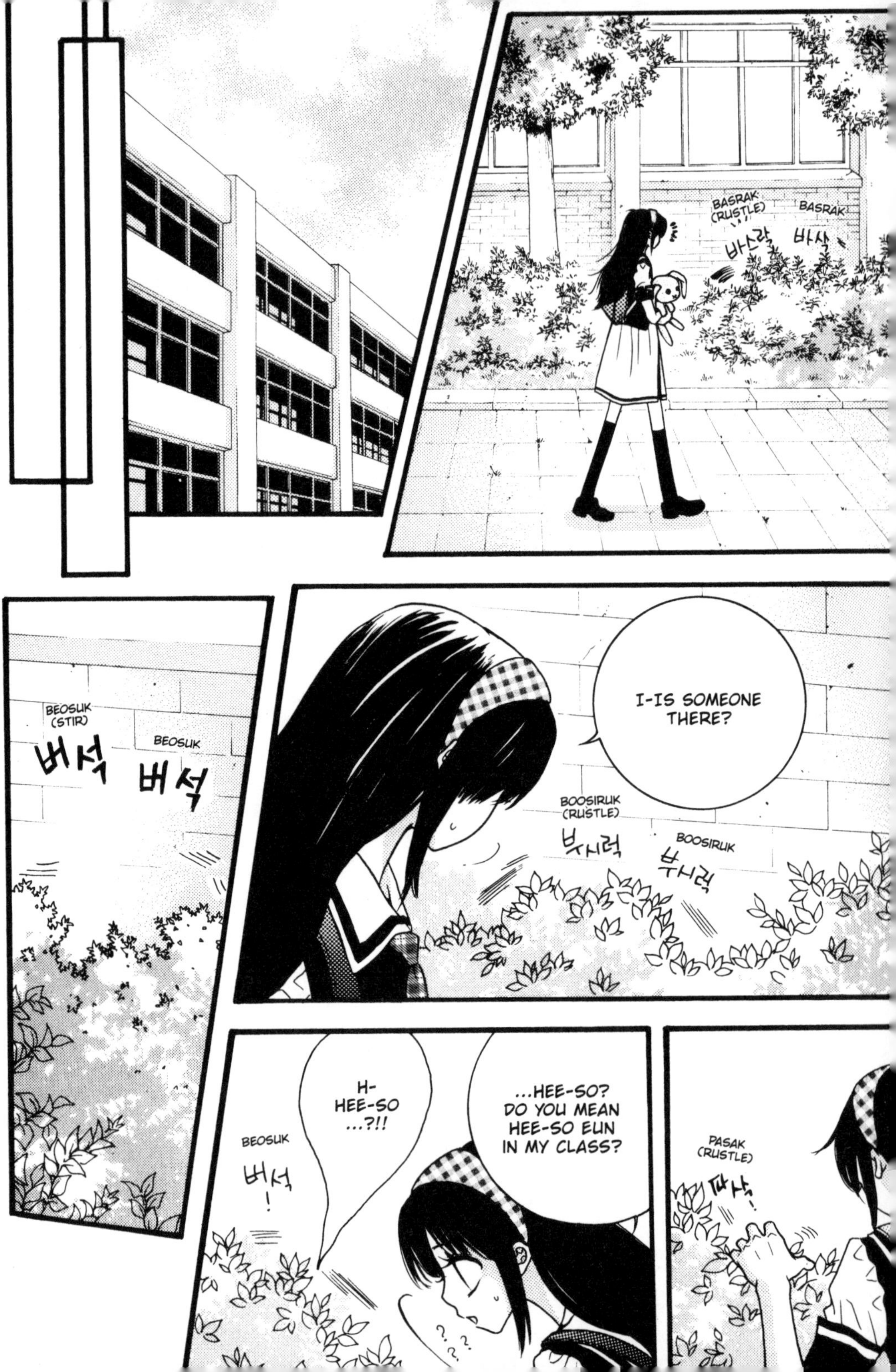
BASRAK (RUSTLE)
바스락
BASRAK
바삭
BEOSUK (STIR)
버석
BEOSUK
버석
I-IS SOMEONE THERE?
BOOSIRUK (RUSTLE)
부시럭
BOOSIRUK
부시럭
BEOSUK
버석!
H-HEE-SO ...?!!
...HEE-SO? DO YOU MEAN HEE-SO EUN IN MY CLASS?
???
PASAK (RUSTLE)
파삭!

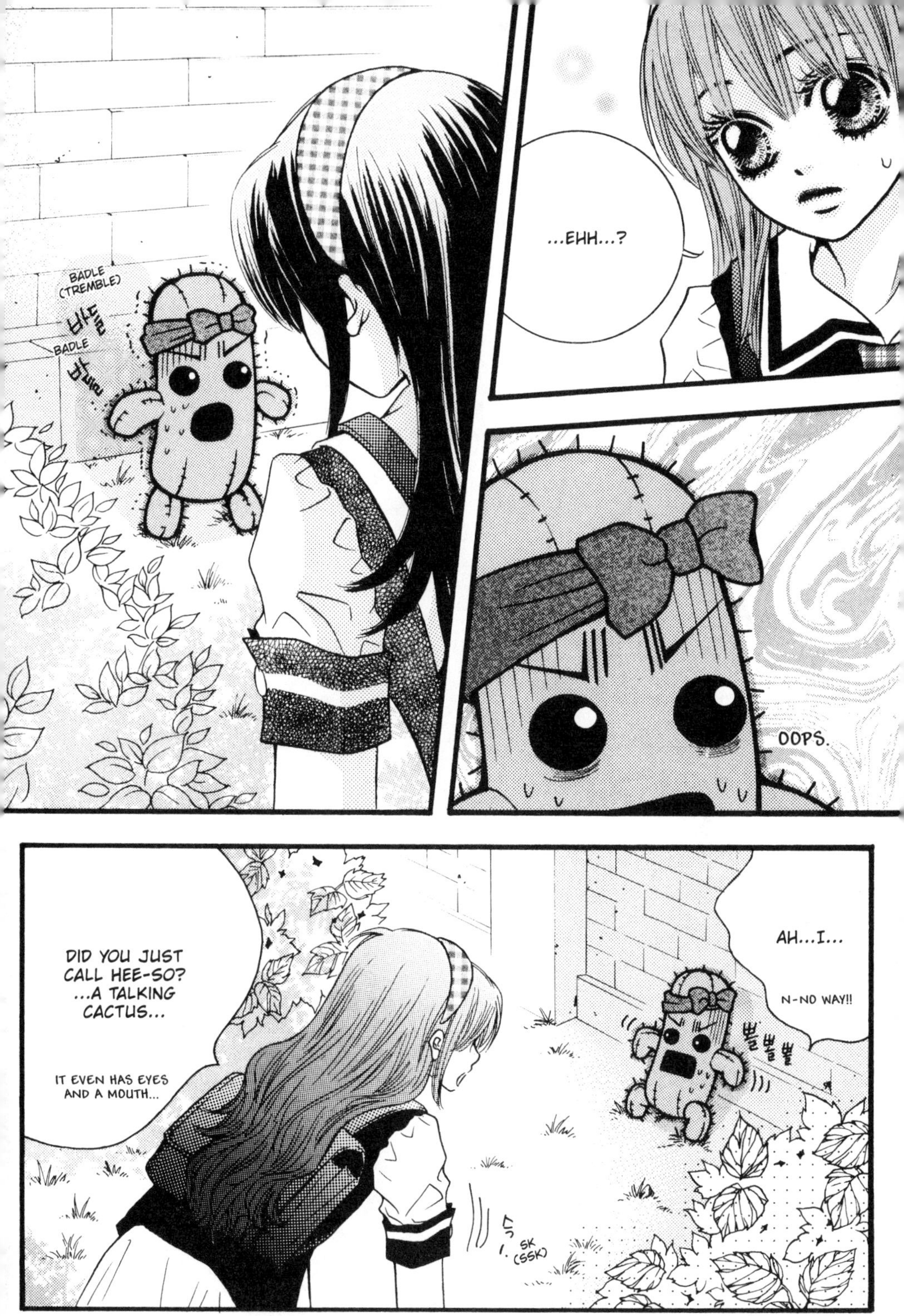
BADLE (TREMBLE)
바들
BADLE
바들
...EHH...?
OOPS.
DID YOU JUST CALL HEE-SO? ...A TALKING CACTUS...
IT EVEN HAS EYES AND A MOUTH...
AH...I...
N-NO WAY!!
뽈뽈뽈
슥
SK (SSK)

SFX: BBOL (SHF) BBOL BBOL

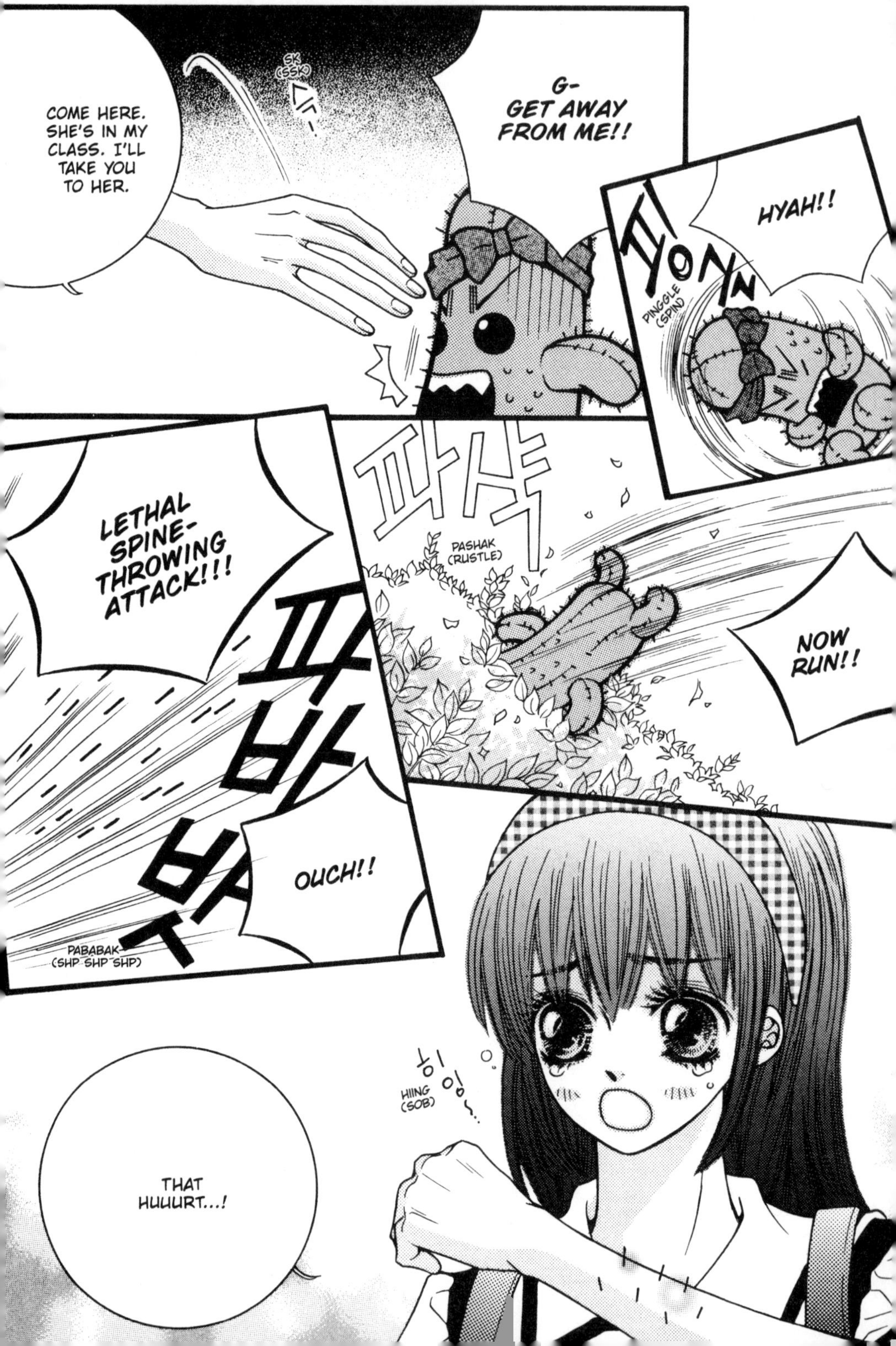
COME HERE. SHE'S IN MY CLASS. I'LL TAKE YOU TO HER.
SK (SSK)
G- GET AWAY FROM ME!!
HYAH!!
PINGGLE (SPIND)
LETHAL SPINE-THROWING ATTACK!!!
OUCH!!
PABABAK (SHP SHP SHP)
PASHAK (RUSTLE)
NOW RUN!!
THAT HUUURT...!
HIING (SOB)

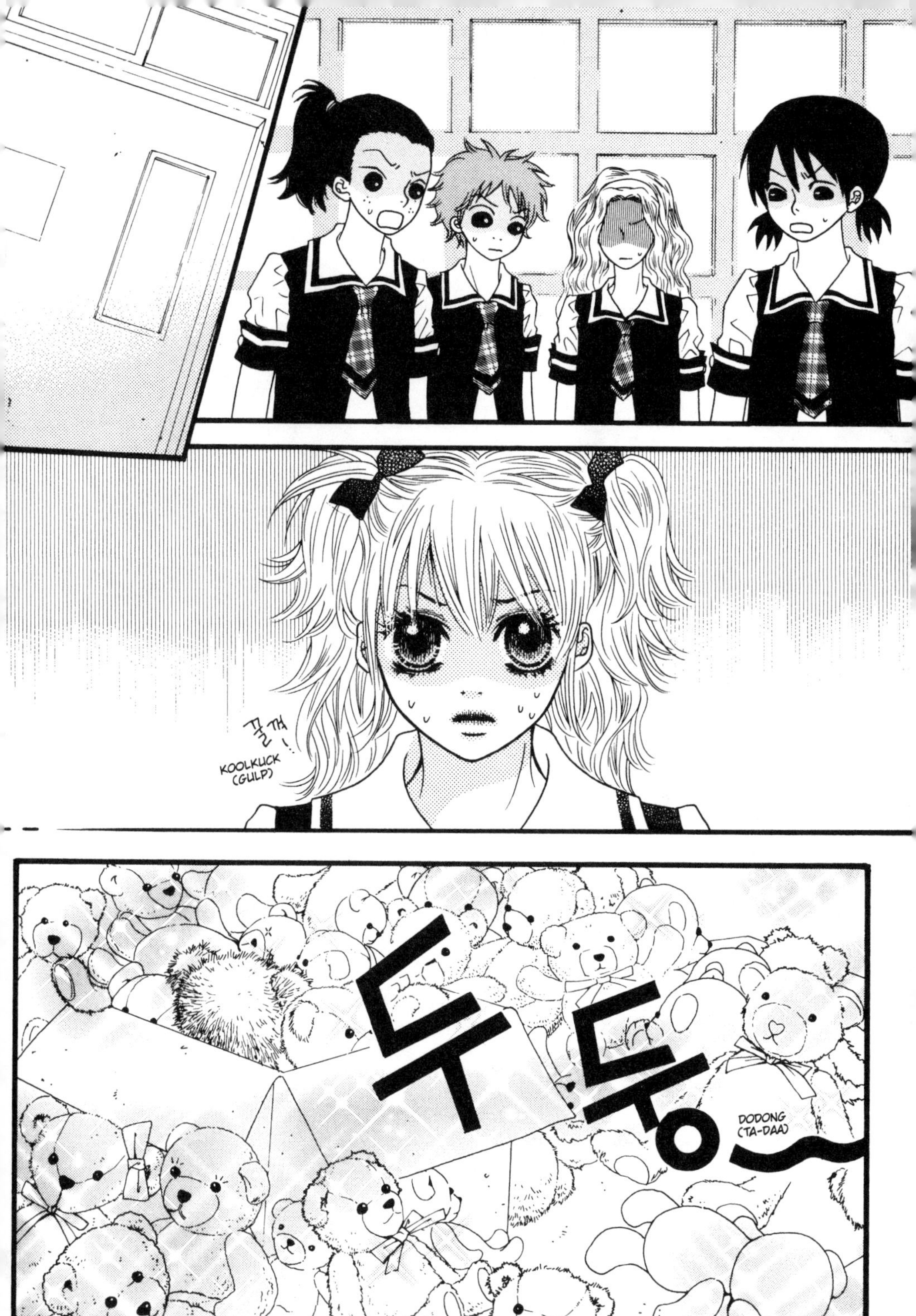
꿀꺽...
KOOLKUCK (GULP)
두둥~
DODONG (TA-DAA)

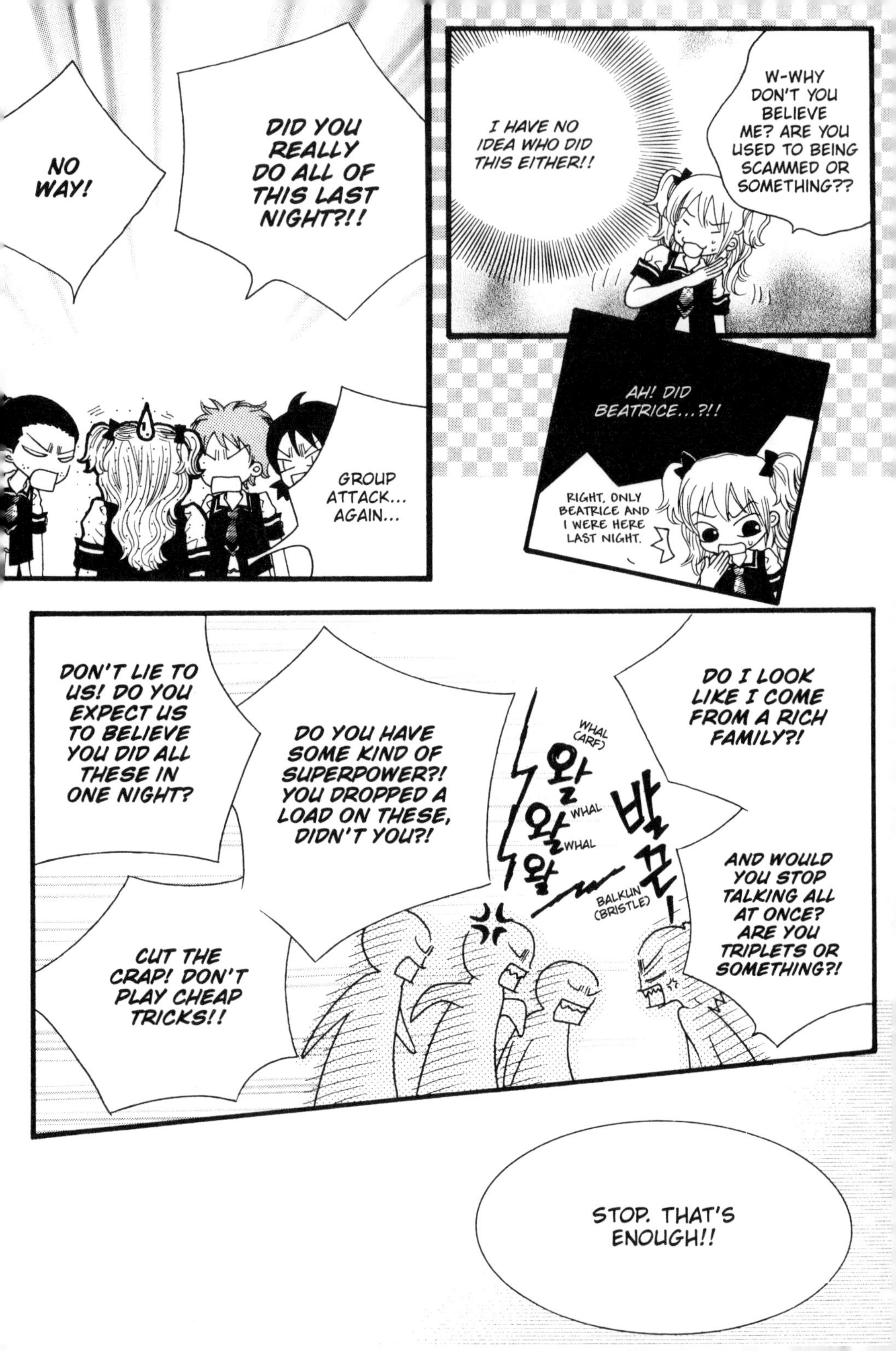
NO WAY!
DID YOU REALLY DO ALL OF THIS LAST NIGHT?!!
GROUP ATTACK... AGAIN...
I HAVE NO IDEA WHO DID THIS EITHER!!
W-WHY DON'T YOU BELIEVE ME? ARE YOU USED TO BEING SCAMMED OR SOMETHING??
AH! DID BEATRICE...?!!
RIGHT, ONLY BEATRICE AND I WERE HERE LAST NIGHT.
DON'T LIE TO US! DO YOU EXPECT US TO BELIEVE YOU DID ALL THESE IN ONE NIGHT?
CUT THE CRAP! DON'T PLAY CHEAP TRICKS!!
DO YOU HAVE SOME KIND OF SUPERPOWER?! YOU DROPPED A LOAD ON THESE, DIDN'T YOU?!
왈 WHAL (ARF)
왈 WHAL
왈 WHAL
발끈 BALKUN (BRISTLE)
DO I LOOK LIKE I COME FROM A RICH FAMILY?!
AND WOULD YOU STOP TALKING ALL AT ONCE? ARE YOU TRIPLETS OR SOMETHING?!
STOP. THAT'S ENOUGH!!

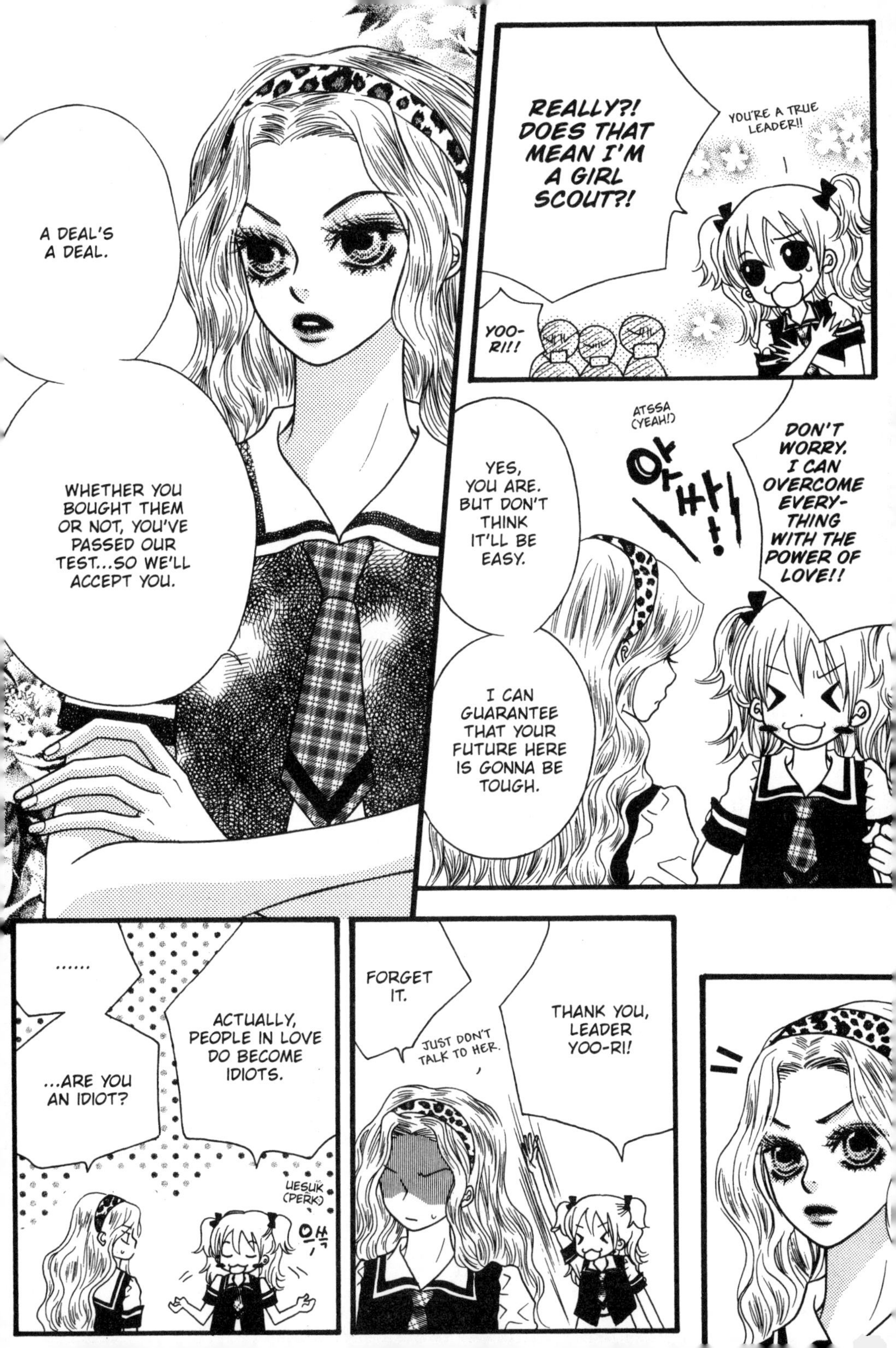
A DEAL'S A DEAL.
WHETHER YOU BOUGHT THEM OR NOT, YOU'VE PASSED OUR TEST...SO WE'LL ACCEPT YOU.
REALLY?! DOES THAT MEAN I'M A GIRL SCOUT?!
YOU'RE A TRUE LEADER!!
YOO-RI!!
YES, YOU ARE. BUT DON'T THINK IT'LL BE EASY.
I CAN GUARANTEE THAT YOUR FUTURE HERE IS GONNA BE TOUGH.
ATSSA (YEAH!)
DON'T WORRY. I CAN OVERCOME EVERY-THING WITH THE POWER OF LOVE!!
......
...ARE YOU AN IDIOT?
ACTUALLY, PEOPLE IN LOVE DO BECOME IDIOTS.
UESUK (PERK)
FORGET IT.
JUST DON'T TALK TO HER.
THANK YOU, LEADER YOO-RI!

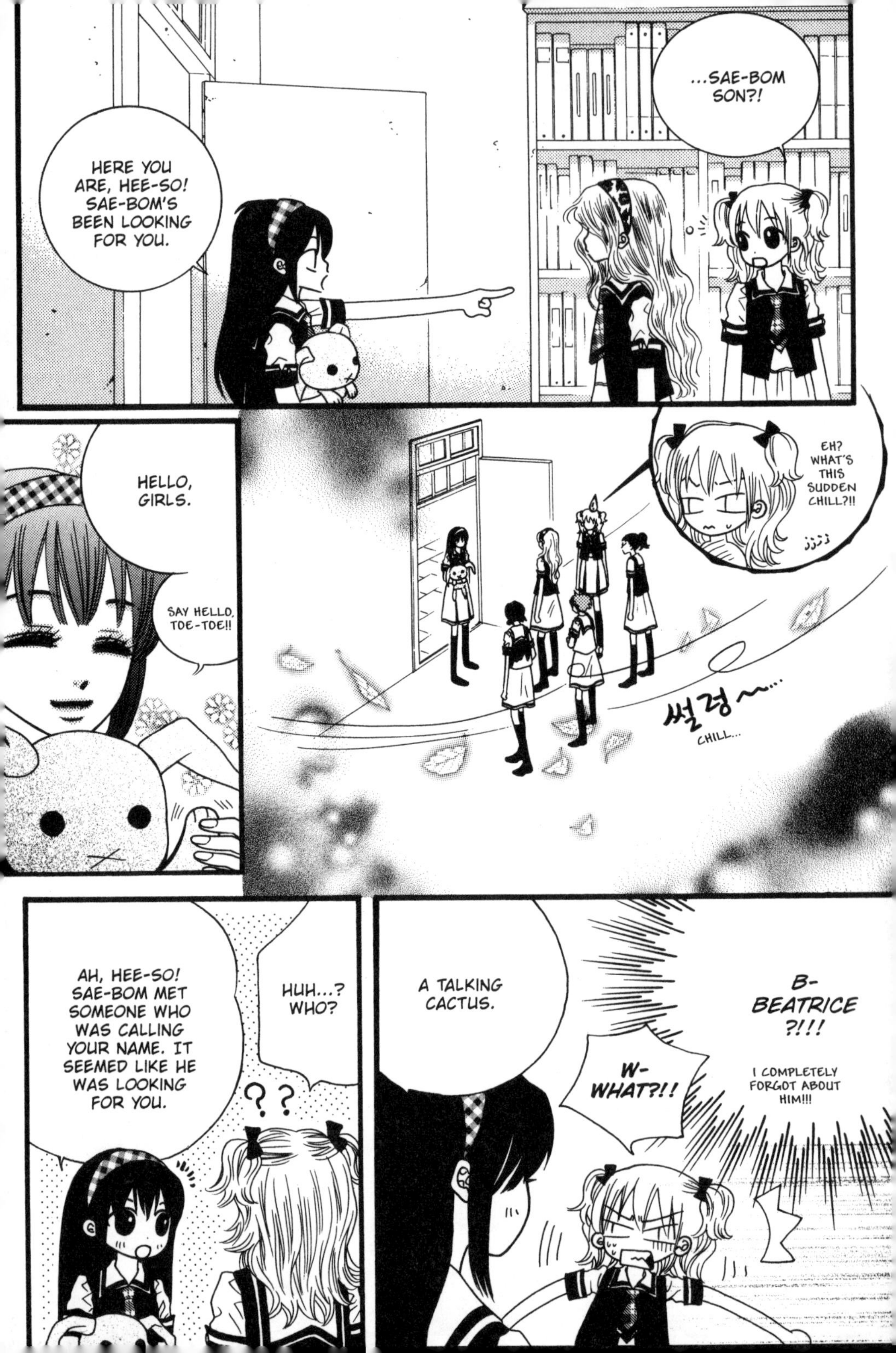
HERE YOU ARE, HEE-SO! SAE-BOM'S BEEN LOOKING FOR YOU.
...SAE-BOM SON?!
HELLO, GIRLS.
SAY HELLO, TOE-TOE!!
EH? WHAT'S THIS SUDDEN CHILL?!!
썰렁~...
CHILL...
AH, HEE-SO! SAE-BOM MET SOMEONE WHO WAS CALLING YOUR NAME. IT SEEMED LIKE HE WAS LOOKING FOR YOU.
HUH...? WHO?
??
A TALKING CACTUS.
W-WHAT?!!
B-BEATRICE?!!!
I COMPLETELY FORGOT ABOUT HIM!!!

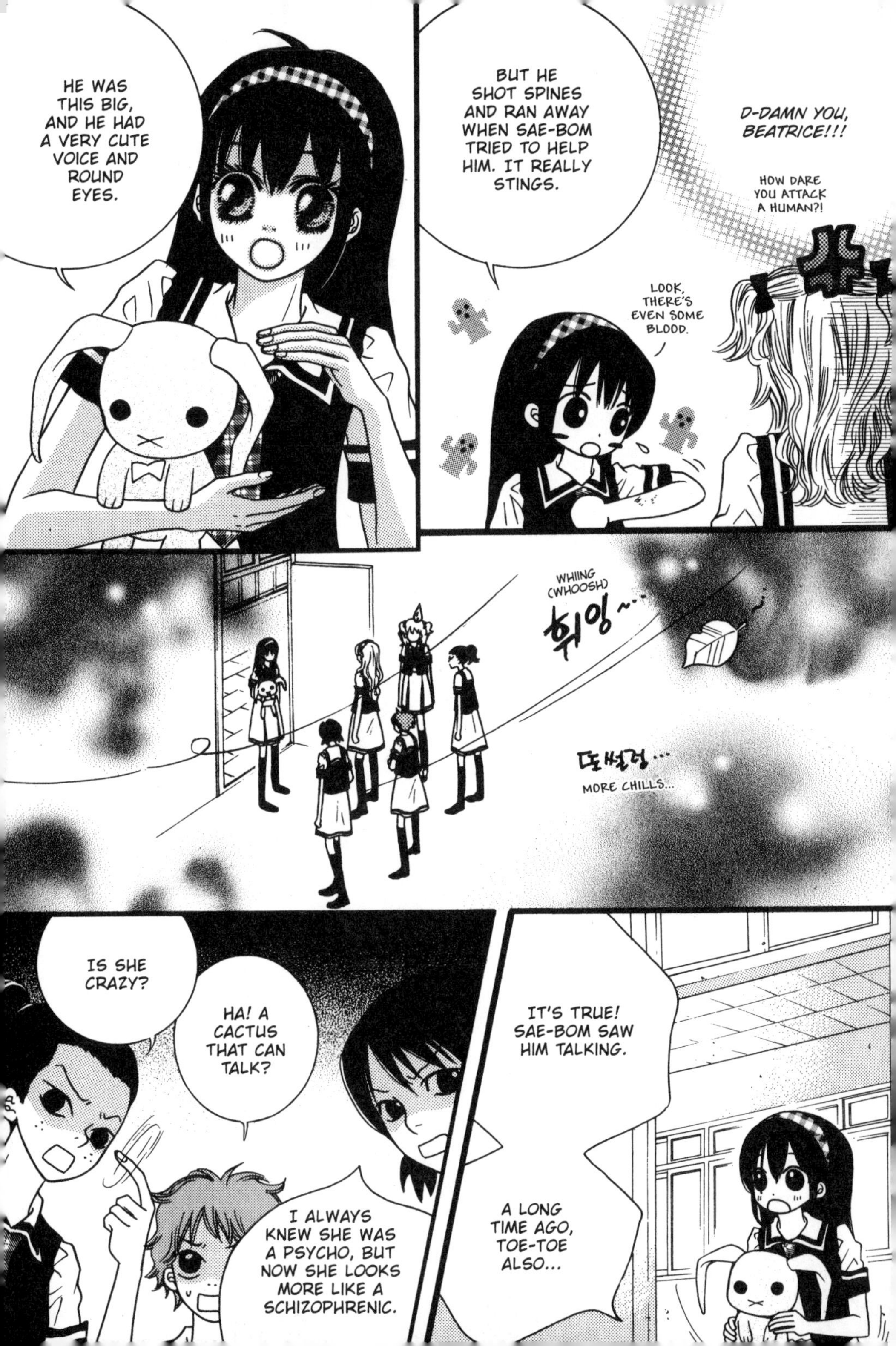
HE WAS THIS BIG, AND HE HAD A VERY CUTE VOICE AND ROUND EYES.
BUT HE SHOT SPINES AND RAN AWAY WHEN SAE-BOM TRIED TO HELP HIM. IT REALLY STINGS.
D-DAMN YOU, BEATRICE!!!
HOW DARE YOU ATTACK A HUMAN?!
LOOK, THERE'S EVEN SOME BLOOD.
WHIING (WHOOSH)
휘잉~...
또벌러...
MORE CHILLS...
IS SHE CRAZY?
HA! A CACTUS THAT CAN TALK?
I ALWAYS KNEW SHE WAS A PSYCHO, BUT NOW SHE LOOKS MORE LIKE A SCHIZOPHRENIC.
IT'S TRUE! SAE-BOM SAW HIM TALKING.
A LONG TIME AGO, TOE-TOE ALSO...

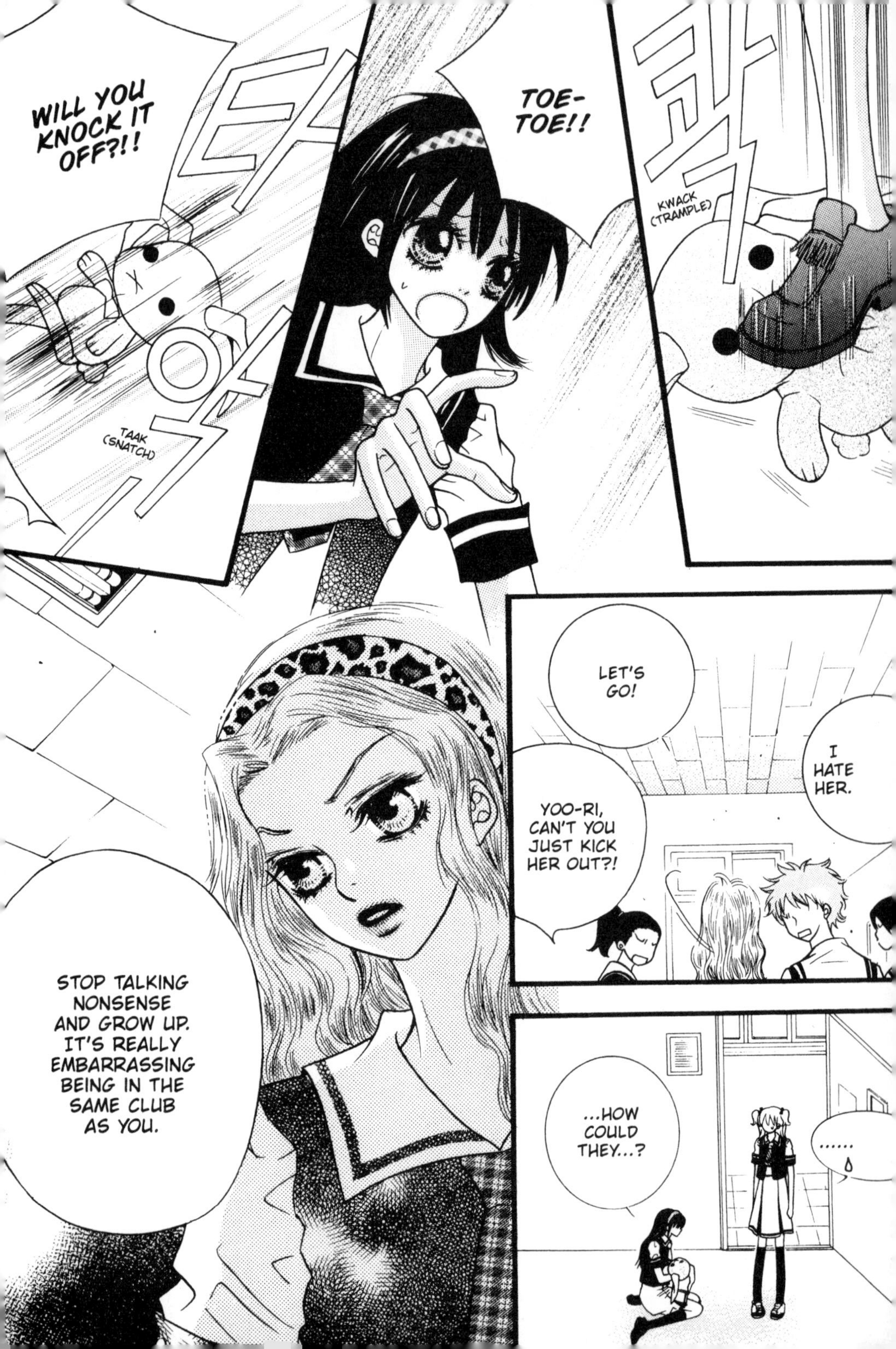
WILL YOU KNOCK IT OFF?!!
TAAK (SNATCH)
TOE-TOE!!
KWACK (TRAMPLE)
STOP TALKING NONSENSE AND GROW UP. IT'S REALLY EMBARRASSING BEING IN THE SAME CLUB AS YOU.
LET'S GO!
YOO-RI, CAN'T YOU JUST KICK HER OUT?!
I HATE HER.
...HOW COULD THEY...?
......

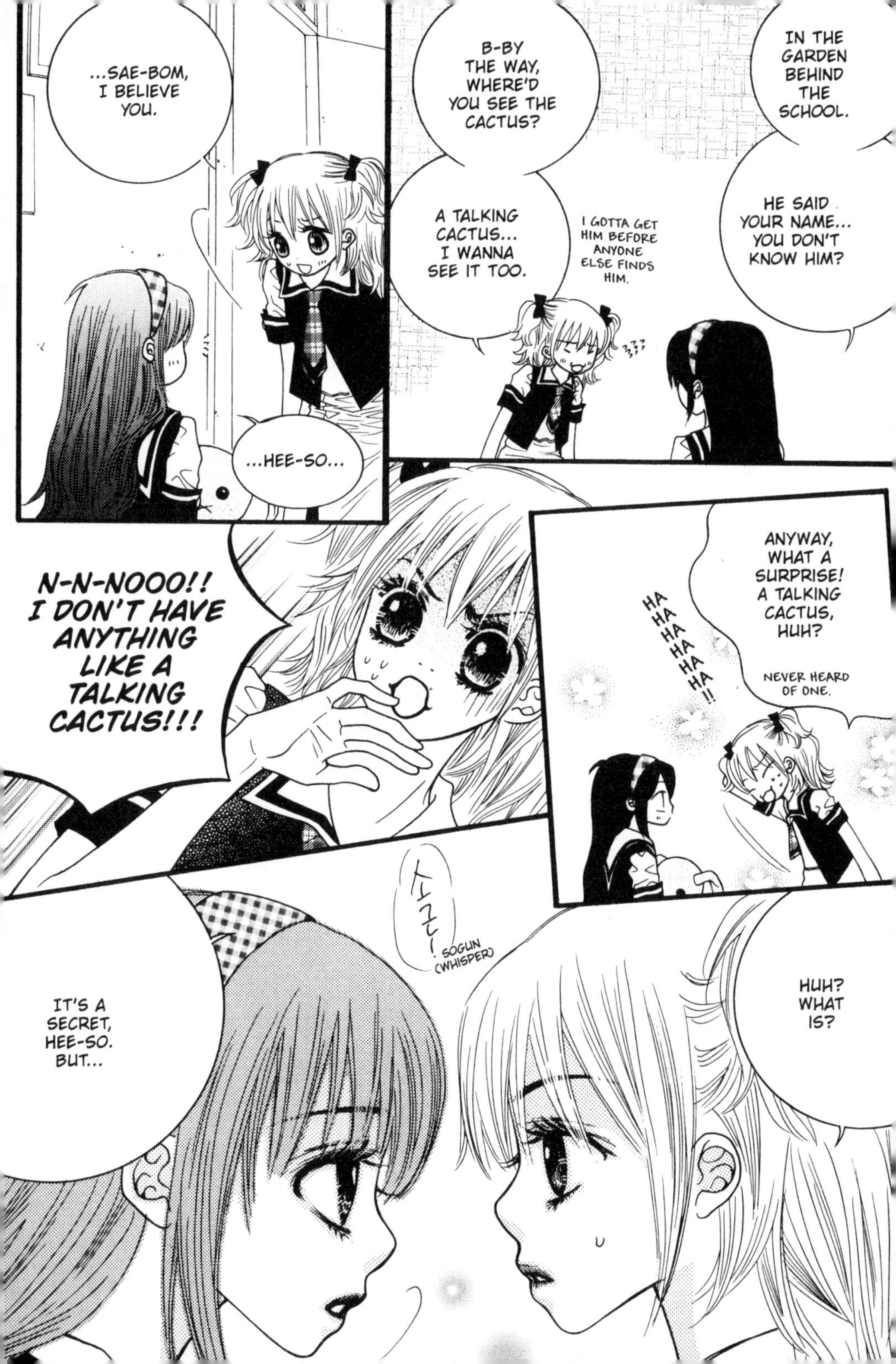
...SAE-BOM, I BELIEVE YOU.
...HEE-SO...
B-BY THE WAY, WHERE'D YOU SEE THE CACTUS?
IN THE GARDEN BEHIND THE SCHOOL.
A TALKING CACTUS... I WANNA SEE IT TOO.
I GOTTA GET HIM BEFORE ANYONE ELSE FINDS HIM.
HE SAID YOUR NAME... YOU DON'T KNOW HIM?
N-N-NOOO!! I DON'T HAVE ANYTHING LIKE A TALKING CACTUS!!!
ANYWAY, WHAT A SURPRISE! A TALKING CACTUS, HUH?
HA HA HA HA HA HA!!
NEVER HEARD OF ONE.
SOGUN (WHISPER)
IT'S A SECRET, HEE-SO. BUT...
HUH? WHAT IS?

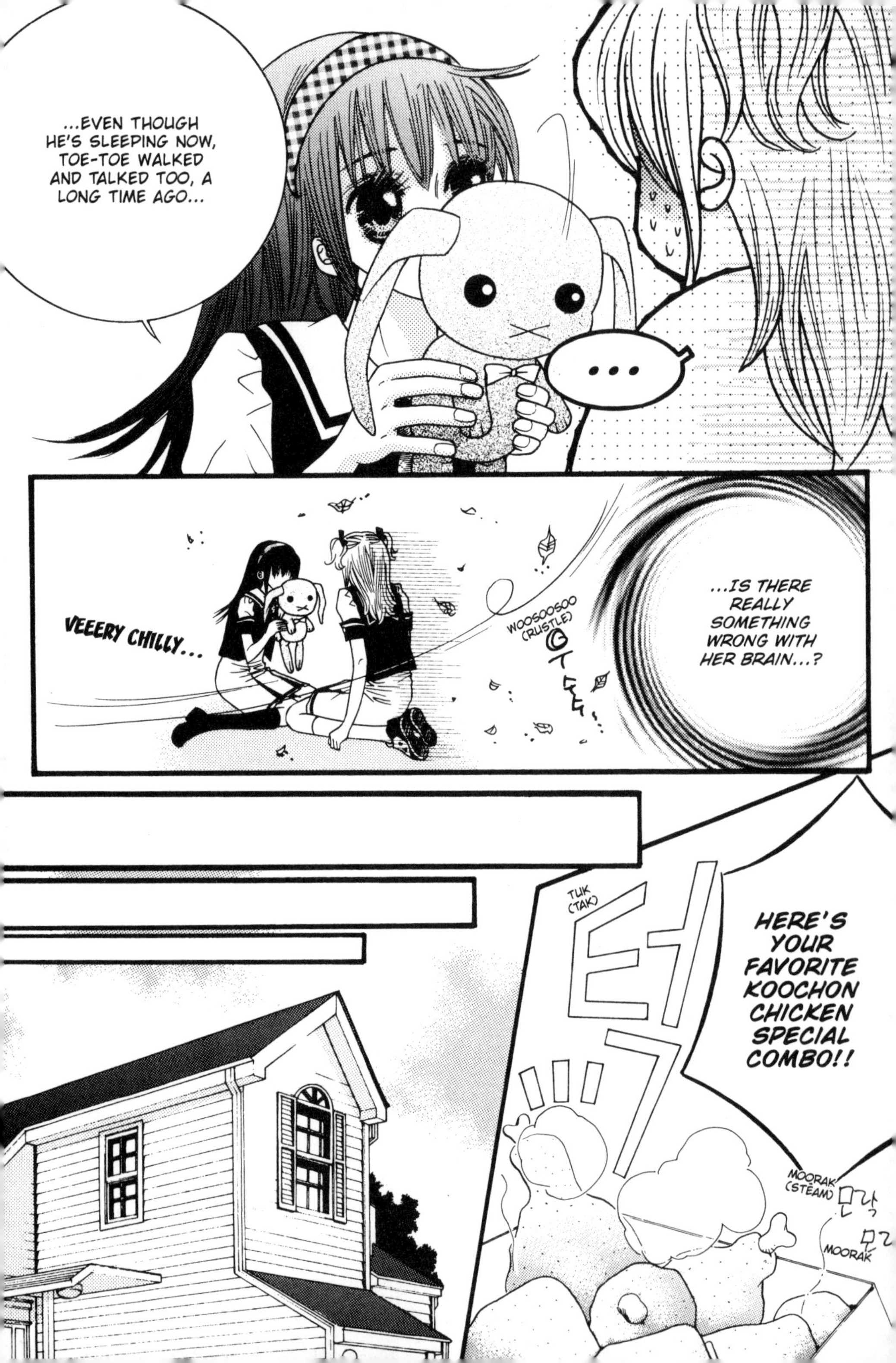
...EVEN THOUGH HE'S SLEEPING NOW, TOE-TOE WALKED AND TALKED TOO, A LONG TIME AGO...
...
VEEERY CHILLY...
WOOSOOSOO (RUSTLE)
...IS THERE REALLY SOMETHING WRONG WITH HER BRAIN...?
TUK (TAK)
HERE'S YOUR FAVORITE KOOCHON CHICKEN SPECIAL COMBO!!
MOORAK (STEAM)
MOORAK

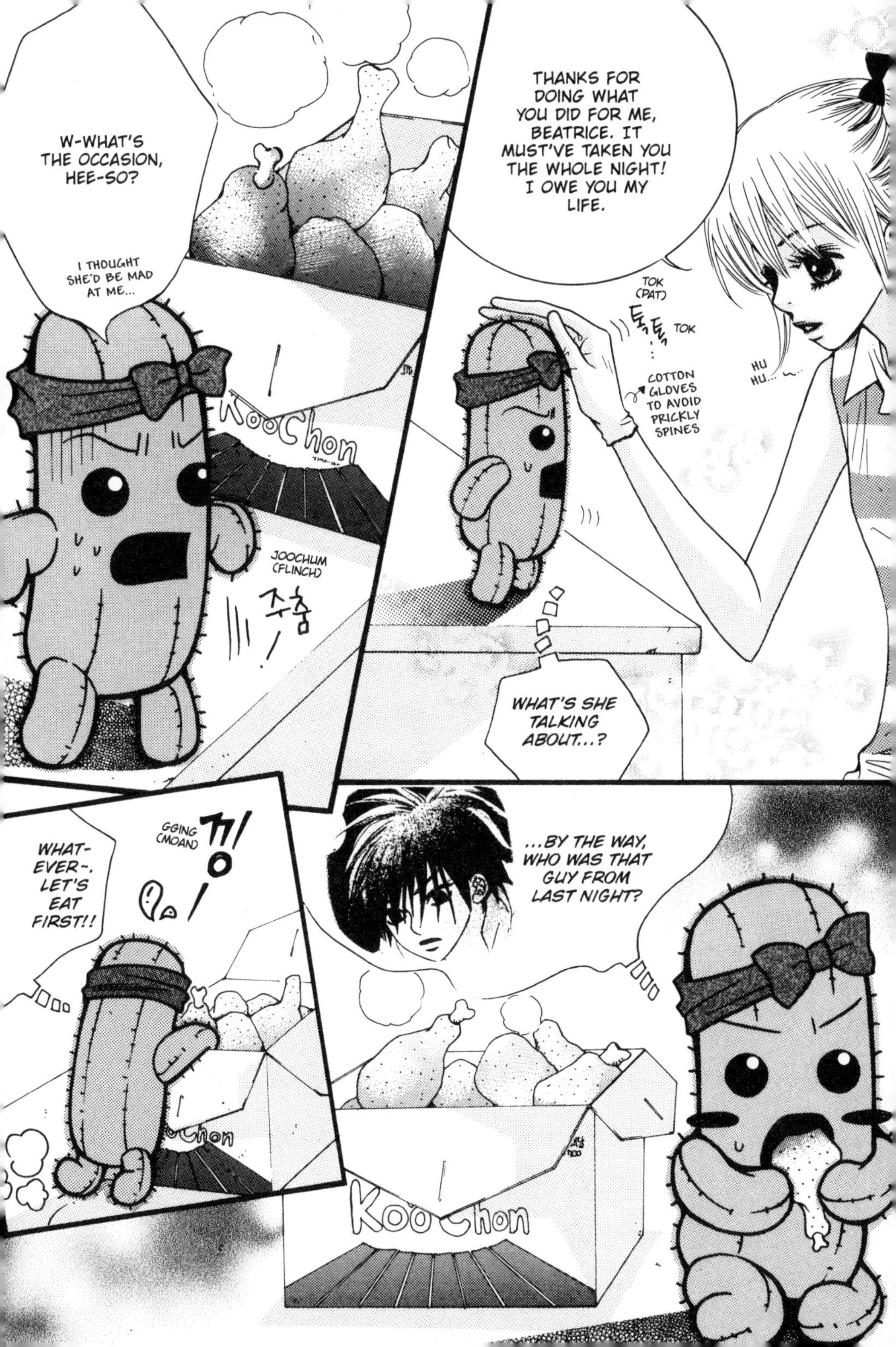
W-WHAT'S THE OCCASION, HEE-SO?
I THOUGHT SHE'D BE MAD AT ME...
KooChon
JOOCHUM (FLINCH)
주춤
THANKS FOR DOING WHAT YOU DID FOR ME, BEATRICE. IT MUST'VE TAKEN YOU THE WHOLE NIGHT! I OWE YOU MY LIFE.
TOK (PAT)
TOK
HU HU...
COTTON GLOVES TO AVOID PRICKLY SPINES
WHAT'S SHE TALKING ABOUT...?
WHAT-EVER~. LET'S EAT FIRST!!
GGING (MOAN)
낑
...BY THE WAY, WHO WAS THAT GUY FROM LAST NIGHT?
KooChon

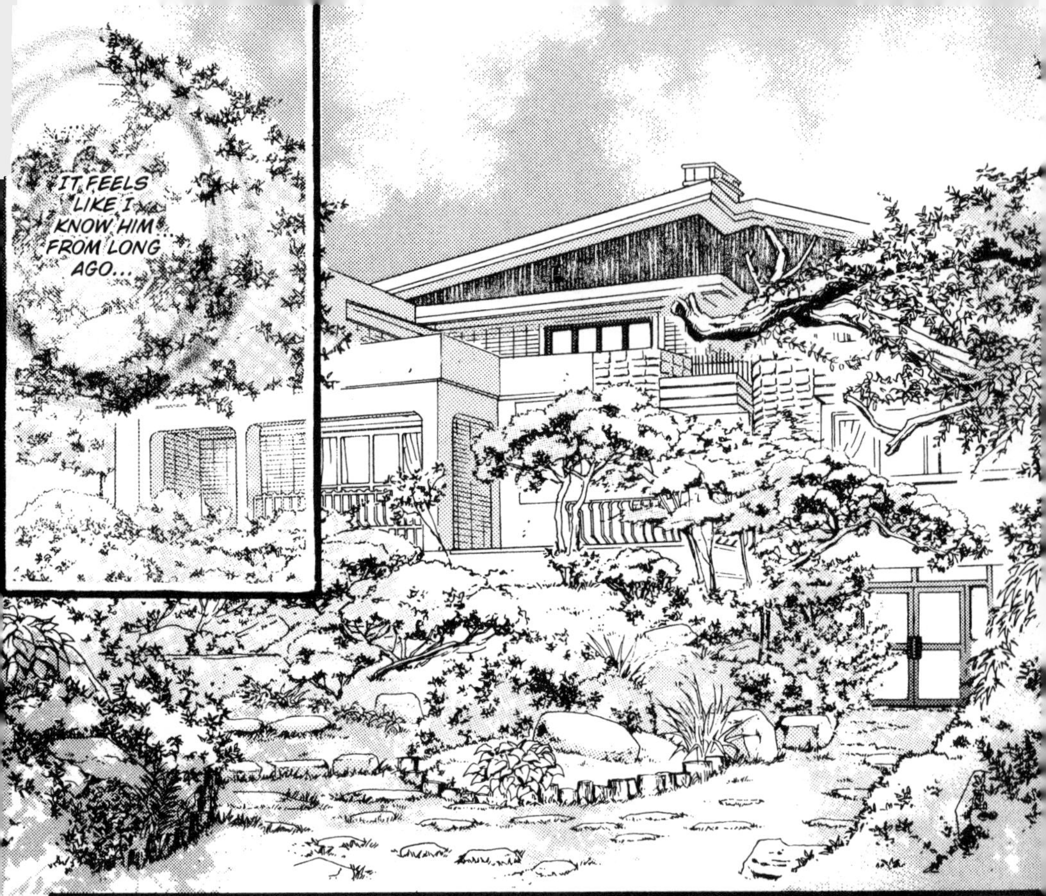
IT FEELS LIKE I KNOW HIM FROM LONG AGO...

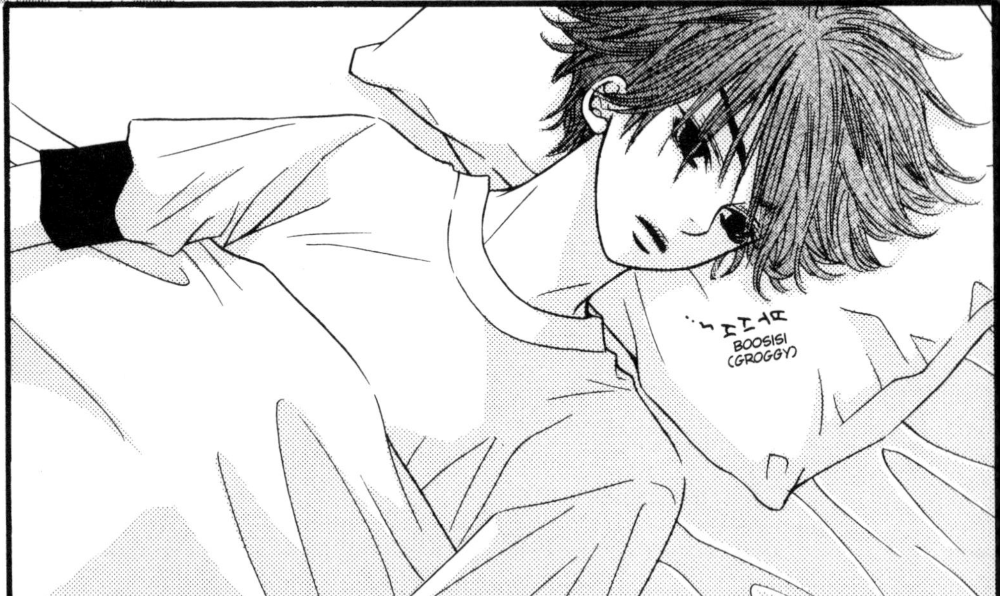
BOOSISI
(GROGGY)

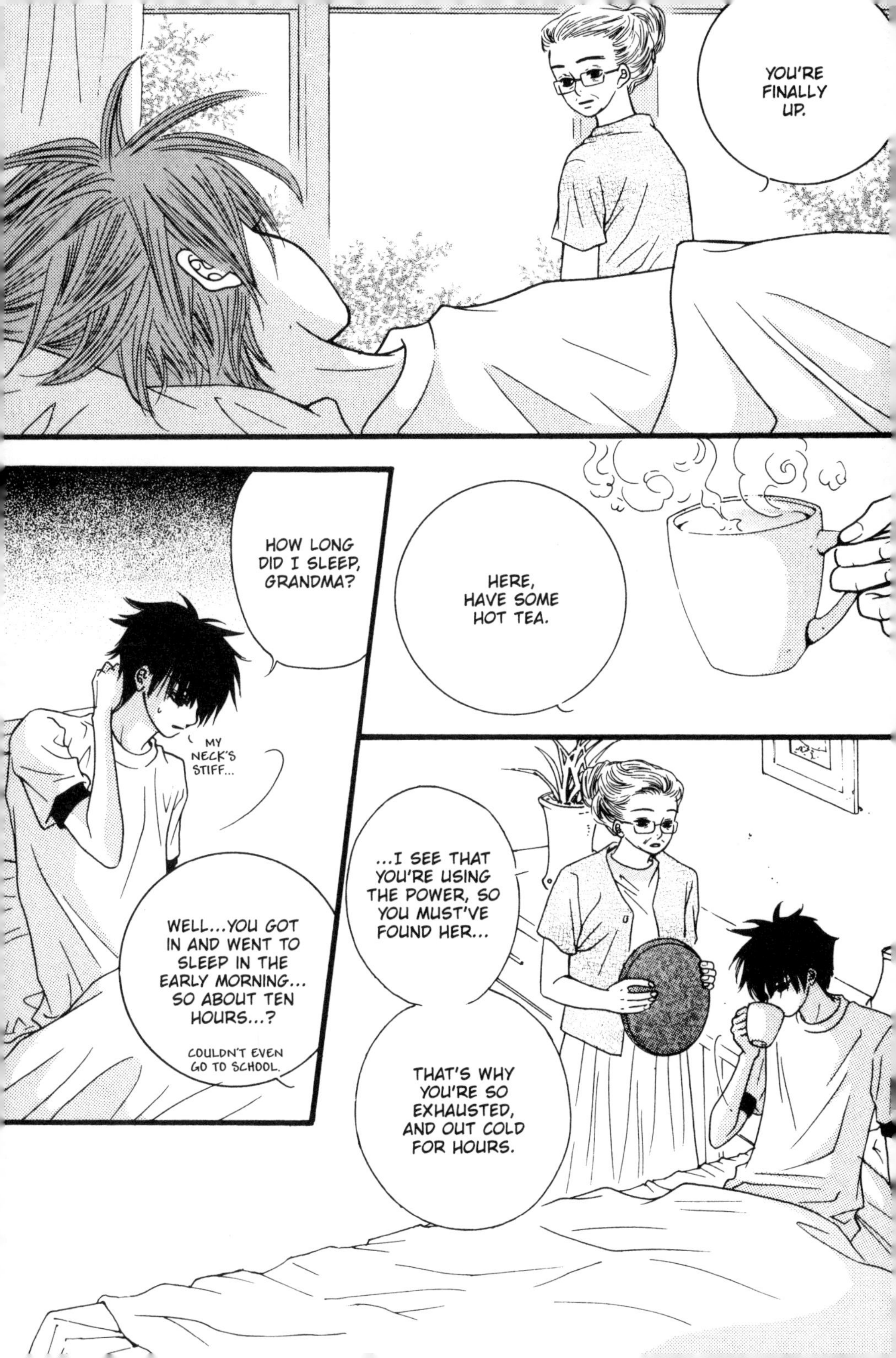
YOU'RE FINALLY UP.
HOW LONG DID I SLEEP, GRANDMA?
MY NECK'S STIFF...
WELL...YOU GOT IN AND WENT TO SLEEP IN THE EARLY MORNING... SO ABOUT TEN HOURS...?
COULDN'T EVEN GO TO SCHOOL.
HERE, HAVE SOME HOT TEA.
...I SEE THAT YOU'RE USING THE POWER, SO YOU MUST'VE FOUND HER...
THAT'S WHY YOU'RE SO EXHAUSTED, AND OUT COLD FOR HOURS.

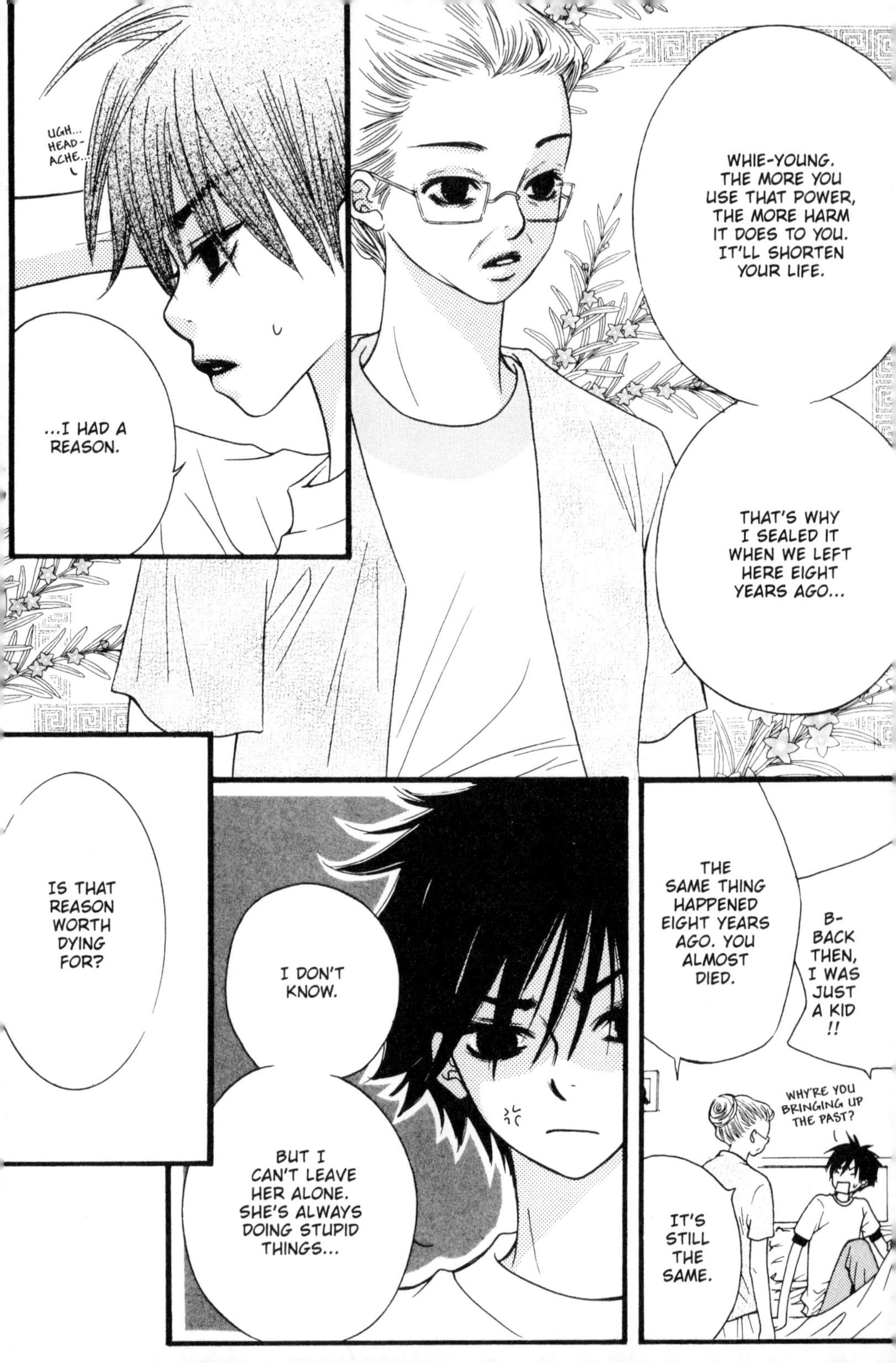
UGH... HEAD-ACHE...
...I HAD A REASON.
WHIE-YOUNG. THE MORE YOU USE THAT POWER, THE MORE HARM IT DOES TO YOU. IT'LL SHORTEN YOUR LIFE.
THAT'S WHY I SEALED IT WHEN WE LEFT HERE EIGHT YEARS AGO...
IS THAT REASON WORTH DYING FOR?
I DON'T KNOW.
BUT I CAN'T LEAVE HER ALONE. SHE'S ALWAYS DOING STUPID THINGS...
THE SAME THING HAPPENED EIGHT YEARS AGO. YOU ALMOST DIED.
B-BACK THEN, I WAS JUST A KID!!
WHY'RE YOU BRINGING UP THE PAST?
IT'S STILL THE SAME.

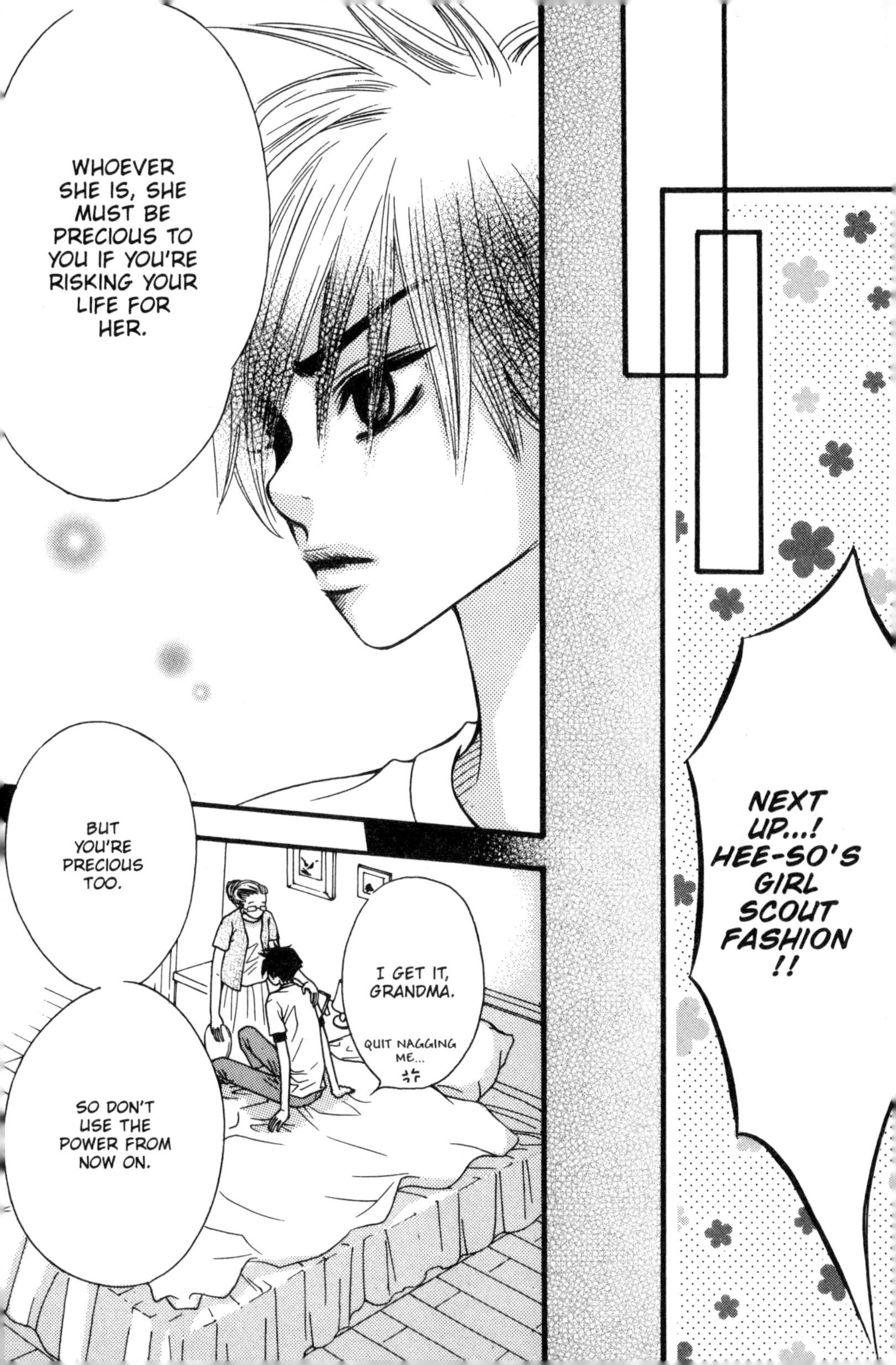
WHOEVER SHE IS, SHE MUST BE PRECIOUS TO YOU IF YOU'RE RISKING YOUR LIFE FOR HER.
BUT YOU'RE PRECIOUS TOO.
SO DON'T USE THE POWER FROM NOW ON.
I GET IT, GRANDMA.
QUIT NAGGING ME...
NEXT UP...! HEE-SO'S GIRL SCOUT FASHION !!

STEP 7. HEE-SO'S STORMY CAMPOUT

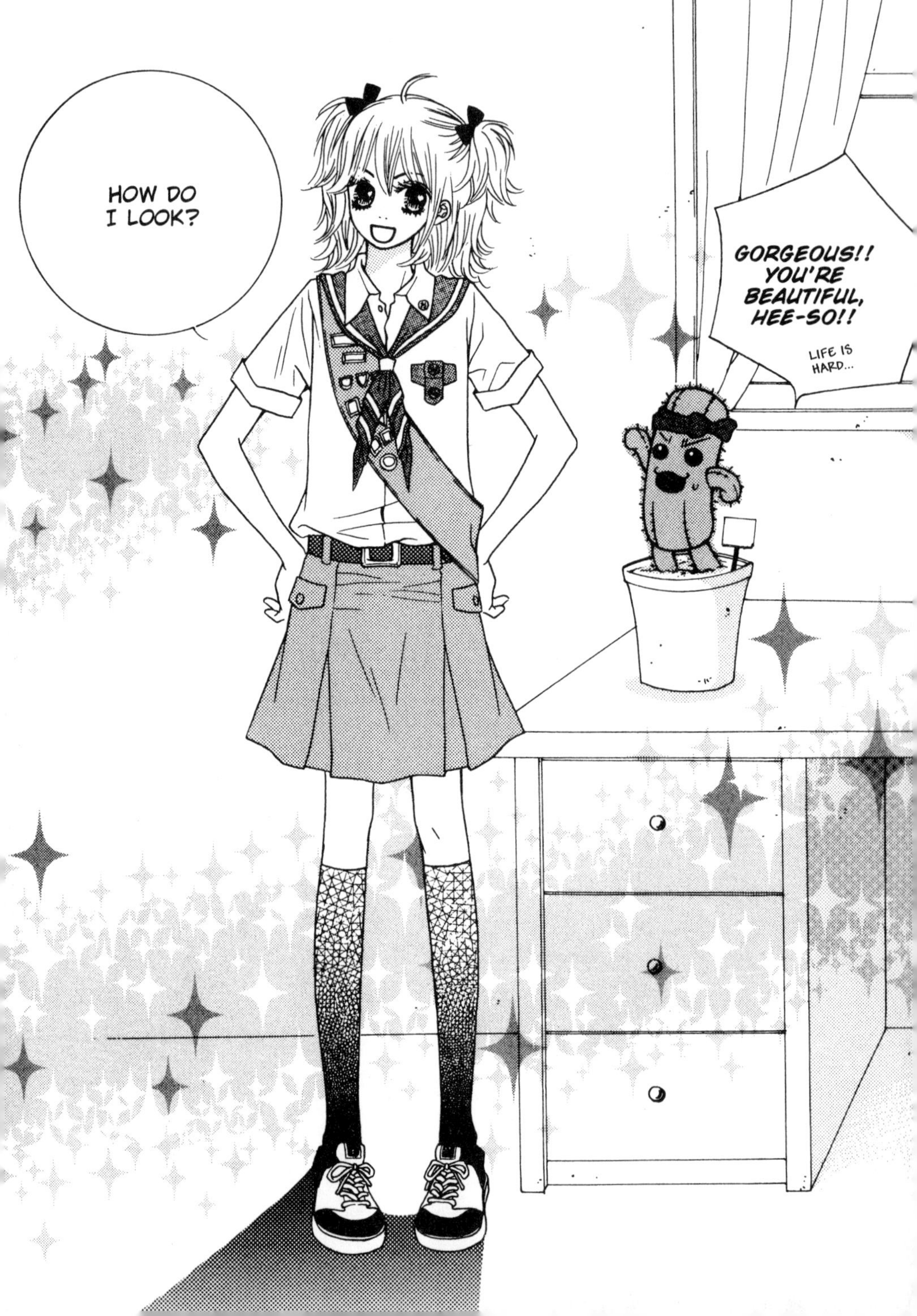
HOW DO I LOOK?
GORGEOUS!! YOU'RE BEAUTIFUL, HEE-SO!!
LIFE IS HARD...

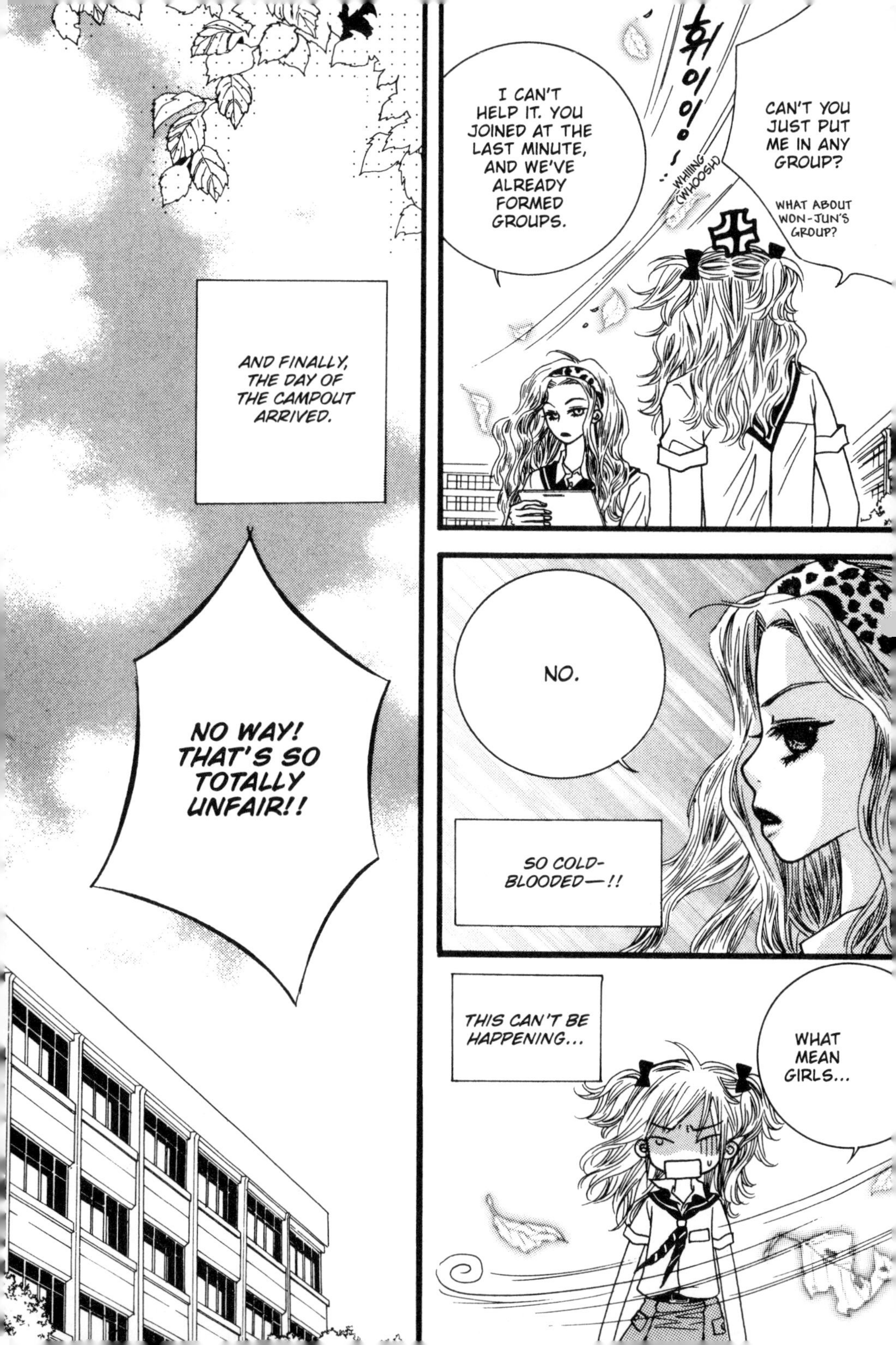
AND FINALLY, THE DAY OF THE CAMPOUT ARRIVED.
NO WAY! THAT'S SO TOTALLY UNFAIR!!
I CAN'T HELP IT. YOU JOINED AT THE LAST MINUTE, AND WE'VE ALREADY FORMED GROUPS.
휘이이잉~
WHIIING (WHOOSH)
CAN'T YOU JUST PUT ME IN ANY GROUP?
WHAT ABOUT WON-JUN'S GROUP?
NO.
SO COLD-BLOODED—!!
THIS CAN'T BE HAPPENING...
WHAT MEAN GIRLS...

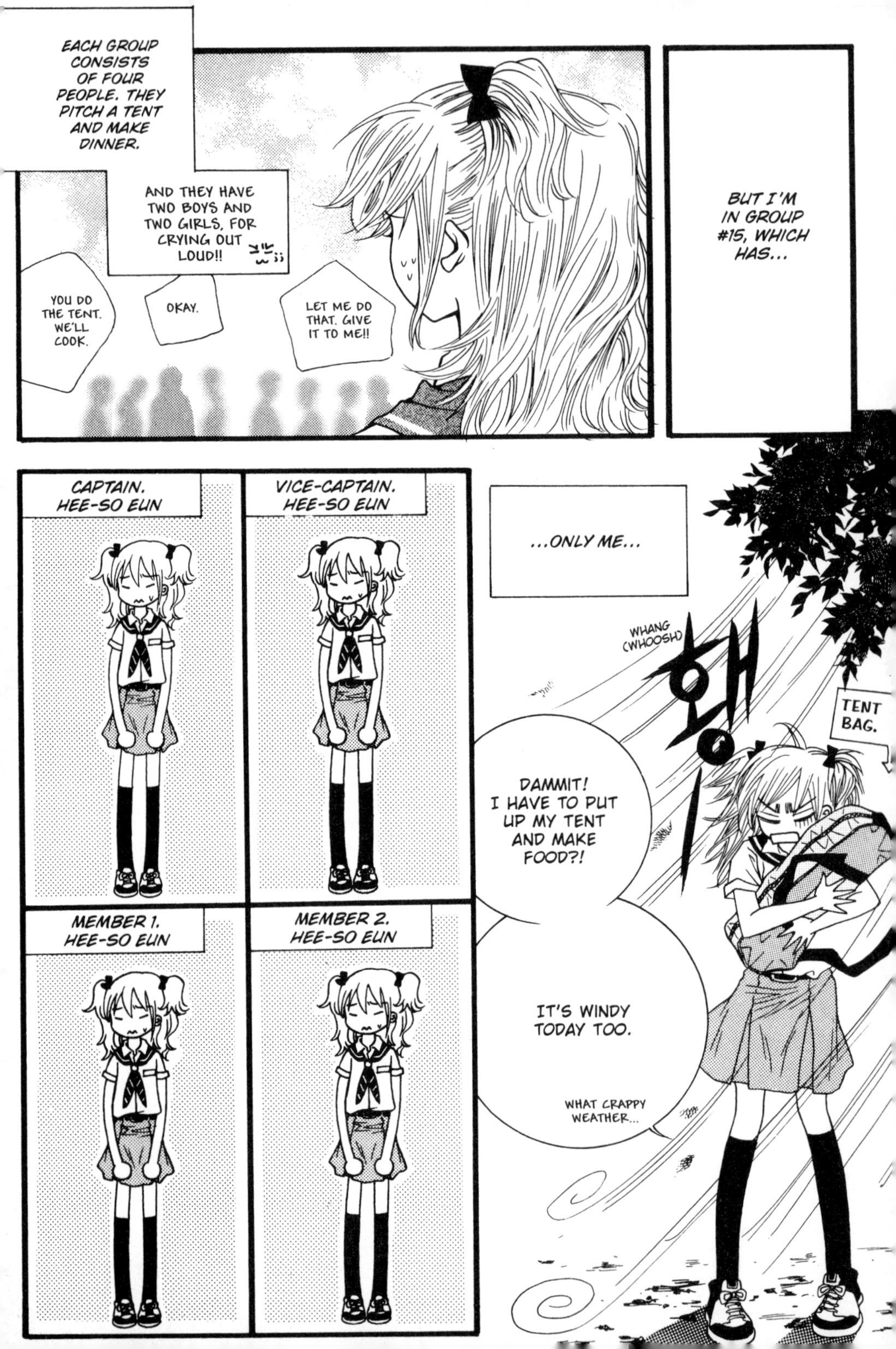
EACH GROUP CONSISTS OF FOUR PEOPLE. THEY PITCH A TENT AND MAKE DINNER.
AND THEY HAVE TWO BOYS AND TWO GIRLS, FOR CRYING OUT LOUD!!
YOU DO THE TENT. WE'LL COOK.
OKAY.
LET ME DO THAT. GIVE IT TO ME!!
BUT I'M IN GROUP #15, WHICH HAS...
CAPTAIN. HEE-SO EUN
VICE-CAPTAIN. HEE-SO EUN
MEMBER 1. HEE-SO EUN
MEMBER 2. HEE-SO EUN
...ONLY ME...
WHANG (WHOOSH)
TENT BAG.
DAMMIT! I HAVE TO PUT UP MY TENT AND MAKE FOOD?!
IT'S WINDY TODAY TOO.
WHAT CRAPPY WEATHER...

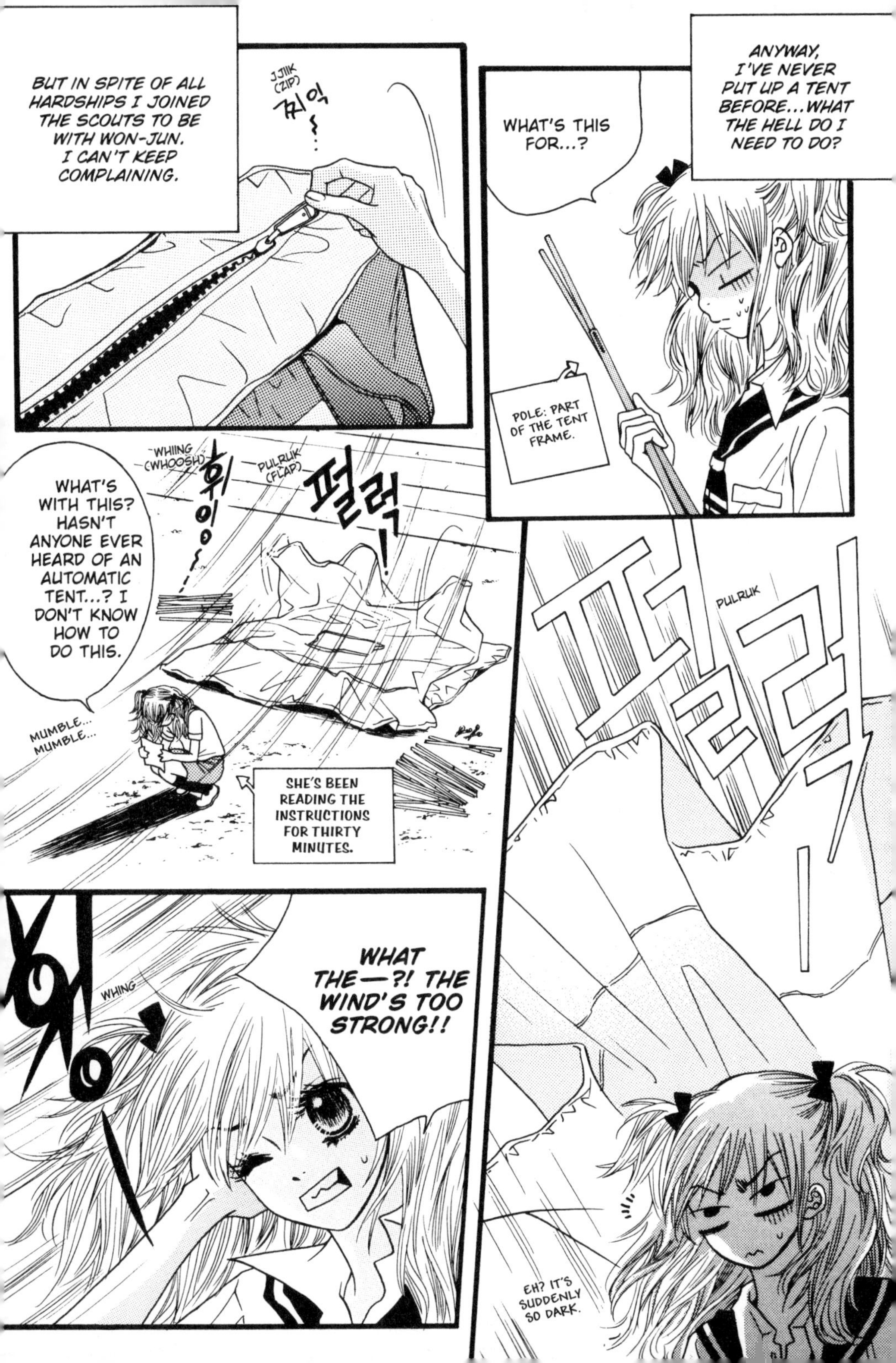

BUT IN SPITE OF ALL HARDSHIPS I JOINED THE SCOUTS TO BE WITH WON-JUN. I CAN'T KEEP COMPLAINING.
JJIIK (ZIP)
찌익~
WHAT'S THIS FOR...?
ANYWAY, I'VE NEVER PUT UP A TENT BEFORE...WHAT THE HELL DO I NEED TO DO?
POLE: PART OF THE TENT FRAME.
WHIING (WHOOSH)
휘이잉~
PULRUK (FLAP)
펄럭!
WHAT'S WITH THIS? HASN'T ANYONE EVER HEARD OF AN AUTOMATIC TENT...? I DON'T KNOW HOW TO DO THIS.
MUMBLE... MUMBLE...
SHE'S BEEN READING THE INSTRUCTIONS FOR THIRTY MINUTES.
WHING
WHAT THE—?! THE WIND'S TOO STRONG!!
PULRUK
펄럭!
EH? IT'S SUDDENLY SO DARK.

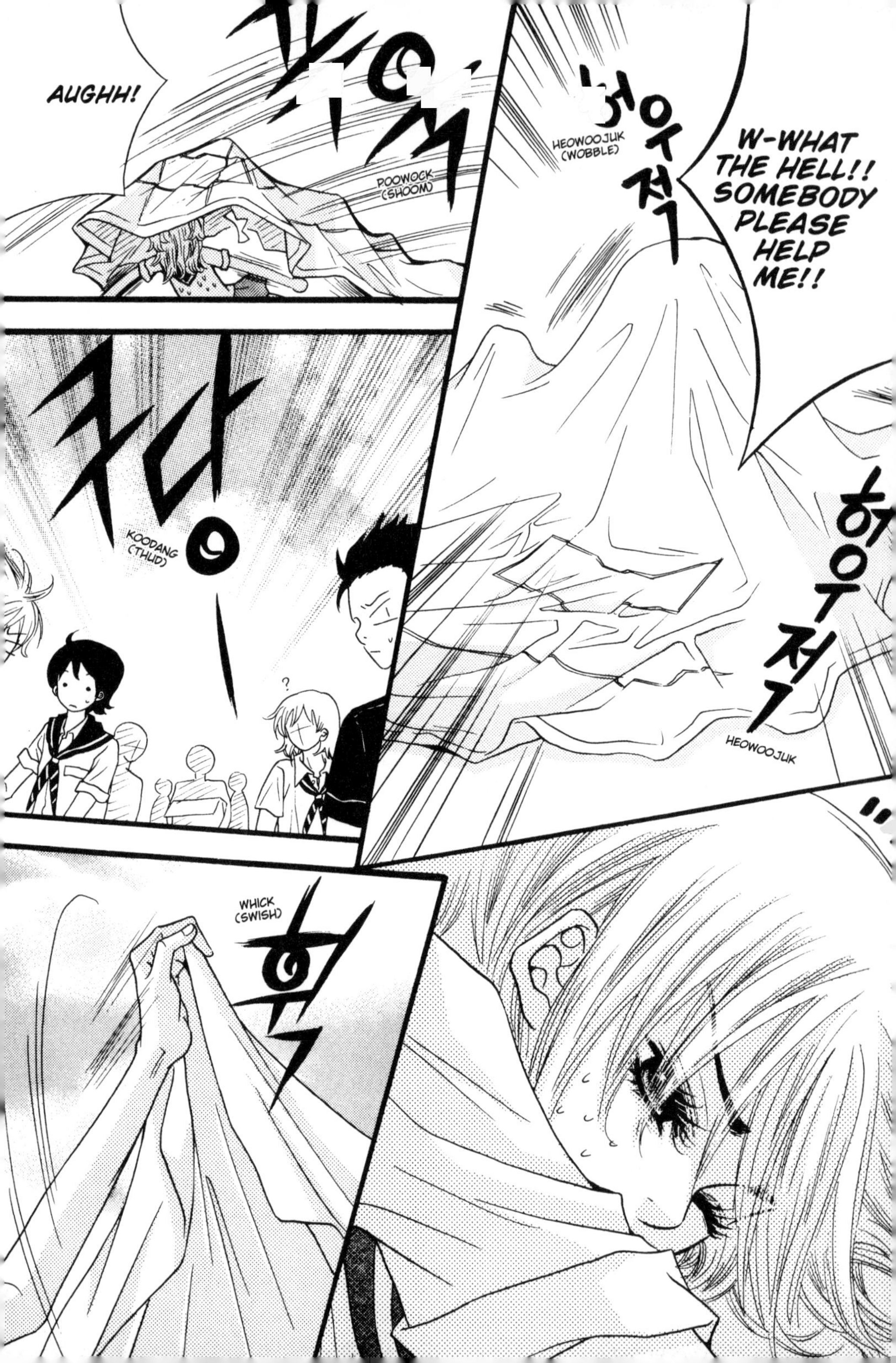
AUGHH!
POOWOCK (SHOOM)
HEOWOOJUK (WOBBLE)
W-WHAT THE HELL!! SOMEBODY PLEASE HELP ME!!
HEOWOOJUK
KOODANG (THUD)
WHICK (SWISH)

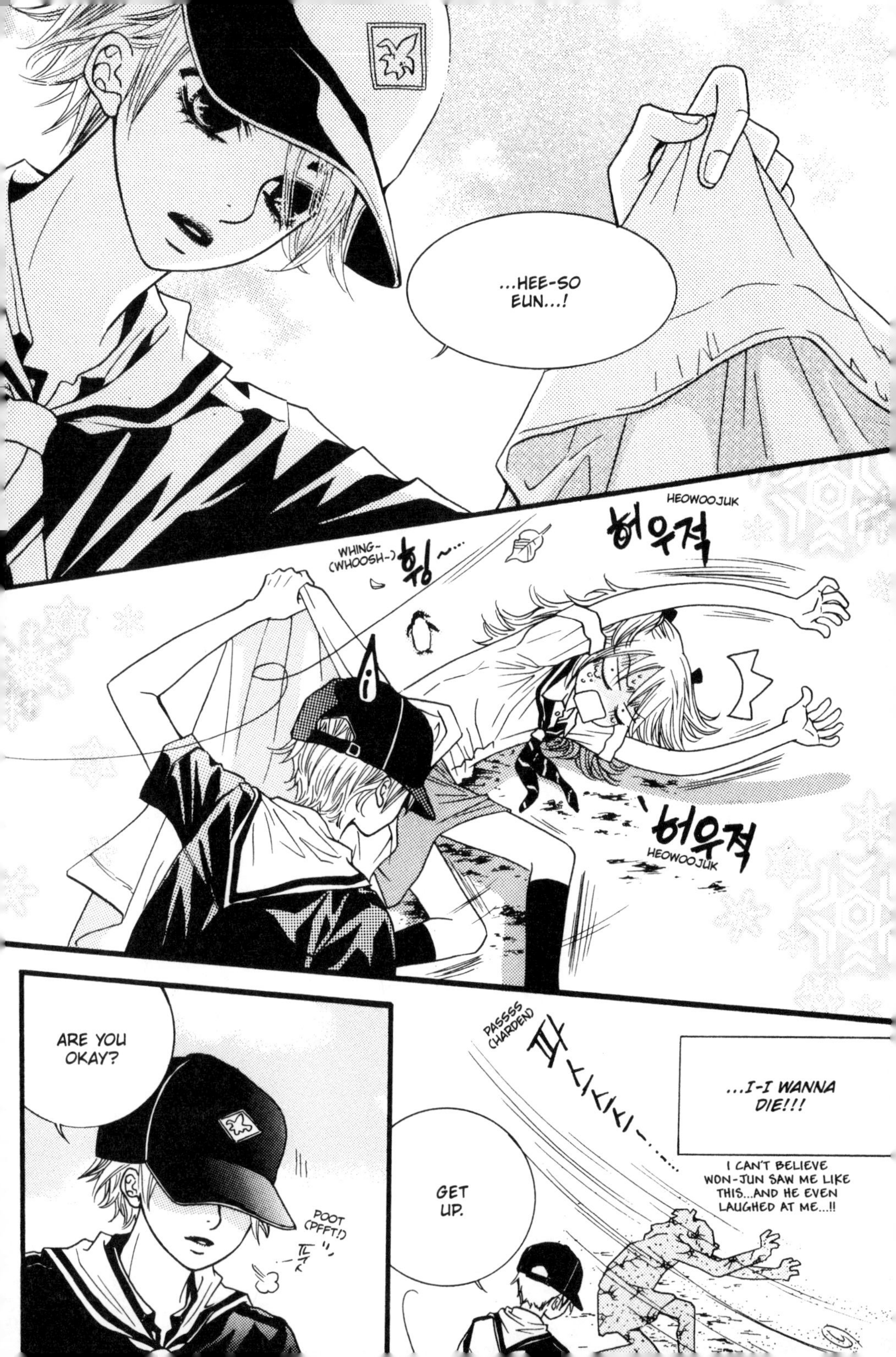
...HEE-SO EUN...!
HEOWOOJUK
허우적
WHING- (WHOOSH-)
휭~...
허우적
HEOWOOJUK
ARE YOU OKAY?
POOT (PFFT!)
PASSSS (HARDEN)
파ㅅㅅㅅㅅ-.....
GET UP.
...I-I WANNA DIE!!!
I CAN'T BELIEVE WON-JUN SAW ME LIKE THIS...AND HE EVEN LAUGHED AT ME...!!

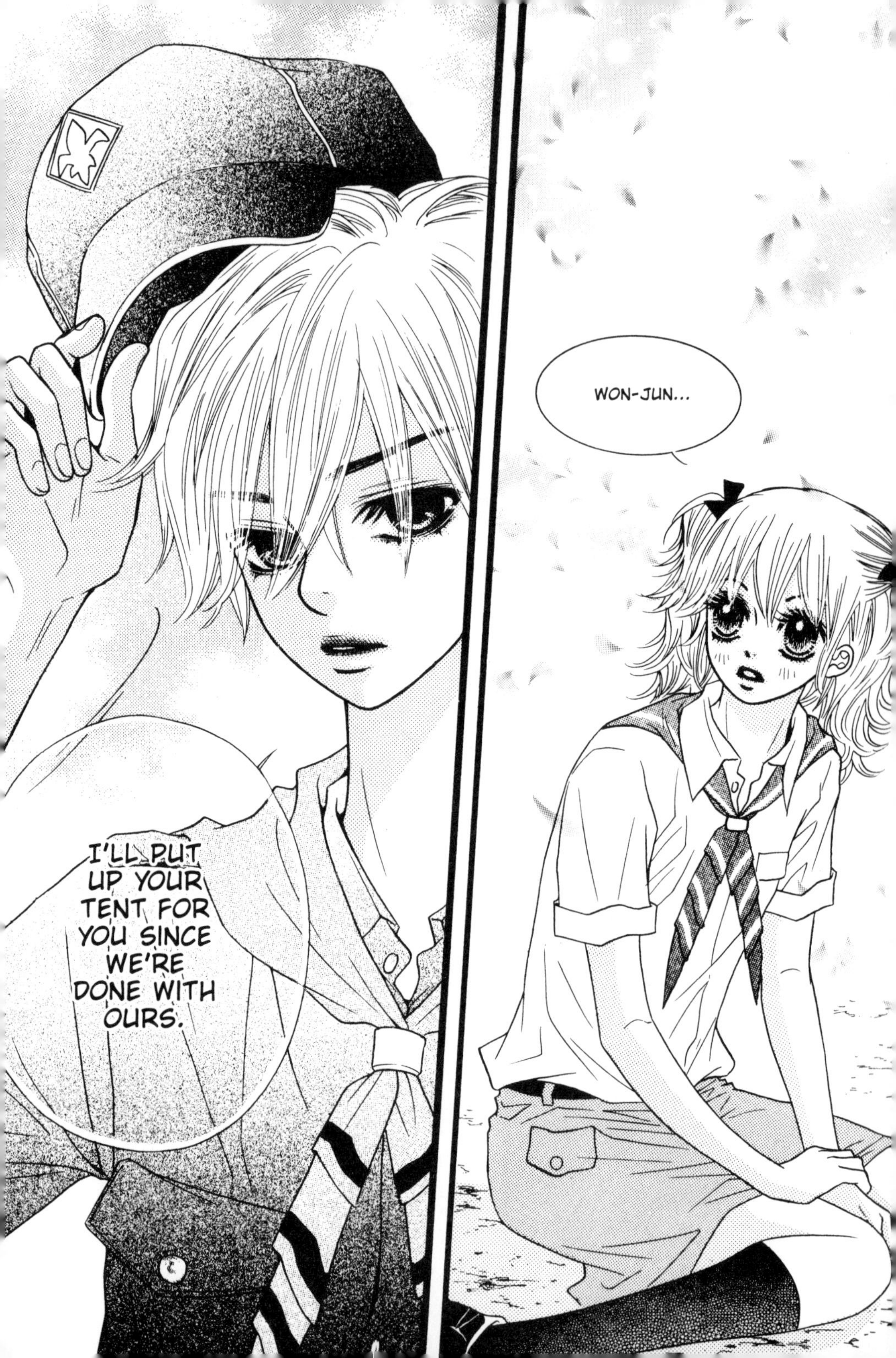
I'LL PUT UP YOUR TENT FOR YOU SINCE WE'RE DONE WITH OURS.
WON-JUN...

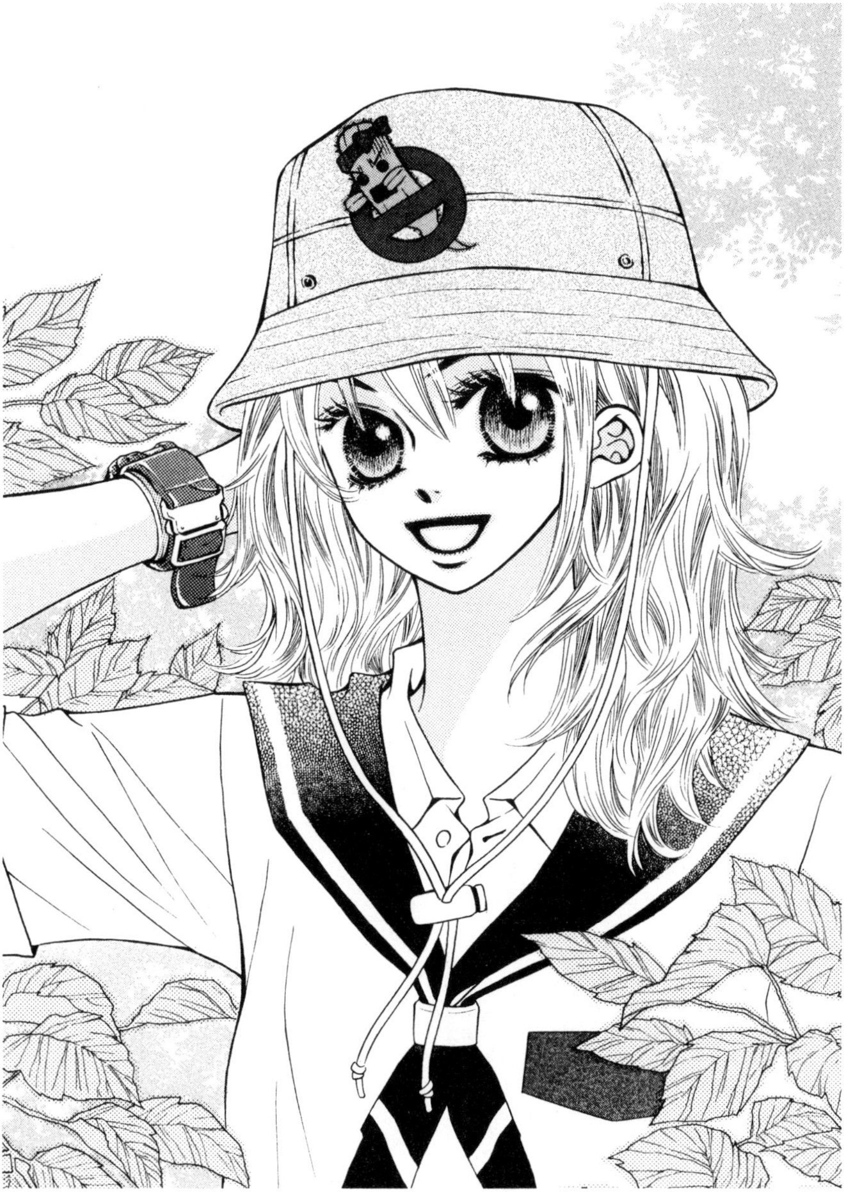

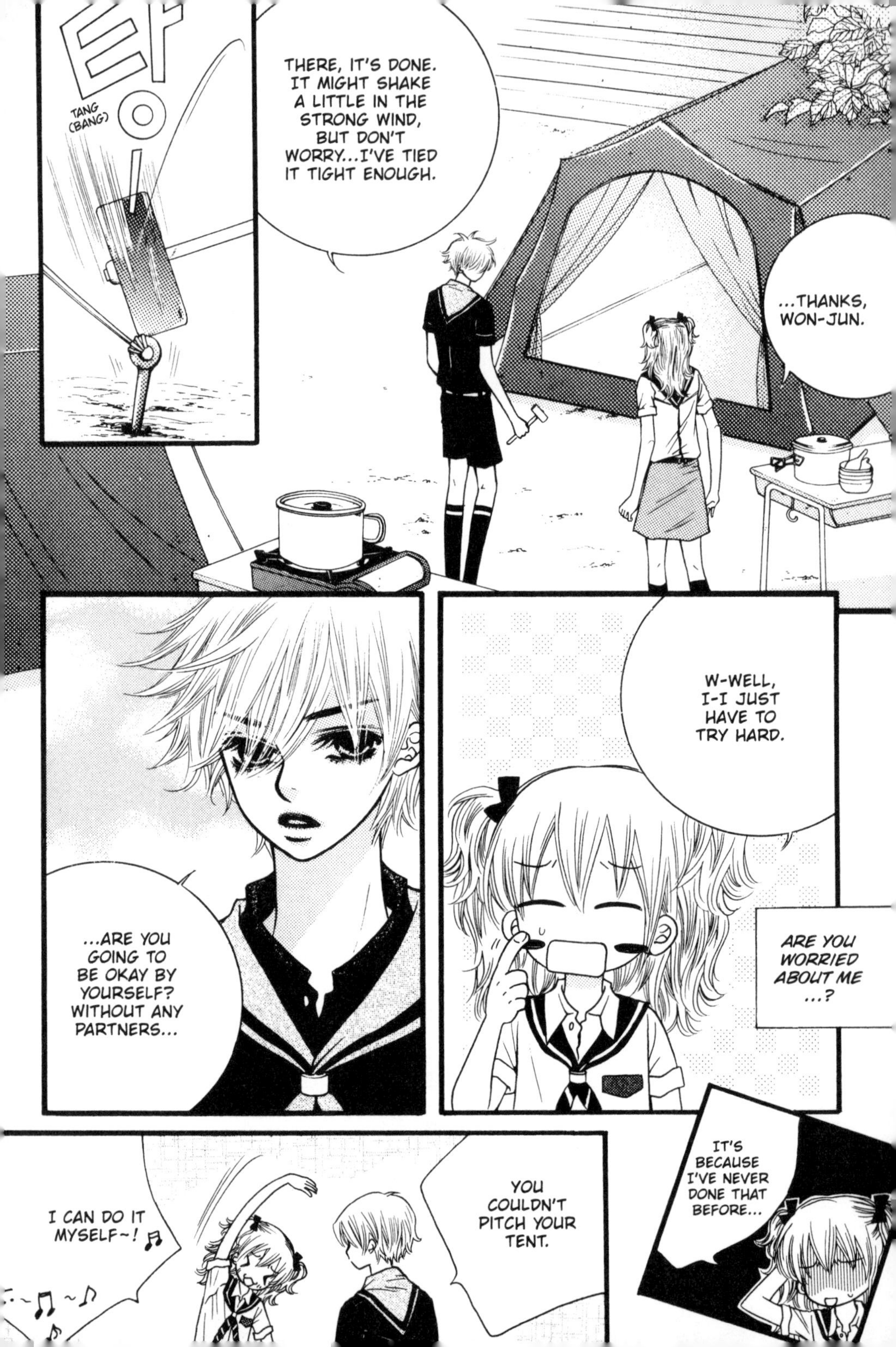
TANG (BANG)
THERE, IT'S DONE. IT MIGHT SHAKE A LITTLE IN THE STRONG WIND, BUT DON'T WORRY...I'VE TIED IT TIGHT ENOUGH.
...THANKS, WON-JUN.
...ARE YOU GOING TO BE OKAY BY YOURSELF? WITHOUT ANY PARTNERS...
W-WELL, I-I JUST HAVE TO TRY HARD.
ARE YOU WORRIED ABOUT ME ...?
I CAN DO IT MYSELF~!
YOU COULDN'T PITCH YOUR TENT.
IT'S BECAUSE I'VE NEVER DONE THAT BEFORE...

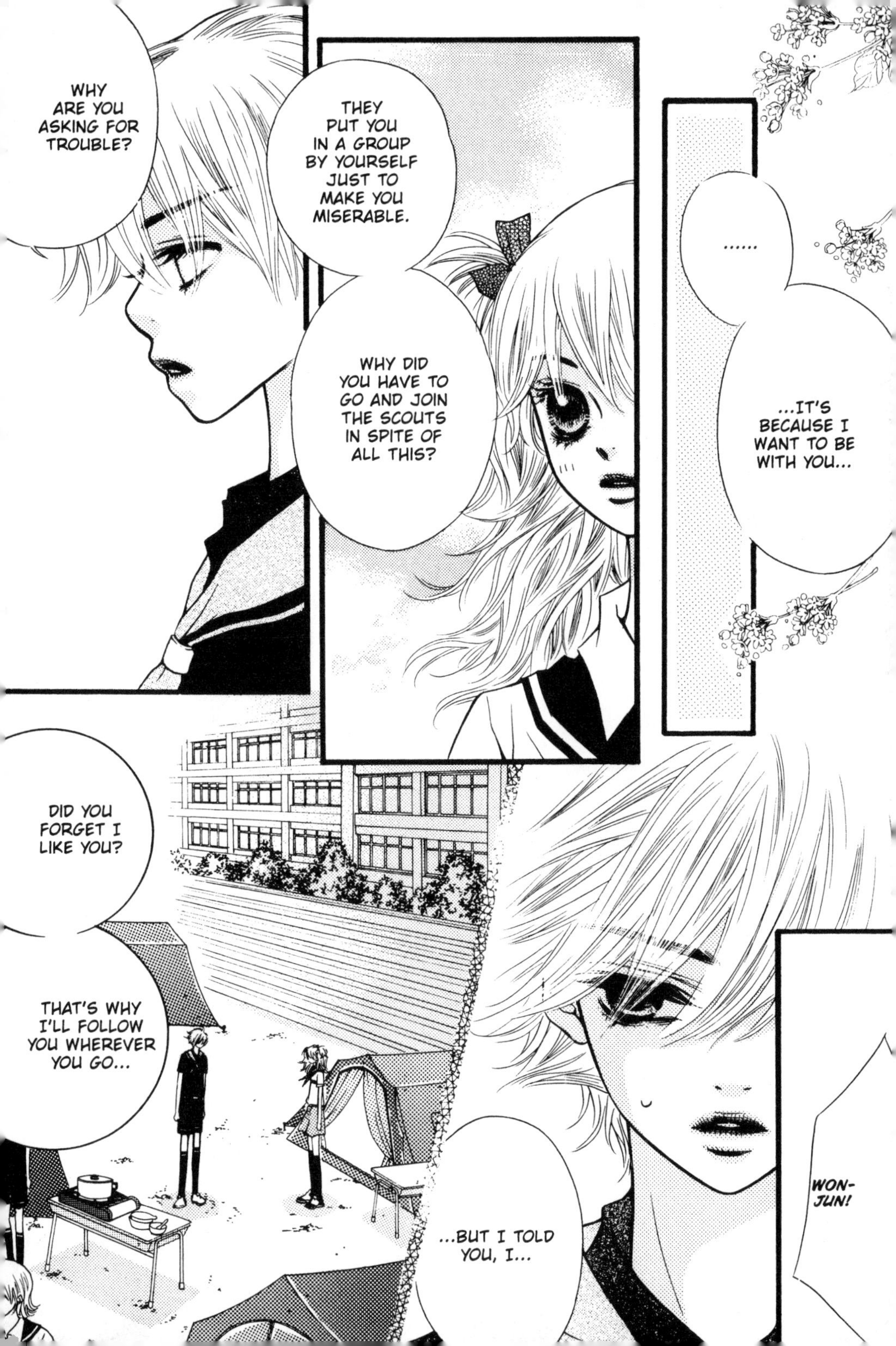
WHY ARE YOU ASKING FOR TROUBLE?
THEY PUT YOU IN A GROUP BY YOURSELF JUST TO MAKE YOU MISERABLE.
WHY DID YOU HAVE TO GO AND JOIN THE SCOUTS IN SPITE OF ALL THIS?
......
...IT'S BECAUSE I WANT TO BE WITH YOU...
DID YOU FORGET I LIKE YOU?
THAT'S WHY I'LL FOLLOW YOU WHEREVER YOU GO...
...BUT I TOLD YOU, I...
WON-JUN!

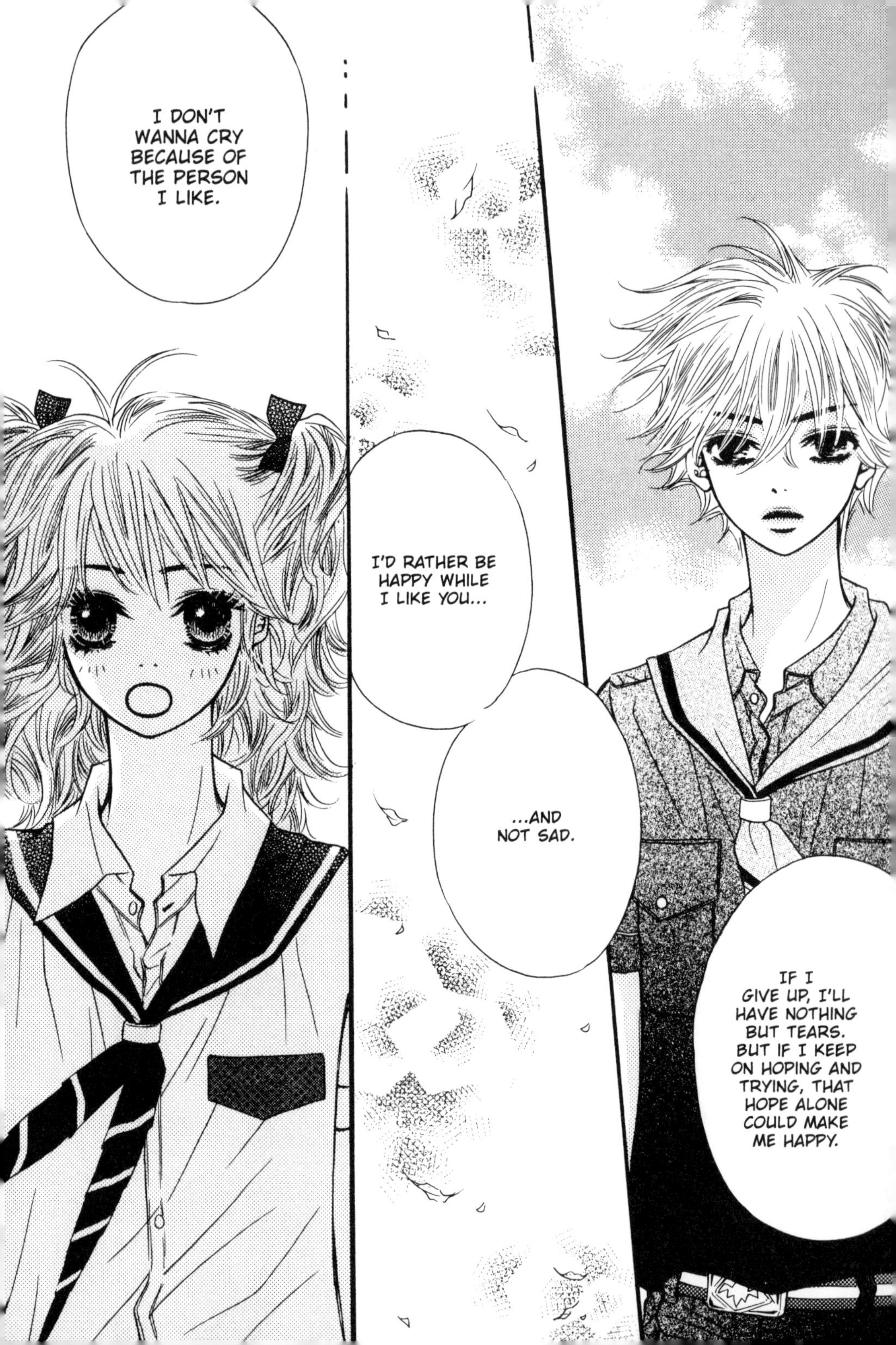
I DON'T WANNA CRY BECAUSE OF THE PERSON I LIKE.
I'D RATHER BE HAPPY WHILE I LIKE YOU...
...AND NOT SAD.
IF I GIVE UP, I'LL HAVE NOTHING BUT TEARS. BUT IF I KEEP ON HOPING AND TRYING, THAT HOPE ALONE COULD MAKE ME HAPPY.

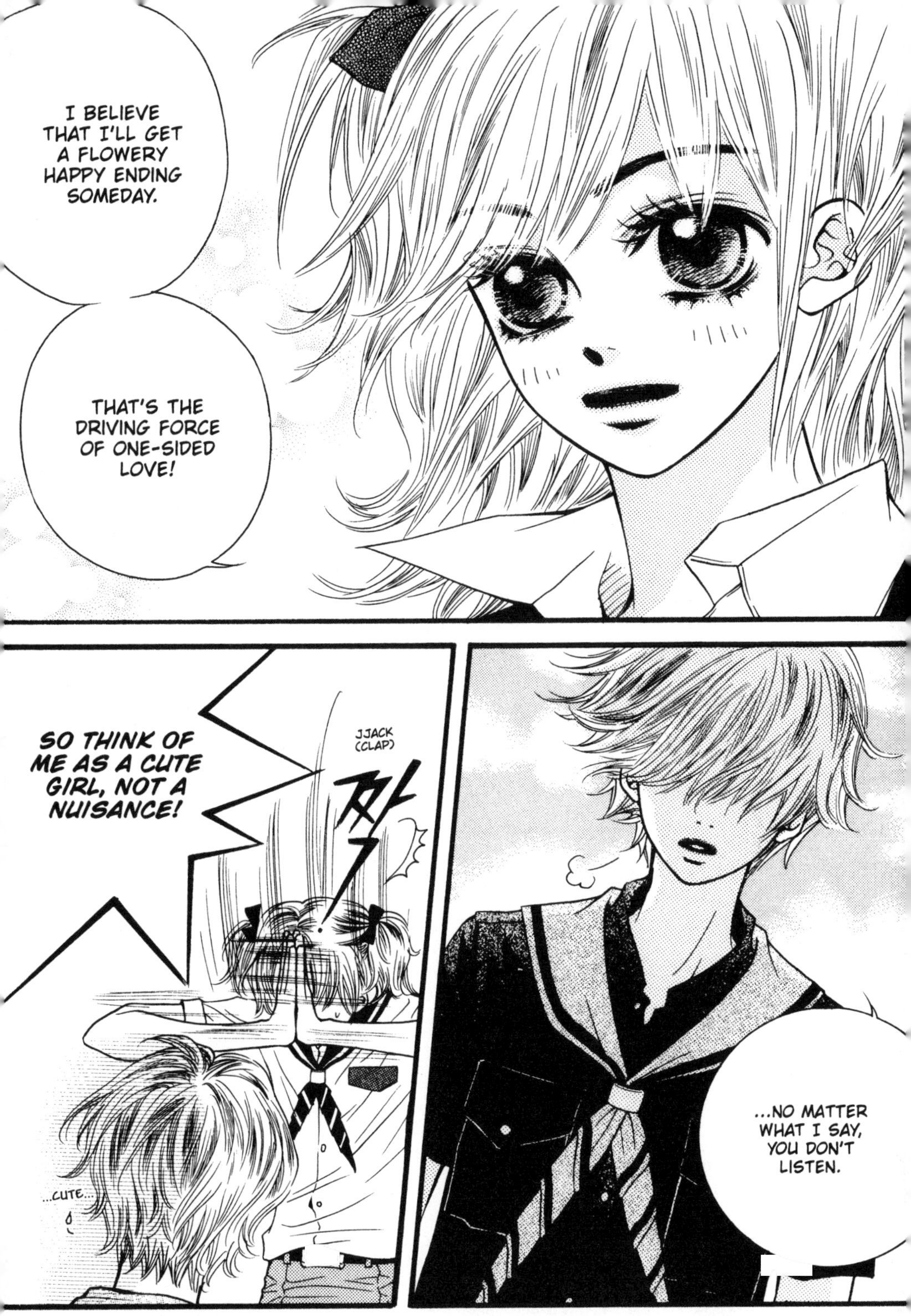
I BELIEVE THAT I'LL GET A FLOWERY HAPPY ENDING SOMEDAY.
THAT'S THE DRIVING FORCE OF ONE-SIDED LOVE!
SO THINK OF ME AS A CUTE GIRL, NOT A NUISANCE!
JJACK (CLAP)
...CUTE...
...NO MATTER WHAT I SAY, YOU DON'T LISTEN.

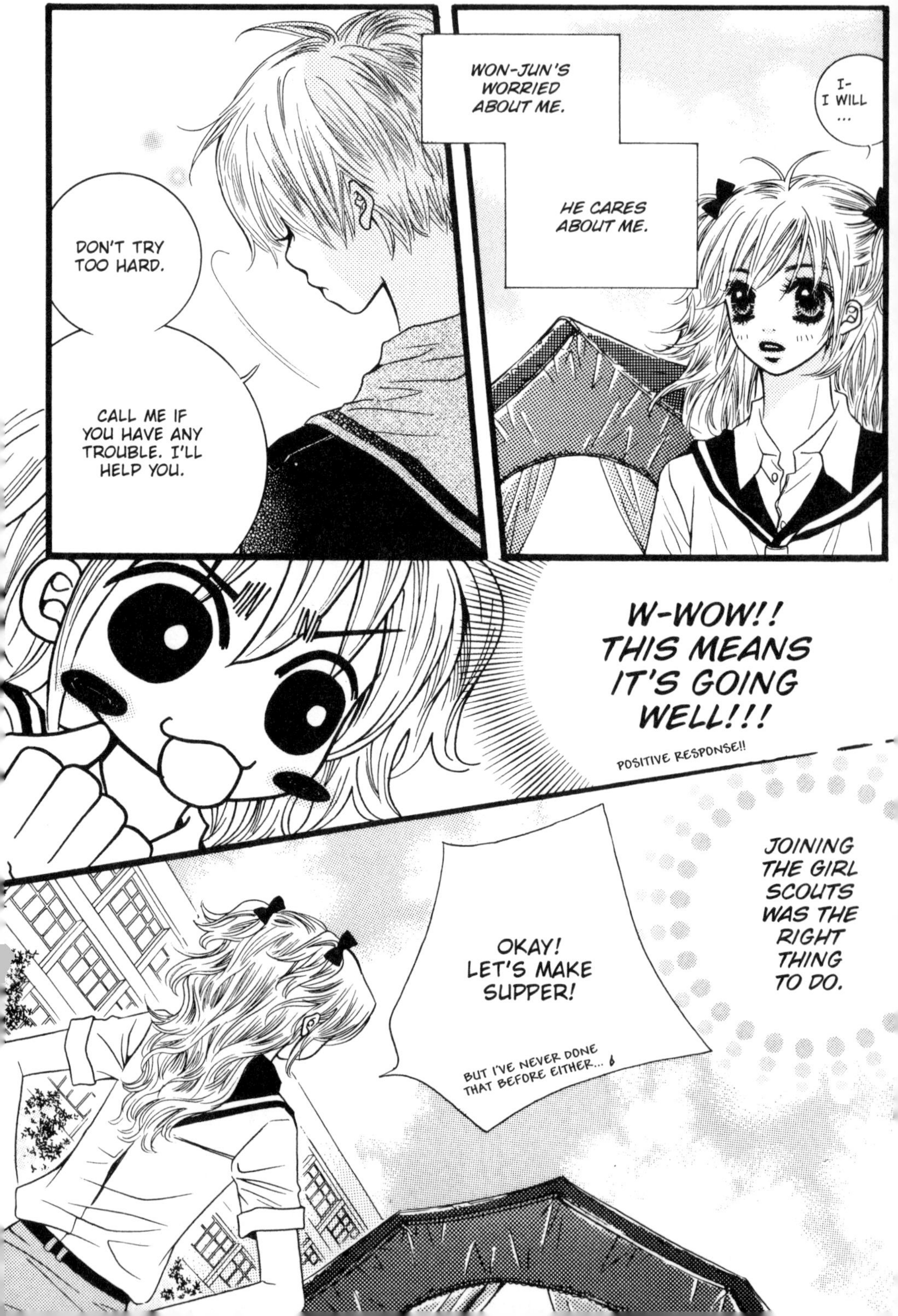
DON'T TRY TOO HARD.
CALL ME IF YOU HAVE ANY TROUBLE. I'LL HELP YOU.
WON-JUN'S WORRIED ABOUT ME.
HE CARES ABOUT ME.
I- I WILL ...
W-WOW!! THIS MEANS IT'S GOING WELL!!!
POSITIVE RESPONSE!!
OKAY! LET'S MAKE SUPPER!
BUT I'VE NEVER DONE THAT BEFORE EITHER...
JOINING THE GIRL SCOUTS WAS THE RIGHT THING TO DO.

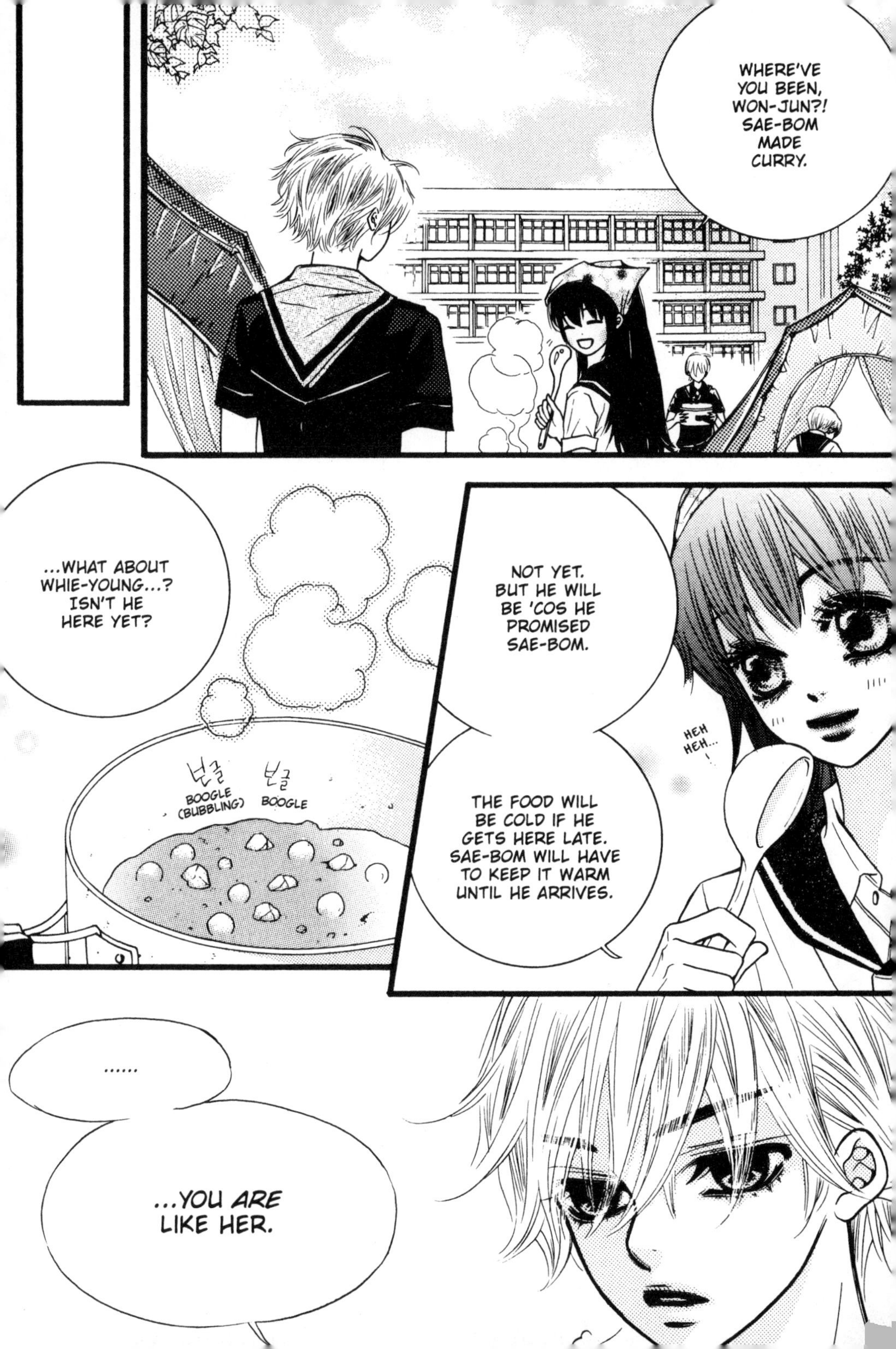
WHERE'VE YOU BEEN, WON-JUN?! SAE-BOM MADE CURRY.
...WHAT ABOUT WHIE-YOUNG...? ISN'T HE HERE YET?
번글
BOOGLE (BUBBLING)
번글
BOOGLE
NOT YET. BUT HE WILL BE 'COS HE PROMISED SAE-BOM.
THE FOOD WILL BE COLD IF HE GETS HERE LATE. SAE-BOM WILL HAVE TO KEEP IT WARM UNTIL HE ARRIVES.
HEH HEH...
......
...YOU ARE LIKE HER.

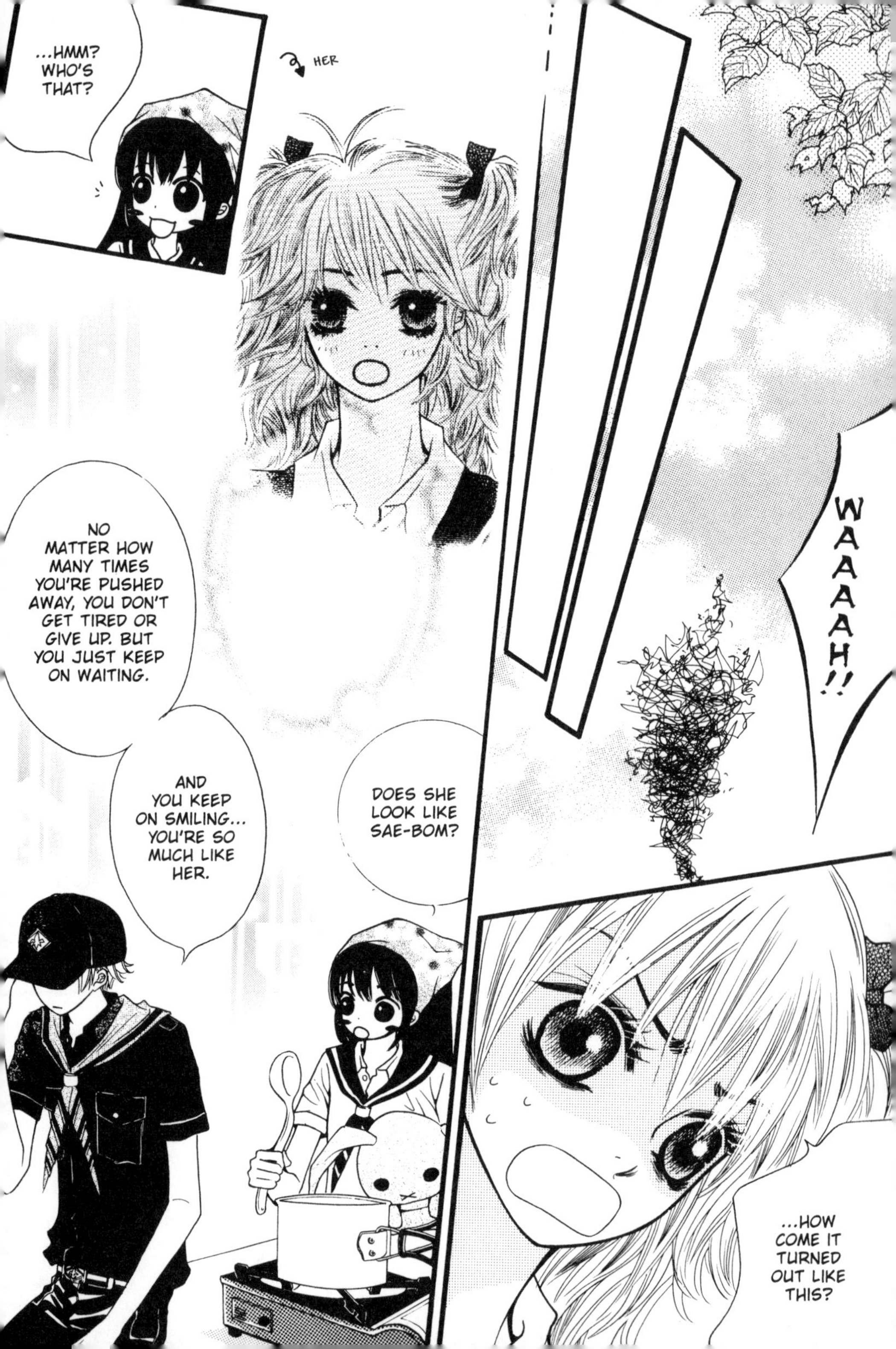
...HMM? WHO'S THAT?
HER
NO MATTER HOW MANY TIMES YOU'RE PUSHED AWAY, YOU DON'T GET TIRED OR GIVE UP. BUT YOU JUST KEEP ON WAITING.
AND YOU KEEP ON SMILING... YOU'RE SO MUCH LIKE HER.
DOES SHE LOOK LIKE SAE-BOM?
WAAAAAH!!
...HOW COME IT TURNED OUT LIKE THIS?

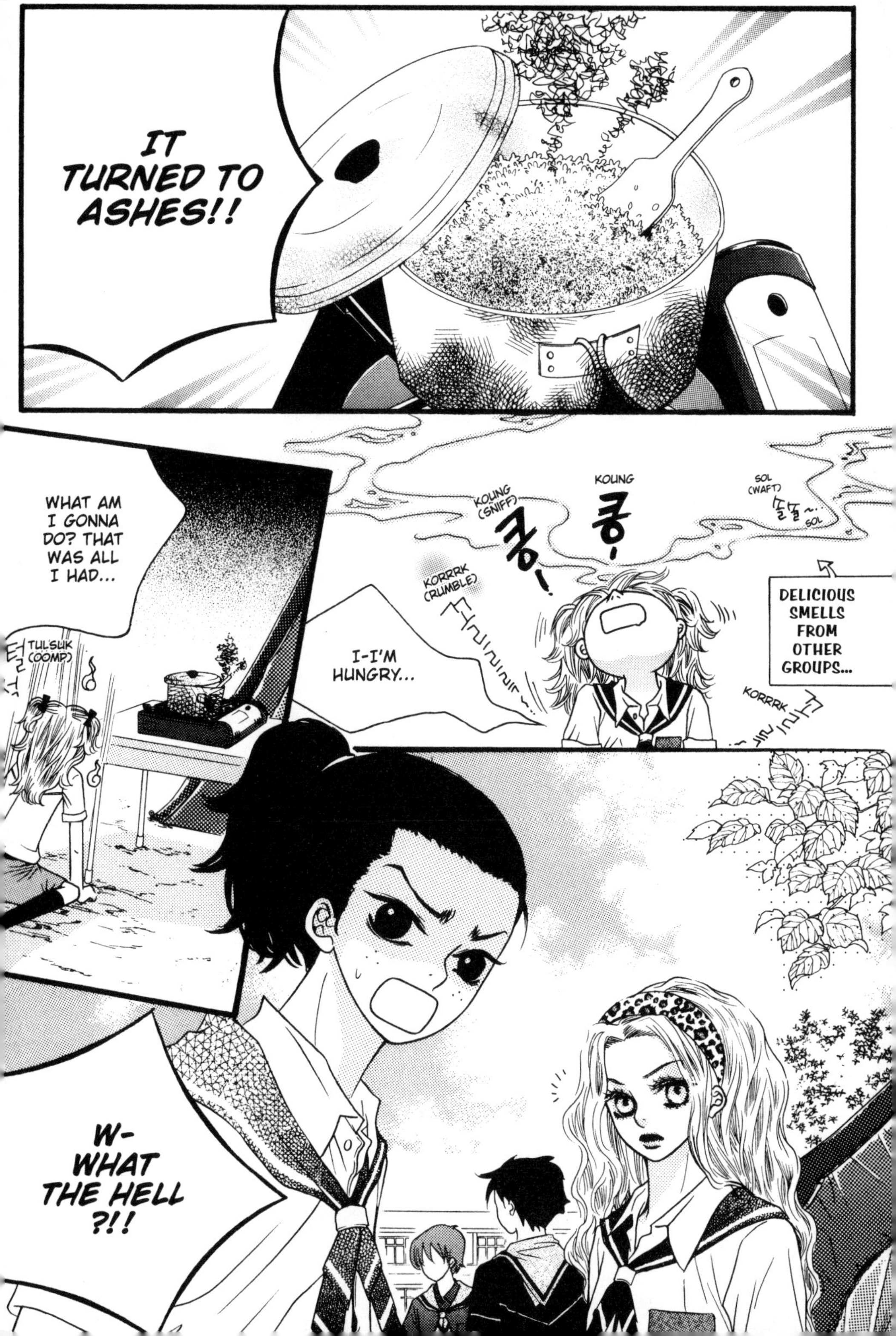
IT TURNED TO ASHES!!
WHAT AM I GONNA DO? THAT WAS ALL I HAD...
TUL'SUK (OOMP)
KOUNG (SNIFF)
쿵
KOUNG
쿵
SOL (WAFT)
솔솔~
SOL
KORRRK (RUMBLE)
I-I'M HUNGRY...
DELICIOUS SMELLS FROM OTHER GROUPS...
KORRRK
W-WHAT THE HELL?!!

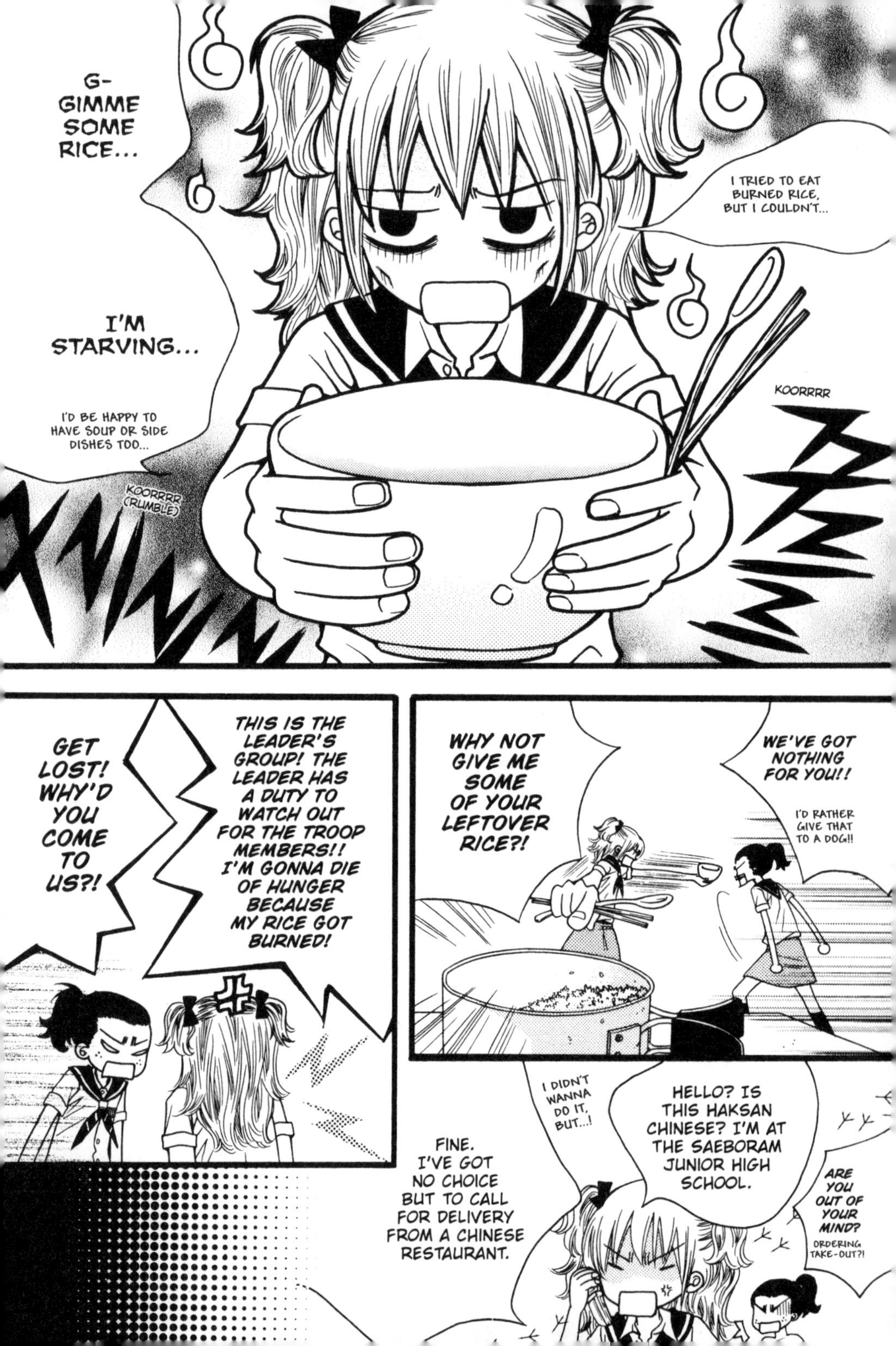
G-GIMME SOME RICE...
I'M STARVING...
I'D BE HAPPY TO HAVE SOUP OR SIDE DISHES TOO...
KOORRRR (RUMBLE)
I TRIED TO EAT BURNED RICE, BUT I COULDN'T...
KOORRRR
GET LOST! WHY'D YOU COME TO US?!
THIS IS THE LEADER'S GROUP! THE LEADER HAS A DUTY TO WATCH OUT FOR THE TROOP MEMBERS!! I'M GONNA DIE OF HUNGER BECAUSE MY RICE GOT BURNED!
WHY NOT GIVE ME SOME OF YOUR LEFTOVER RICE?!
WE'VE GOT NOTHING FOR YOU!!
I'D RATHER GIVE THAT TO A DOG!!
FINE. I'VE GOT NO CHOICE BUT TO CALL FOR DELIVERY FROM A CHINESE RESTAURANT.
I DIDN'T WANNA DO IT, BUT...!
HELLO? IS THIS HAKSAN CHINESE? I'M AT THE SAEBORAM JUNIOR HIGH SCHOOL.
ARE YOU OUT OF YOUR MIND?
ORDERING TAKE-OUT?!

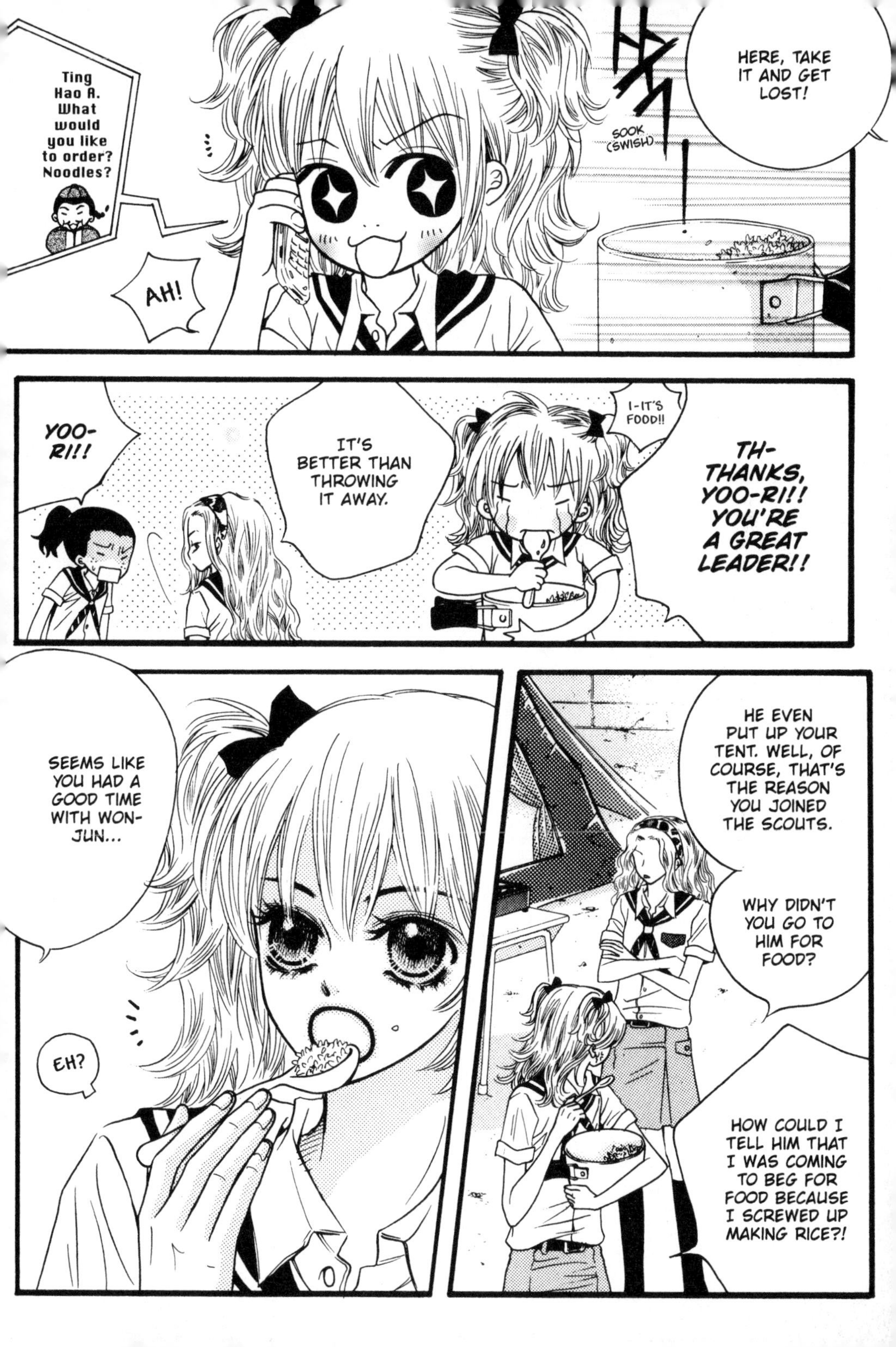

Ting Hao A. What would you like to order? Noodles?
AH!
SOOK (SWISH)
HERE, TAKE IT AND GET LOST!
YOO-RI!!
IT'S BETTER THAN THROWING IT AWAY.
I-IT'S FOOD!!
TH-THANKS, YOO-RI!! YOU'RE A GREAT LEADER!!
SEEMS LIKE YOU HAD A GOOD TIME WITH WON-JUN...
EH?
HE EVEN PUT UP YOUR TENT. WELL, OF COURSE, THAT'S THE REASON YOU JOINED THE SCOUTS.
WHY DIDN'T YOU GO TO HIM FOR FOOD?
HOW COULD I TELL HIM THAT I WAS COMING TO BEG FOR FOOD BECAUSE I SCREWED UP MAKING RICE?!

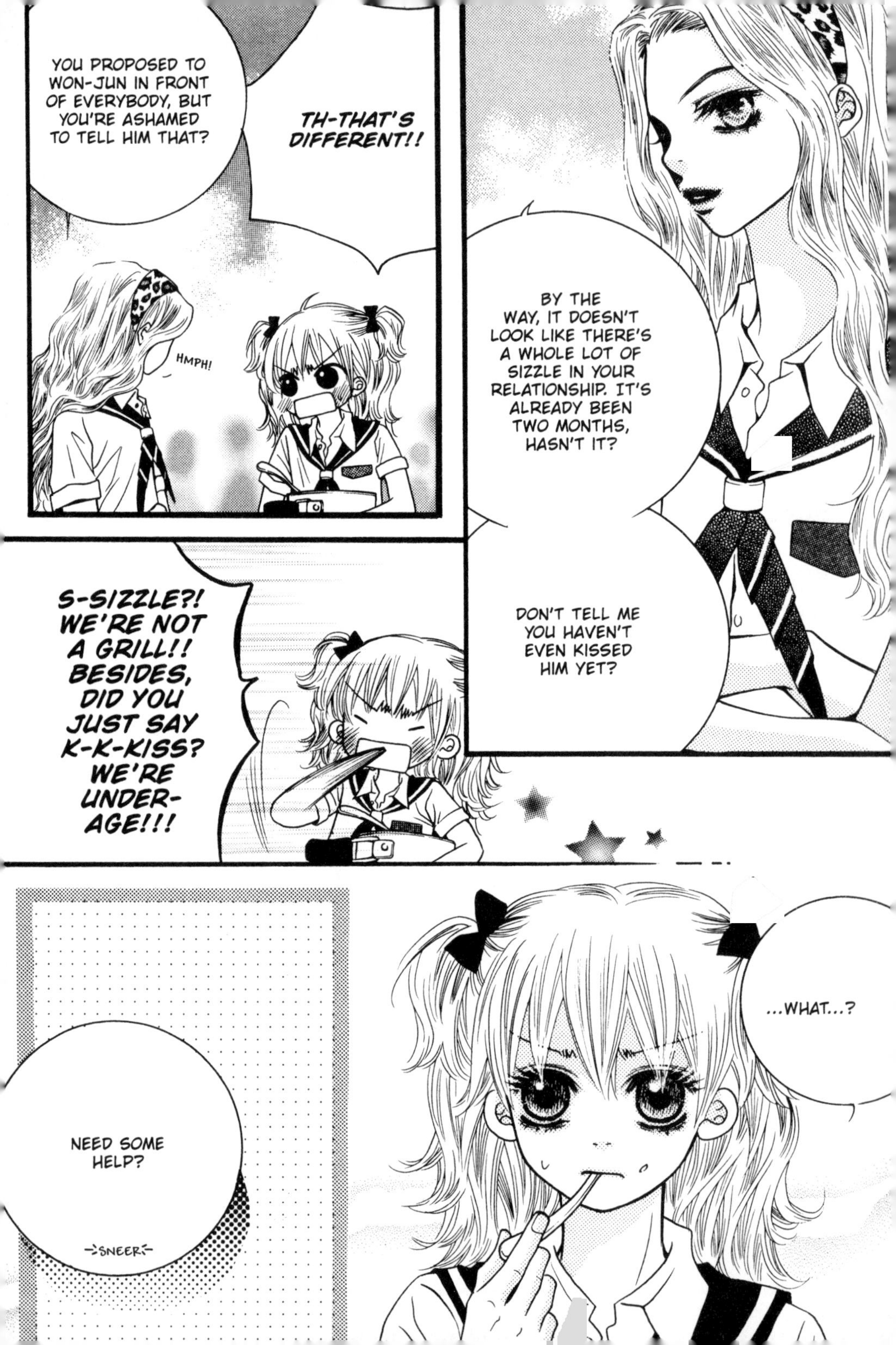
YOU PROPOSED TO WON-JUN IN FRONT OF EVERYBODY, BUT YOU'RE ASHAMED TO TELL HIM THAT?
TH-THAT'S DIFFERENT!!
HMPH!
BY THE WAY, IT DOESN'T LOOK LIKE THERE'S A WHOLE LOT OF SIZZLE IN YOUR RELATIONSHIP. IT'S ALREADY BEEN TWO MONTHS, HASN'T IT?
DON'T TELL ME YOU HAVEN'T EVEN KISSED HIM YET?
S-SIZZLE?! WE'RE NOT A GRILL!! BESIDES, DID YOU JUST SAY K-K-KISS? WE'RE UNDER-AGE!!!
NEED SOME HELP?
SNEER
...WHAT...?

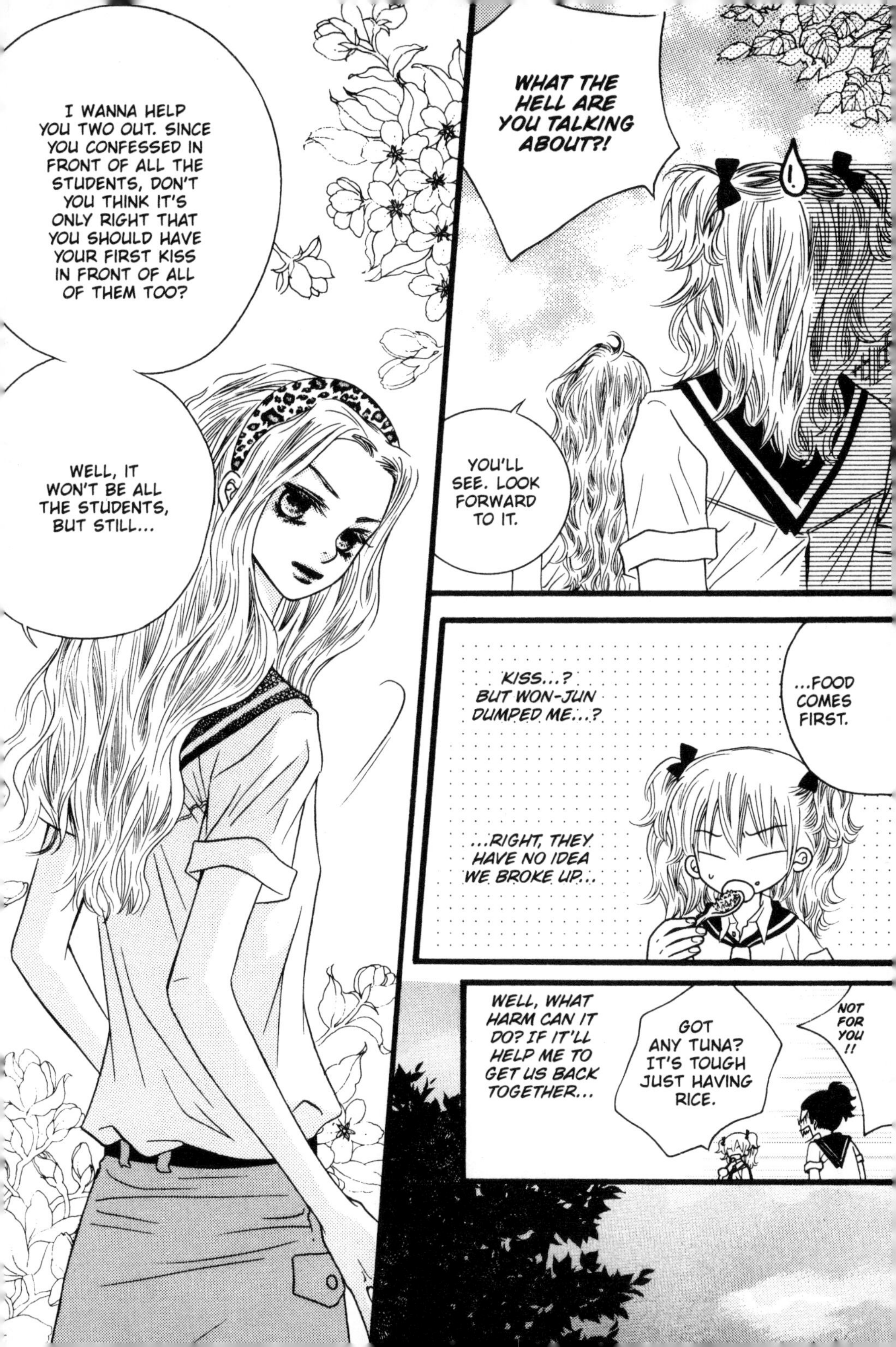
I WANNA HELP YOU TWO OUT. SINCE YOU CONFESSED IN FRONT OF ALL THE STUDENTS, DON'T YOU THINK IT'S ONLY RIGHT THAT YOU SHOULD HAVE YOUR FIRST KISS IN FRONT OF ALL OF THEM TOO?
WELL, IT WON'T BE ALL THE STUDENTS, BUT STILL...
WHAT THE HELL ARE YOU TALKING ABOUT?!
YOU'LL SEE. LOOK FORWARD TO IT.
KISS...? BUT WON-JUN DUMPED ME...?
...FOOD COMES FIRST.
...RIGHT, THEY HAVE NO IDEA WE BROKE UP...
WELL, WHAT HARM CAN IT DO? IF IT'LL HELP ME TO GET US BACK TOGETHER...
GOT ANY TUNA? IT'S TOUGH JUST HAVING RICE.
NOT FOR YOU!!

AND THE CAMPFIRE...

Let's have a night of fun and games here at the Scouts' joint campout!!

WHAL
(FWOOM)

WHAL

How about we get things warmed up with a newspaper game?

One couple from each group, please come forward!!

HE'S THE EMCEE.

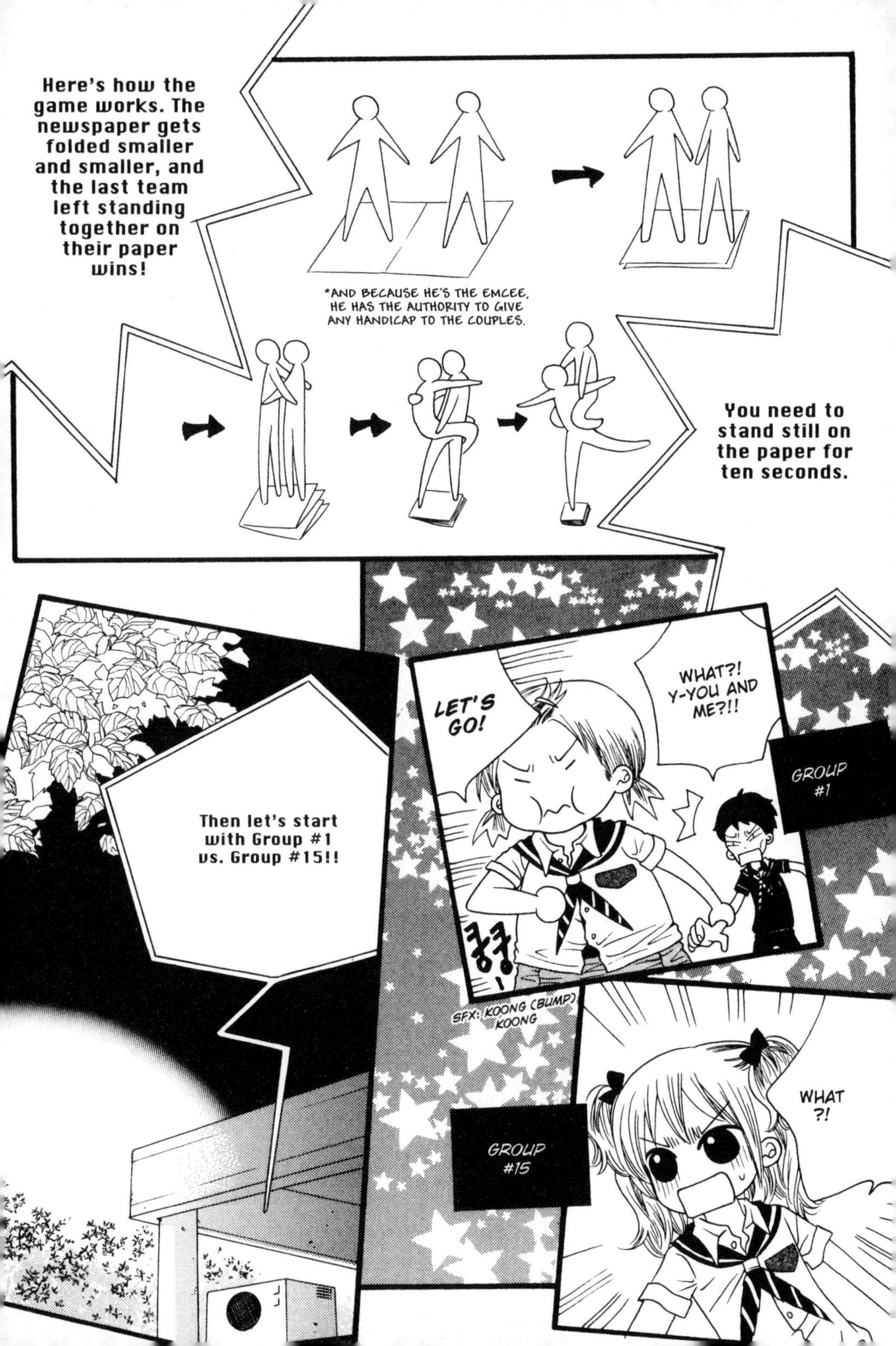
Here's how the game works. The newspaper gets folded smaller and smaller, and the last team left standing together on their paper wins!
*AND BECAUSE HE'S THE EMCEE, HE HAS THE AUTHORITY TO GIVE ANY HANDICAP TO THE COUPLES.
You need to stand still on the paper for ten seconds.
Then let's start with Group #1 vs. Group #15!!
LET'S GO!
WHAT?! Y-YOU AND ME?!!
GROUP #1
쿵쿵
SFX: KOONG (BUMP) KOONG
GROUP #15
WHAT ?!

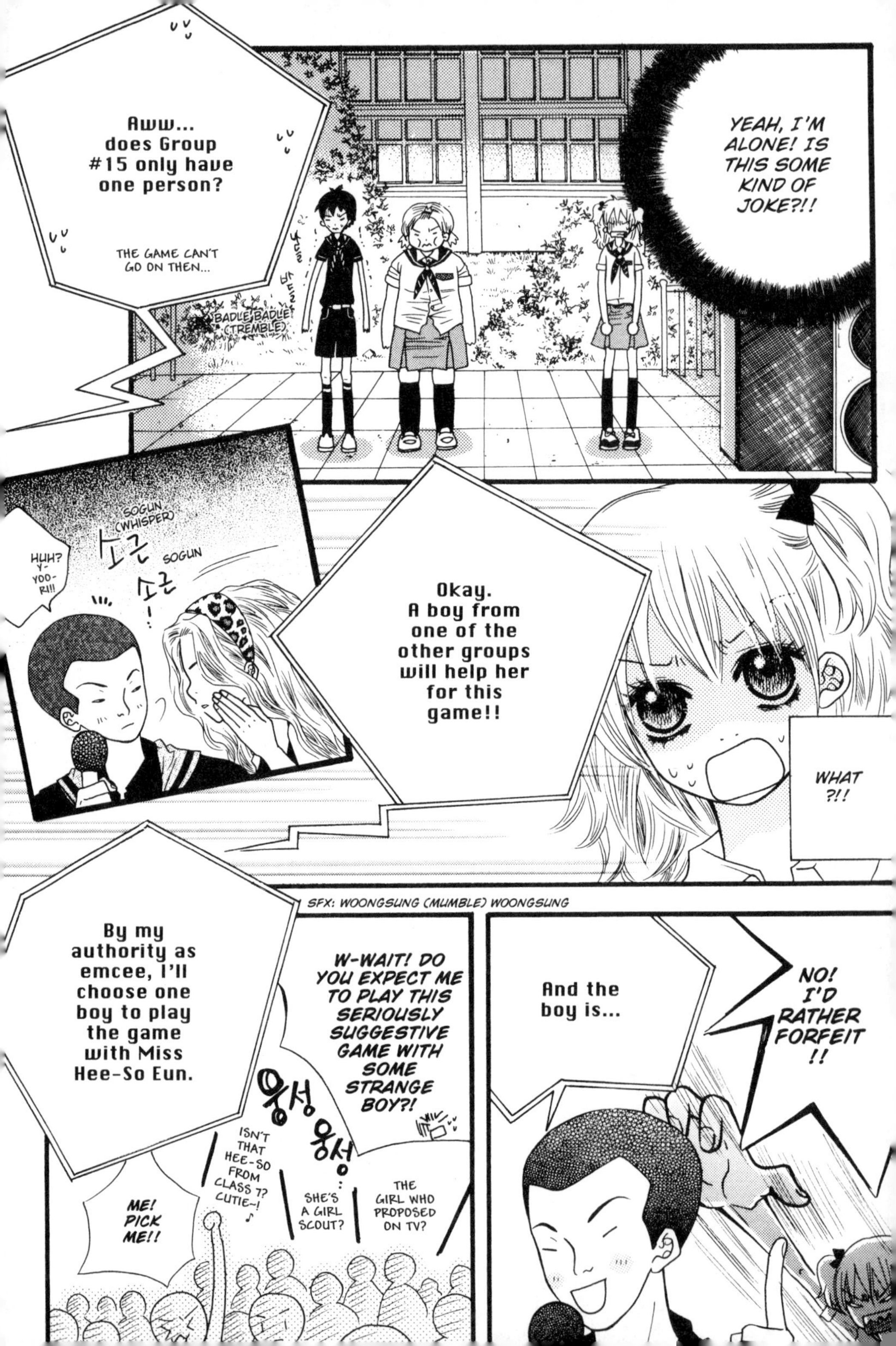
Aww... does Group #15 only have one person?
THE GAME CAN'T GO ON THEN...
BADLE BADLE (TREMBLE)
YEAH, I'M ALONE! IS THIS SOME KIND OF JOKE?!!
SOGUN (WHISPER)
소곤
SOGUN
소곤
HUH? Y-YOORI!!
Okay. A boy from one of the other groups will help her for this game!!
WHAT ?!!
SFX: WOONGSUNG (MUMBLE) WOONGSUNG
By my authority as emcee, I'll choose one boy to play the game with Miss Hee-So Eun.
W-WAIT! DO YOU EXPECT ME TO PLAY THIS SERIOUSLY SUGGESTIVE GAME WITH SOME STRANGE BOY?!
웅성
웅성
ISN'T THAT HEE-SO FROM CLASS 7? CUTIE~! ♪
ME! PICK ME!!
SHE'S A GIRL SCOUT?
THE GIRL WHO PROPOSED ON TV?
And the boy is...
NO! I'D RATHER FORFEIT!!

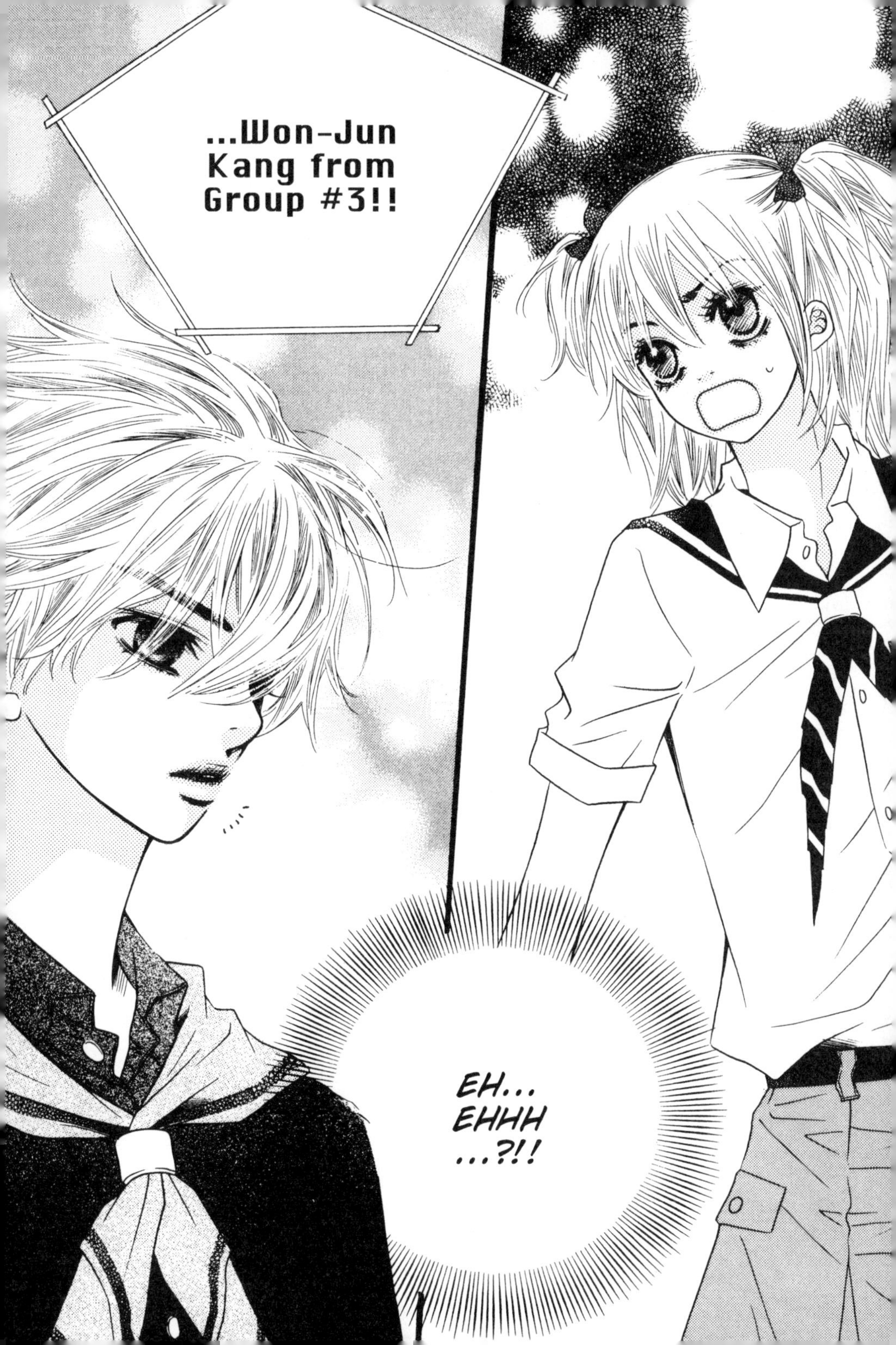
...Won-Jun Kang from Group #3!!
EH... EHHH ...?!!

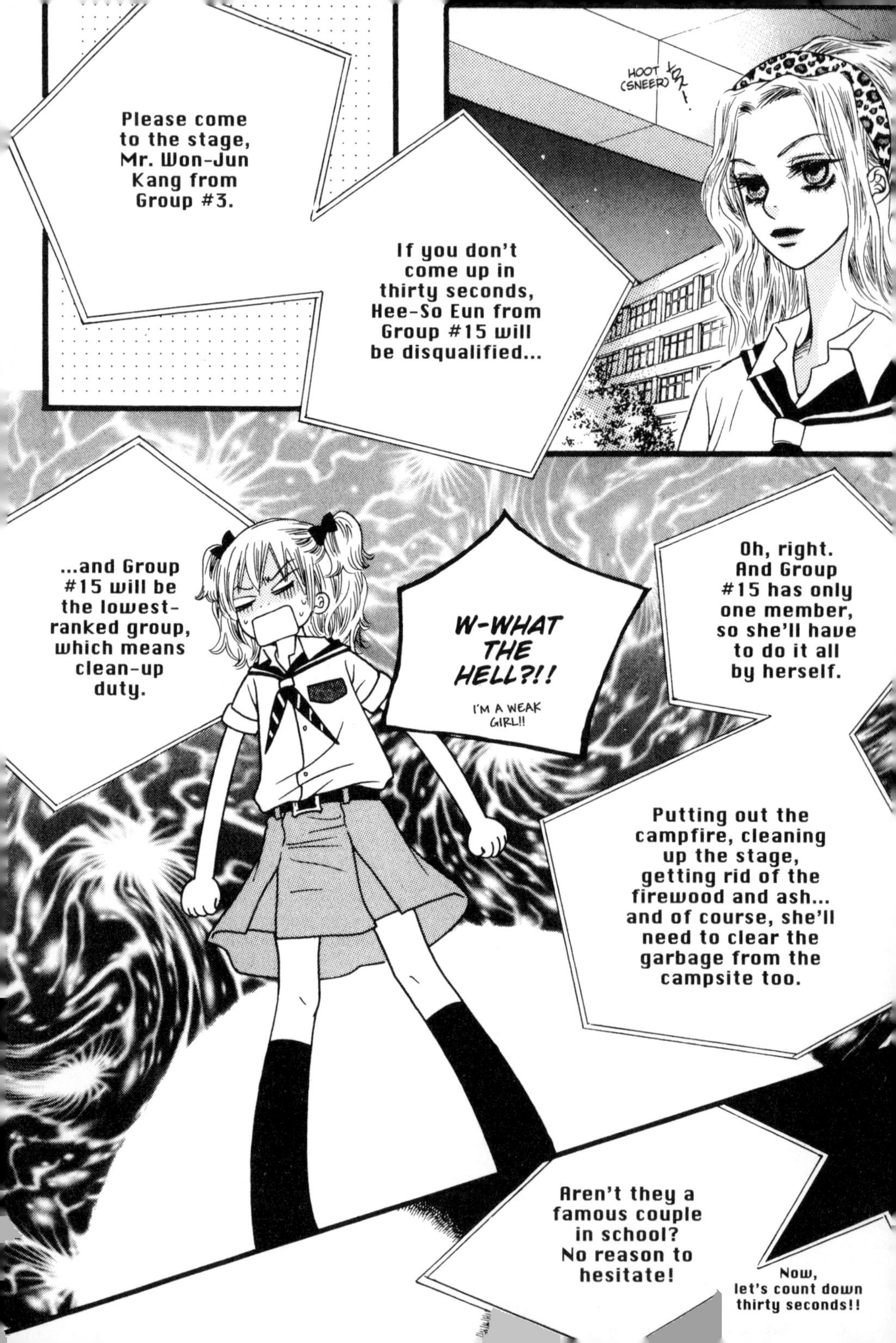
Please come to the stage, Mr. Won-Jun Kang from Group #3.
If you don't come up in thirty seconds, Hee-So Eun from Group #15 will be disqualified...
HOOT (SNEER)
...and Group #15 will be the lowest-ranked group, which means clean-up duty.
W-WHAT THE HELL?!!
I'M A WEAK GIRL!!
Oh, right. And Group #15 has only one member, so she'll have to do it all by herself.
Putting out the campfire, cleaning up the stage, getting rid of the firewood and ash... and of course, she'll need to clear the garbage from the campsite too.
Aren't they a famous couple in school? No reason to hesitate!
Now, let's count down thirty seconds!!

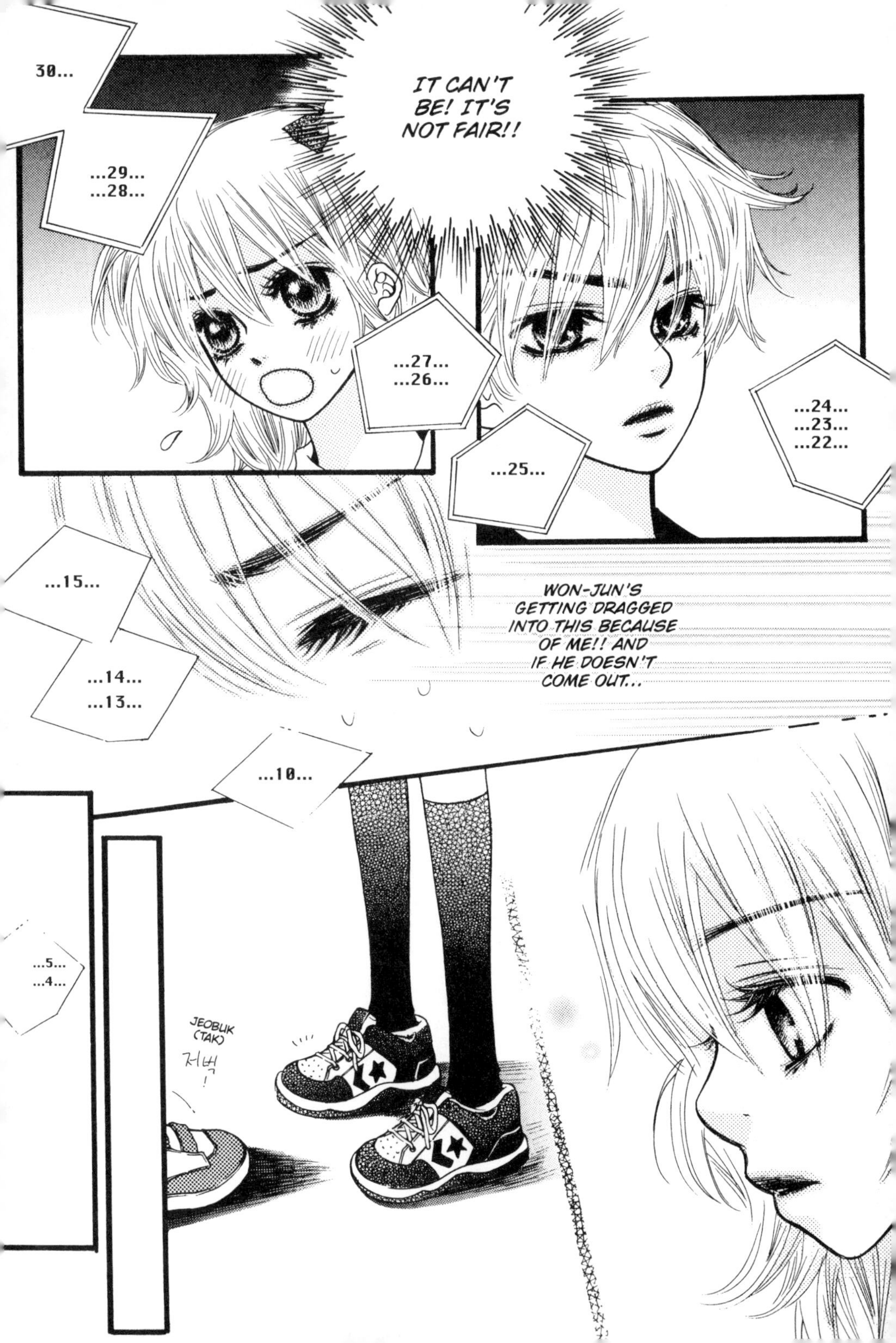
30...
...29...
...28...
IT CAN'T BE! IT'S NOT FAIR!!
...27...
...26...
...25...
...24...
...23...
...22...
...15...
...14...
...13...
WON-JUN'S GETTING DRAGGED INTO THIS BECAUSE OF ME!! AND IF HE DOESN'T COME OUT...
...10...
...5...
...4...
JEOBUK (TAK)
저벅
!

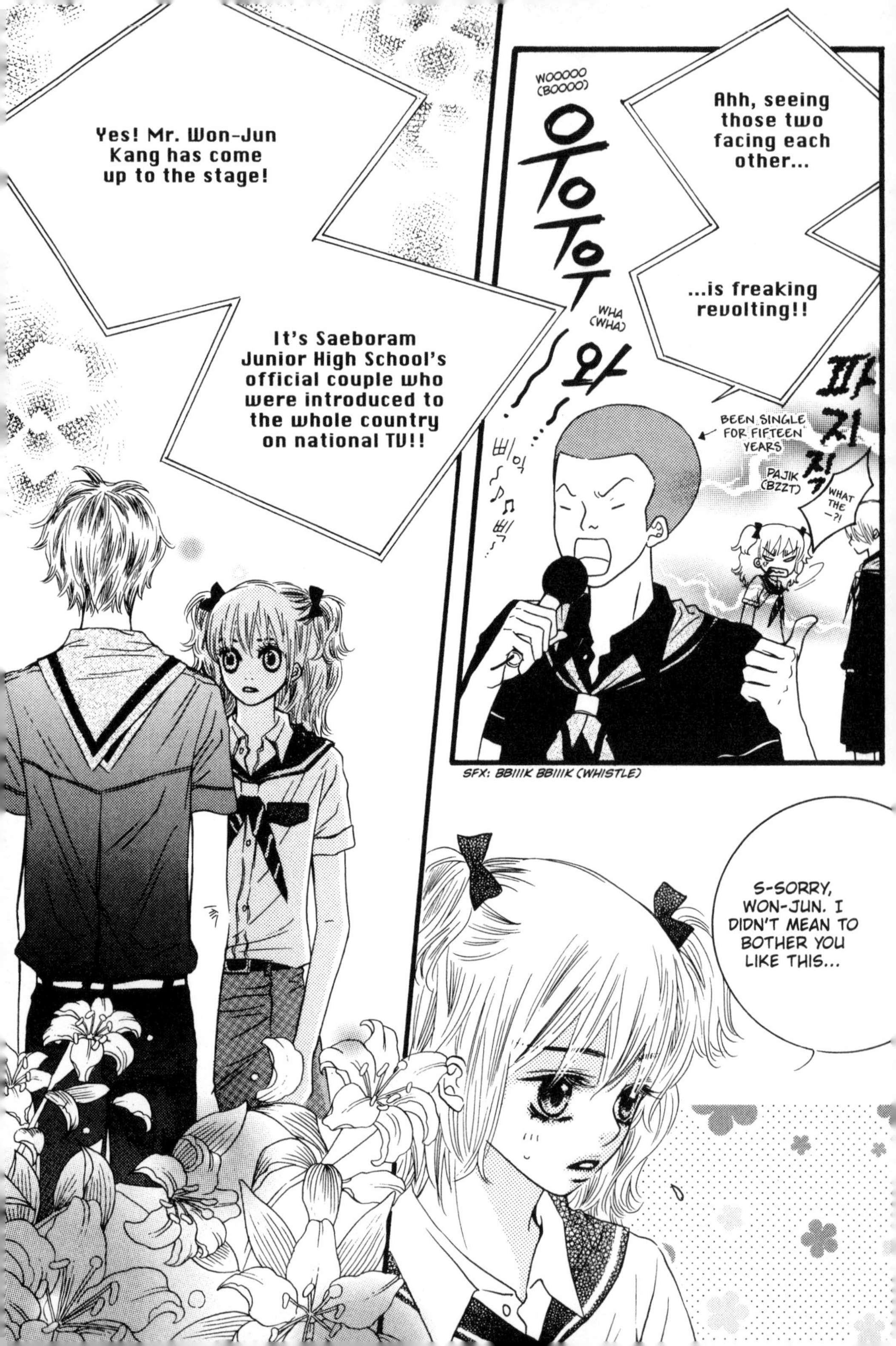
Yes! Mr. Won-Jun Kang has come up to the stage!
It's Saeboram Junior High School's official couple who were introduced to the whole country on national TV!!
WOOOOO (BOOOO)
Ahh, seeing those two facing each other...
...is freaking revolting!!
WHA (WHA)
와
BEEN SINGLE FOR FIFTEEN YEARS
파지직
PAJIK (BZZT)
WHAT THE —?!
SFX: BBIIIK BBIIIK (WHISTLE)
S-SORRY, WON-JUN. I DIDN'T MEAN TO BOTHER YOU LIKE THIS...

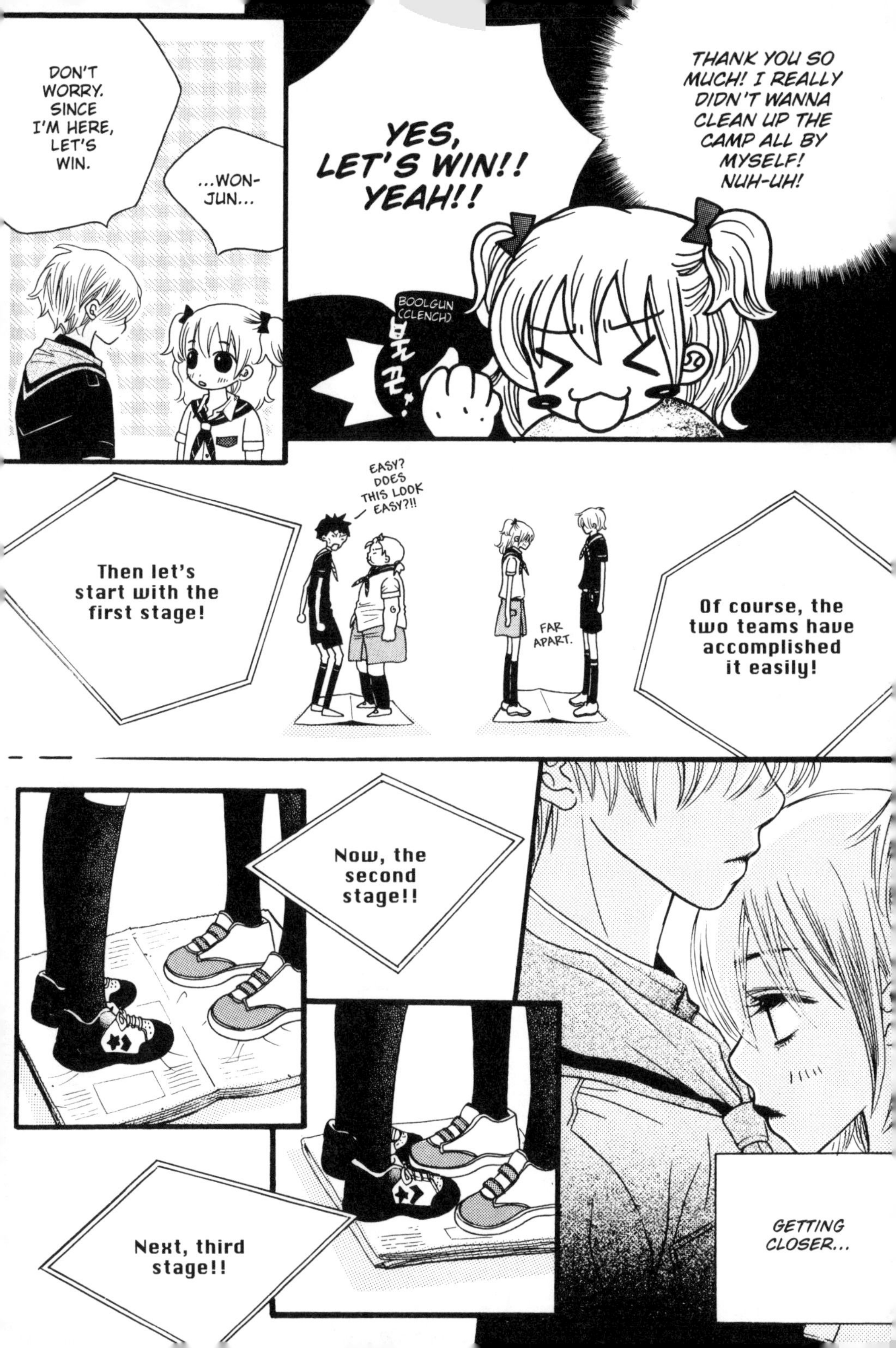
DON'T WORRY. SINCE I'M HERE, LET'S WIN.
...WON-JUN...
YES, LET'S WIN!! YEAH!!
THANK YOU SO MUCH! I REALLY DIDN'T WANNA CLEAN UP THE CAMP ALL BY MYSELF! NUH-UH!
BOOLGUN (CLENCH)
불끈
Then let's start with the first stage!
EASY? DOES THIS LOOK EASY?!!
FAR APART.
Of course, the two teams have accomplished it easily!
Now, the second stage!!
Next, third stage!!
GETTING CLOSER...

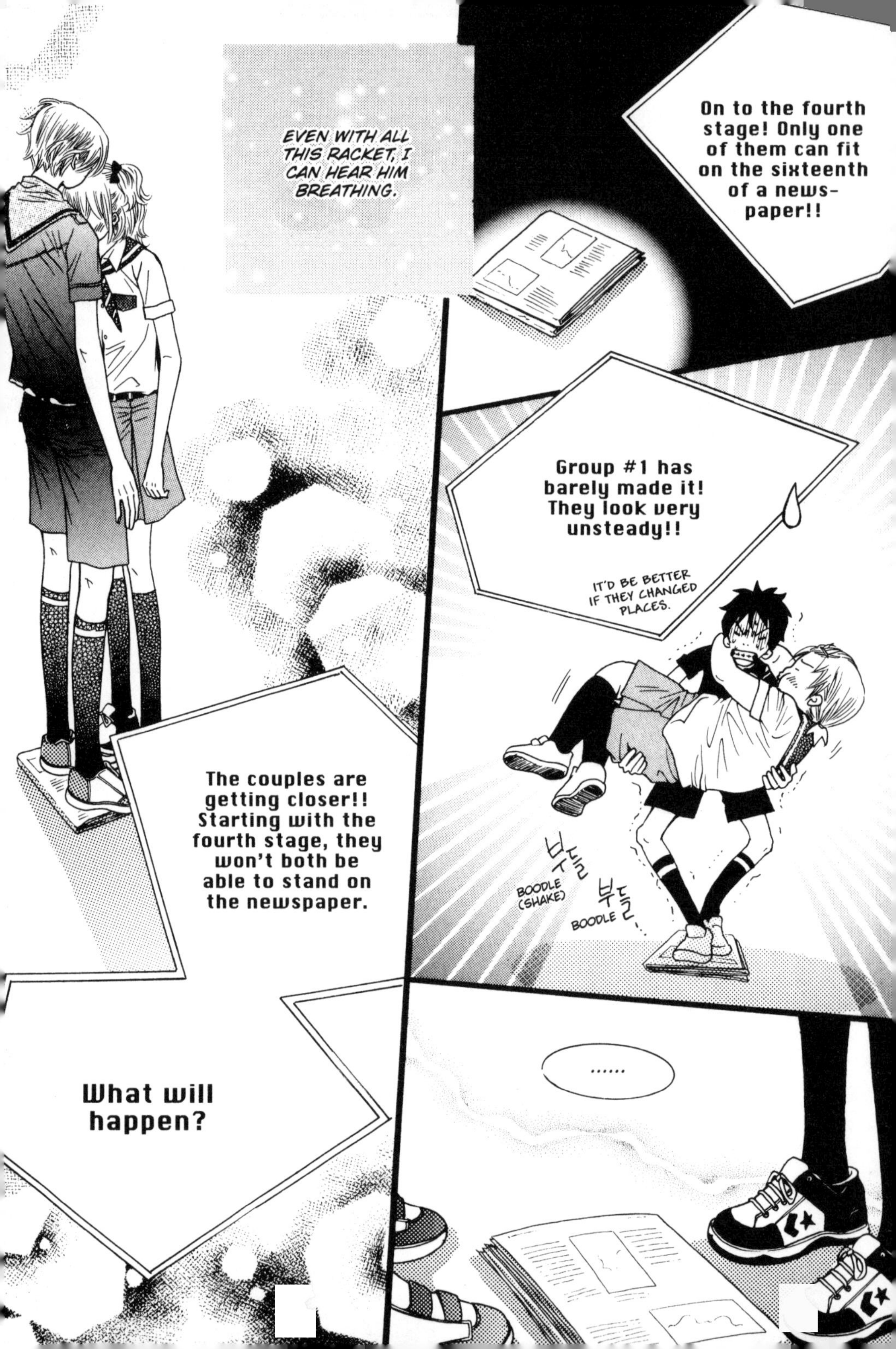
EVEN WITH ALL THIS RACKET, I CAN HEAR HIM BREATHING.
On to the fourth stage! Only one of them can fit on the sixteenth of a news-paper!!
The couples are getting closer!! Starting with the fourth stage, they won't both be able to stand on the newspaper.
Group #1 has barely made it! They look very unsteady!!
IT'D BE BETTER IF THEY CHANGED PLACES.
부들
BOODLE (SHAKE)
부들
BOODLE
What will happen?
......

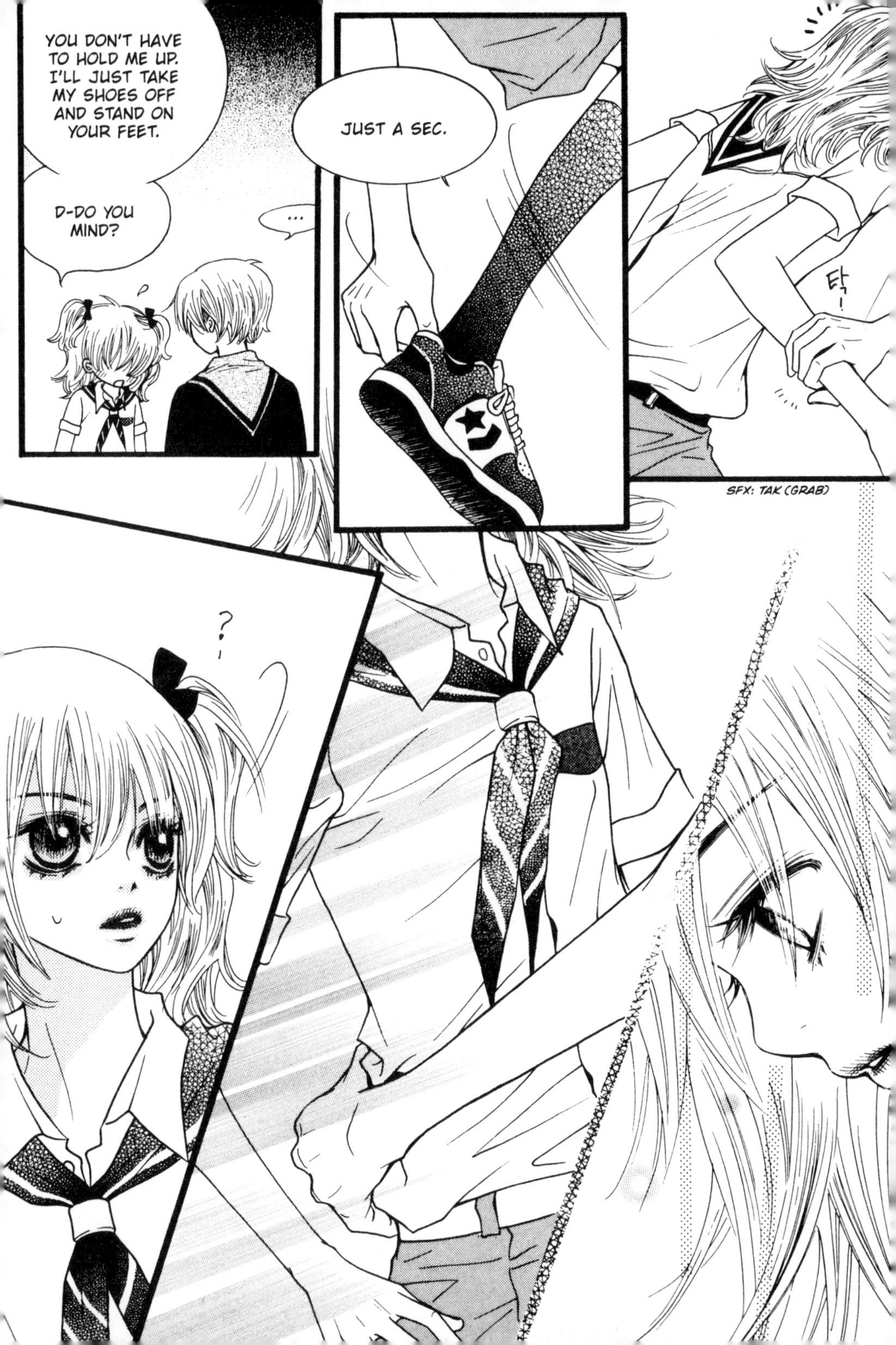
YOU DON'T HAVE TO HOLD ME UP. I'LL JUST TAKE MY SHOES OFF AND STAND ON YOUR FEET.
D-DO YOU MIND?
...
JUST A SEC.
탁
SFX: TAK (GRAB)
?

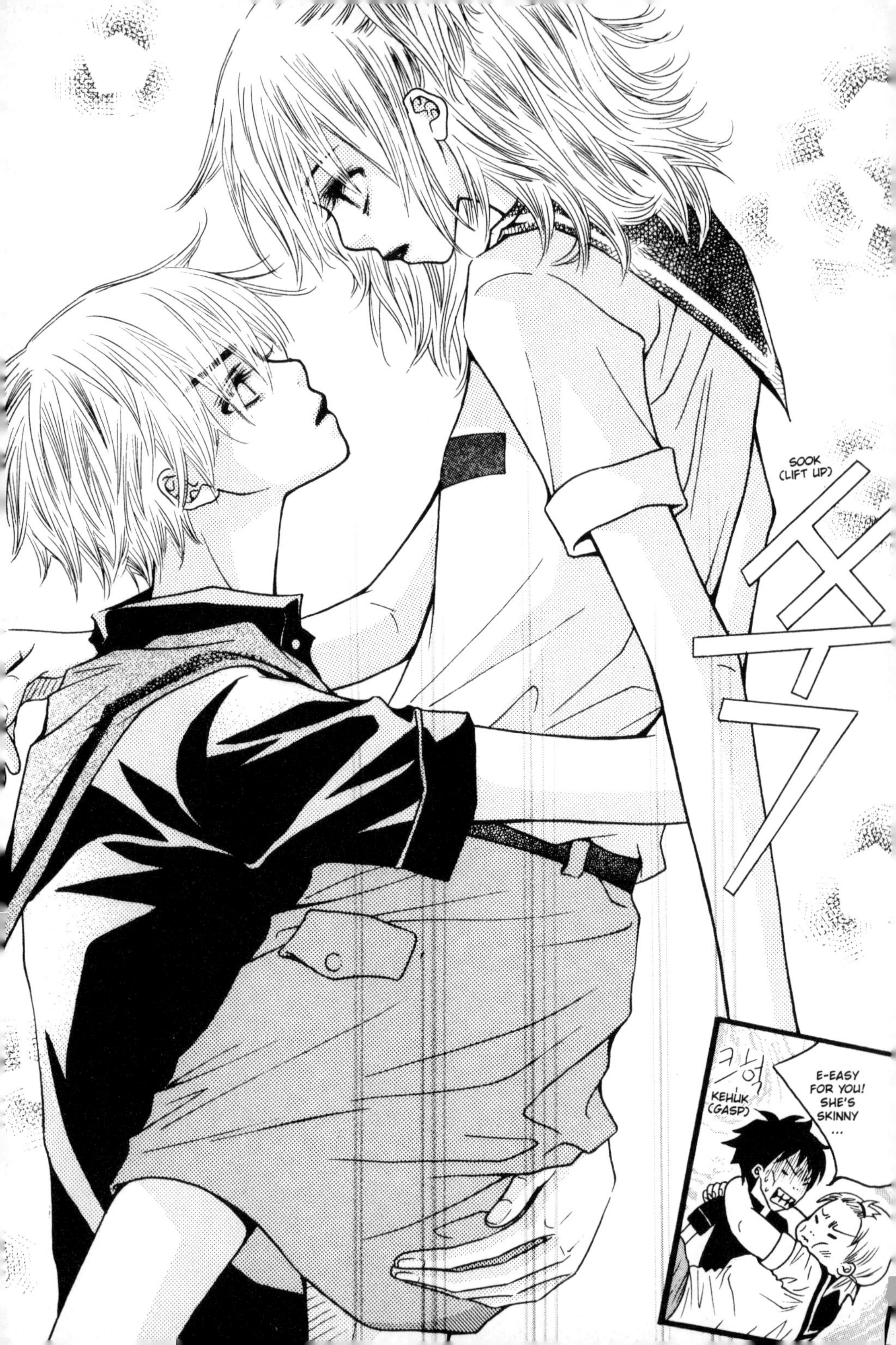
SOOK (LIFT UP)
KEHUK (GASP)
E-EASY FOR YOU! SHE'S SKINNY ...

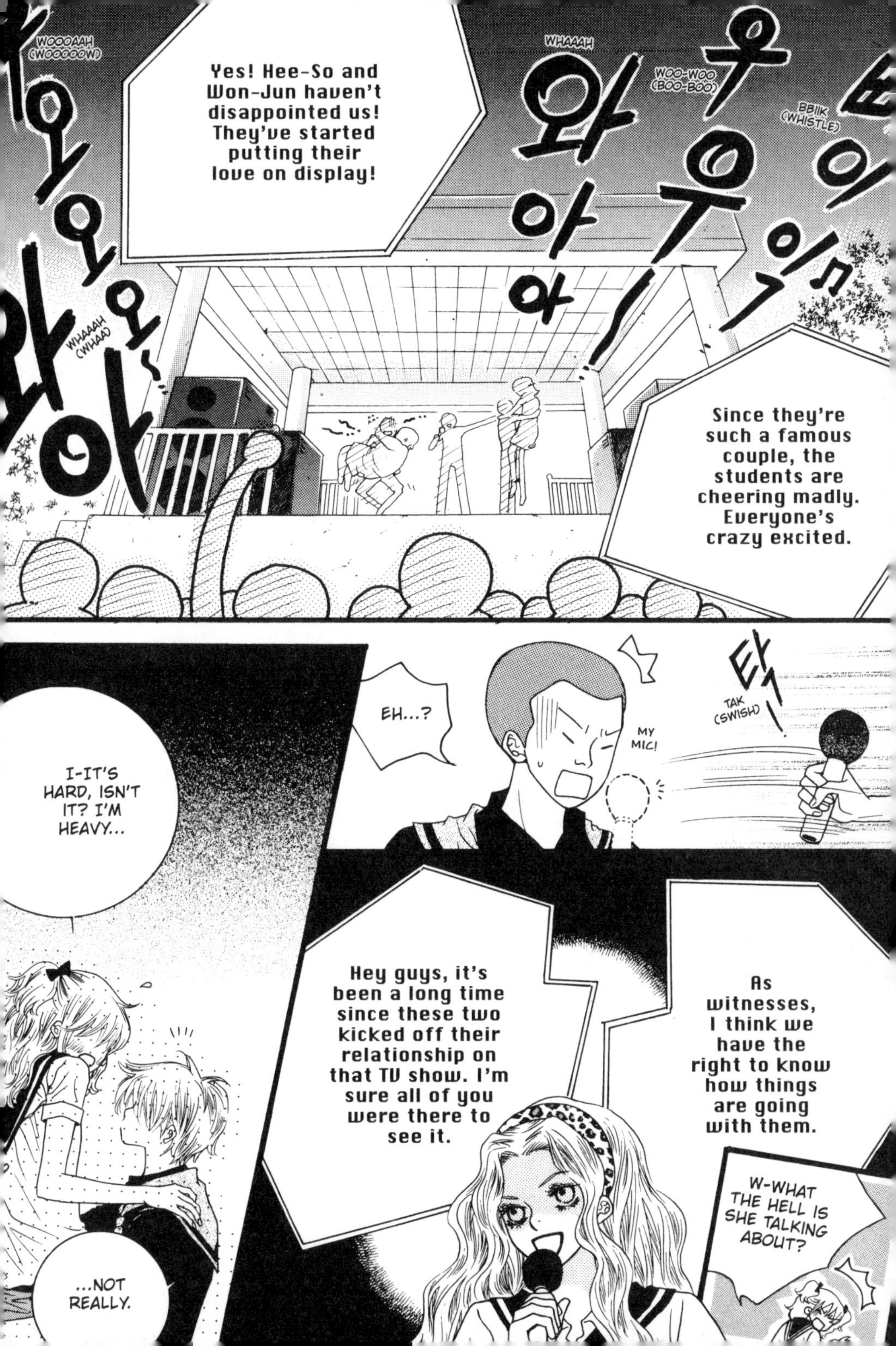
WOOOAAH (WOOOOOW)
Yes! Hee-So and Won-Jun haven't disappointed us! They've started putting their love on display!
WHAAAH
WOO-WOO (BOO-BOO)
BBIIK (WHISTLE)
WHAAAH (WHAA)
Since they're such a famous couple, the students are cheering madly. Everyone's crazy excited.
I-IT'S HARD, ISN'T IT? I'M HEAVY...
...NOT REALLY.
EH...?
MY MIC!
TAK (SWISH)
Hey guys, it's been a long time since these two kicked off their relationship on that TV show. I'm sure all of you were there to see it.
As witnesses, I think we have the right to know how things are going with them.
W-WHAT THE HELL IS SHE TALKING ABOUT?

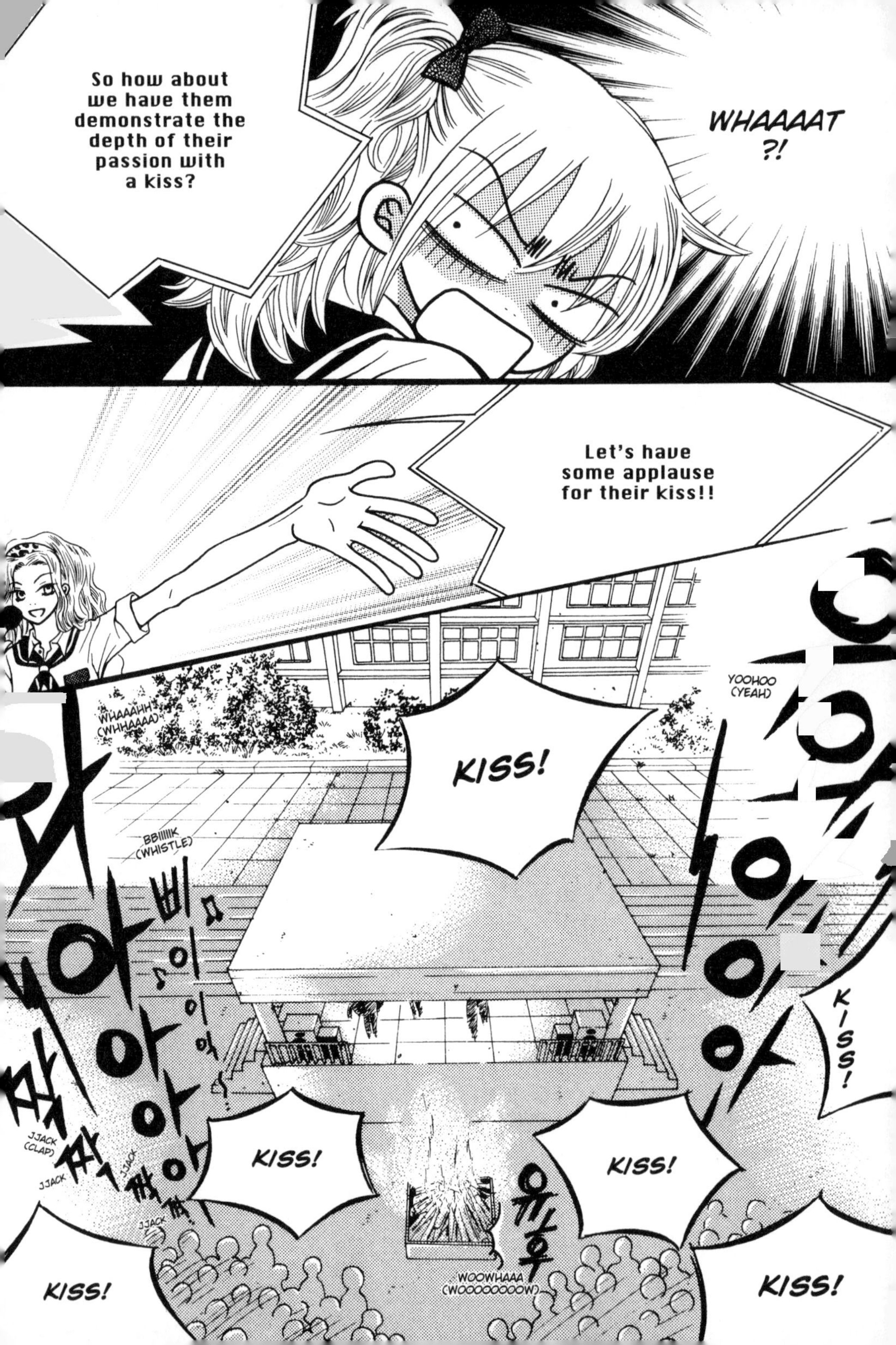
So how about we have them demonstrate the depth of their passion with a kiss?
WHAAAAT ?!
Let's have some applause for their kiss!!
WHAAAHH (WHHAAAA)
KISS!
YOOHOO (YEAH)
BBIIIIIK (WHISTLE)
KISS!
JJACK (CLAP)
JJACK
JJACK
JJACK
KISS!
KISS!
WOOWHAAA (WOOOOOOOOW)
KISS!
KISS!

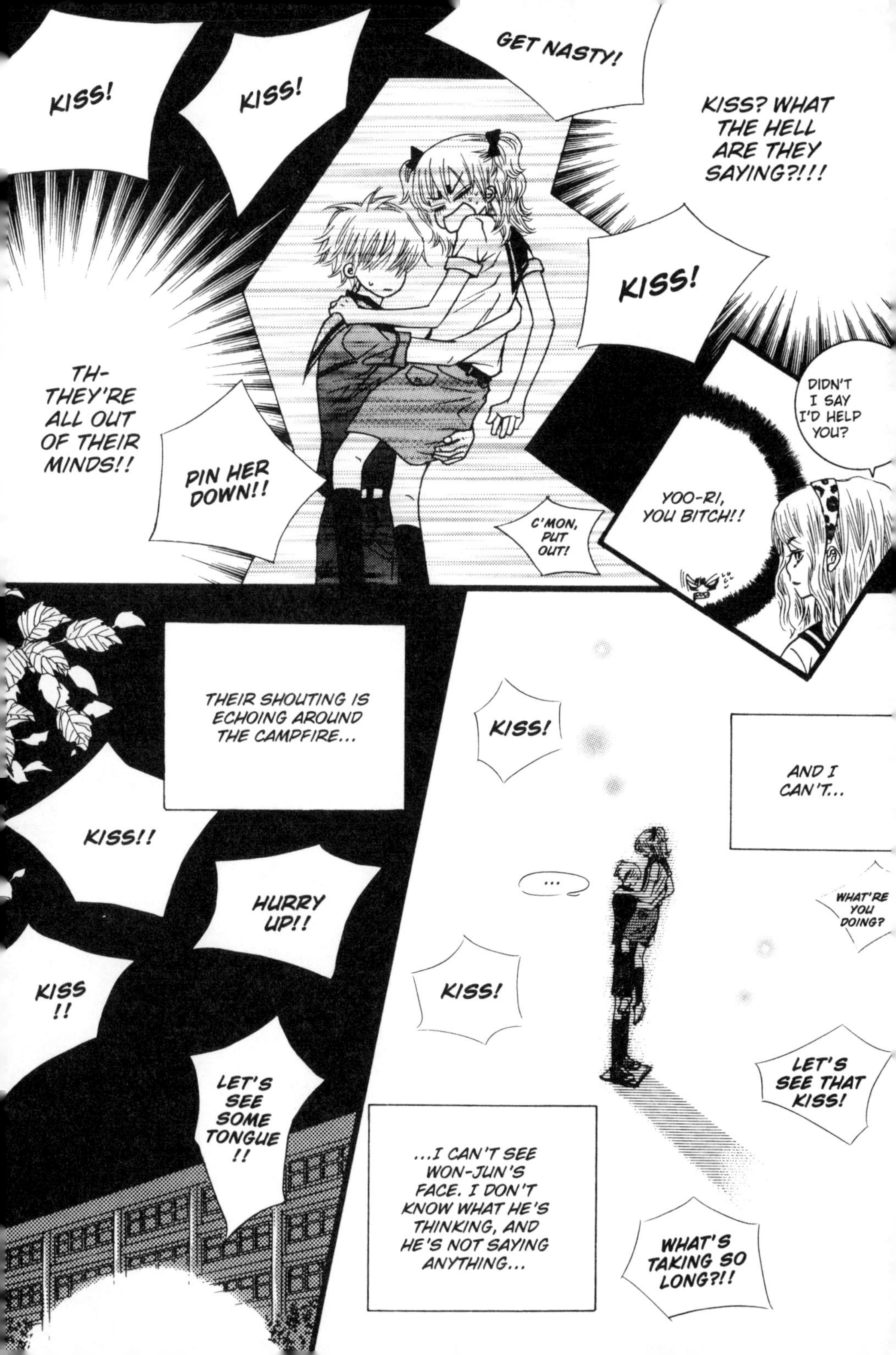
KISS!
KISS!
GET NASTY!
KISS? WHAT THE HELL ARE THEY SAYING?!!!
KISS!
TH- THEY'RE ALL OUT OF THEIR MINDS!!
PIN HER DOWN!!
C'MON, PUT OUT!
DIDN'T I SAY I'D HELP YOU?
YOO-RI, YOU BITCH!!
THEIR SHOUTING IS ECHOING AROUND THE CAMPFIRE...
KISS!!
HURRY UP!!
KISS !!
LET'S SEE SOME TONGUE !!
KISS!
AND I CAN'T...
...
WHAT'RE YOU DOING?
KISS!
LET'S SEE THAT KISS!
...I CAN'T SEE WON-JUN'S FACE. I DON'T KNOW WHAT HE'S THINKING, AND HE'S NOT SAYING ANYTHING...
WHAT'S TAKING SO LONG?!!

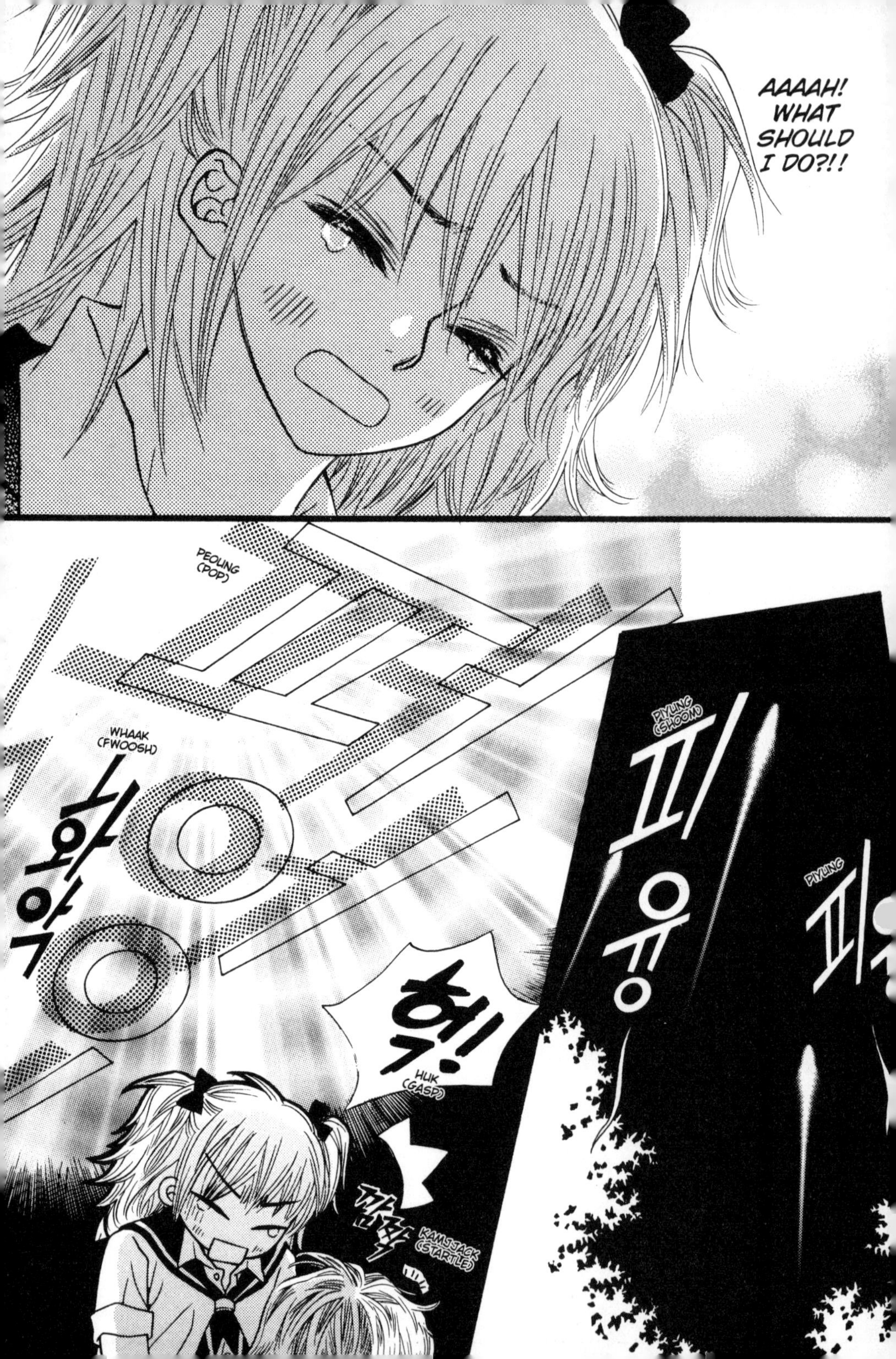
AAAAH! WHAT SHOULD I DO?!!
PEOLING (POP)
WHAAK (FWOOSH)
헉!
HUK (GASP)
KAMJJACK (STARTLE)
피융
PIYUNG (CHOOM)
PIYUNG

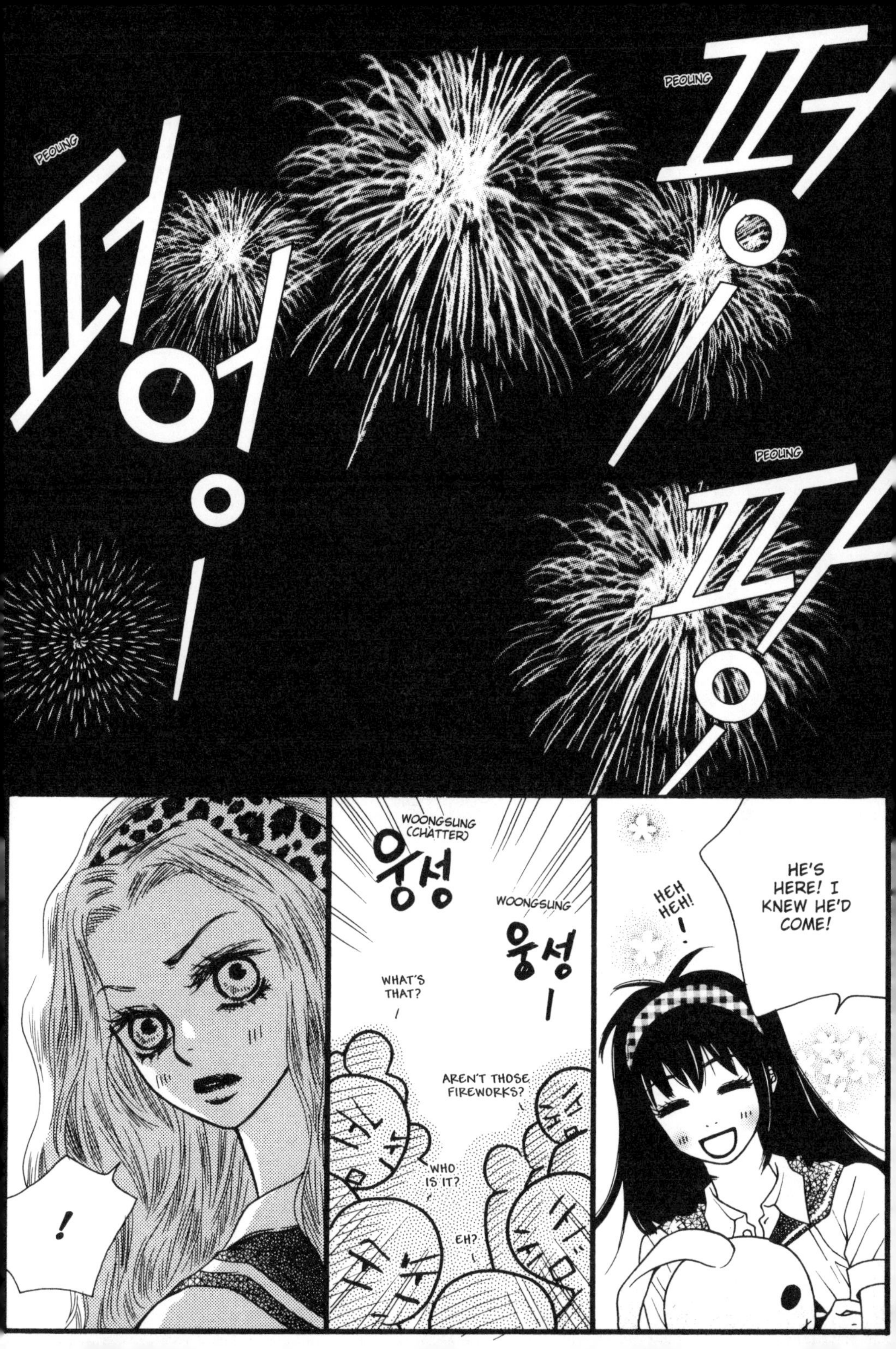

PEOUNG
PEOUNG
PEOUNG
!
WOONGSUNG (CHATTER)
웅성
WOONGSUNG
웅성
WHAT'S THAT?
AREN'T THOSE FIREWORKS?
WHO IS IT?
EH?
HEH HEH!
!
HE'S HERE! I KNEW HE'D COME!

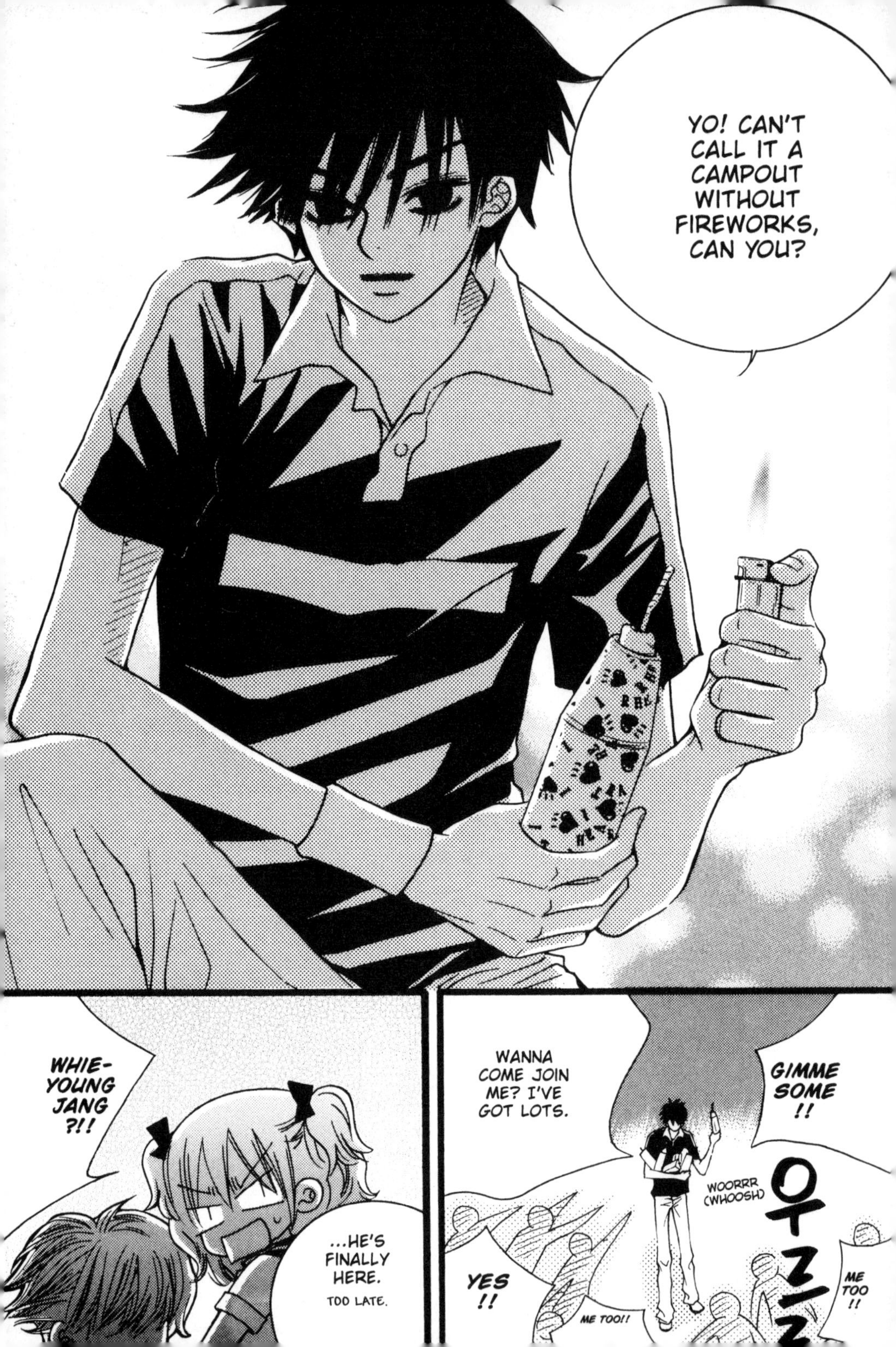
YO! CAN'T CALL IT A CAMPOUT WITHOUT FIREWORKS, CAN YOU?
WHIE-YOUNG JANG?!!
...HE'S FINALLY HERE.
TOO LATE.
WANNA COME JOIN ME? I'VE GOT LOTS.
GIMME SOME!!
WOORRR (WHOOSH)
YES!!
ME TOO!!
ME TOO!!

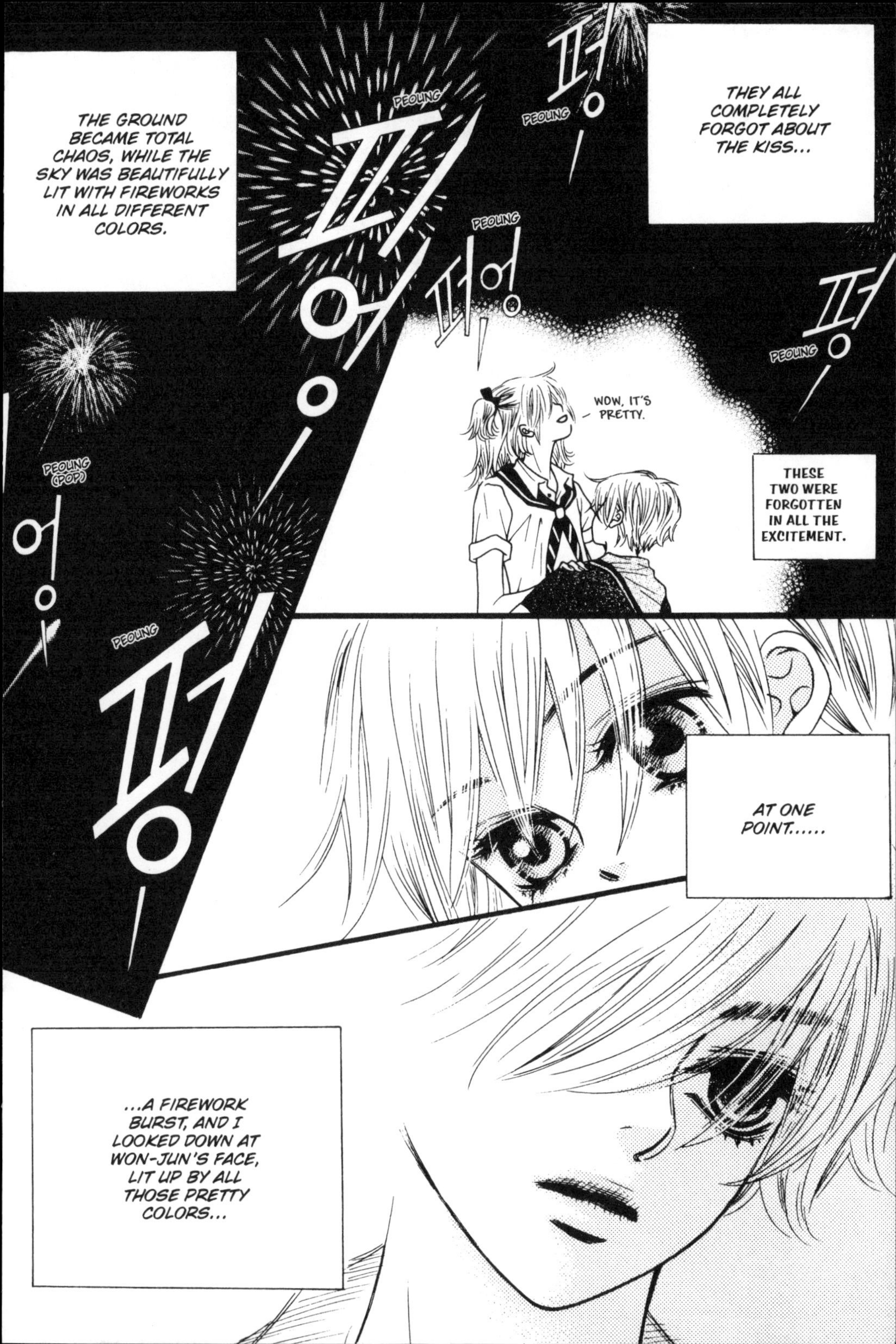
THE GROUND BECAME TOTAL CHAOS, WHILE THE SKY WAS BEAUTIFULLY LIT WITH FIREWORKS IN ALL DIFFERENT COLORS.
PEOUNG
PEOUNG
PEOUNG
THEY ALL COMPLETELY FORGOT ABOUT THE KISS...
PEOUNG
PEOUNG (POP)
WOW, IT'S PRETTY.
THESE TWO WERE FORGOTTEN IN ALL THE EXCITEMENT.
PEOUNG
AT ONE POINT......
...A FIREWORK BURST, AND I LOOKED DOWN AT WON-JUN'S FACE, LIT UP BY ALL THOSE PRETTY COLORS...

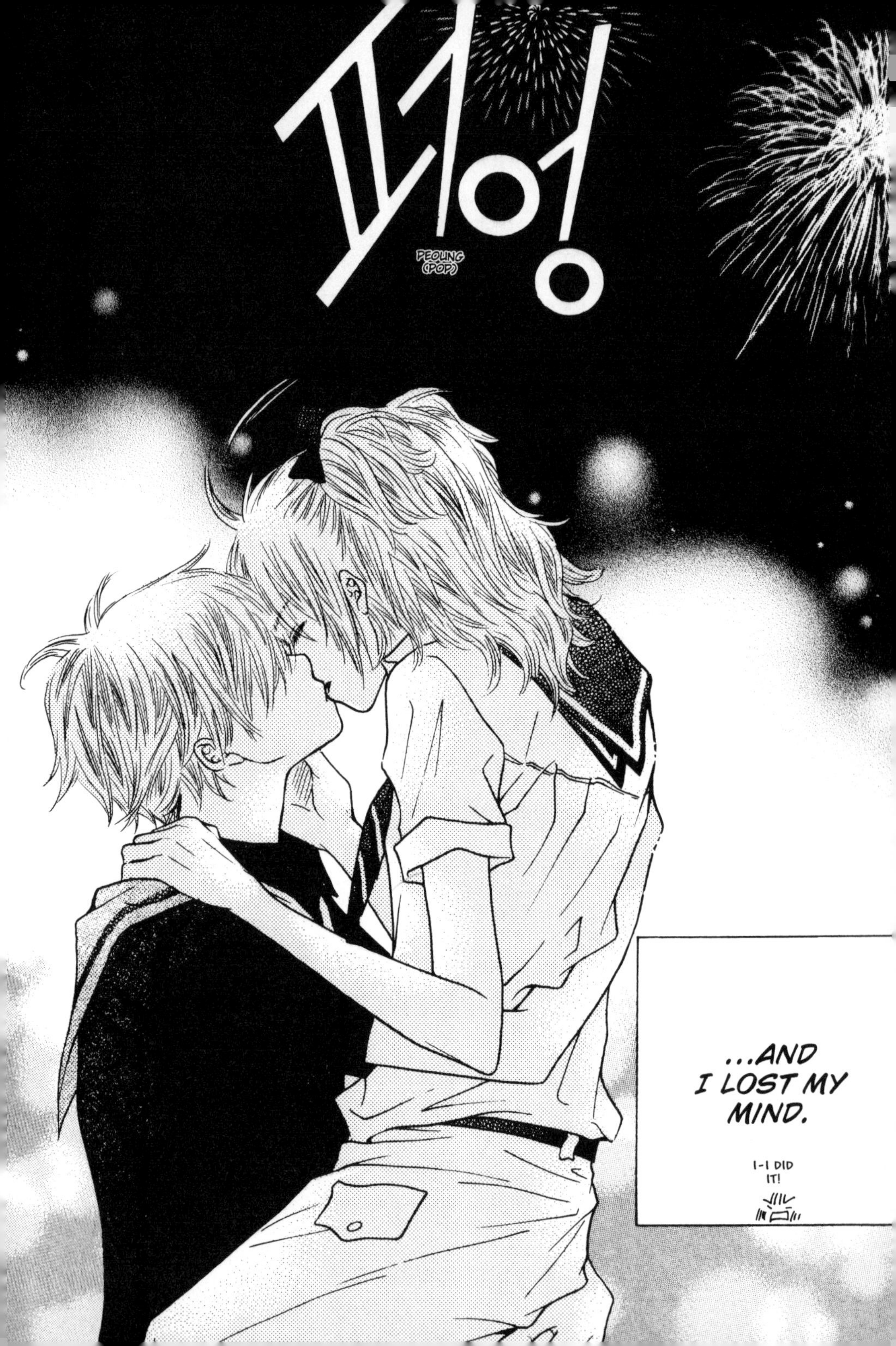
펑!
PEOUNG (POP)
...AND I LOST MY MIND.
I-I DID IT!

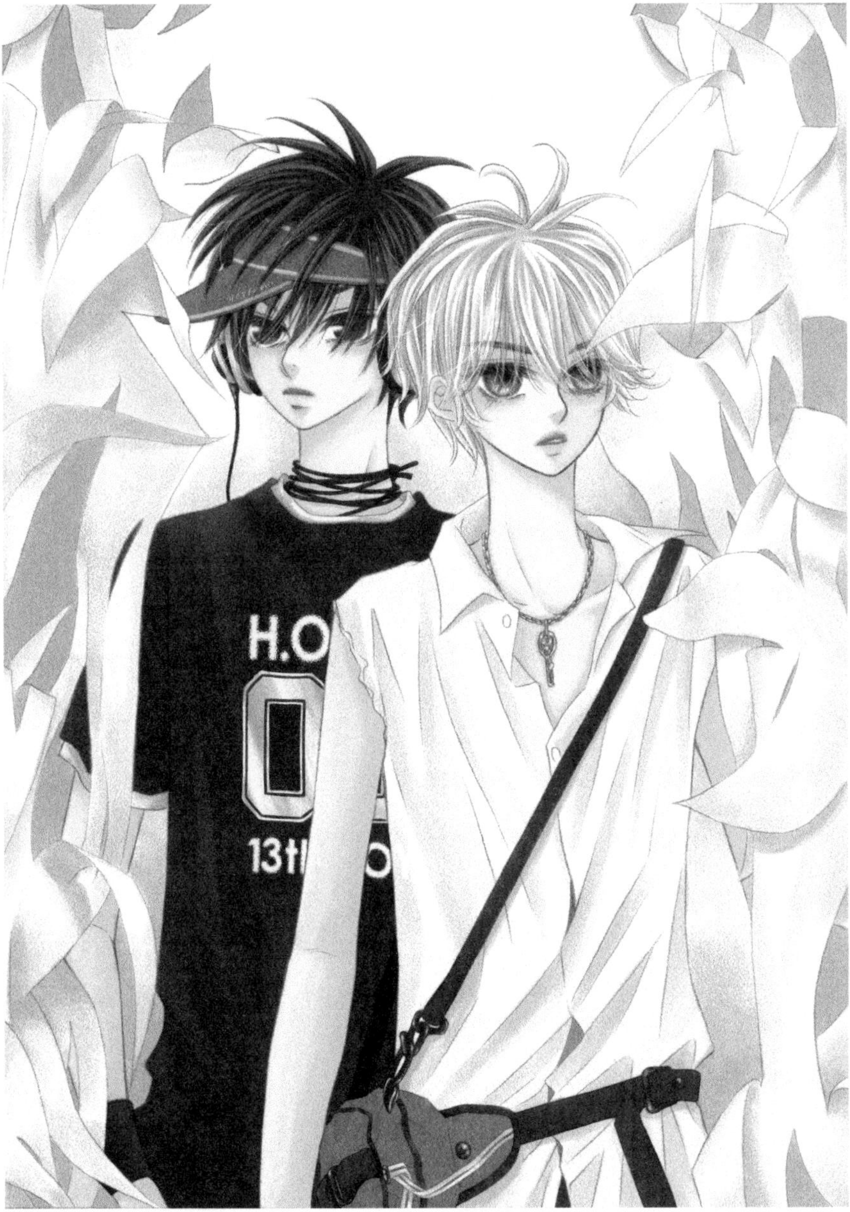

13th Boy

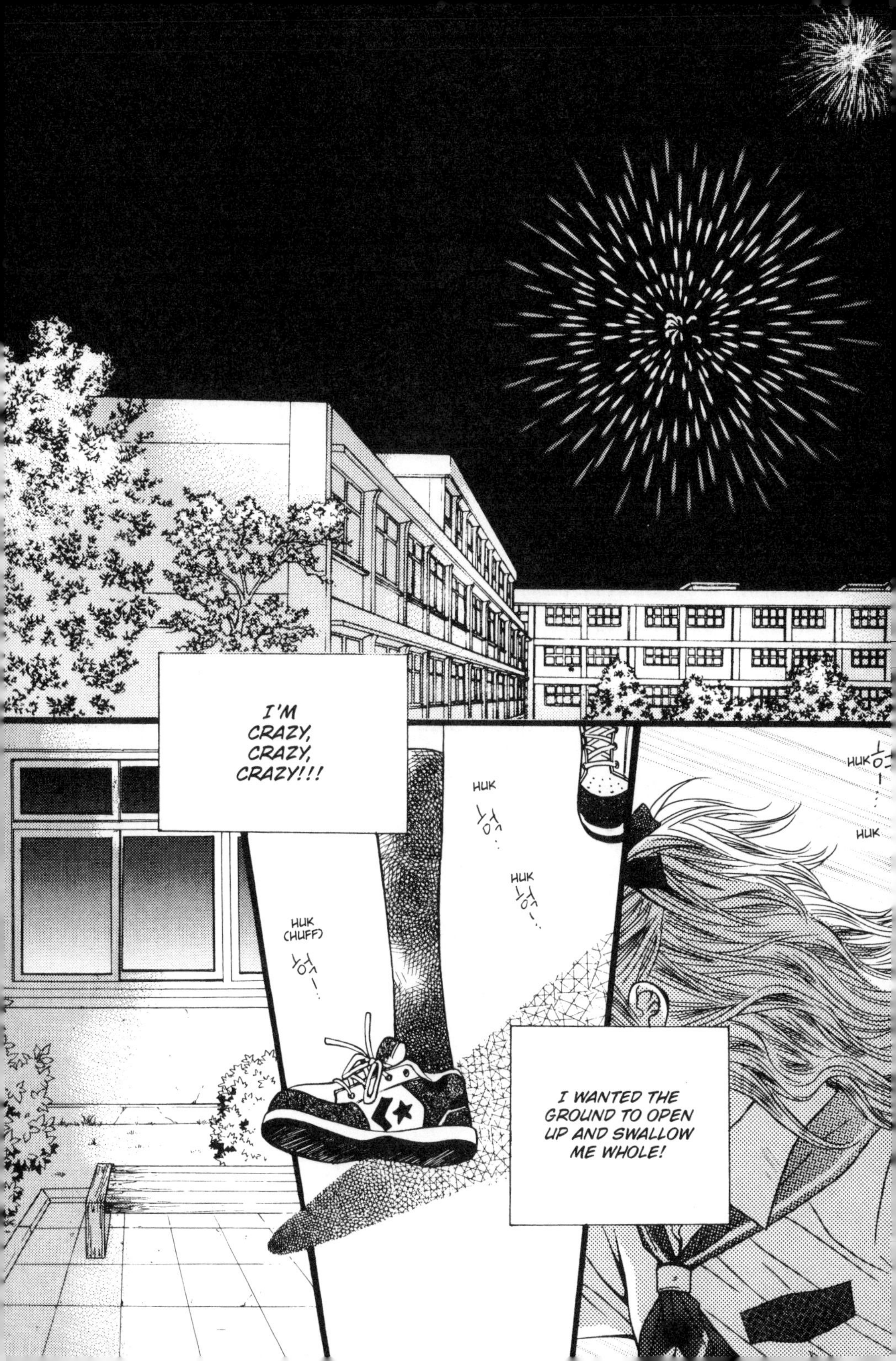
I'M CRAZY, CRAZY, CRAZY!!!
HUK
HUK
HUK (HUFF)
HUK
HUK
I WANTED THE GROUND TO OPEN UP AND SWALLOW ME WHOLE!

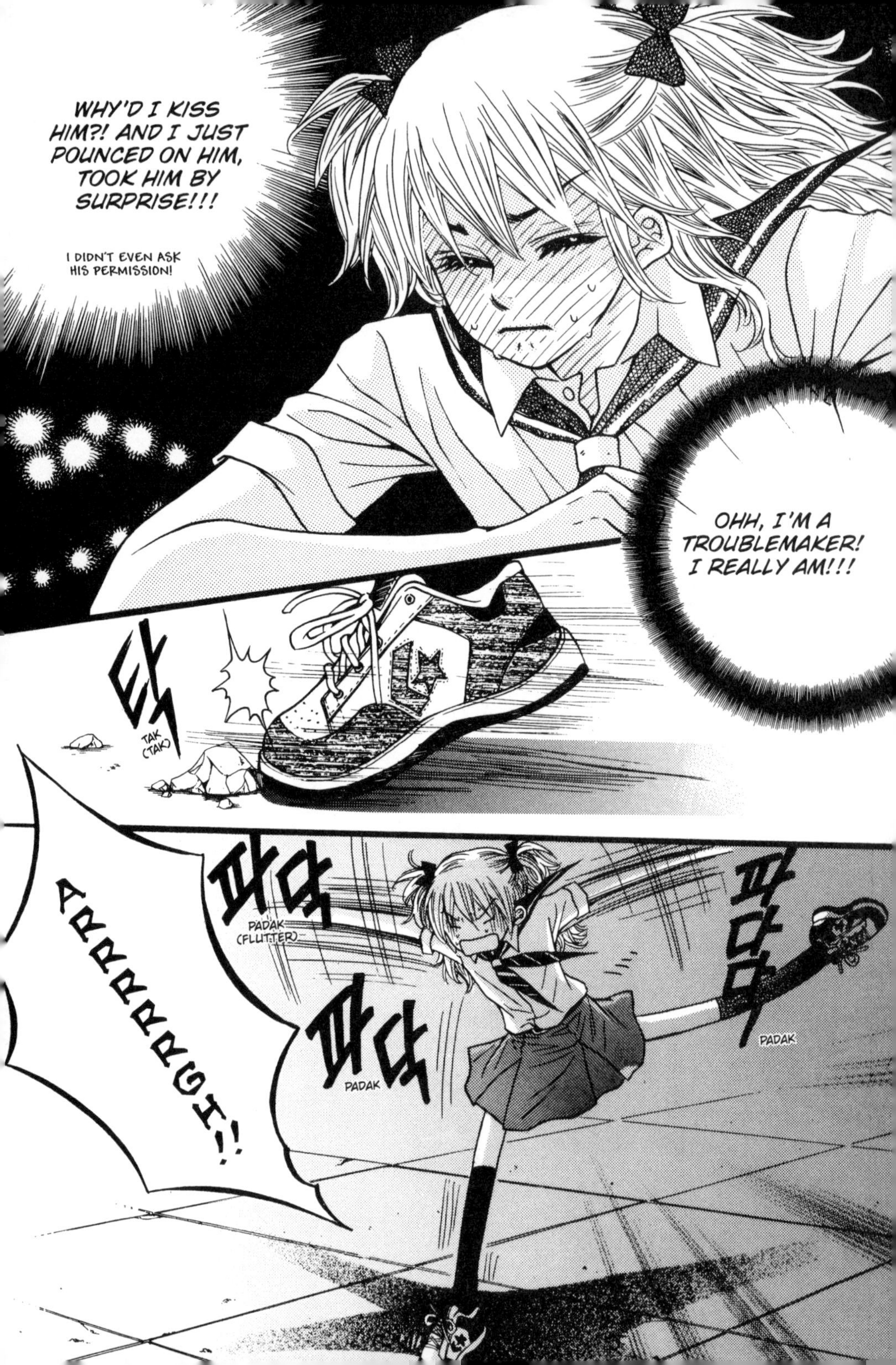
WHY'D I KISS HIM?! AND I JUST POUNCED ON HIM, TOOK HIM BY SURPRISE!!!
I DIDN'T EVEN ASK HIS PERMISSION!
OHH, I'M A TROUBLEMAKER! I REALLY AM!!!
탁
TAK (TAK)
ARRRRRGH!!
파닥
PADAK (FLUTTER)
파닥
PADAK
파닥
PADAK

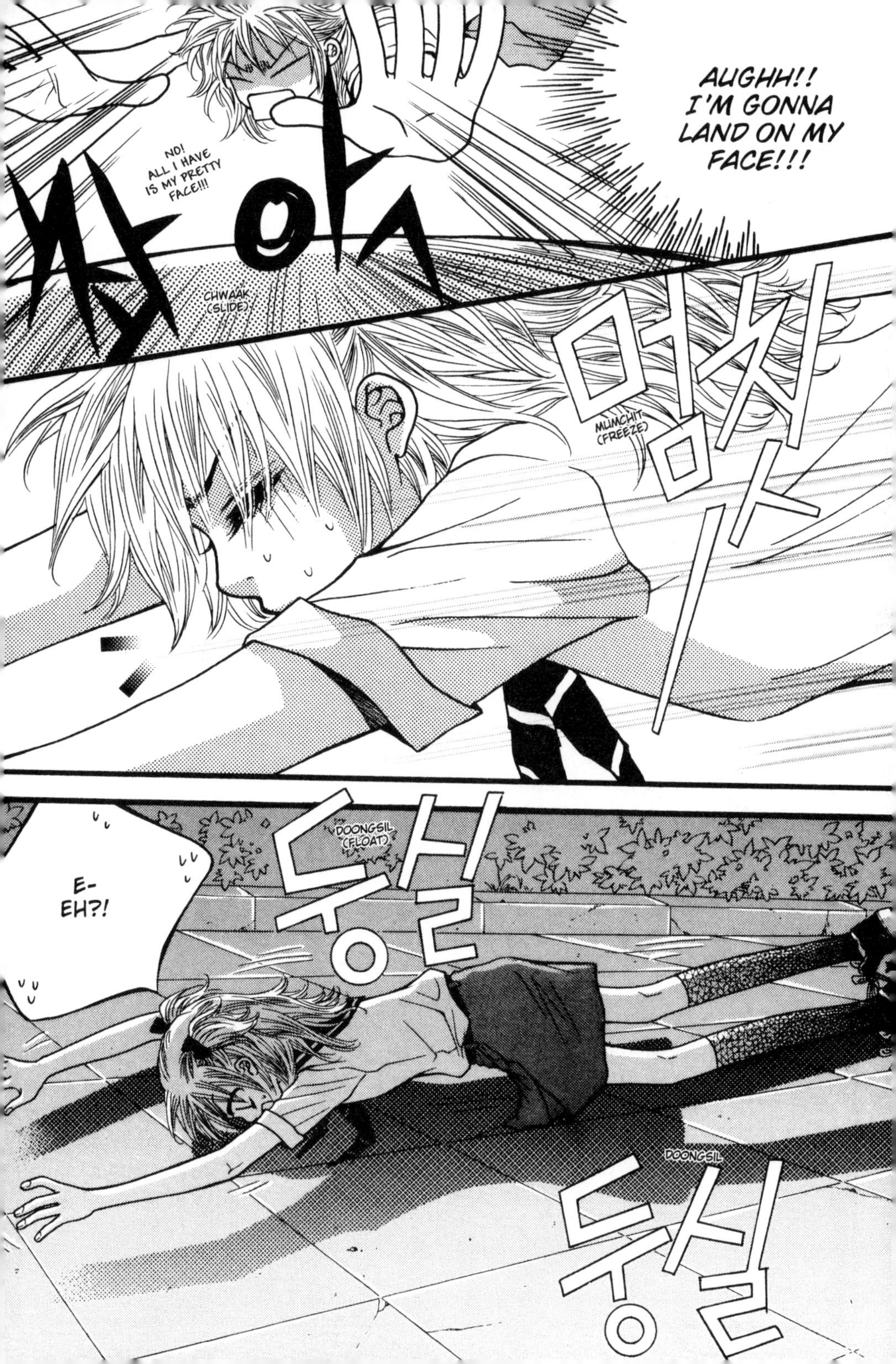
NO! ALL I HAVE IS MY PRETTY FACE!!!
AUGHH!! I'M GONNA LAND ON MY FACE!!!
CHWAAK (SLIDE)
멈칫
MUMCHIT (FREEZE)
E- EH?!
둥실
DOONGSIL (FLOAT)
둥실
DOONGSIL

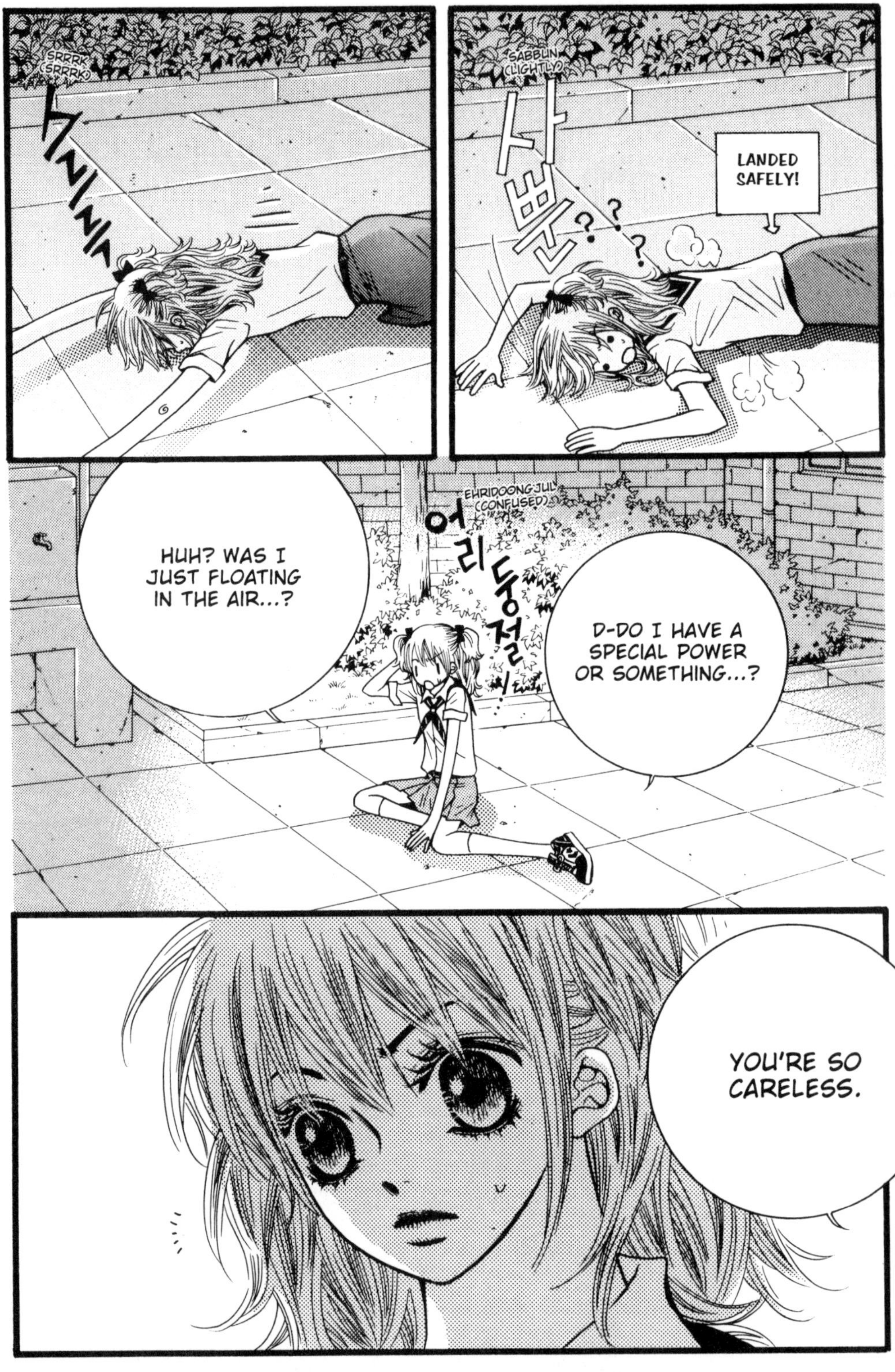
SRRRK (SRRRK)
SABBUN (LIGHTLY)
사뿐
LANDED SAFELY!
HUH? WAS I JUST FLOATING IN THE AIR...?
EHRIDOONGJUL (CONFUSED)
어리둥절
D-DO I HAVE A SPECIAL POWER OR SOMETHING...?
YOU'RE SO CARELESS.

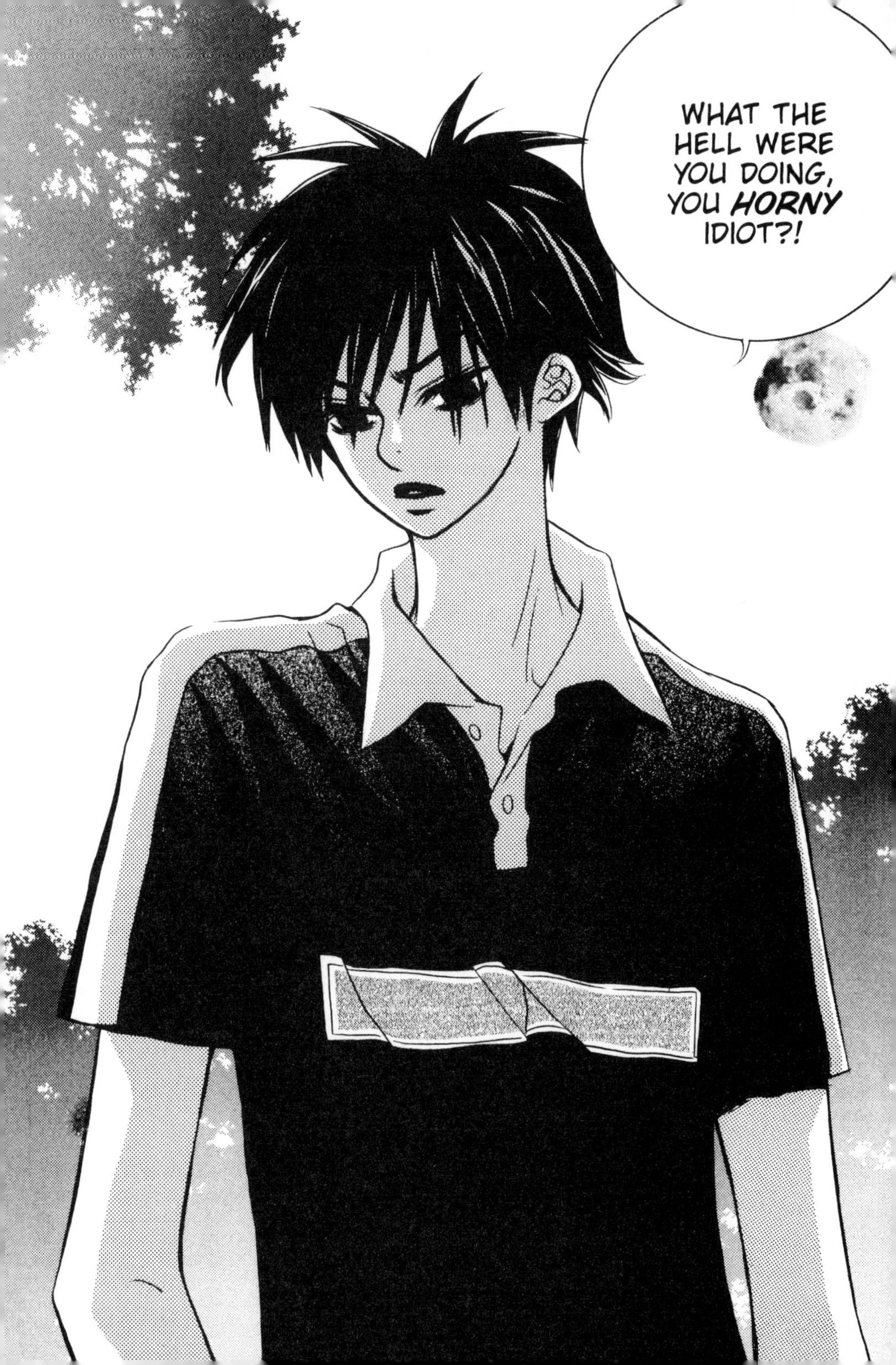
WHAT THE HELL WERE YOU DOING, YOU ***HORNY*** IDIOT?!

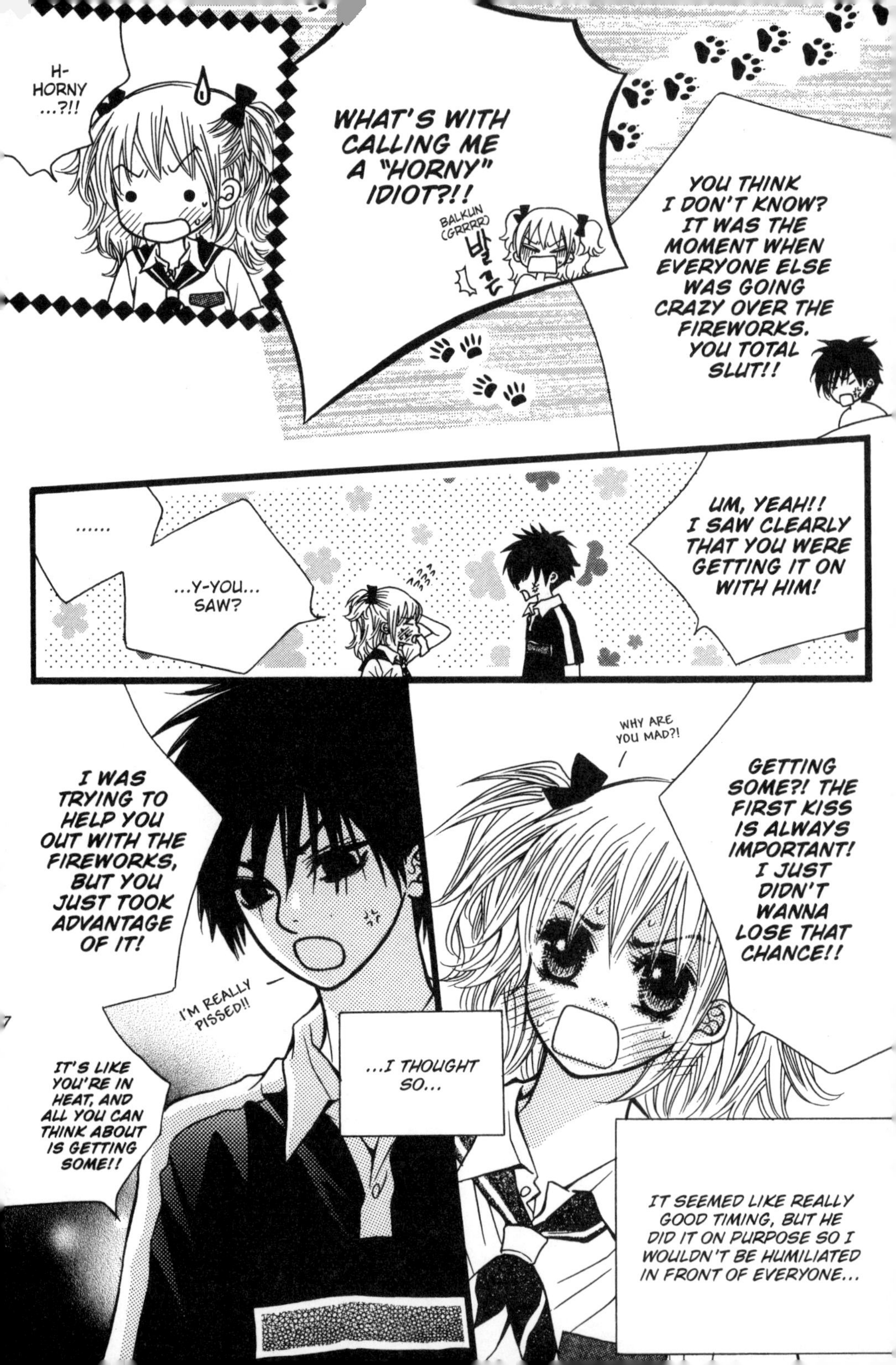
H-HORNY ...?!!
WHAT'S WITH CALLING ME A "HORNY" IDIOT?!!
BALKUN (GRRRR)
발끈
YOU THINK I DON'T KNOW? IT WAS THE MOMENT WHEN EVERYONE ELSE WAS GOING CRAZY OVER THE FIREWORKS. YOU TOTAL SLUT!!
......
...Y-YOU... SAW?
UM, YEAH!! I SAW CLEARLY THAT YOU WERE GETTING IT ON WITH HIM!
I WAS TRYING TO HELP YOU OUT WITH THE FIREWORKS, BUT YOU JUST TOOK ADVANTAGE OF IT!
I'M REALLY PISSED!!
IT'S LIKE YOU'RE IN HEAT, AND ALL YOU CAN THINK ABOUT IS GETTING SOME!!
...I THOUGHT SO...
WHY ARE YOU MAD?!
GETTING SOME?! THE FIRST KISS IS ALWAYS IMPORTANT! I JUST DIDN'T WANNA LOSE THAT CHANCE!!
IT SEEMED LIKE REALLY GOOD TIMING, BUT HE DID IT ON PURPOSE SO I WOULDN'T BE HUMILIATED IN FRONT OF EVERYONE...

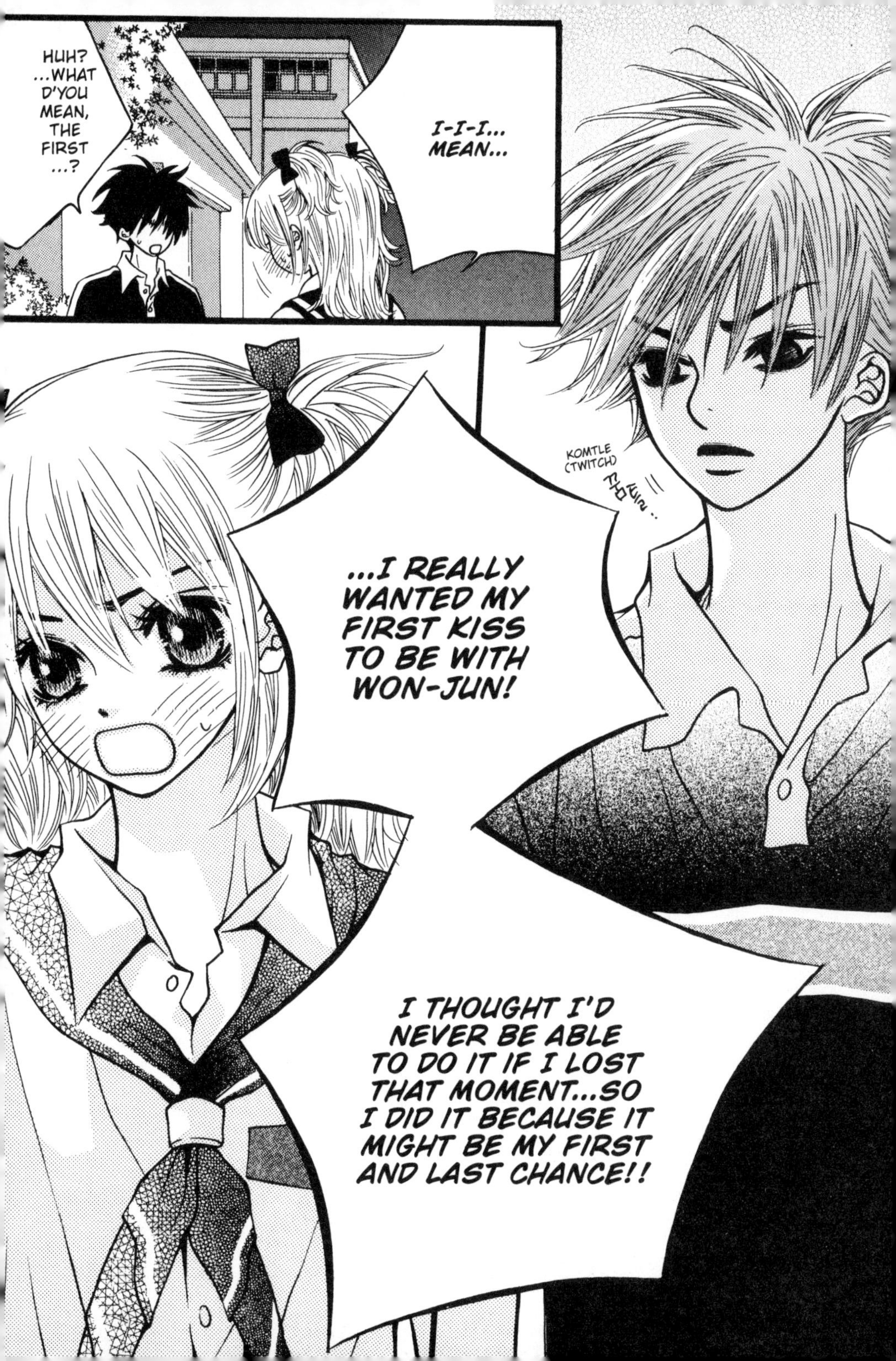
HUH? ...WHAT D'YOU MEAN, THE FIRST ...?
I-I-I... MEAN...
KOMTLE (TWITCH)
...I REALLY WANTED MY FIRST KISS TO BE WITH WON-JUN!
I THOUGHT I'D NEVER BE ABLE TO DO IT IF I LOST THAT MOMENT...SO I DID IT BECAUSE IT MIGHT BE MY FIRST AND LAST CHANCE!!

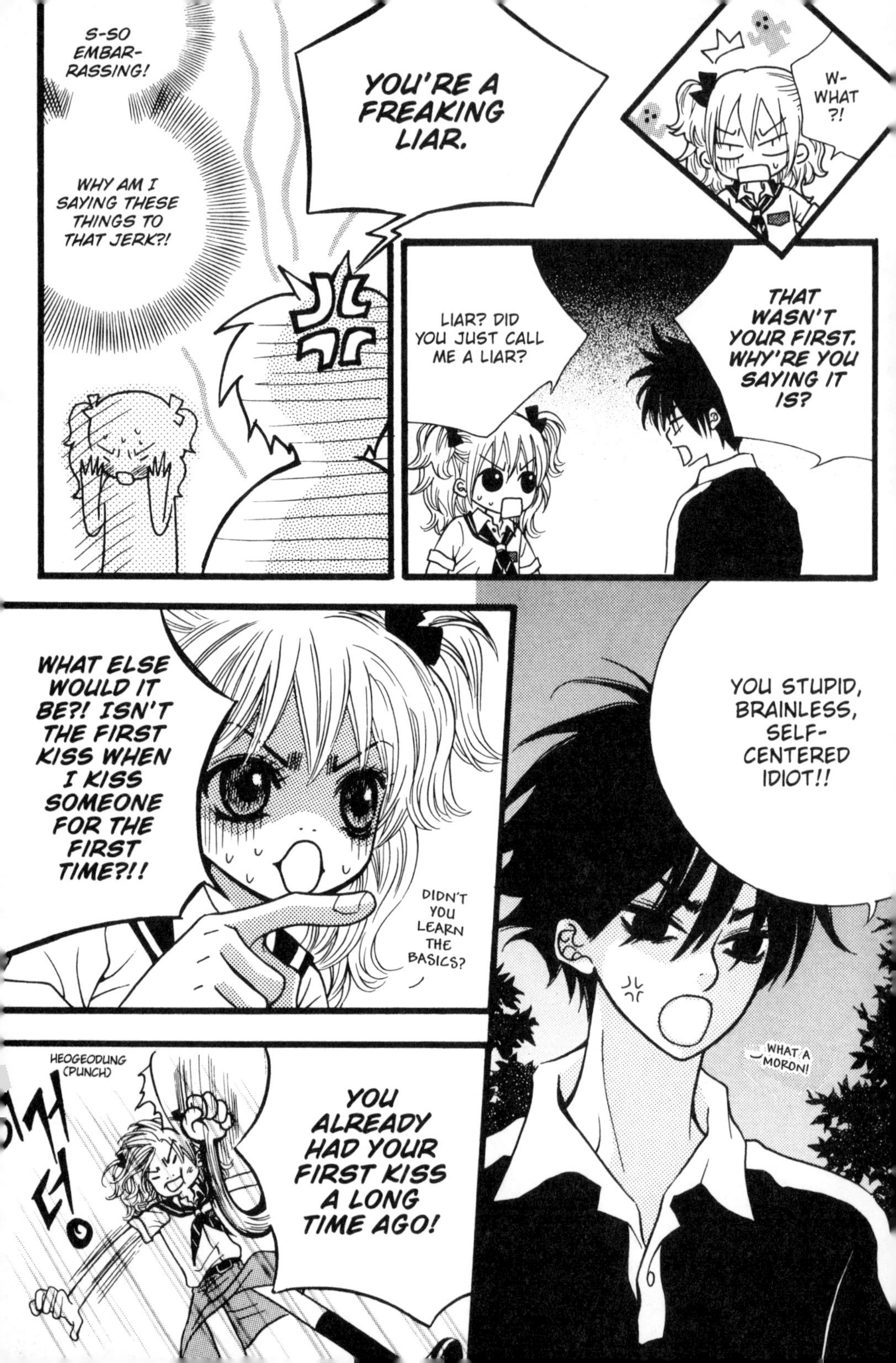
S-SO EMBAR-RASSING!
WHY AM I SAYING THESE THINGS TO THAT JERK?!
YOU'RE A FREAKING LIAR.
W-WHAT?!
LIAR? DID YOU JUST CALL ME A LIAR?
THAT WASN'T YOUR FIRST. WHY'RE YOU SAYING IT IS?
WHAT ELSE WOULD IT BE?! ISN'T THE FIRST KISS WHEN I KISS SOMEONE FOR THE FIRST TIME?!!
DIDN'T YOU LEARN THE BASICS?
HEOGEODUNG (PUNCH)
YOU ALREADY HAD YOUR FIRST KISS A LONG TIME AGO!
YOU STUPID, BRAINLESS, SELF-CENTERED IDIOT!!
WHAT A MORON!

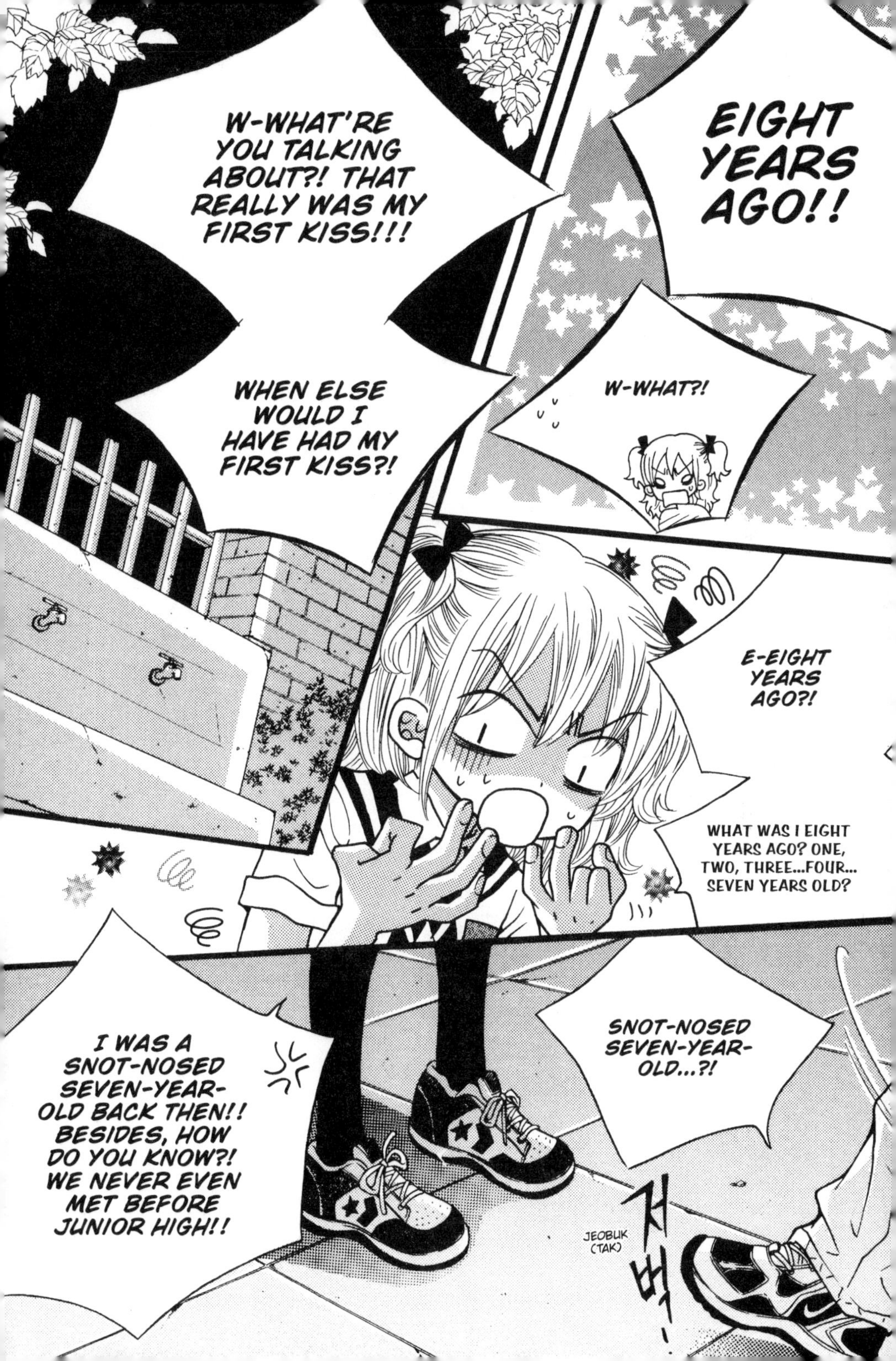
W-WHAT'RE YOU TALKING ABOUT?! THAT REALLY WAS MY FIRST KISS!!!
WHEN ELSE WOULD I HAVE HAD MY FIRST KISS?!
EIGHT YEARS AGO!!
W-WHAT?!
E-EIGHT YEARS AGO?!
WHAT WAS I EIGHT YEARS AGO? ONE, TWO, THREE...FOUR... SEVEN YEARS OLD?
I WAS A SNOT-NOSED SEVEN-YEAR-OLD BACK THEN!! BESIDES, HOW DO YOU KNOW?! WE NEVER EVEN MET BEFORE JUNIOR HIGH!!
SNOT-NOSED SEVEN-YEAR-OLD...?!
저벅
JEOBUK (TAK)

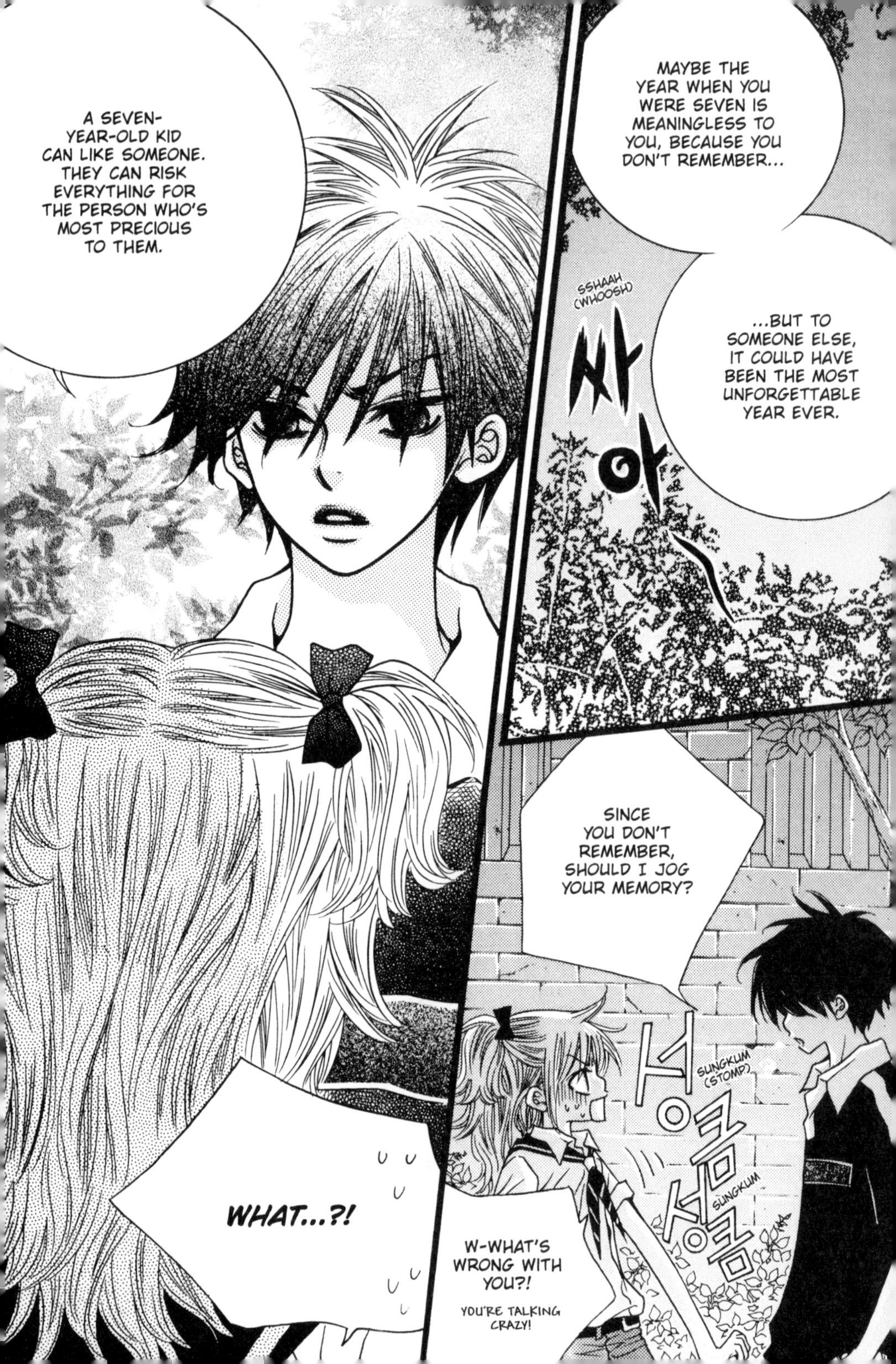
A SEVEN-YEAR-OLD KID CAN LIKE SOMEONE. THEY CAN RISK EVERYTHING FOR THE PERSON WHO'S MOST PRECIOUS TO THEM.
WHAT...?!
MAYBE THE YEAR WHEN YOU WERE SEVEN IS MEANINGLESS TO YOU, BECAUSE YOU DON'T REMEMBER...
SSHAAH (WHOOSH)
...BUT TO SOMEONE ELSE, IT COULD HAVE BEEN THE MOST UNFORGETTABLE YEAR EVER.
SINCE YOU DON'T REMEMBER, SHOULD I JOG YOUR MEMORY?
SUNGKUM (STOMP)
SUNGKUM
W-WHAT'S WRONG WITH YOU?!
YOU'RE TALKING CRAZY!

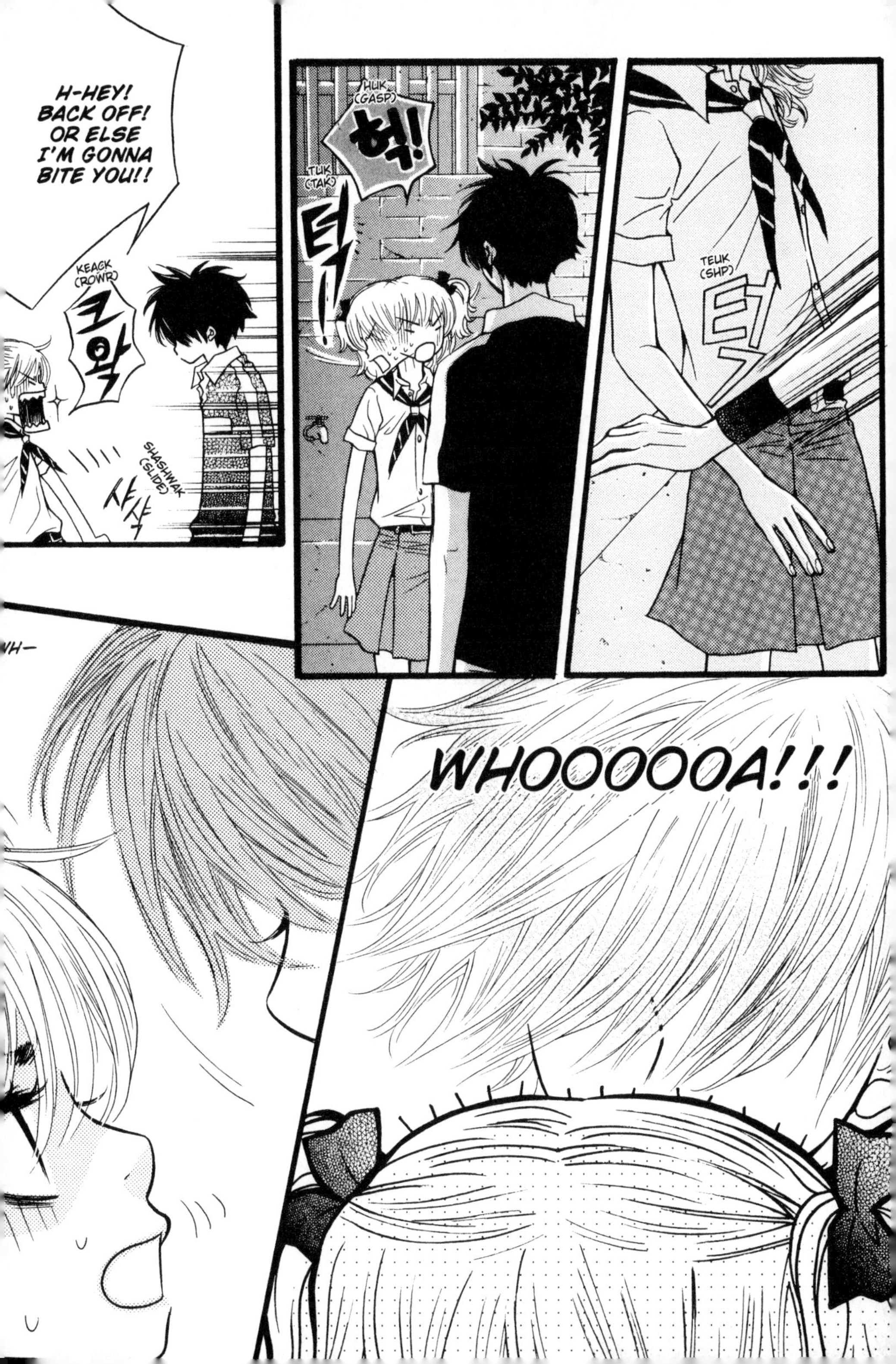
H-HEY! BACK OFF! OR ELSE I'M GONNA BITE YOU!!
KEACK (ROWR)
크왁
SHASHWAK (SLIDE)
샤샥
HUK (GASP)
헉!
TUK (TAK)
턱!
TEUK (SHP)
턱
NH—
WHOOOOOA!!!

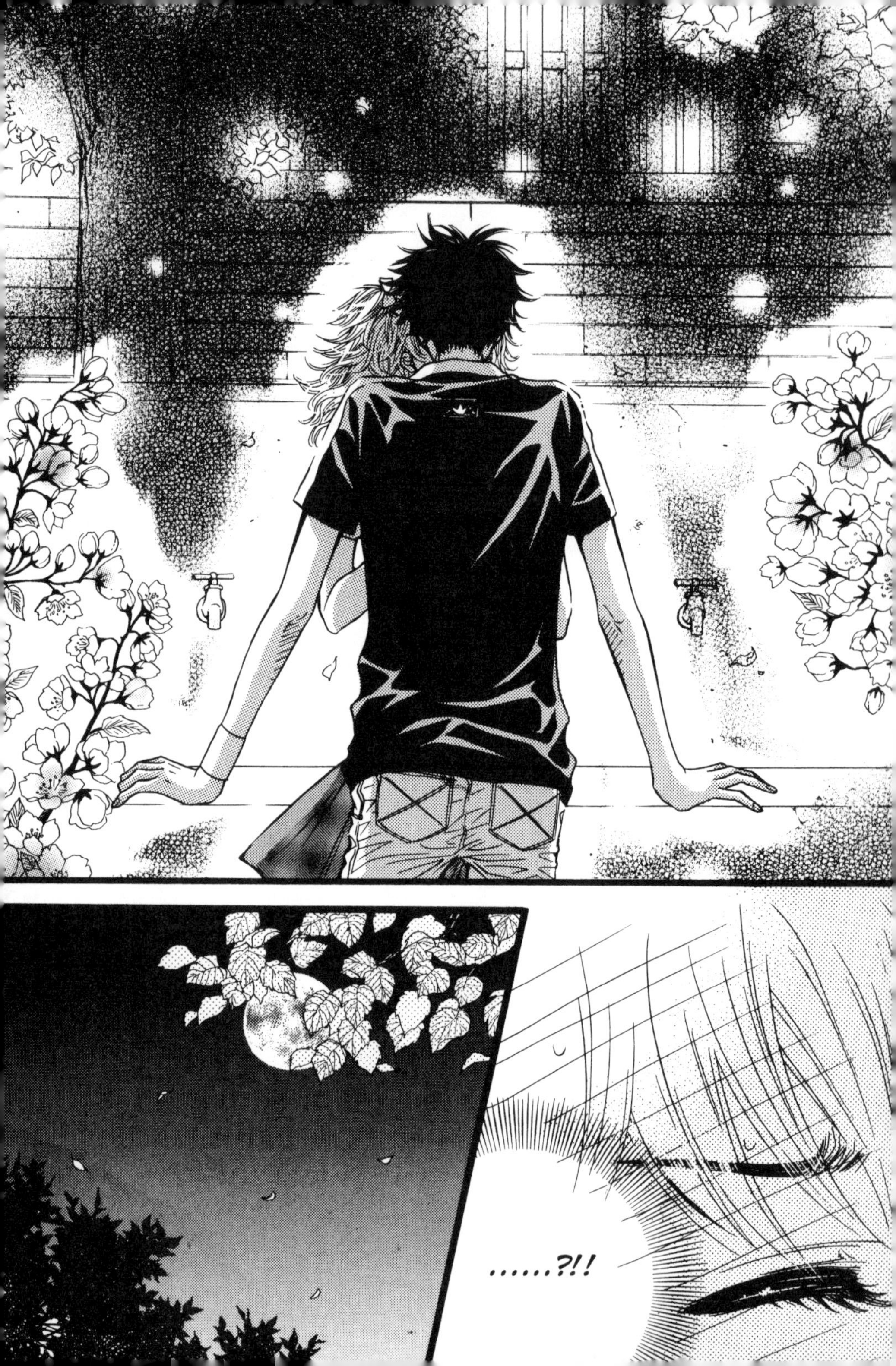
......?!!

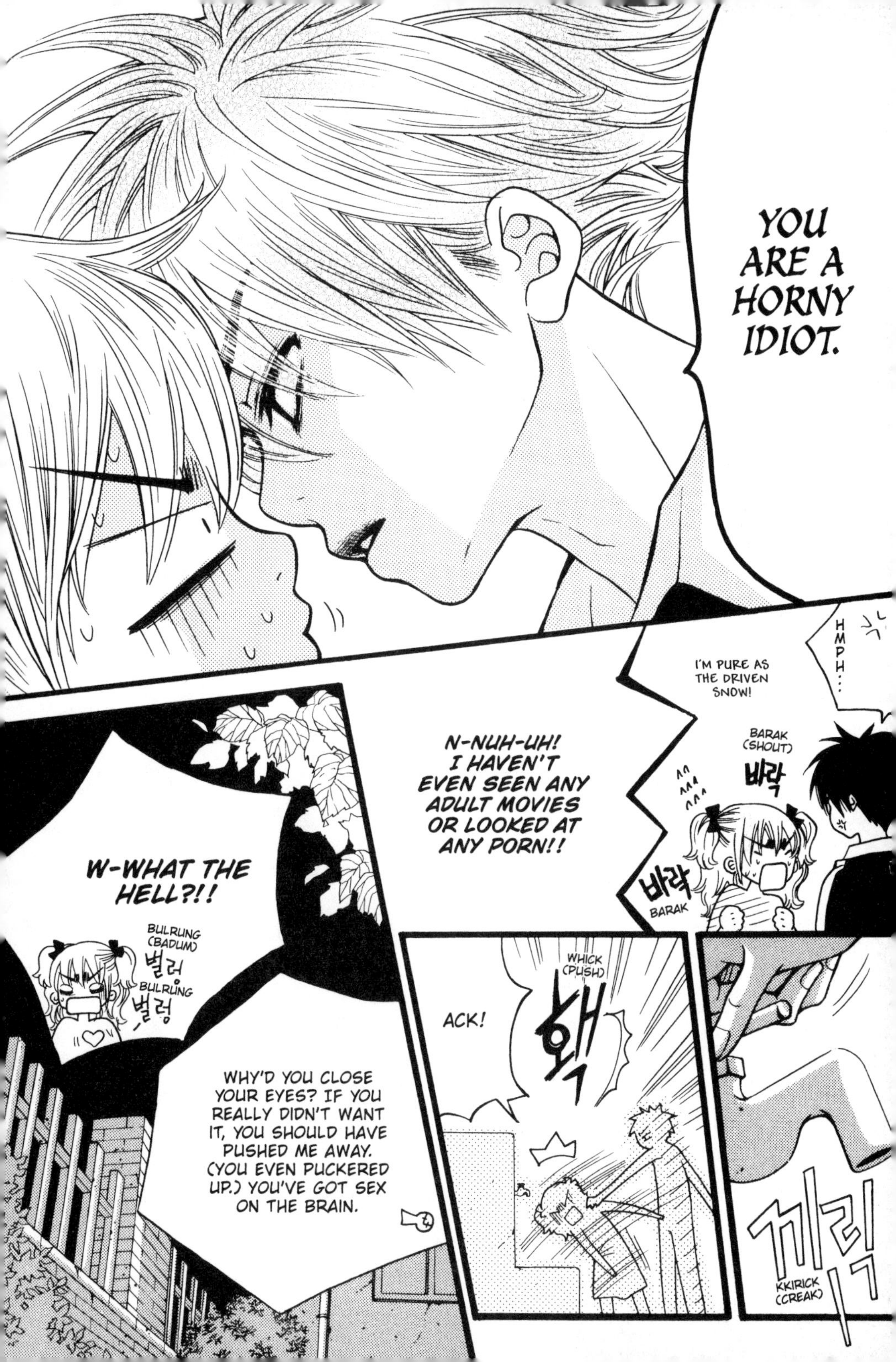
YOU ARE A HORNY IDIOT.
W-WHAT THE HELL?!!
BULRUNG (BADUM)
벌러
BULRUNG
벌렁
WHY'D YOU CLOSE YOUR EYES? IF YOU REALLY DIDN'T WANT IT, YOU SHOULD HAVE PUSHED ME AWAY. (YOU EVEN PUCKERED UP.) YOU'VE GOT SEX ON THE BRAIN.
N-NUH-UH! I HAVEN'T EVEN SEEN ANY ADULT MOVIES OR LOOKED AT ANY PORN!!
I'M PURE AS THE DRIVEN SNOW!
HMPH...
BARAK (SHOUT)
바락
바락
BARAK
ACK!
WHICK (PUSH)
홱
KKIRICK (CREAK)
끼릭

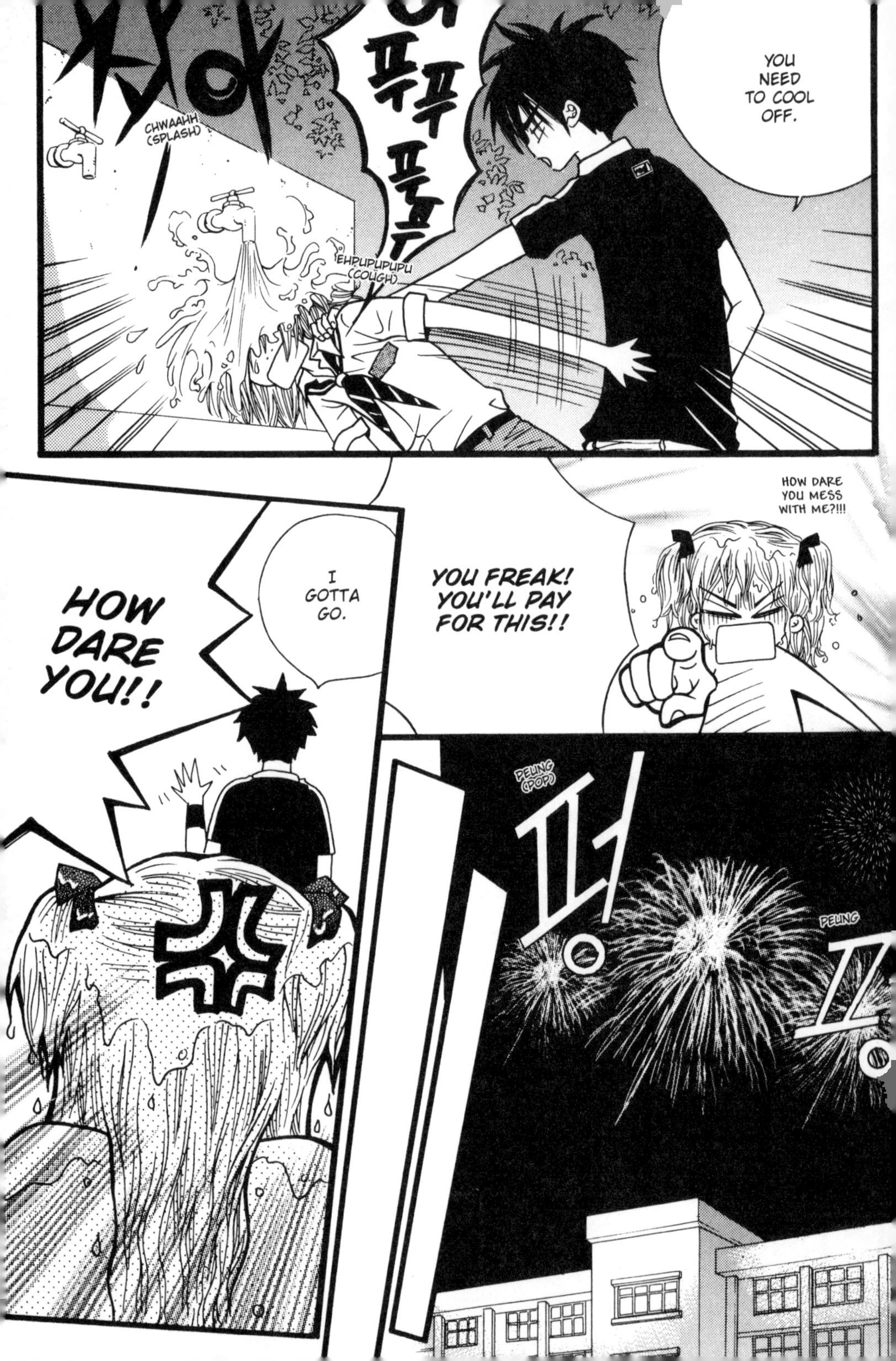
CHWAAHH (SPLASH)
EHPUPUPUPU (COUGH)
YOU NEED TO COOL OFF.
HOW DARE YOU!!
I GOTTA GO.
YOU FREAK! YOU'LL PAY FOR THIS!!
HOW DARE YOU MESS WITH ME?!!!
PEUNG (POP)
PEUNG

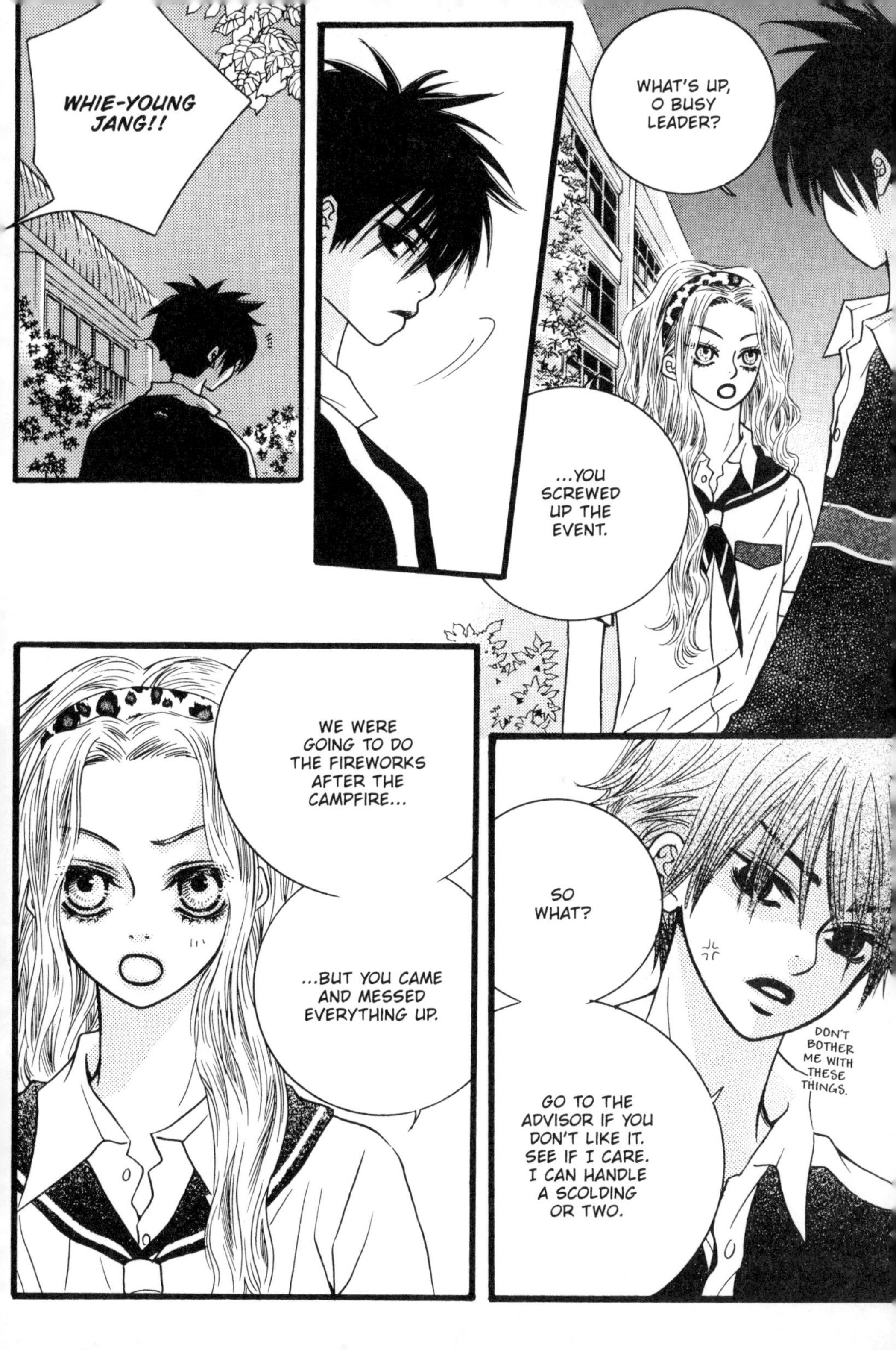
WHIE-YOUNG JANG!!
WHAT'S UP, O BUSY LEADER?
...YOU SCREWED UP THE EVENT.
WE WERE GOING TO DO THE FIREWORKS AFTER THE CAMPFIRE...
...BUT YOU CAME AND MESSED EVERYTHING UP.
SO WHAT?
DON'T BOTHER ME WITH THESE THINGS.
GO TO THE ADVISOR IF YOU DON'T LIKE IT. SEE IF I CARE. I CAN HANDLE A SCOLDING OR TWO.

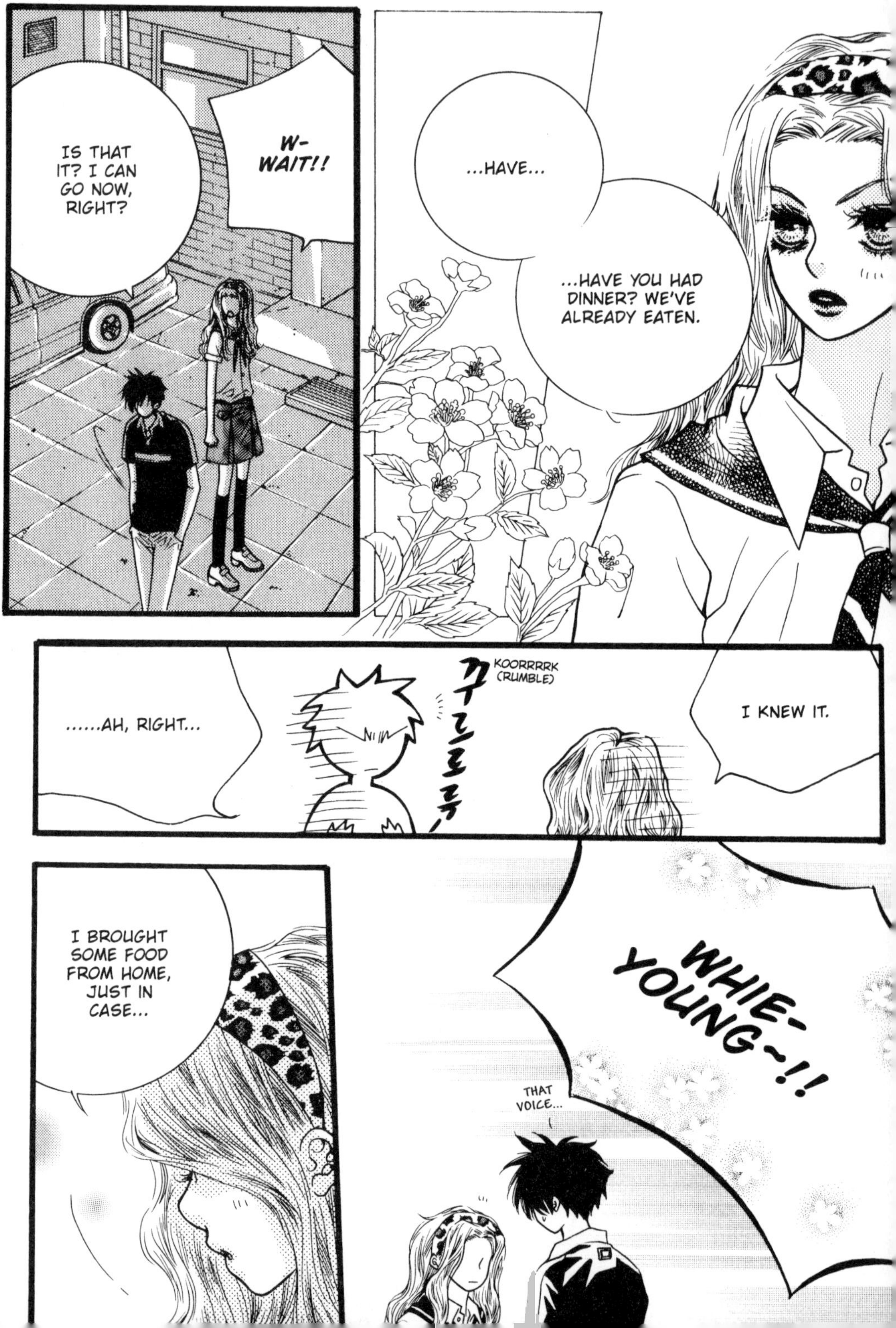
IS THAT IT? I CAN GO NOW, RIGHT?
W-WAIT!!
...HAVE...
...HAVE YOU HAD DINNER? WE'VE ALREADY EATEN.
......AH, RIGHT...
KOORRRRK (RUMBLE)
꾸르르륵
I KNEW IT.
I BROUGHT SOME FOOD FROM HOME, JUST IN CASE...
WHIE-YOUNG~!!
THAT VOICE...

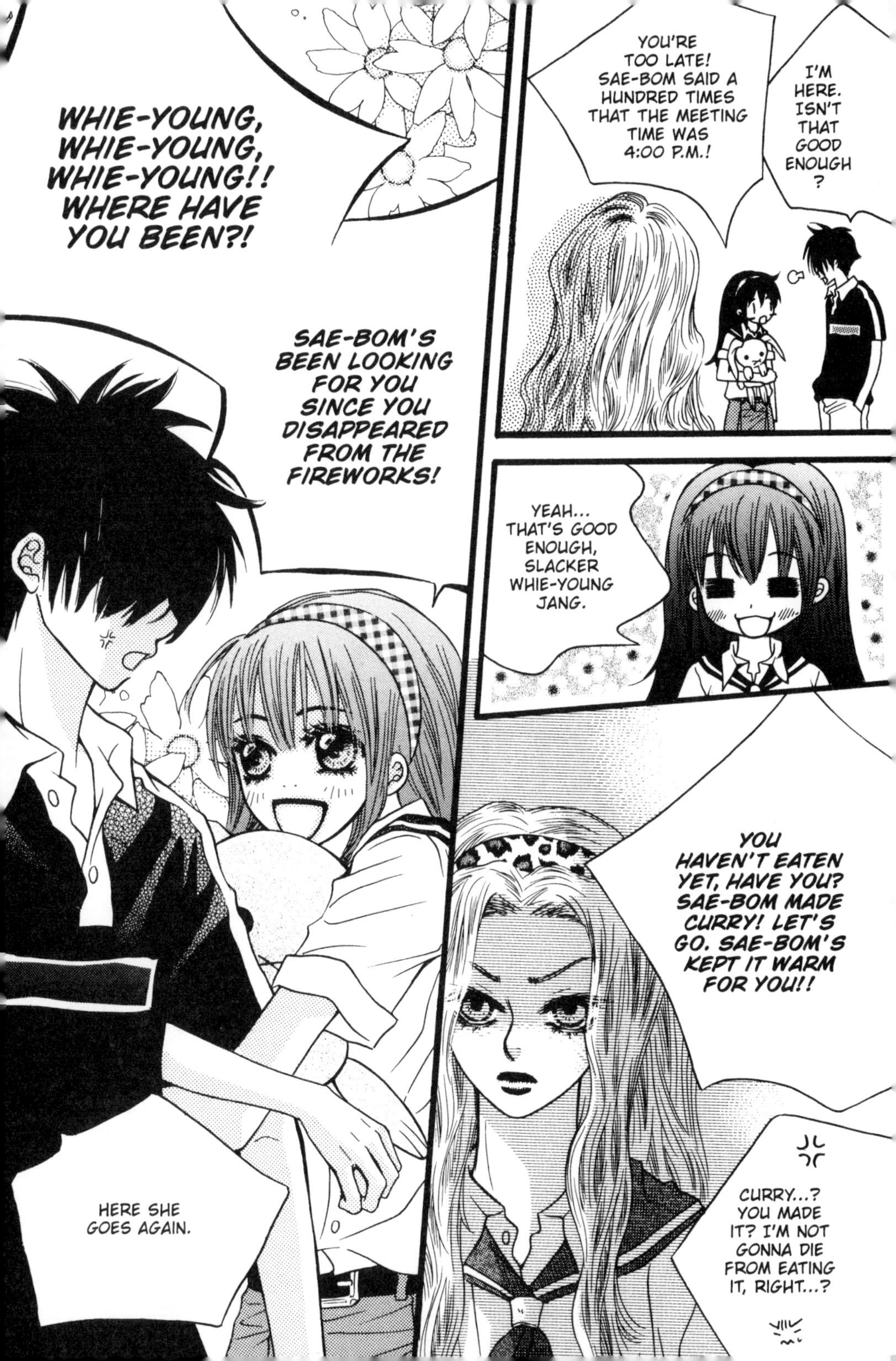
WHIE-YOUNG, WHIE-YOUNG, WHIE-YOUNG!! WHERE HAVE YOU BEEN?!
SAE-BOM'S BEEN LOOKING FOR YOU SINCE YOU DISAPPEARED FROM THE FIREWORKS!
HERE SHE GOES AGAIN.
YOU'RE TOO LATE! SAE-BOM SAID A HUNDRED TIMES THAT THE MEETING TIME WAS 4:00 P.M.!
I'M HERE. ISN'T THAT GOOD ENOUGH?
YEAH... THAT'S GOOD ENOUGH, SLACKER WHIE-YOUNG JANG.
YOU HAVEN'T EATEN YET, HAVE YOU? SAE-BOM MADE CURRY! LET'S GO. SAE-BOM'S KEPT IT WARM FOR YOU!!
CURRY...? YOU MADE IT? I'M NOT GONNA DIE FROM EATING IT, RIGHT...?

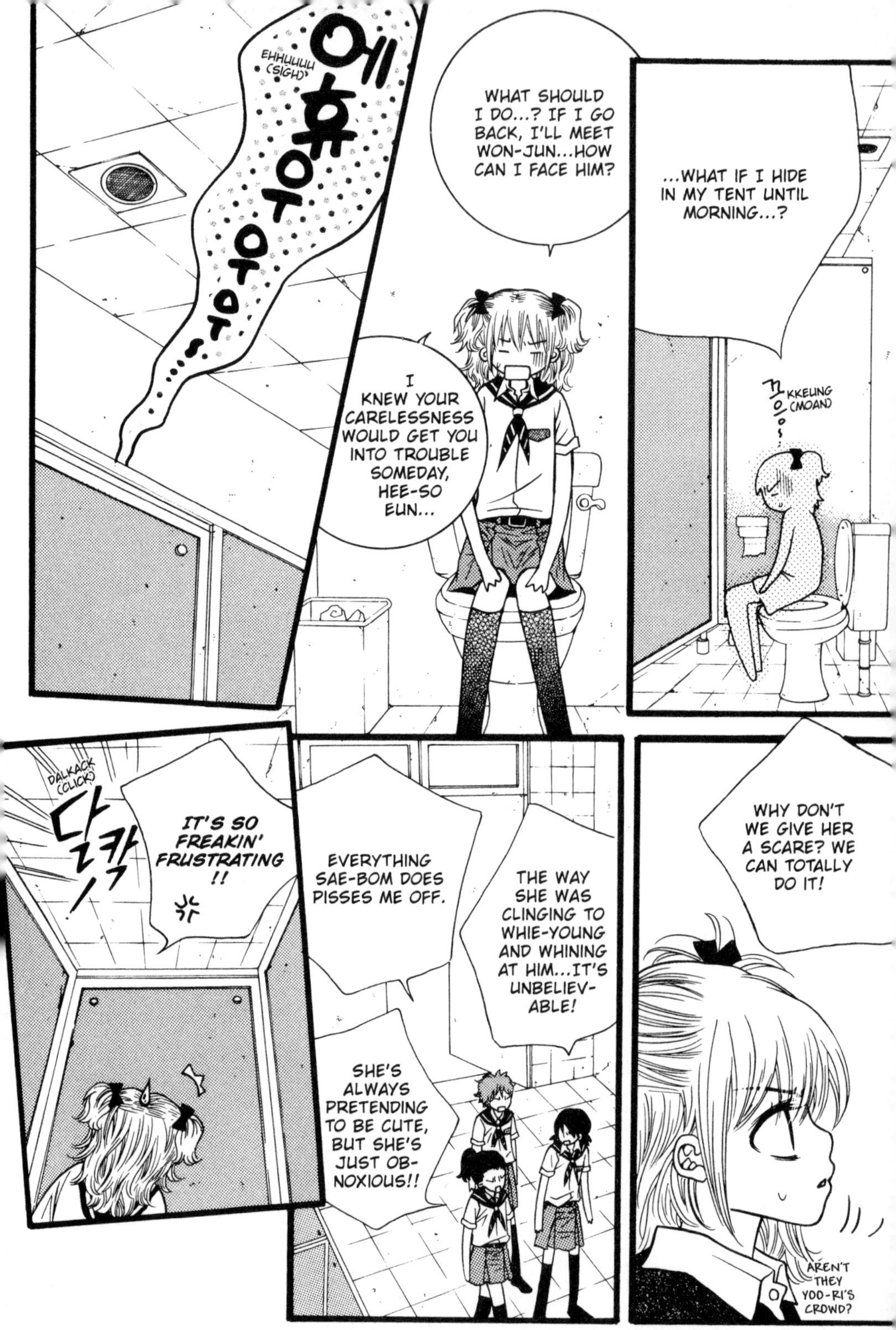

에휴우우우...
EHHUUUU (SIGH)
WHAT SHOULD I DO...? IF I GO BACK, I'LL MEET WON-JUN...HOW CAN I FACE HIM?
I KNEW YOUR CARELESSNESS WOULD GET YOU INTO TROUBLE SOMEDAY, HEE-SO EUN...
...WHAT IF I HIDE IN MY TENT UNTIL MORNING...?
끄응...
KKEUNG (MOAN)
달칵!
DALKACK (CLICK)
IT'S SO FREAKIN' FRUSTRATING!!
EVERYTHING SAE-BOM DOES PISSES ME OFF.
THE WAY SHE WAS CLINGING TO WHIE-YOUNG AND WHINING AT HIM...IT'S UNBELIEVABLE!
SHE'S ALWAYS PRETENDING TO BE CUTE, BUT SHE'S JUST OBNOXIOUS!!
WHY DON'T WE GIVE HER A SCARE? WE CAN TOTALLY DO IT!
AREN'T THEY YOO-RI'S CROWD?

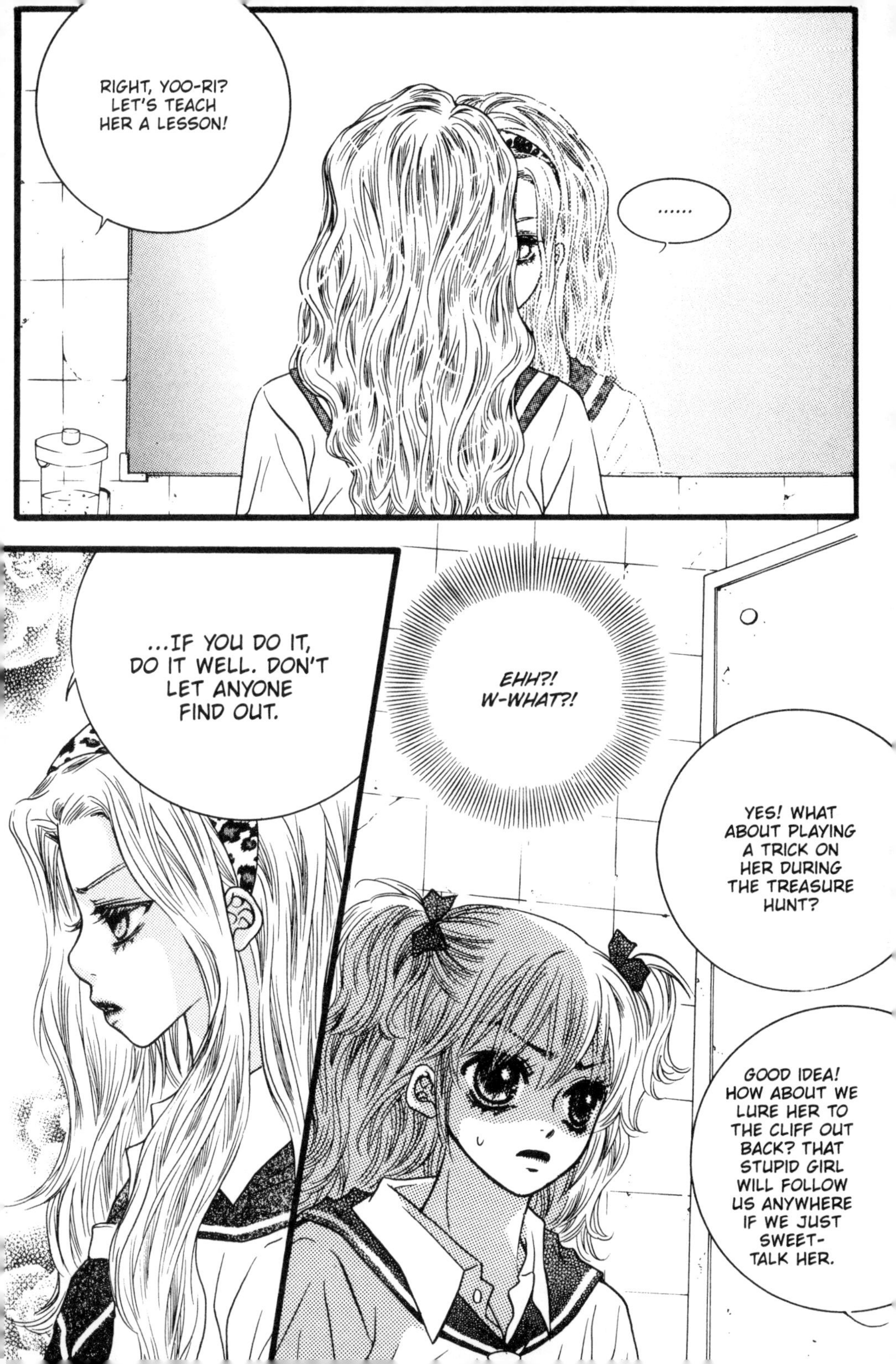
RIGHT, YOO-RI? LET'S TEACH HER A LESSON!
......
...IF YOU DO IT, DO IT WELL. DON'T LET ANYONE FIND OUT.
EHH?! W-WHAT?!
YES! WHAT ABOUT PLAYING A TRICK ON HER DURING THE TREASURE HUNT?
GOOD IDEA! HOW ABOUT WE LURE HER TO THE CLIFF OUT BACK? THAT STUPID GIRL WILL FOLLOW US ANYWHERE IF WE JUST SWEET-TALK HER.

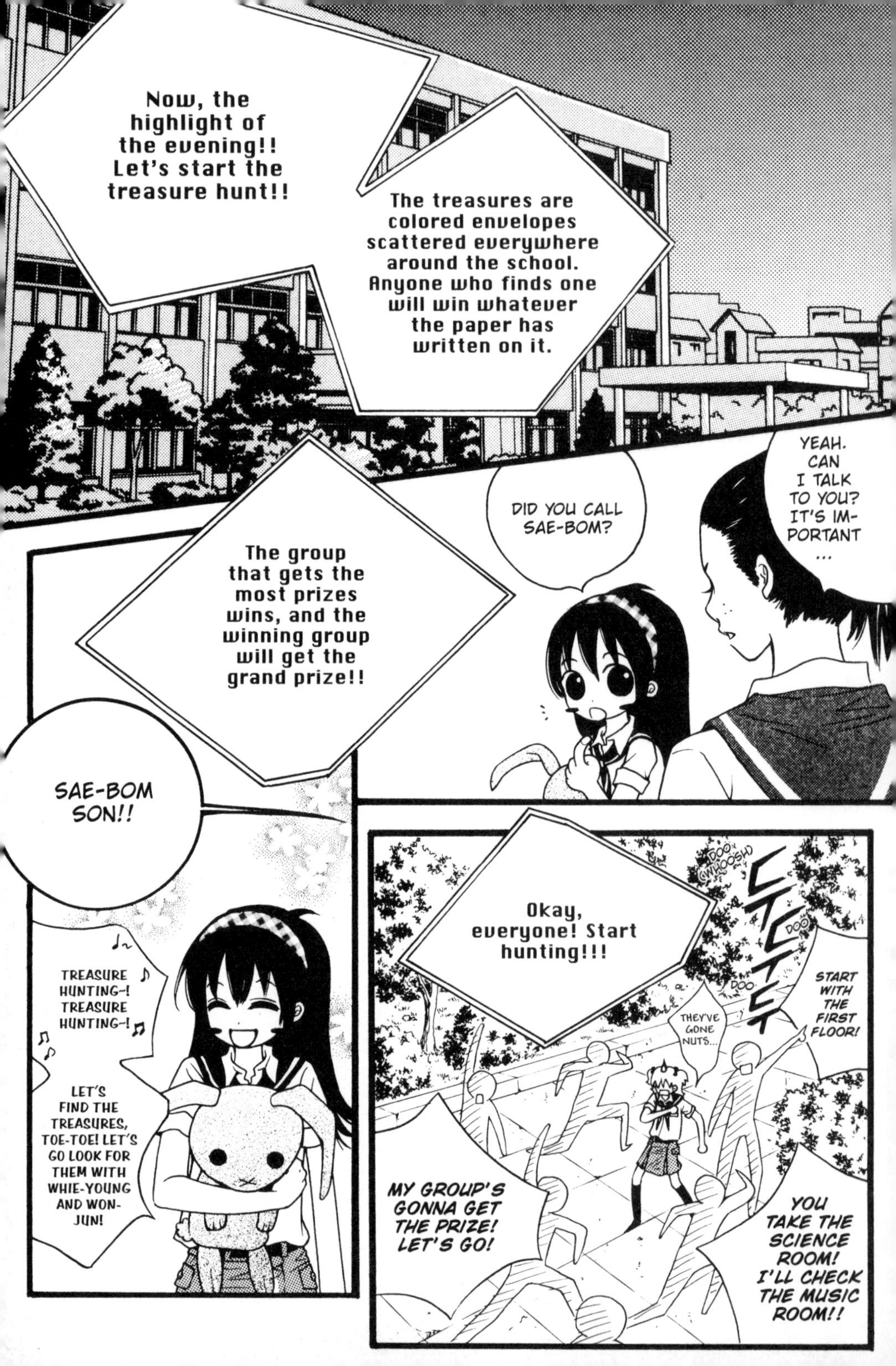
Now, the highlight of the evening!! Let's start the treasure hunt!!
The treasures are colored envelopes scattered everywhere around the school. Anyone who finds one will win whatever the paper has written on it.
The group that gets the most prizes wins, and the winning group will get the grand prize!!
SAE-BOM SON!!
TREASURE HUNTING-! TREASURE HUNTING-!
LET'S FIND THE TREASURES, TOE-TOE! LET'S GO LOOK FOR THEM WITH WHIE-YOUNG AND WON-JUN!
DID YOU CALL SAE-BOM?
YEAH. CAN I TALK TO YOU? IT'S IM-PORTANT ...
Okay, everyone! Start hunting!!!
DOO (WHOOSH)
DOO
DOO
THEY'VE GONE NUTS...
START WITH THE FIRST FLOOR!
MY GROUP'S GONNA GET THE PRIZE! LET'S GO!
YOU TAKE THE SCIENCE ROOM! I'LL CHECK THE MUSIC ROOM!!

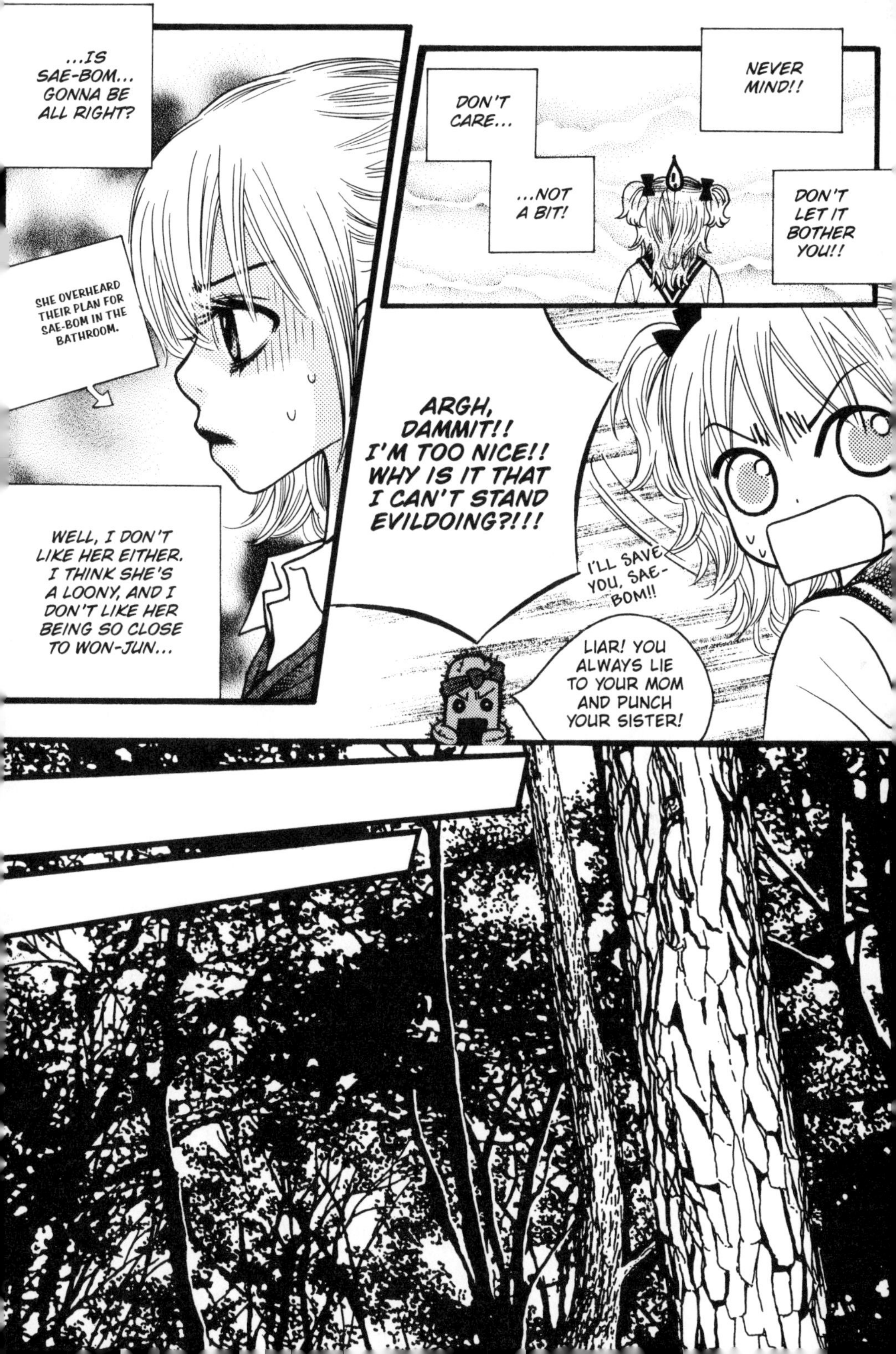
...IS SAE-BOM... GONNA BE ALL RIGHT?
SHE OVERHEARD THEIR PLAN FOR SAE-BOM IN THE BATHROOM.
WELL, I DON'T LIKE HER EITHER. I THINK SHE'S A LOONY, AND I DON'T LIKE HER BEING SO CLOSE TO WON-JUN...
DON'T CARE...
...NOT A BIT!
NEVER MIND!!
DON'T LET IT BOTHER YOU!!
ARGH, DAMMIT!! I'M TOO NICE!! WHY IS IT THAT I CAN'T STAND EVILDOING?!!!
I'LL SAVE YOU, SAE-BOM!!
LIAR! YOU ALWAYS LIE TO YOUR MOM AND PUNCH YOUR SISTER!

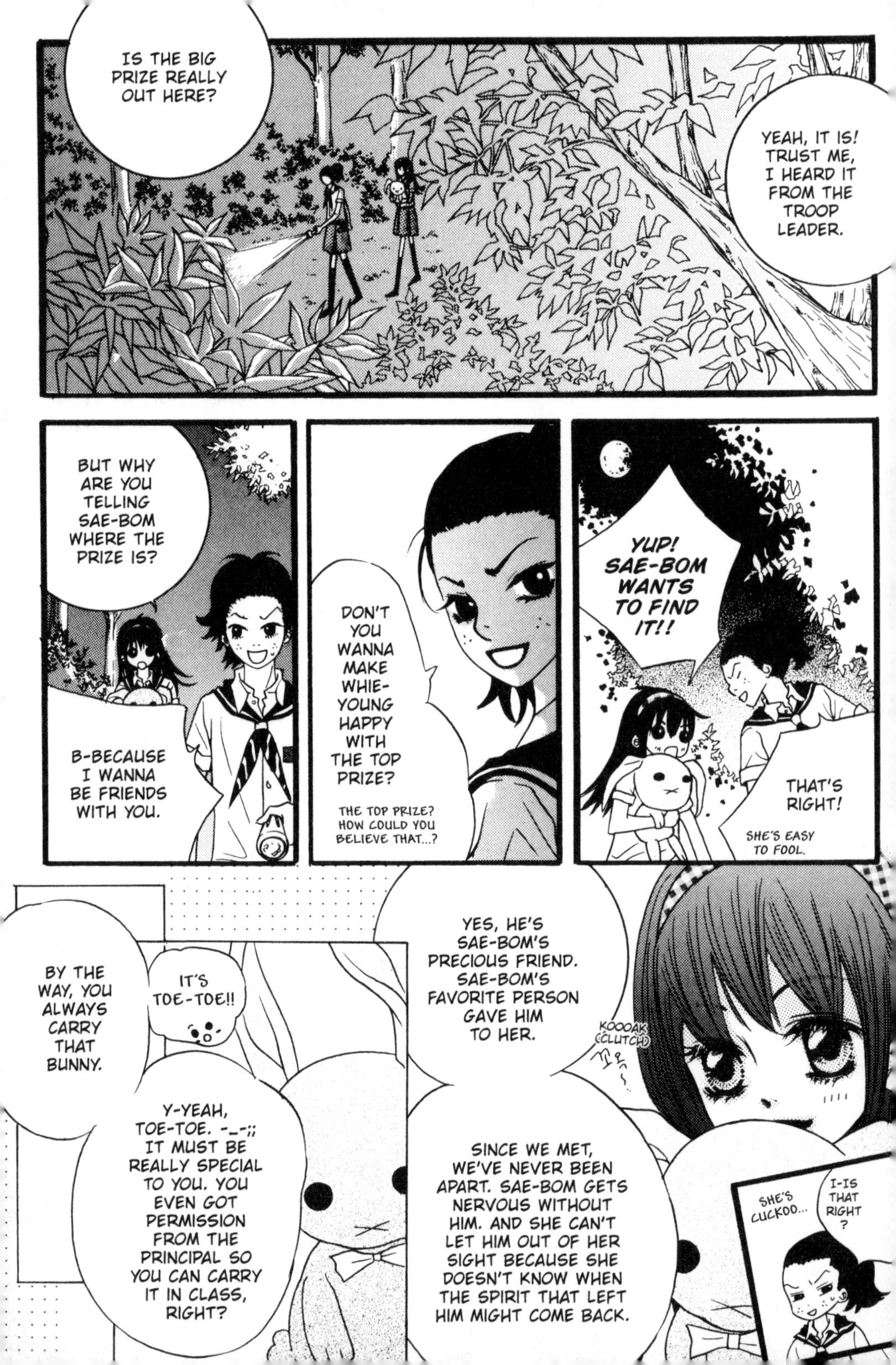

IS THE BIG PRIZE REALLY OUT HERE?
YEAH, IT IS! TRUST ME, I HEARD IT FROM THE TROOP LEADER.
BUT WHY ARE YOU TELLING SAE-BOM WHERE THE PRIZE IS?
B-BECAUSE I WANNA BE FRIENDS WITH YOU.
DON'T YOU WANNA MAKE WHIE-YOUNG HAPPY WITH THE TOP PRIZE?
THE TOP PRIZE? HOW COULD YOU BELIEVE THAT...?
YUP! SAE-BOM WANTS TO FIND IT!!
THAT'S RIGHT!
SHE'S EASY TO FOOL.
BY THE WAY, YOU ALWAYS CARRY THAT BUNNY.
IT'S TOE-TOE!!
Y-YEAH, TOE-TOE. -_-;; IT MUST BE REALLY SPECIAL TO YOU. YOU EVEN GOT PERMISSION FROM THE PRINCIPAL SO YOU CAN CARRY IT IN CLASS, RIGHT?
YES, HE'S SAE-BOM'S PRECIOUS FRIEND. SAE-BOM'S FAVORITE PERSON GAVE HIM TO HER.
KOOOAK (CLUTCH)
SINCE WE MET, WE'VE NEVER BEEN APART. SAE-BOM GETS NERVOUS WITHOUT HIM. AND SHE CAN'T LET HIM OUT OF HER SIGHT BECAUSE SHE DOESN'T KNOW WHEN THE SPIRIT THAT LEFT HIM MIGHT COME BACK.
SHE'S CUCKOO...
I-IS THAT RIGHT?

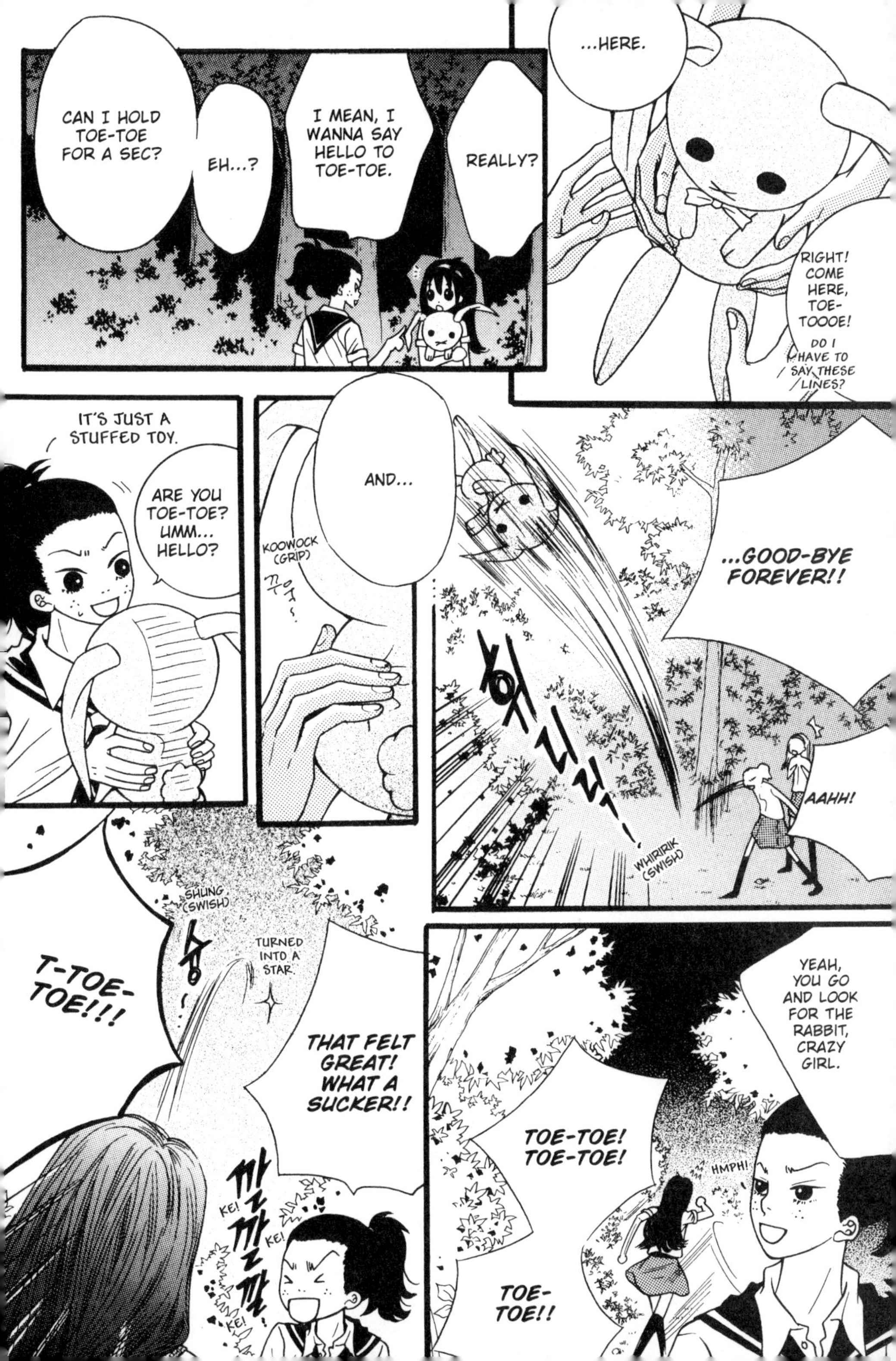
CAN I HOLD TOE-TOE FOR A SEC?
EH...?
I MEAN, I WANNA SAY HELLO TO TOE-TOE.
REALLY?
...HERE.
RIGHT! COME HERE, TOE-TOOOE!
DO I HAVE TO SAY THESE LINES?
IT'S JUST A STUFFED TOY.
ARE YOU TOE-TOE? UMM... HELLO?
AND...
KOOWOCK (GRIP)
...GOOD-BYE FOREVER!!
AAHH!
WHIRIRIK (SWISH)
SHUNG (SWISH)
T-TOE-TOE!!!
TURNED INTO A STAR.
THAT FELT GREAT! WHAT A SUCKER!!
KE!
KE!
KE!
YEAH, YOU GO AND LOOK FOR THE RABBIT, CRAZY GIRL.
TOE-TOE! TOE-TOE!
HMPH!
TOE-TOE!!

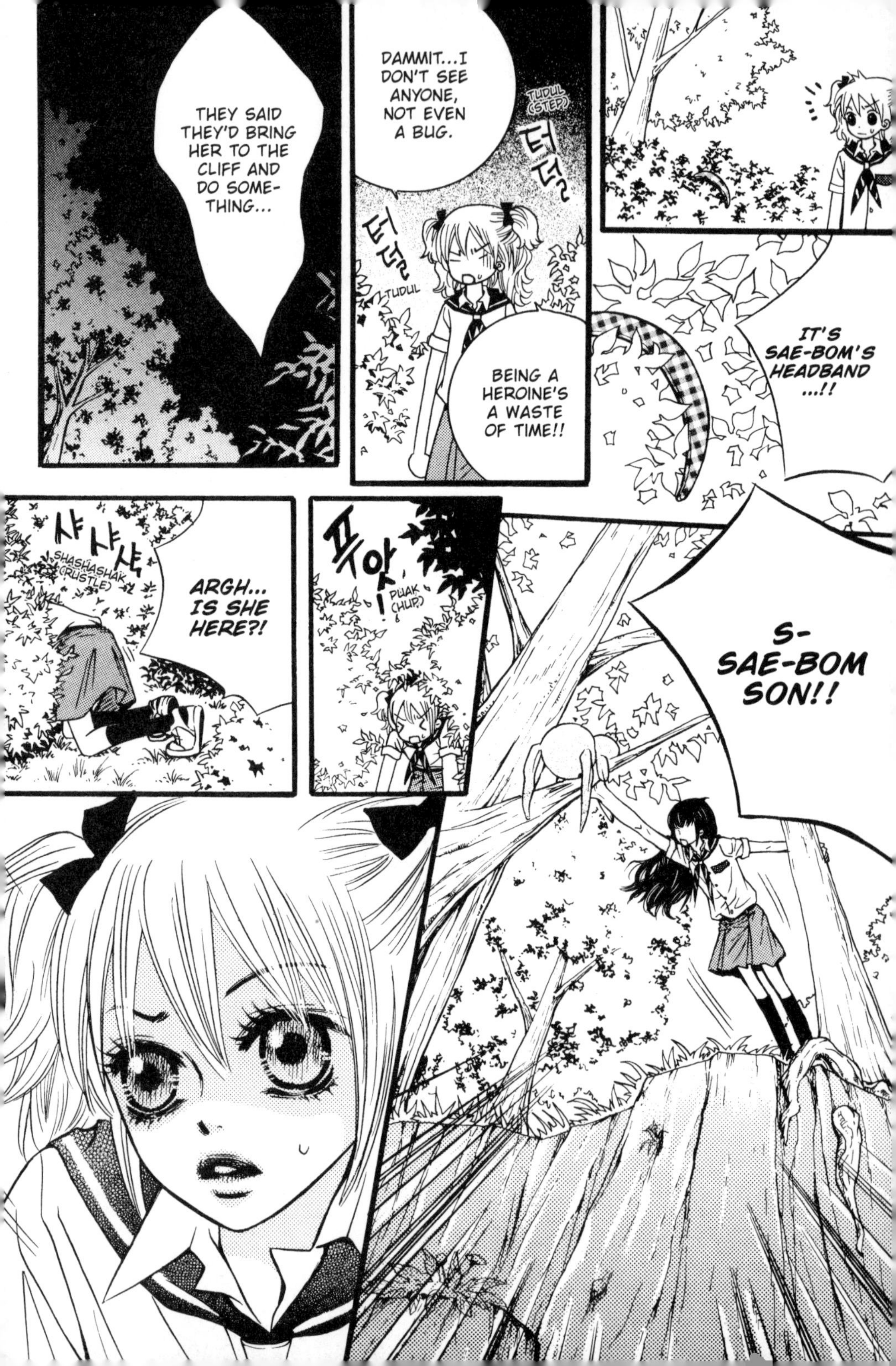
THEY SAID THEY'D BRING HER TO THE CLIFF AND DO SOME-THING...
DAMMIT...I DON'T SEE ANYONE, NOT EVEN A BUG.
터덜
TUDUL (STEP)
터덜
TUDUL
BEING A HEROINE'S A WASTE OF TIME!!
IT'S SAE-BOM'S HEADBAND ...!!
샤샤샥
SHASHASHAK (RUSTLE)
ARGH... IS SHE HERE?!
푸앗!
PUAK (HUP)
S-SAE-BOM SON!!

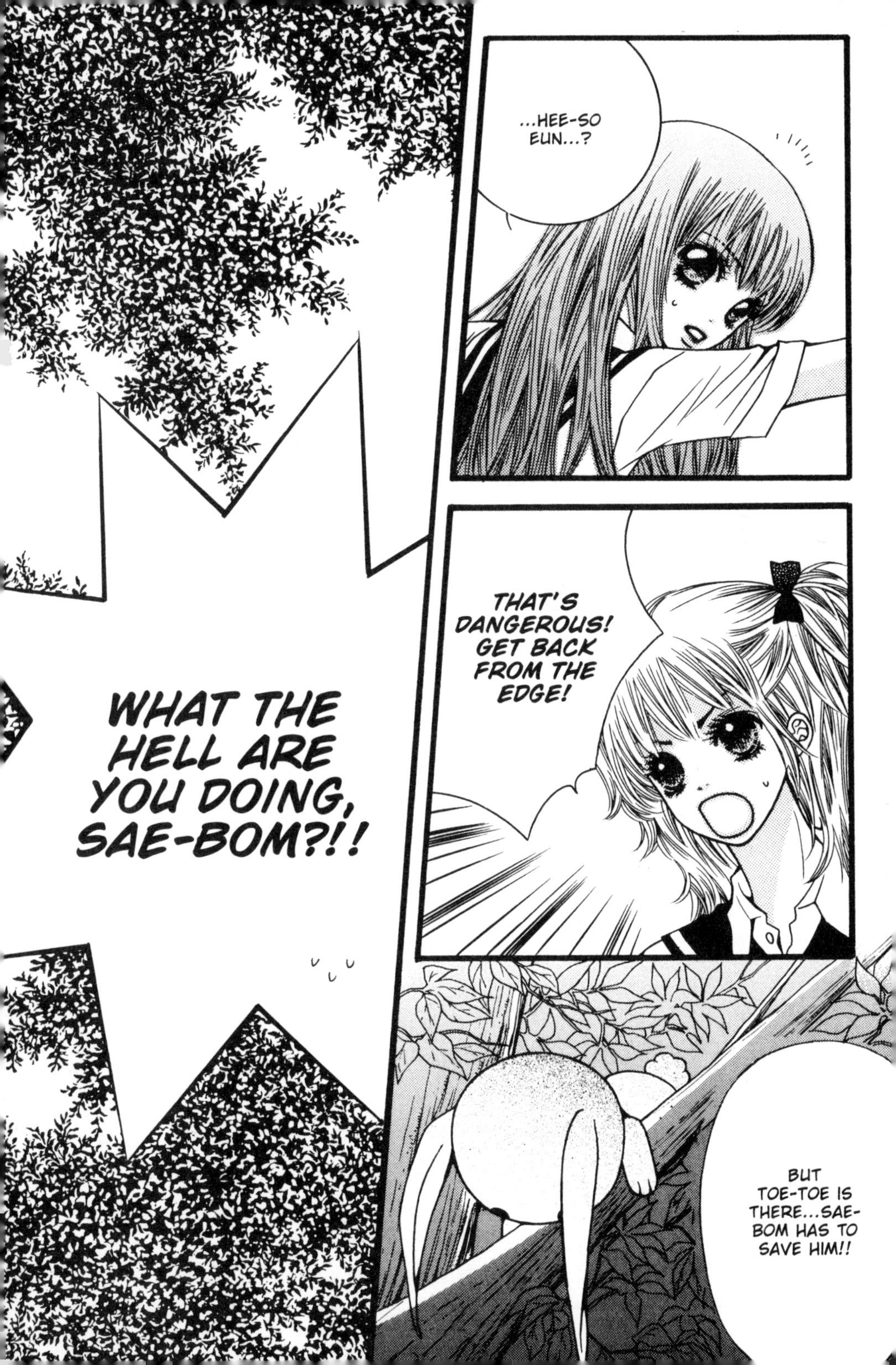
WHAT THE HELL ARE YOU DOING, SAE-BOM?!!
...HEE-SO EUN...?
THAT'S DANGEROUS! GET BACK FROM THE EDGE!
BUT TOE-TOE IS THERE...SAE-BOM HAS TO SAVE HIM!!

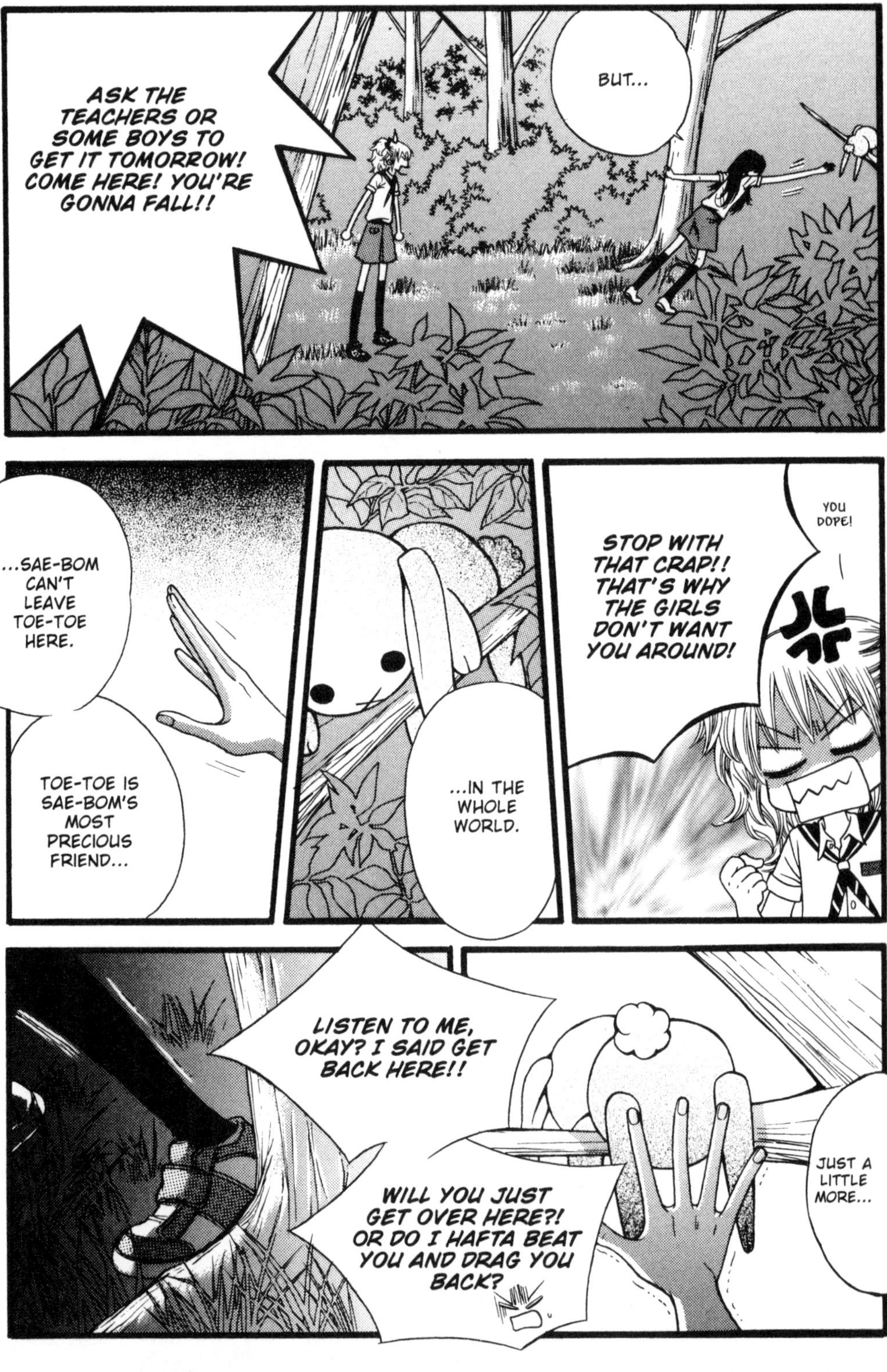
ASK THE TEACHERS OR SOME BOYS TO GET IT TOMORROW! COME HERE! YOU'RE GONNA FALL!!
BUT...
...SAE-BOM CAN'T LEAVE TOE-TOE HERE.
TOE-TOE IS SAE-BOM'S MOST PRECIOUS FRIEND...
...IN THE WHOLE WORLD.
STOP WITH THAT CRAP!! THAT'S WHY THE GIRLS DON'T WANT YOU AROUND!
YOU DOPE!
LISTEN TO ME, OKAY? I SAID GET BACK HERE!!
WILL YOU JUST GET OVER HERE?! OR DO I HAFTA BEAT YOU AND DRAG YOU BACK?
JUST A LITTLE MORE...

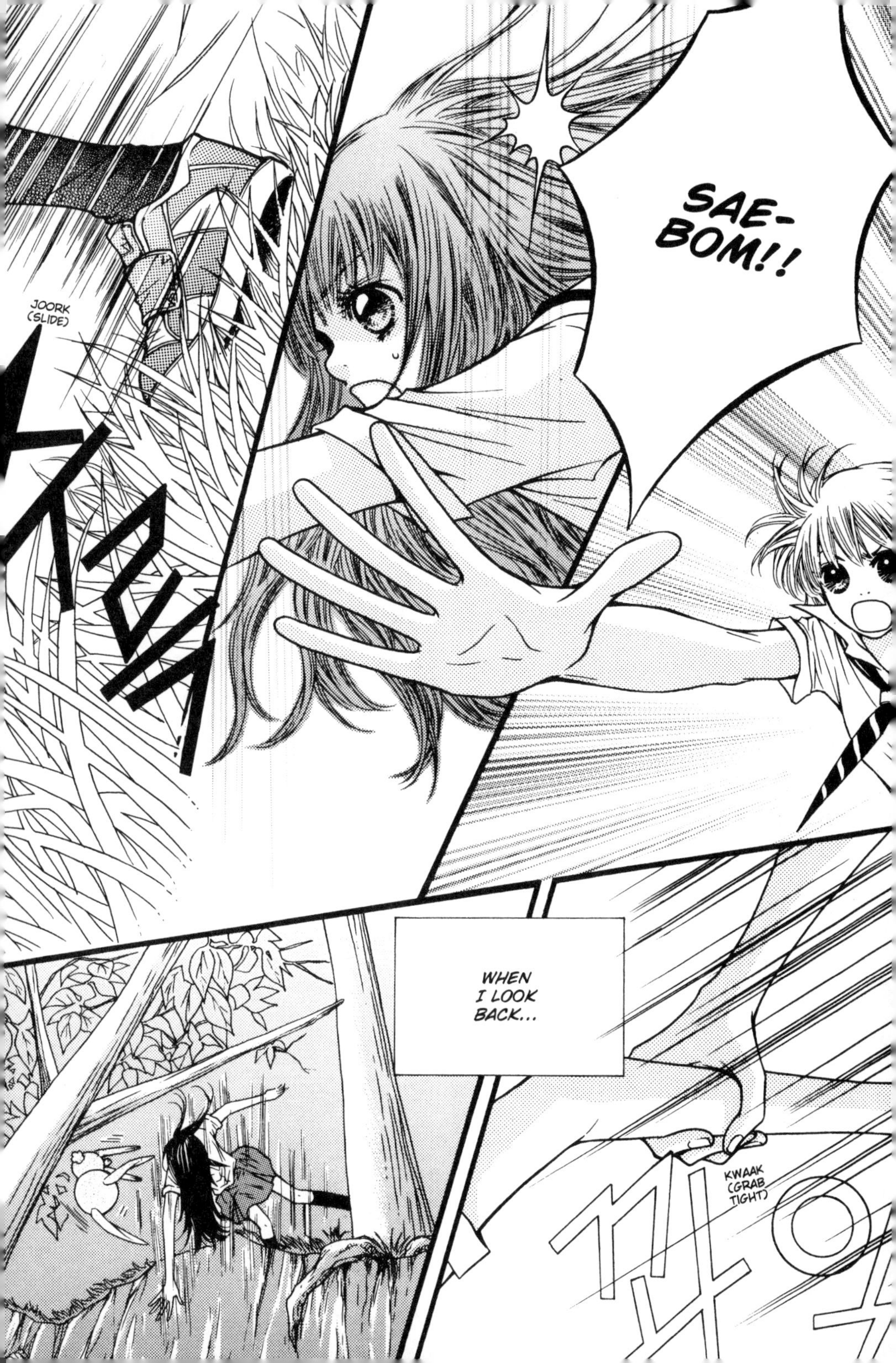

JOORK (SLIDE)
SAE-BOM!!
WHEN I LOOK BACK...
KWAAK (GRAB TIGHT)

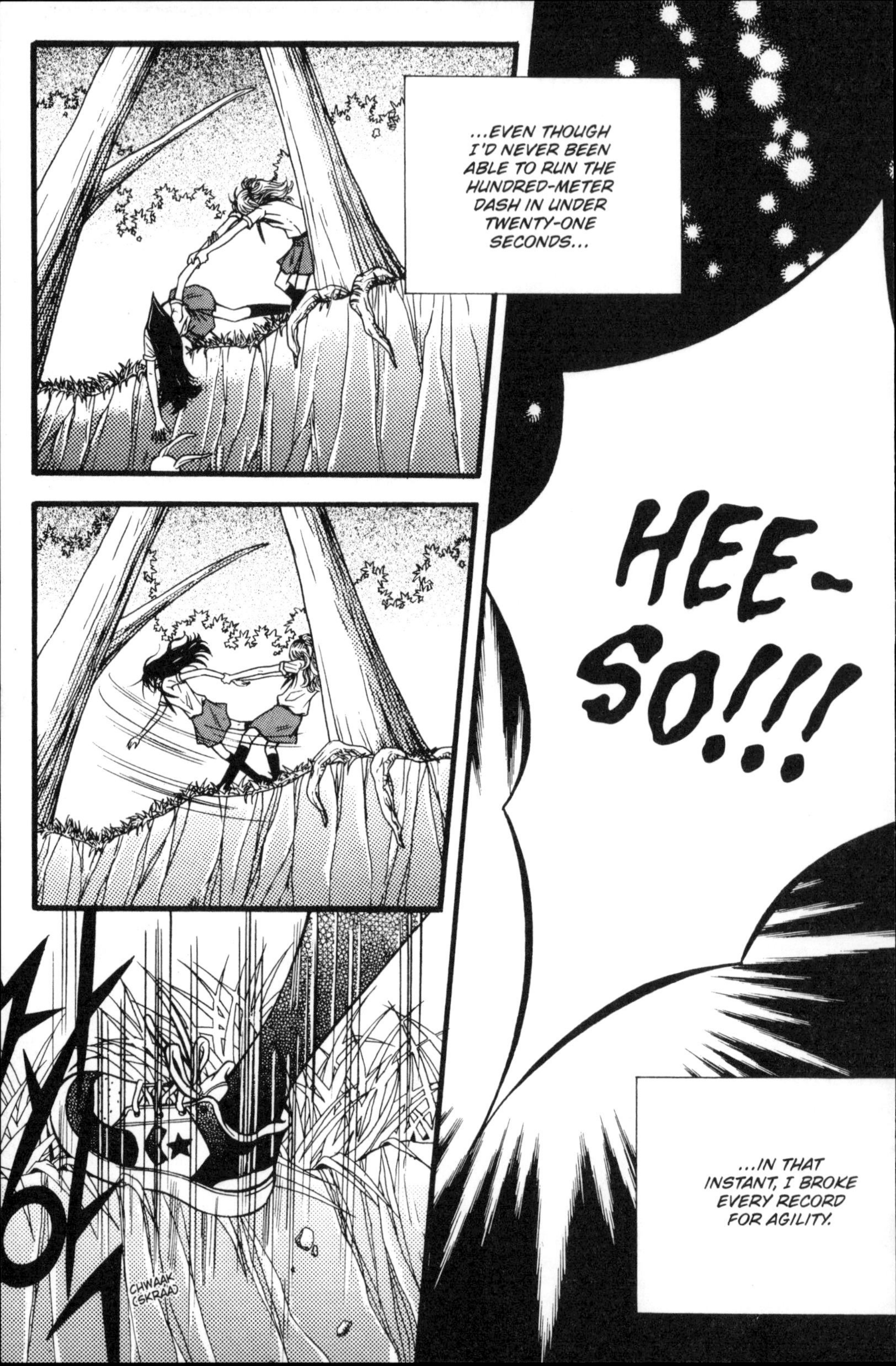
...EVEN THOUGH I'D NEVER BEEN ABLE TO RUN THE HUNDRED-METER DASH IN UNDER TWENTY-ONE SECONDS...
HEE-SO!!!
CHWAAK (SKRAA)
...IN THAT INSTANT, I BROKE EVERY RECORD FOR AGILITY.

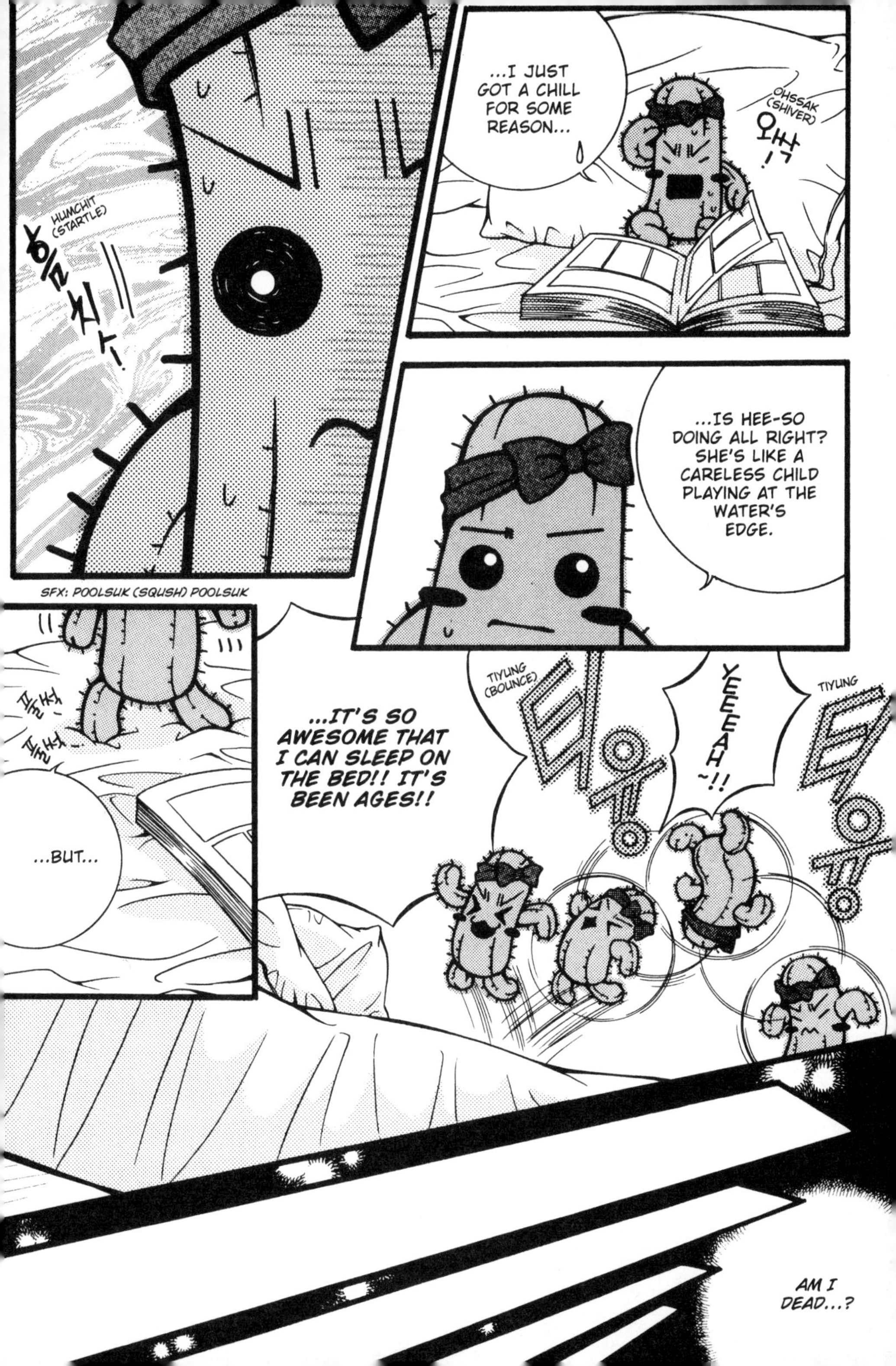

HUMCHIT (STARTLE)
흠칫!
...I JUST GOT A CHILL FOR SOME REASON...
OHSSAK (SHIVER)
오싹!
...IS HEE-SO DOING ALL RIGHT? SHE'S LIKE A CARELESS CHILD PLAYING AT THE WATER'S EDGE.
SFX: POOLSUK (SQUSH) POOLSUK
풀썩
풀썩
...BUT...
...IT'S SO AWESOME THAT I CAN SLEEP ON THE BED!! IT'S BEEN AGES!!
TIYUNG (BOUNCE)
YEEEAH~!!
TIYUNG
AM I DEAD...?

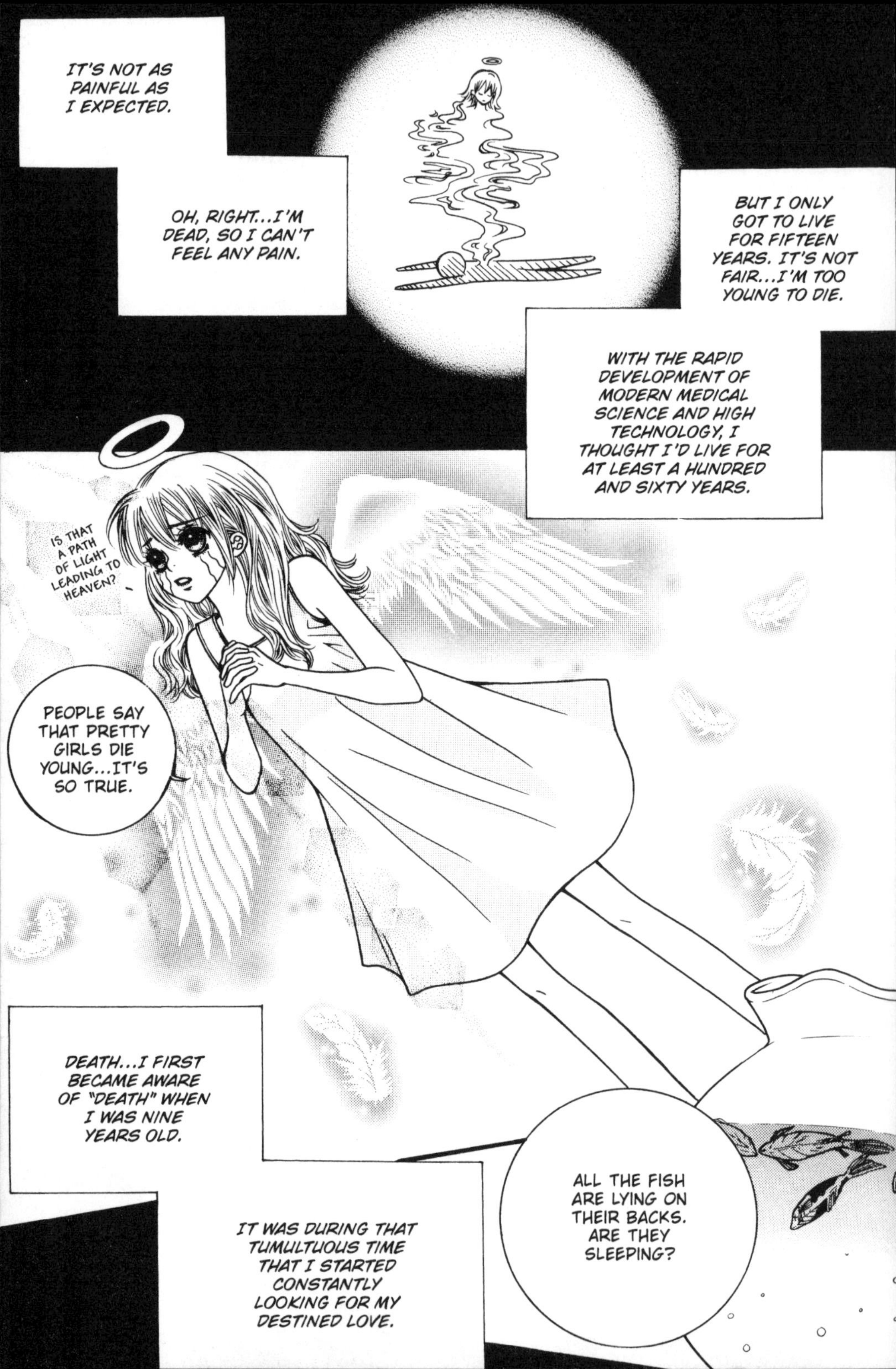
IT'S NOT AS PAINFUL AS I EXPECTED.
OH, RIGHT...I'M DEAD, SO I CAN'T FEEL ANY PAIN.
BUT I ONLY GOT TO LIVE FOR FIFTEEN YEARS. IT'S NOT FAIR...I'M TOO YOUNG TO DIE.
WITH THE RAPID DEVELOPMENT OF MODERN MEDICAL SCIENCE AND HIGH TECHNOLOGY, I THOUGHT I'D LIVE FOR AT LEAST A HUNDRED AND SIXTY YEARS.
IS THAT A PATH OF LIGHT LEADING TO HEAVEN?
PEOPLE SAY THAT PRETTY GIRLS DIE YOUNG...IT'S SO TRUE.
DEATH...I FIRST BECAME AWARE OF "DEATH" WHEN I WAS NINE YEARS OLD.
IT WAS DURING THAT TUMULTUOUS TIME THAT I STARTED CONSTANTLY LOOKING FOR MY DESTINED LOVE.
ALL THE FISH ARE LYING ON THEIR BACKS. ARE THEY SLEEPING?

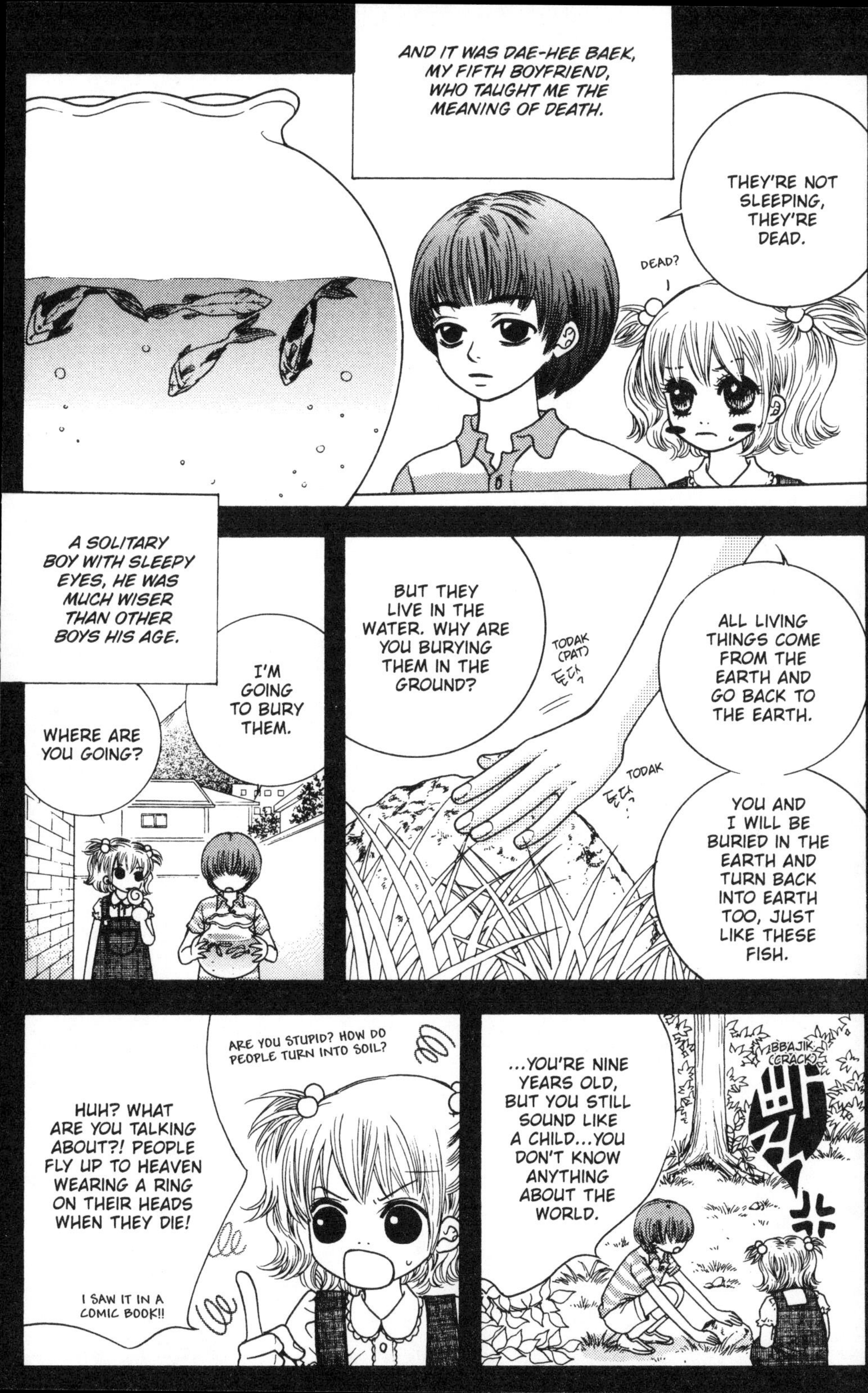
AND IT WAS DAE-HEE BAEK, MY FIFTH BOYFRIEND, WHO TAUGHT ME THE MEANING OF DEATH.
THEY'RE NOT SLEEPING, THEY'RE DEAD.
DEAD?
A SOLITARY BOY WITH SLEEPY EYES, HE WAS MUCH WISER THAN OTHER BOYS HIS AGE.
WHERE ARE YOU GOING?
I'M GOING TO BURY THEM.
BUT THEY LIVE IN THE WATER. WHY ARE YOU BURYING THEM IN THE GROUND?
TODAK (PAT)
ALL LIVING THINGS COME FROM THE EARTH AND GO BACK TO THE EARTH.
TODAK
YOU AND I WILL BE BURIED IN THE EARTH AND TURN BACK INTO EARTH TOO, JUST LIKE THESE FISH.
HUH? WHAT ARE YOU TALKING ABOUT?! PEOPLE FLY UP TO HEAVEN WEARING A RING ON THEIR HEADS WHEN THEY DIE!
ARE YOU STUPID? HOW DO PEOPLE TURN INTO SOIL?
I SAW IT IN A COMIC BOOK!!
...YOU'RE NINE YEARS OLD, BUT YOU STILL SOUND LIKE A CHILD...YOU DON'T KNOW ANYTHING ABOUT THE WORLD.
BBAJIK (CRACK)

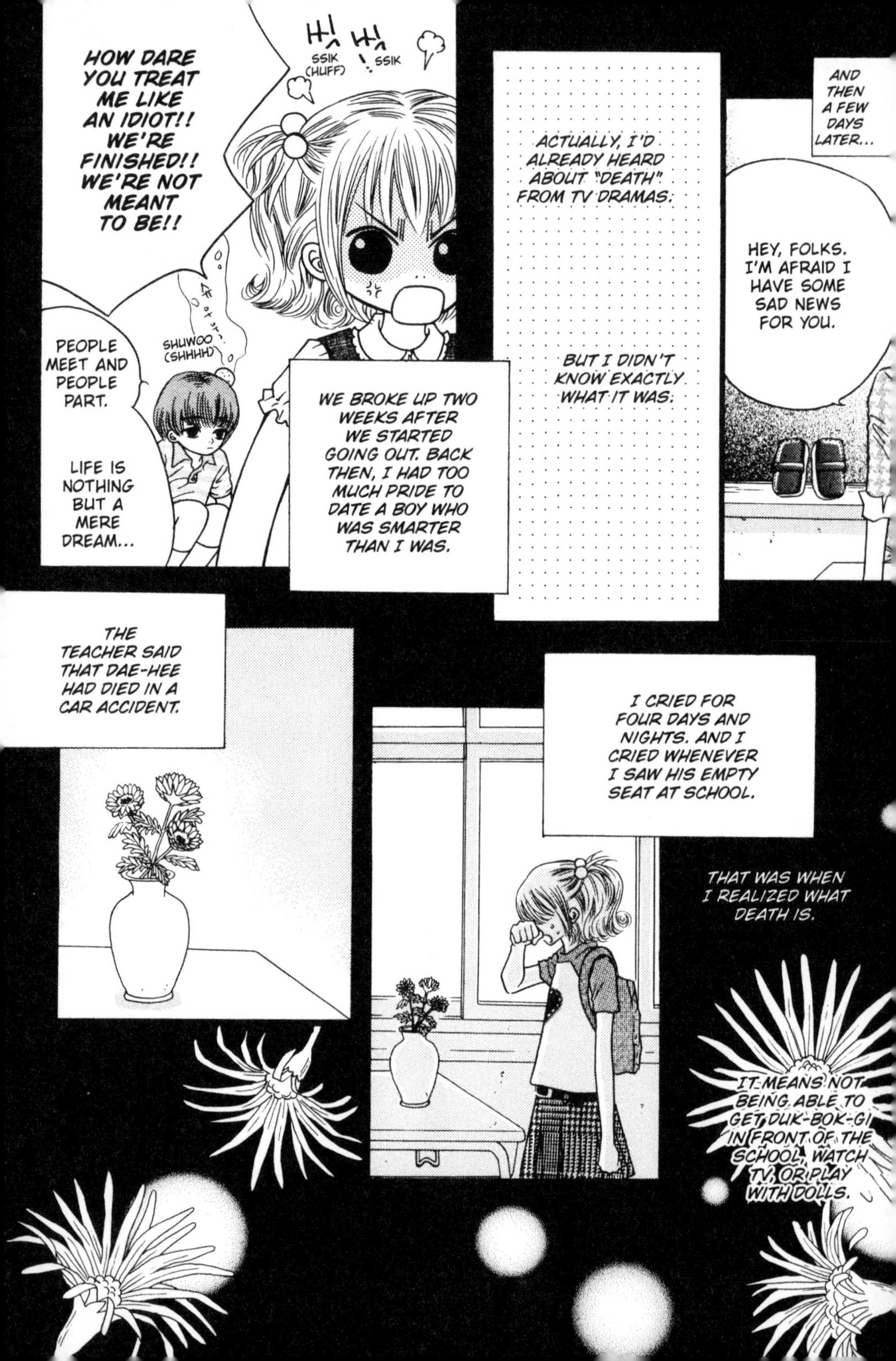
HOW DARE YOU TREAT ME LIKE AN IDIOT!! WE'RE FINISHED!! WE'RE NOT MEANT TO BE!!
SSIK (HUFF)
SSIK
PEOPLE MEET AND PEOPLE PART.
SHUWOO (SHHHH)
LIFE IS NOTHING BUT A MERE DREAM...
WE BROKE UP TWO WEEKS AFTER WE STARTED GOING OUT. BACK THEN, I HAD TOO MUCH PRIDE TO DATE A BOY WHO WAS SMARTER THAN I WAS.
ACTUALLY, I'D ALREADY HEARD ABOUT "DEATH" FROM TV DRAMAS.
BUT I DIDN'T KNOW EXACTLY WHAT IT WAS.
AND THEN A FEW DAYS LATER...
HEY, FOLKS. I'M AFRAID I HAVE SOME SAD NEWS FOR YOU.
THE TEACHER SAID THAT DAE-HEE HAD DIED IN A CAR ACCIDENT.
I CRIED FOR FOUR DAYS AND NIGHTS. AND I CRIED WHENEVER I SAW HIS EMPTY SEAT AT SCHOOL.
THAT WAS WHEN I REALIZED WHAT DEATH IS.
IT MEANS NOT BEING ABLE TO GET DUK-BOK-GI IN FRONT OF THE SCHOOL, WATCH TV, OR PLAY WITH DOLLS.

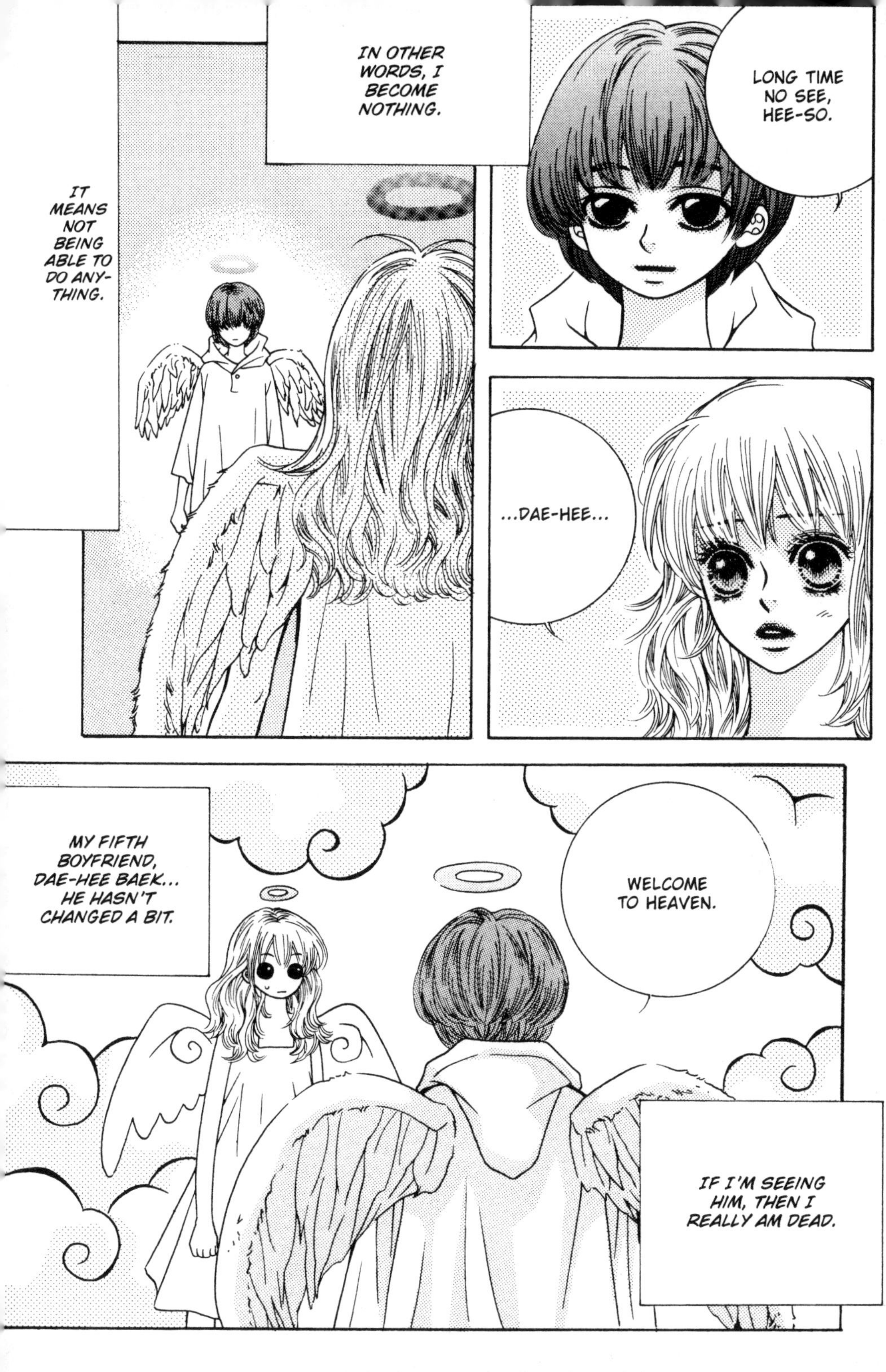
IT MEANS NOT BEING ABLE TO DO ANY-THING.
IN OTHER WORDS, I BECOME NOTHING.
LONG TIME NO SEE, HEE-SO.
...DAE-HEE...
MY FIFTH BOYFRIEND, DAE-HEE BAEK... HE HASN'T CHANGED A BIT.
WELCOME TO HEAVEN.
IF I'M SEEING HIM, THEN I REALLY AM DEAD.

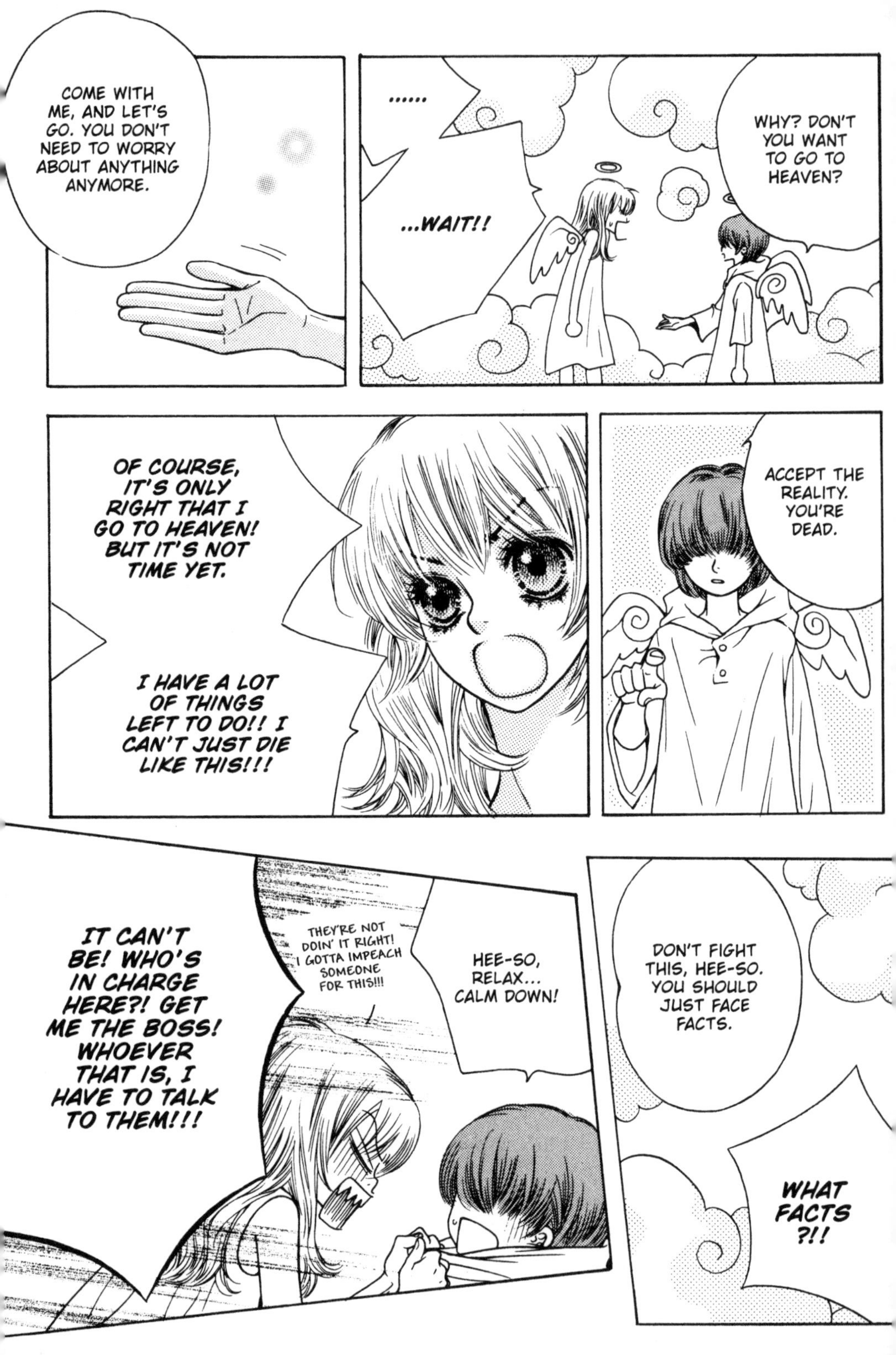
COME WITH ME, AND LET'S GO. YOU DON'T NEED TO WORRY ABOUT ANYTHING ANYMORE.
......
...WAIT!!
WHY? DON'T YOU WANT TO GO TO HEAVEN?
OF COURSE, IT'S ONLY RIGHT THAT I GO TO HEAVEN! BUT IT'S NOT TIME YET.
I HAVE A LOT OF THINGS LEFT TO DO!! I CAN'T JUST DIE LIKE THIS!!!
ACCEPT THE REALITY. YOU'RE DEAD.
IT CAN'T BE! WHO'S IN CHARGE HERE?! GET ME THE BOSS! WHOEVER THAT IS, I HAVE TO TALK TO THEM!!!
THEY'RE NOT DOIN' IT RIGHT! I GOTTA IMPEACH SOMEONE FOR THIS!!!
HEE-SO, RELAX... CALM DOWN!
DON'T FIGHT THIS, HEE-SO. YOU SHOULD JUST FACE FACTS.
WHAT FACTS?!!

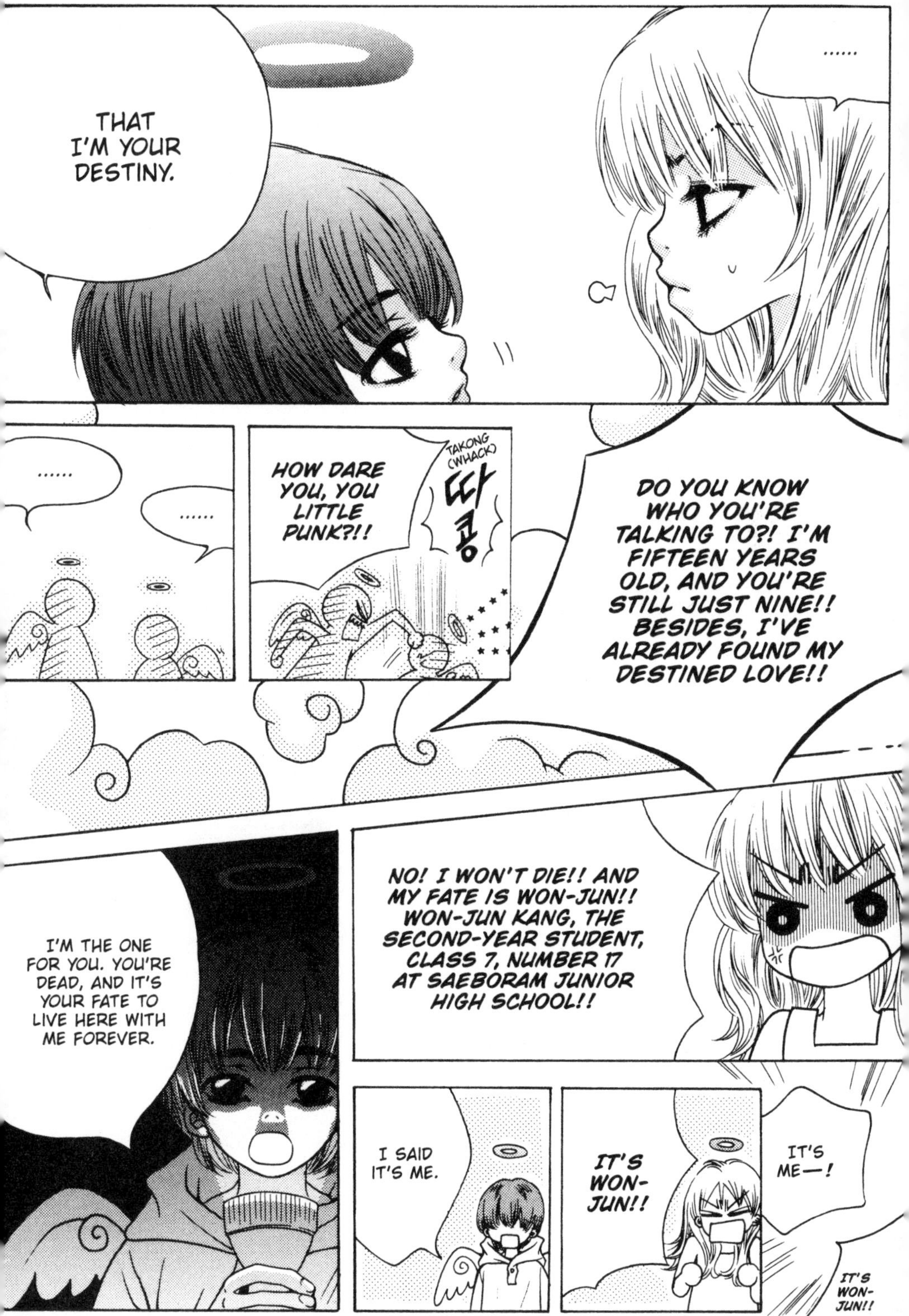
THAT I'M YOUR DESTINY.
......
......
......
HOW DARE YOU, YOU LITTLE PUNK?!!
TAKONG (WHACK)
따콩
DO YOU KNOW WHO YOU'RE TALKING TO?! I'M FIFTEEN YEARS OLD, AND YOU'RE STILL JUST NINE!! BESIDES, I'VE ALREADY FOUND MY DESTINED LOVE!!
I'M THE ONE FOR YOU. YOU'RE DEAD, AND IT'S YOUR FATE TO LIVE HERE WITH ME FOREVER.
NO! I WON'T DIE!! AND MY FATE IS WON-JUN!! WON-JUN KANG, THE SECOND-YEAR STUDENT, CLASS 7, NUMBER 17 AT SAEBORAM JUNIOR HIGH SCHOOL!!
I SAID IT'S ME.
IT'S WON-JUN!!
IT'S ME—!
IT'S WON-JUN!!

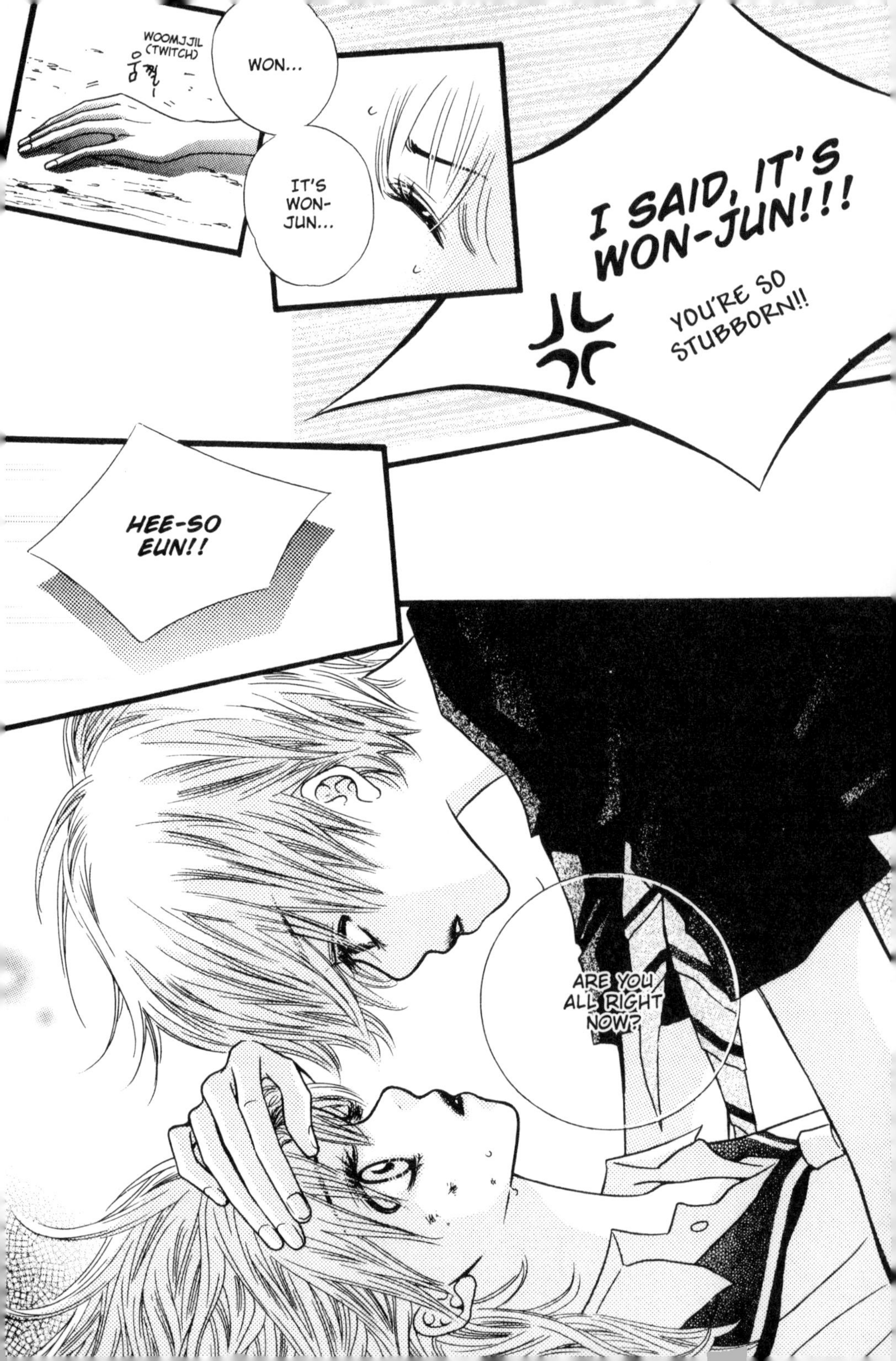
WOOMJJIL (TWITCH)
움찔
WON...
IT'S WON-JUN...
I SAID, IT'S WON-JUN!!!
YOU'RE SO STUBBORN!!
HEE-SO EUN!!
ARE YOU ALL RIGHT NOW?

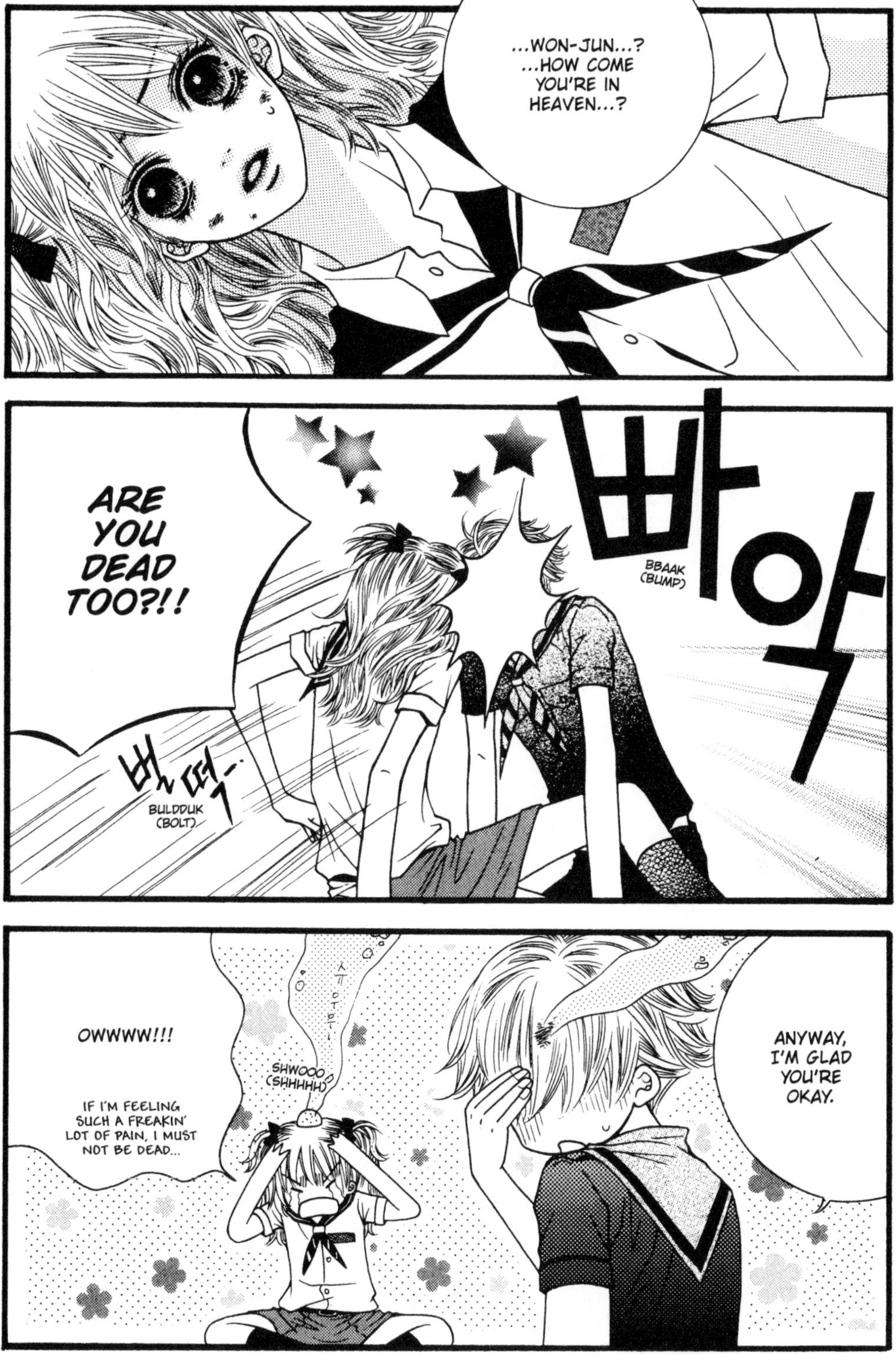
...WON-JUN...? ...HOW COME YOU'RE IN HEAVEN...?
ARE YOU DEAD TOO?!!
빠악
BBAAK (BUMP)
BULDDUK (BOLT)
OWWWW!!!
IF I'M FEELING SUCH A FREAKIN' LOT OF PAIN, I MUST NOT BE DEAD...
SHWOOO (SHHHHH)
ANYWAY, I'M GLAD YOU'RE OKAY.

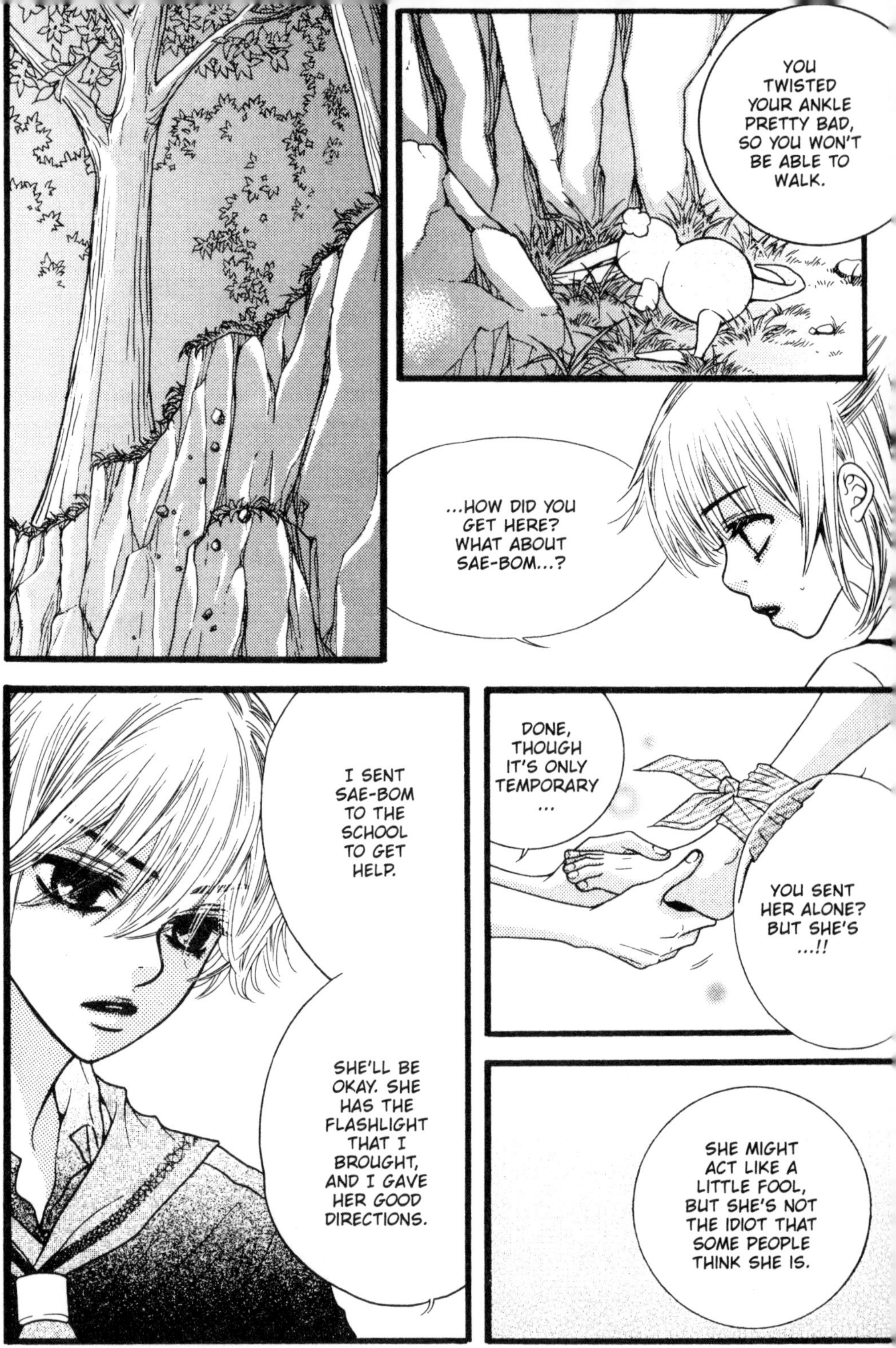
YOU TWISTED YOUR ANKLE PRETTY BAD, SO YOU WON'T BE ABLE TO WALK.
...HOW DID YOU GET HERE? WHAT ABOUT SAE-BOM...?
I SENT SAE-BOM TO THE SCHOOL TO GET HELP.
SHE'LL BE OKAY. SHE HAS THE FLASHLIGHT THAT I BROUGHT, AND I GAVE HER GOOD DIRECTIONS.
DONE, THOUGH IT'S ONLY TEMPORARY ...
YOU SENT HER ALONE? BUT SHE'S ...!!
SHE MIGHT ACT LIKE A LITTLE FOOL, BUT SHE'S NOT THE IDIOT THAT SOME PEOPLE THINK SHE IS.

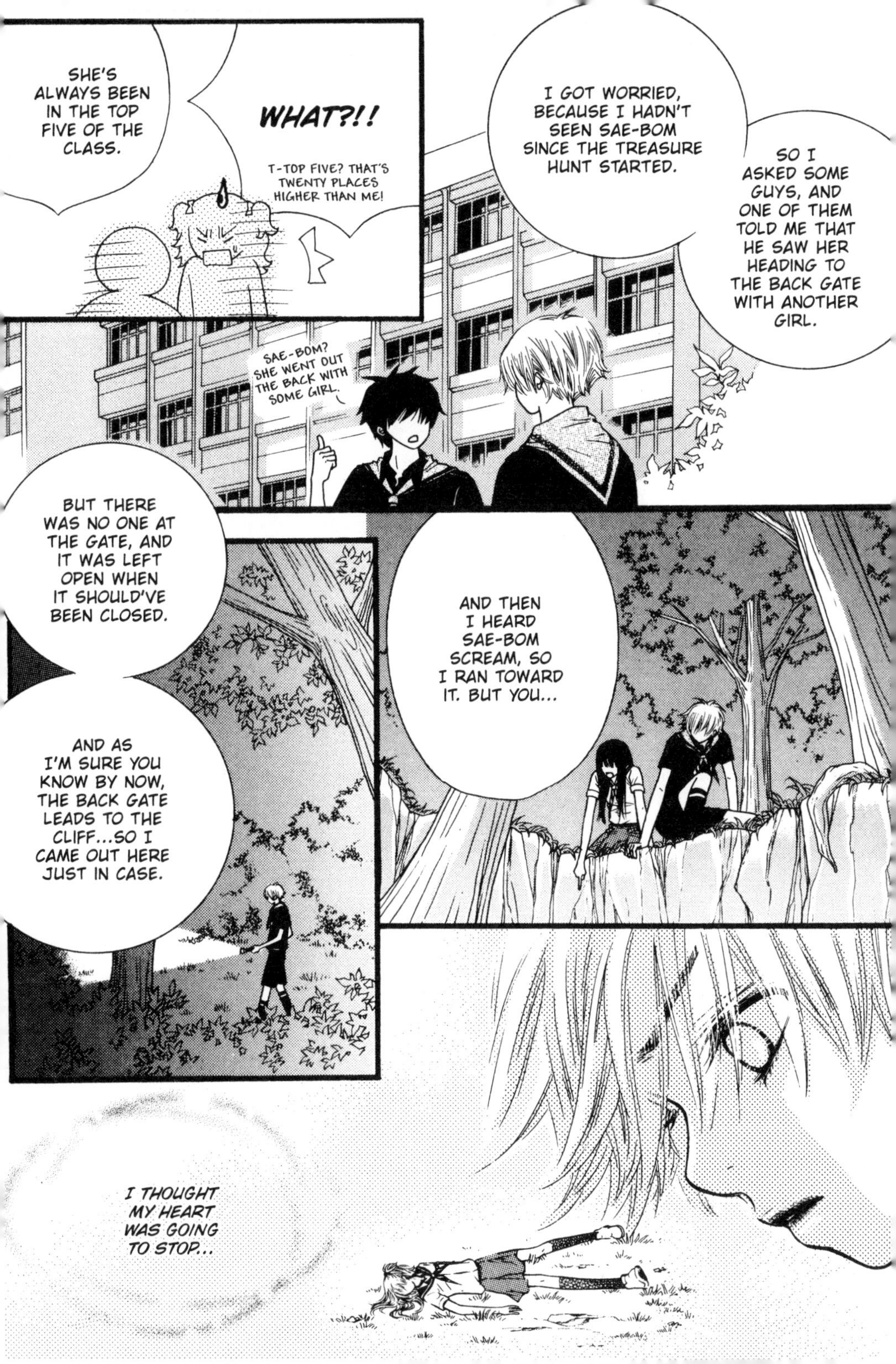
SHE'S ALWAYS BEEN IN THE TOP FIVE OF THE CLASS.
WHAT?!!
T-TOP FIVE? THAT'S TWENTY PLACES HIGHER THAN ME!
I GOT WORRIED, BECAUSE I HADN'T SEEN SAE-BOM SINCE THE TREASURE HUNT STARTED.
SO I ASKED SOME GUYS, AND ONE OF THEM TOLD ME THAT HE SAW HER HEADING TO THE BACK GATE WITH ANOTHER GIRL.
SAE-BOM? SHE WENT OUT THE BACK WITH SOME GIRL.
BUT THERE WAS NO ONE AT THE GATE, AND IT WAS LEFT OPEN WHEN IT SHOULD'VE BEEN CLOSED.
AND AS I'M SURE YOU KNOW BY NOW, THE BACK GATE LEADS TO THE CLIFF...SO I CAME OUT HERE JUST IN CASE.
AND THEN I HEARD SAE-BOM SCREAM, SO I RAN TOWARD IT. BUT YOU...
I THOUGHT MY HEART WAS GOING TO STOP...

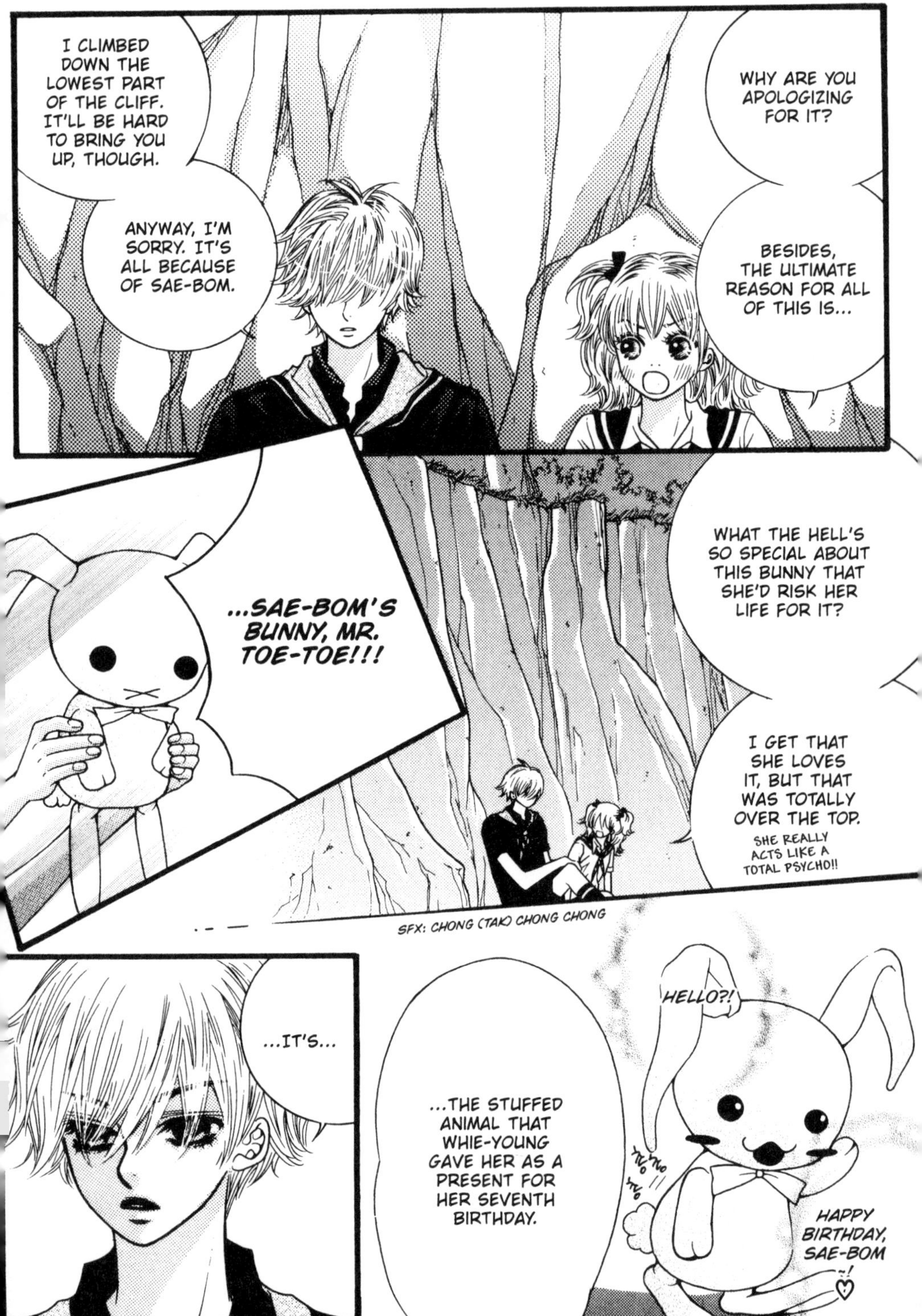
I CLIMBED DOWN THE LOWEST PART OF THE CLIFF. IT'LL BE HARD TO BRING YOU UP, THOUGH.
ANYWAY, I'M SORRY. IT'S ALL BECAUSE OF SAE-BOM.
WHY ARE YOU APOLOGIZING FOR IT?
BESIDES, THE ULTIMATE REASON FOR ALL OF THIS IS...
...SAE-BOM'S BUNNY, MR. TOE-TOE!!!
WHAT THE HELL'S SO SPECIAL ABOUT THIS BUNNY THAT SHE'D RISK HER LIFE FOR IT?
I GET THAT SHE LOVES IT, BUT THAT WAS TOTALLY OVER THE TOP.
SHE REALLY ACTS LIKE A TOTAL PSYCHO!!
SFX: CHONG (TAK) CHONG CHONG
...IT'S...
...THE STUFFED ANIMAL THAT WHIE-YOUNG GAVE HER AS A PRESENT FOR HER SEVENTH BIRTHDAY.
HELLO?!
HAPPY BIRTHDAY, SAE-BOM~!

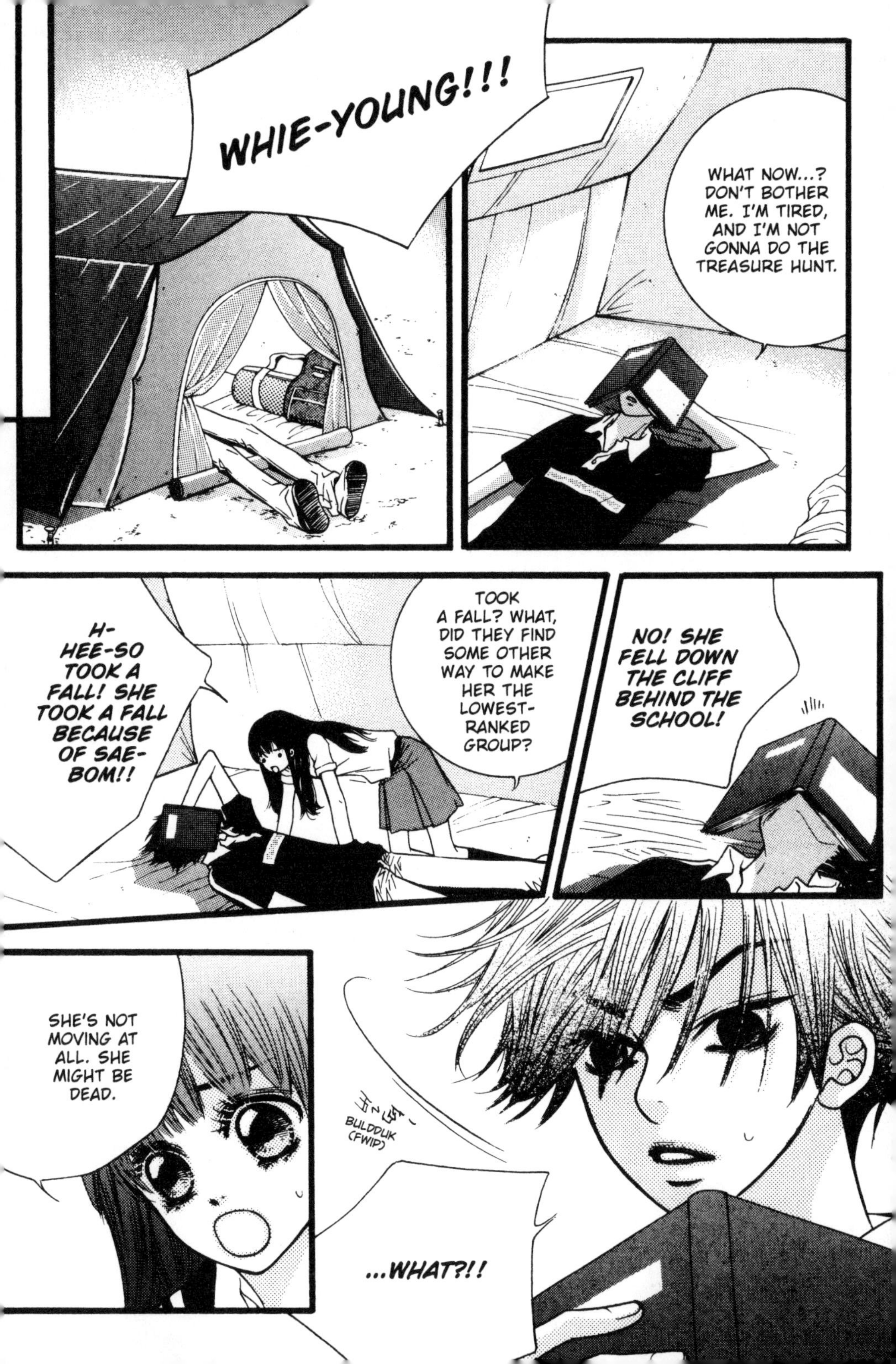

WHIE-YOUNG!!!
WHAT NOW...? DON'T BOTHER ME. I'M TIRED, AND I'M NOT GONNA DO THE TREASURE HUNT.
H-HEE-SO TOOK A FALL! SHE TOOK A FALL BECAUSE OF SAE-BOM!!
TOOK A FALL? WHAT, DID THEY FIND SOME OTHER WAY TO MAKE HER THE LOWEST-RANKED GROUP?
NO! SHE FELL DOWN THE CLIFF BEHIND THE SCHOOL!
SHE'S NOT MOVING AT ALL. SHE MIGHT BE DEAD.
BULDDUK (FWIP)
...WHAT?!!

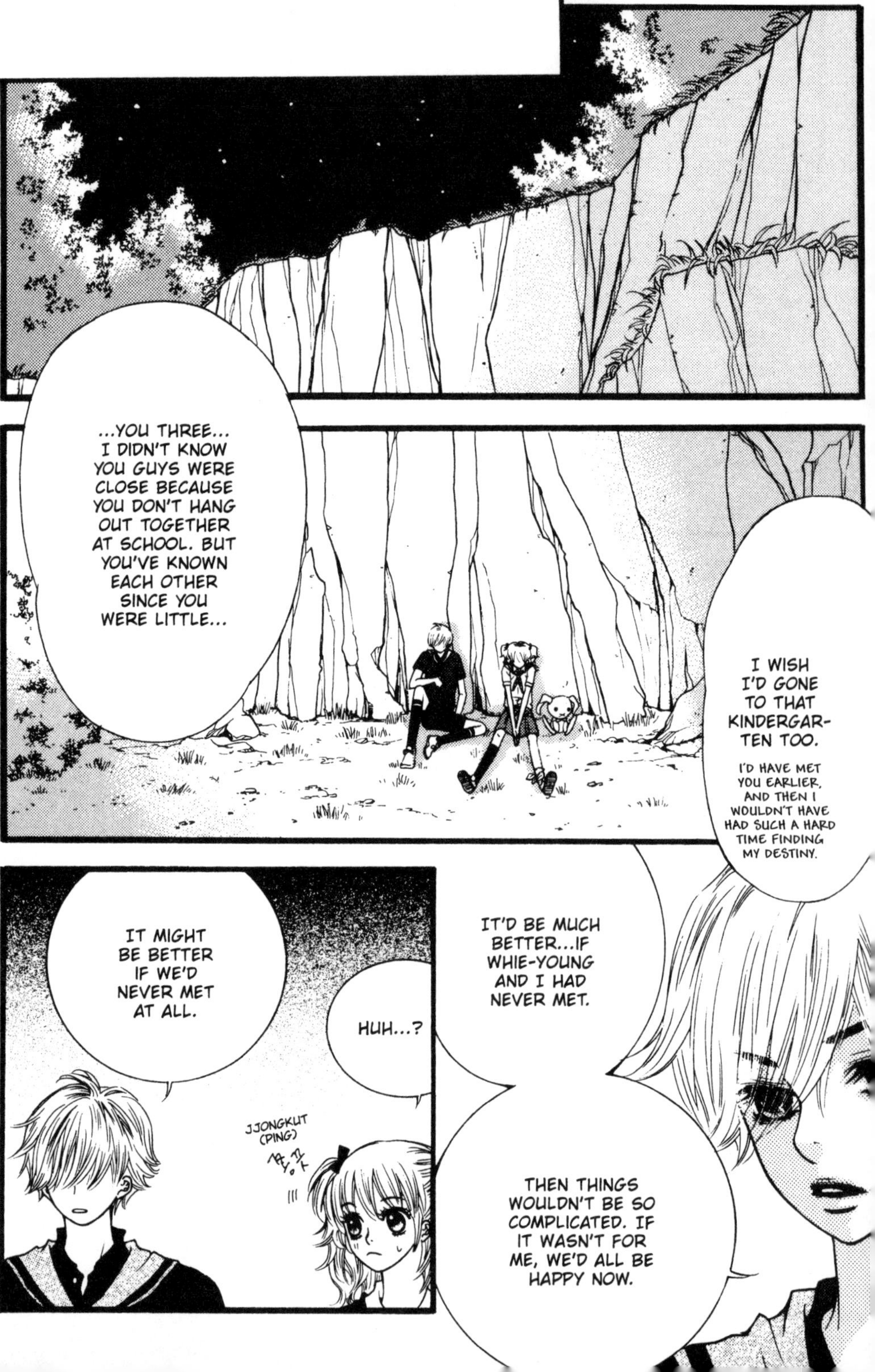
...YOU THREE... I DIDN'T KNOW YOU GUYS WERE CLOSE BECAUSE YOU DON'T HANG OUT TOGETHER AT SCHOOL. BUT YOU'VE KNOWN EACH OTHER SINCE YOU WERE LITTLE...
I WISH I'D GONE TO THAT KINDERGAR-TEN TOO.
I'D HAVE MET YOU EARLIER, AND THEN I WOULDN'T HAVE HAD SUCH A HARD TIME FINDING MY DESTINY.
IT MIGHT BE BETTER IF WE'D NEVER MET AT ALL.
HUH...?
JJONGKUT (PING)
IT'D BE MUCH BETTER...IF WHIE-YOUNG AND I HAD NEVER MET.
THEN THINGS WOULDN'T BE SO COMPLICATED. IF IT WASN'T FOR ME, WE'D ALL BE HAPPY NOW.

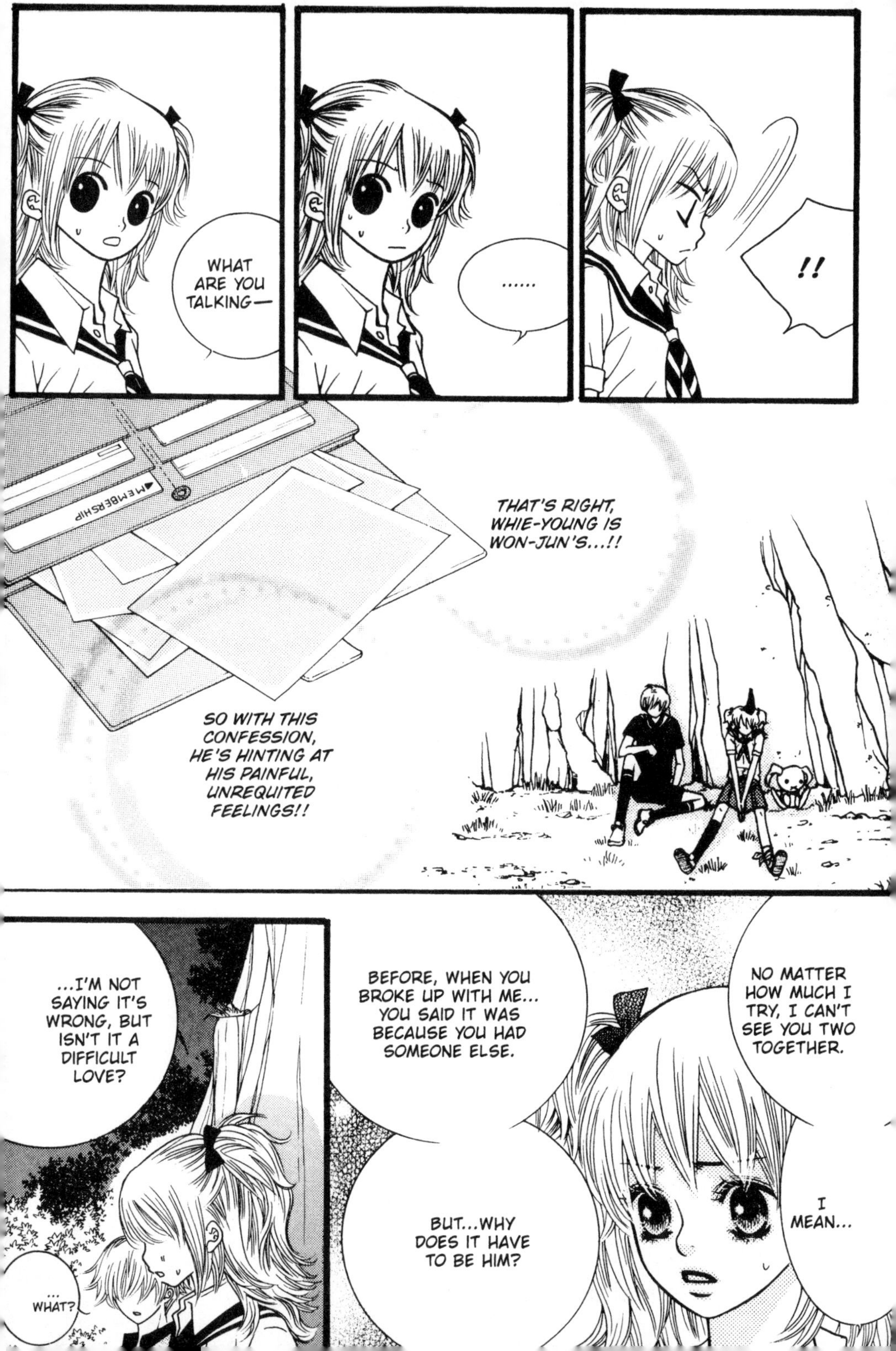

WHAT ARE YOU TALKING—
......
!!
THAT'S RIGHT, WHIE-YOUNG IS WON-JUN'S...!!
SO WITH THIS CONFESSION, HE'S HINTING AT HIS PAINFUL, UNREQUITED FEELINGS!!
MEMBERSHIP
...I'M NOT SAYING IT'S WRONG, BUT ISN'T IT A DIFFICULT LOVE?
...WHAT?
BEFORE, WHEN YOU BROKE UP WITH ME... YOU SAID IT WAS BECAUSE YOU HAD SOMEONE ELSE.
BUT...WHY DOES IT HAVE TO BE HIM?
NO MATTER HOW MUCH I TRY, I CAN'T SEE YOU TWO TOGETHER.
I MEAN...

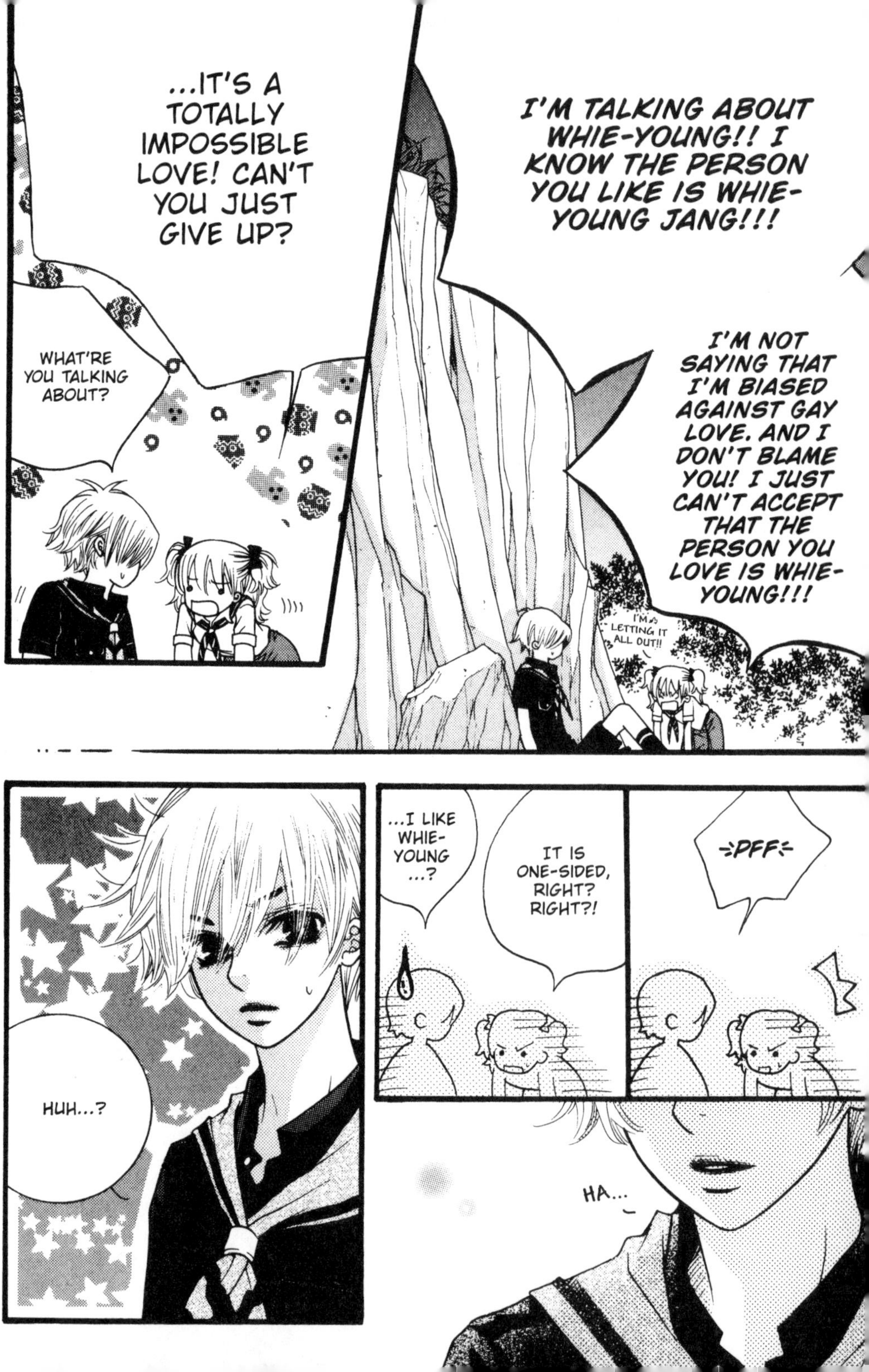
...IT'S A TOTALLY IMPOSSIBLE LOVE! CAN'T YOU JUST GIVE UP?
WHAT'RE YOU TALKING ABOUT?
I'M TALKING ABOUT WHIE-YOUNG!! I KNOW THE PERSON YOU LIKE IS WHIE-YOUNG JANG!!!
I'M NOT SAYING THAT I'M BIASED AGAINST GAY LOVE. AND I DON'T BLAME YOU! I JUST CAN'T ACCEPT THAT THE PERSON YOU LOVE IS WHIE-YOUNG!!!
I'M LETTING IT ALL OUT!!
HUH...?
...I LIKE WHIE-YOUNG ...?
IT IS ONE-SIDED, RIGHT? RIGHT?!
PFF
HA...

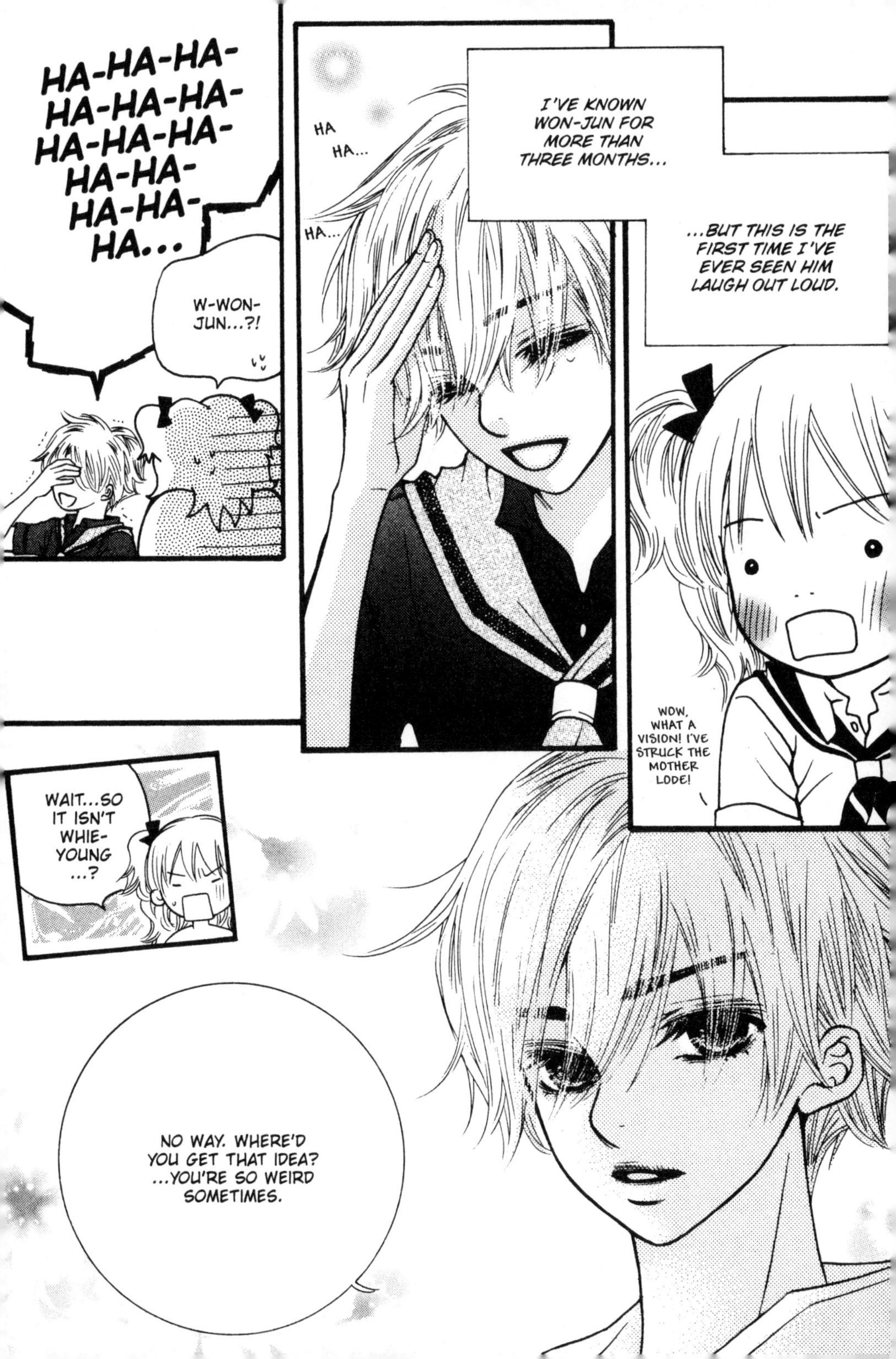
HA-HA-HA-HA-HA-HA-HA-HA-HA-HA-HA-HA-HA-HA...
W-WON-JUN...?!
HA HA...
HA...
I'VE KNOWN WON-JUN FOR MORE THAN THREE MONTHS...
...BUT THIS IS THE FIRST TIME I'VE EVER SEEN HIM LAUGH OUT LOUD.
WOW, WHAT A VISION! I'VE STRUCK THE MOTHER LODE!
WAIT...SO IT ISN'T WHIE-YOUNG...?
NO WAY. WHERE'D YOU GET THAT IDEA? ...YOU'RE SO WEIRD SOMETIMES.

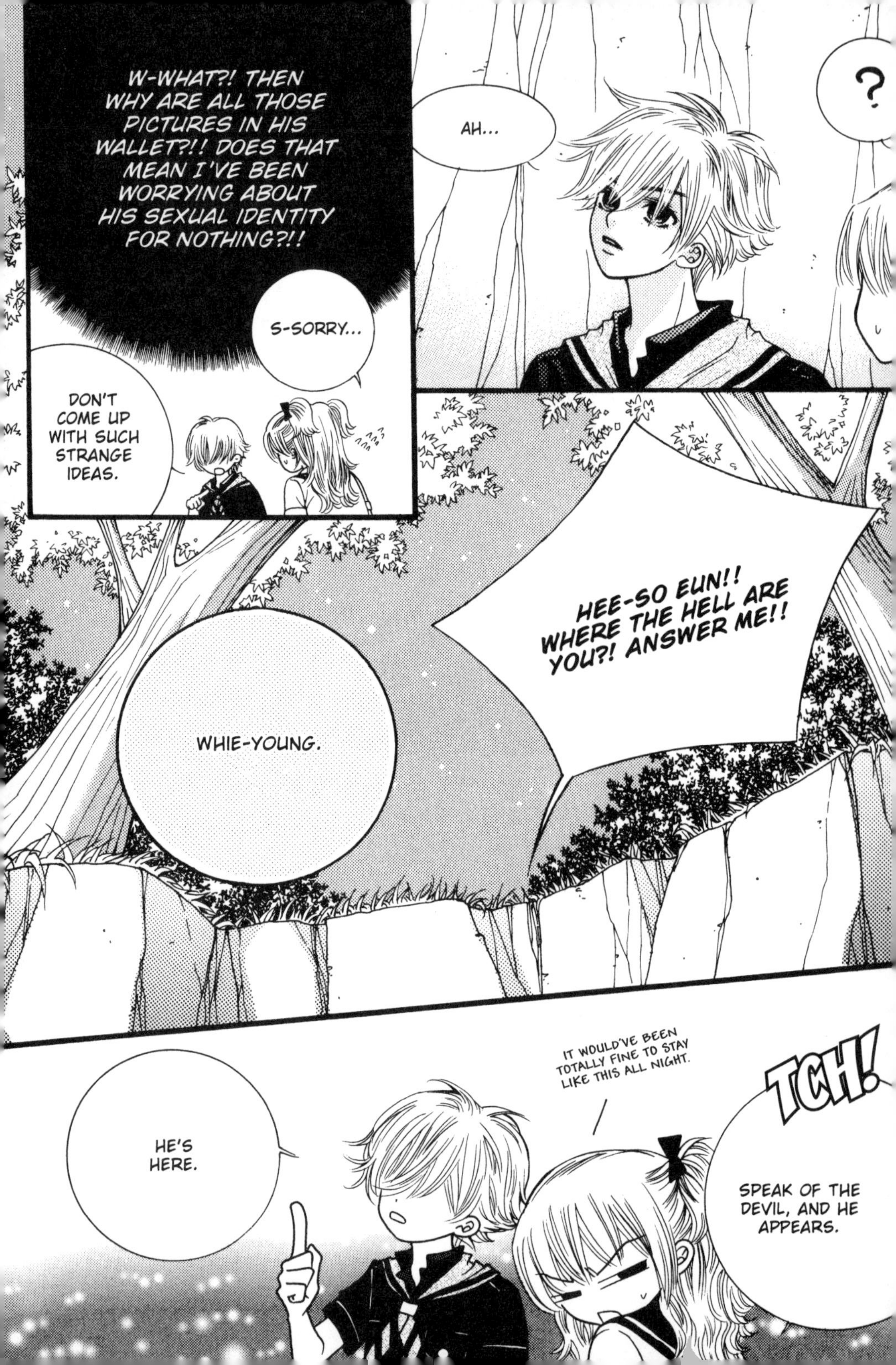
W-WHAT?! THEN WHY ARE ALL THOSE PICTURES IN HIS WALLET?!! DOES THAT MEAN I'VE BEEN WORRYING ABOUT HIS SEXUAL IDENTITY FOR NOTHING?!!
S-SORRY...
DON'T COME UP WITH SUCH STRANGE IDEAS.
AH...
?
WHIE-YOUNG.
HEE-SO EUN!! WHERE THE HELL ARE YOU?! ANSWER ME!!
HE'S HERE.
IT WOULD'VE BEEN TOTALLY FINE TO STAY LIKE THIS ALL NIGHT.
TCH!
SPEAK OF THE DEVIL, AND HE APPEARS.

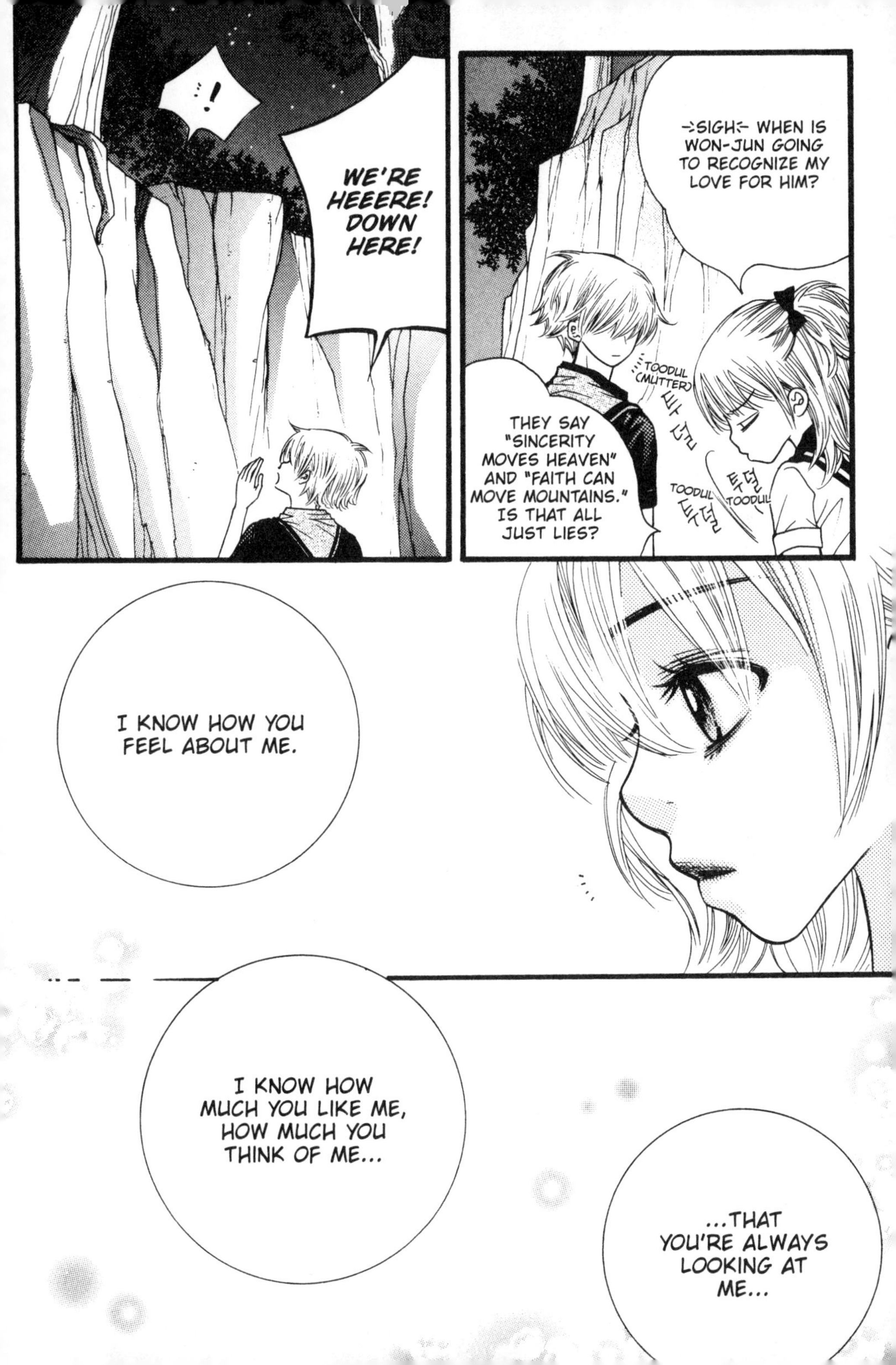

!
WE'RE HEEERE! DOWN HERE!
-SIGH- WHEN IS WON-JUN GOING TO RECOGNIZE MY LOVE FOR HIM?
TOODUL (MUTTER)
THEY SAY "SINCERITY MOVES HEAVEN" AND "FAITH CAN MOVE MOUNTAINS." IS THAT ALL JUST LIES?
TOODUL TOODUL
I KNOW HOW YOU FEEL ABOUT ME.
I KNOW HOW MUCH YOU LIKE ME, HOW MUCH YOU THINK OF ME...
...THAT YOU'RE ALWAYS LOOKING AT ME...

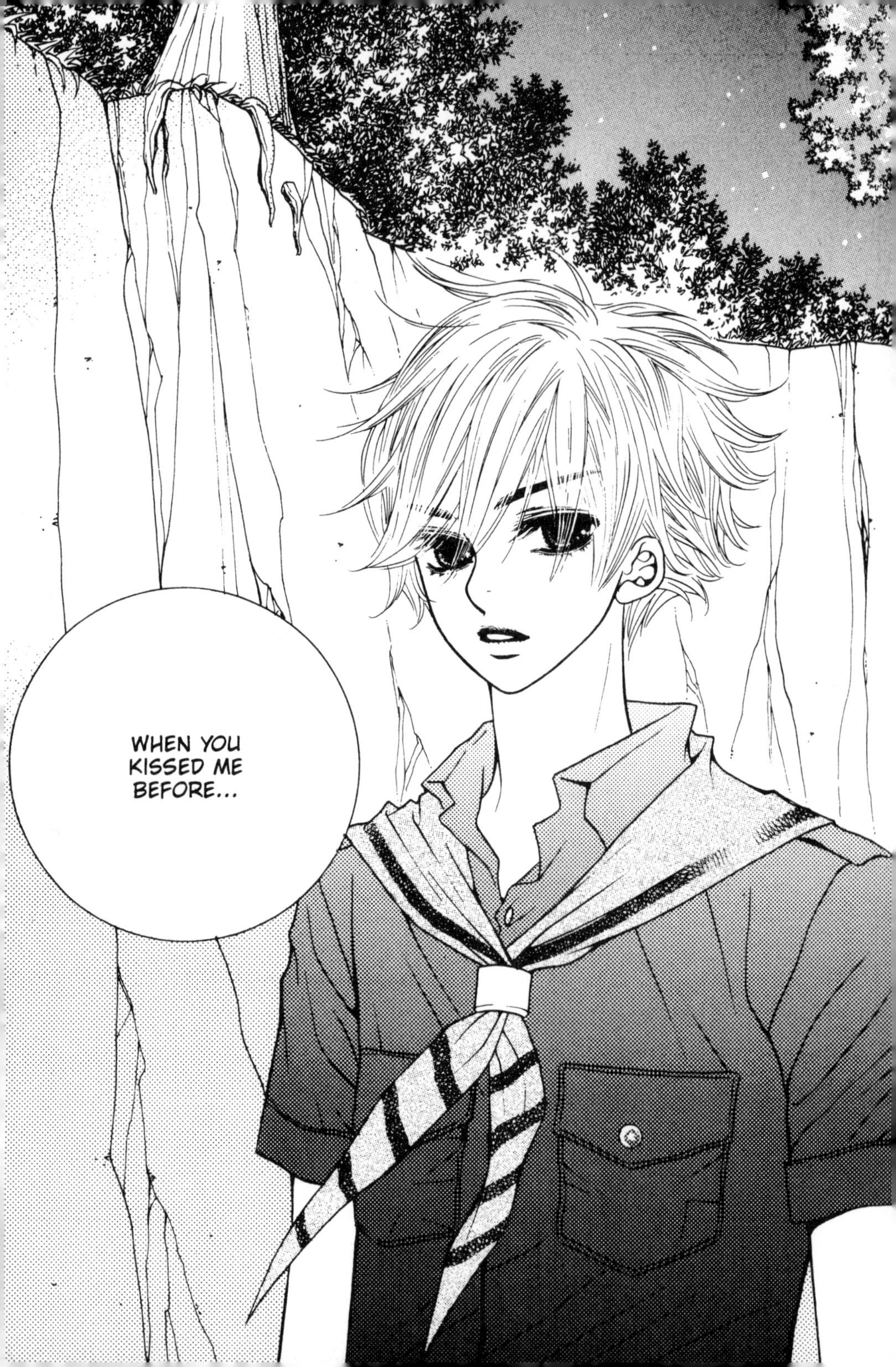
WHEN YOU KISSED ME BEFORE...

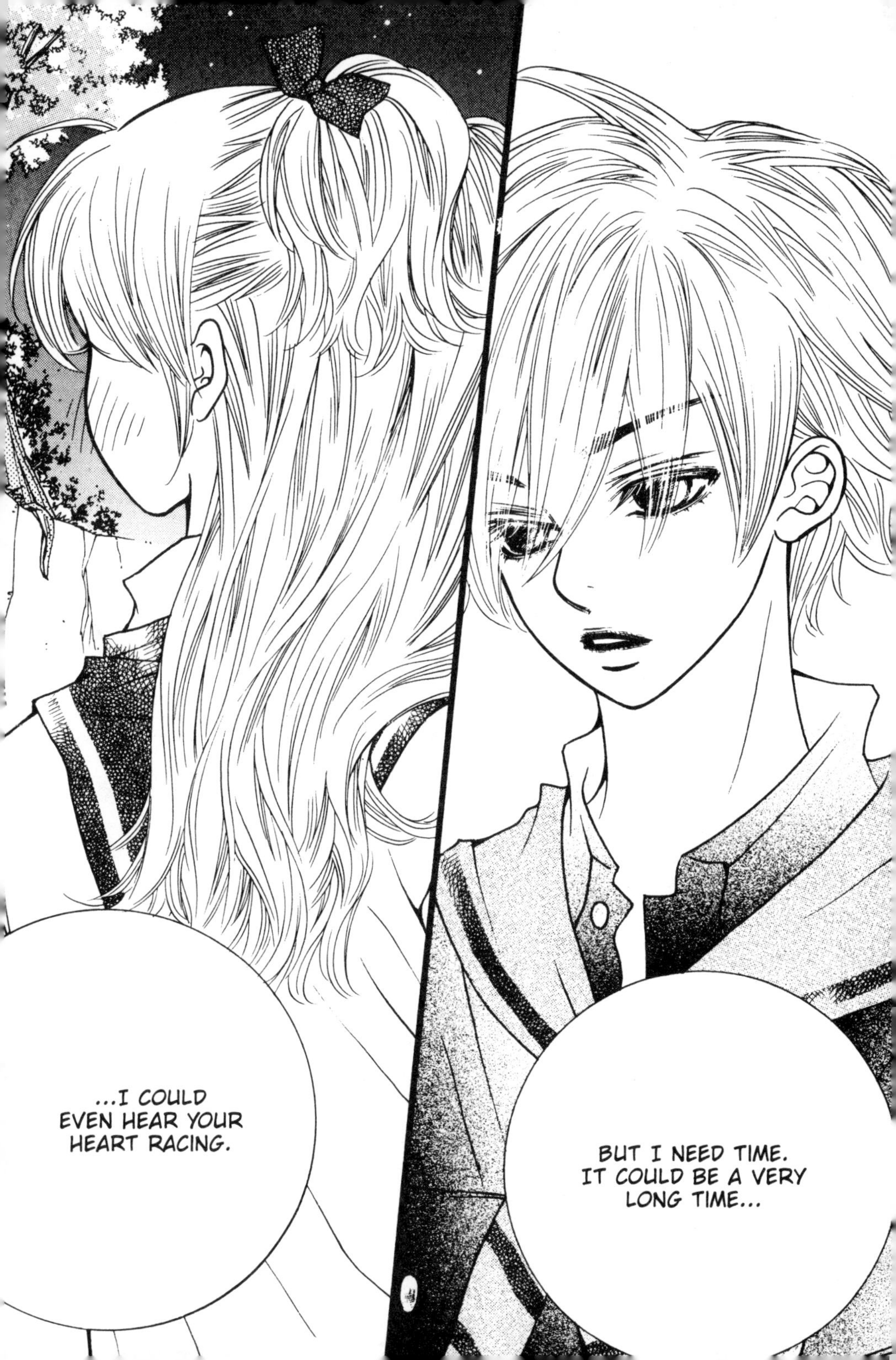
...I COULD EVEN HEAR YOUR HEART RACING.
BUT I NEED TIME. IT COULD BE A VERY LONG TIME...

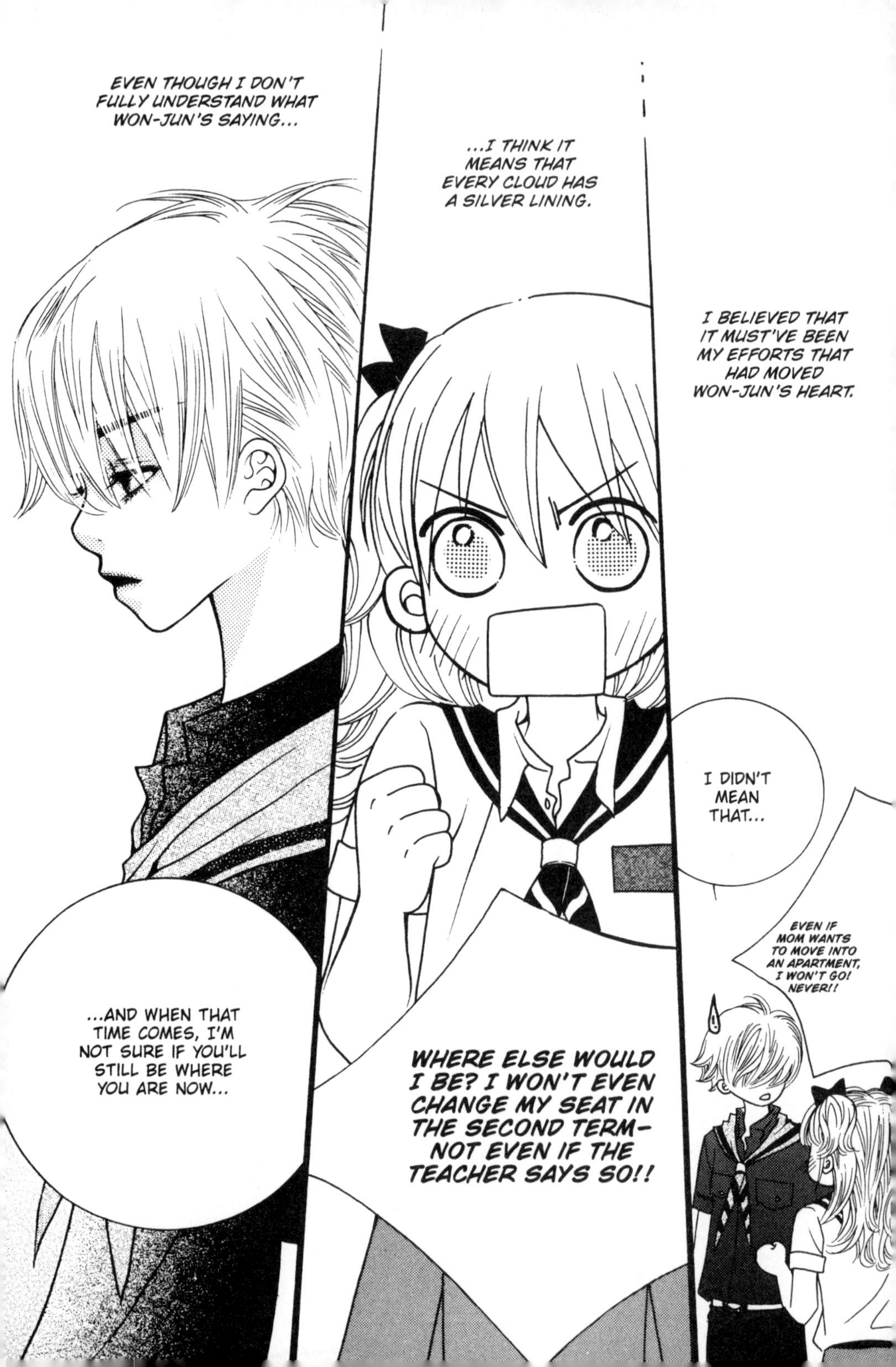
EVEN THOUGH I DON'T FULLY UNDERSTAND WHAT WON-JUN'S SAYING...
...AND WHEN THAT TIME COMES, I'M NOT SURE IF YOU'LL STILL BE WHERE YOU ARE NOW...
...I THINK IT MEANS THAT EVERY CLOUD HAS A SILVER LINING.
WHERE ELSE WOULD I BE? I WON'T EVEN CHANGE MY SEAT IN THE SECOND TERM-NOT EVEN IF THE TEACHER SAYS SO!!
I BELIEVED THAT IT MUST'VE BEEN MY EFFORTS THAT HAD MOVED WON-JUN'S HEART.
I DIDN'T MEAN THAT...
EVEN IF MOM WANTS TO MOVE INTO AN APARTMENT, I WON'T GO! NEVER!!

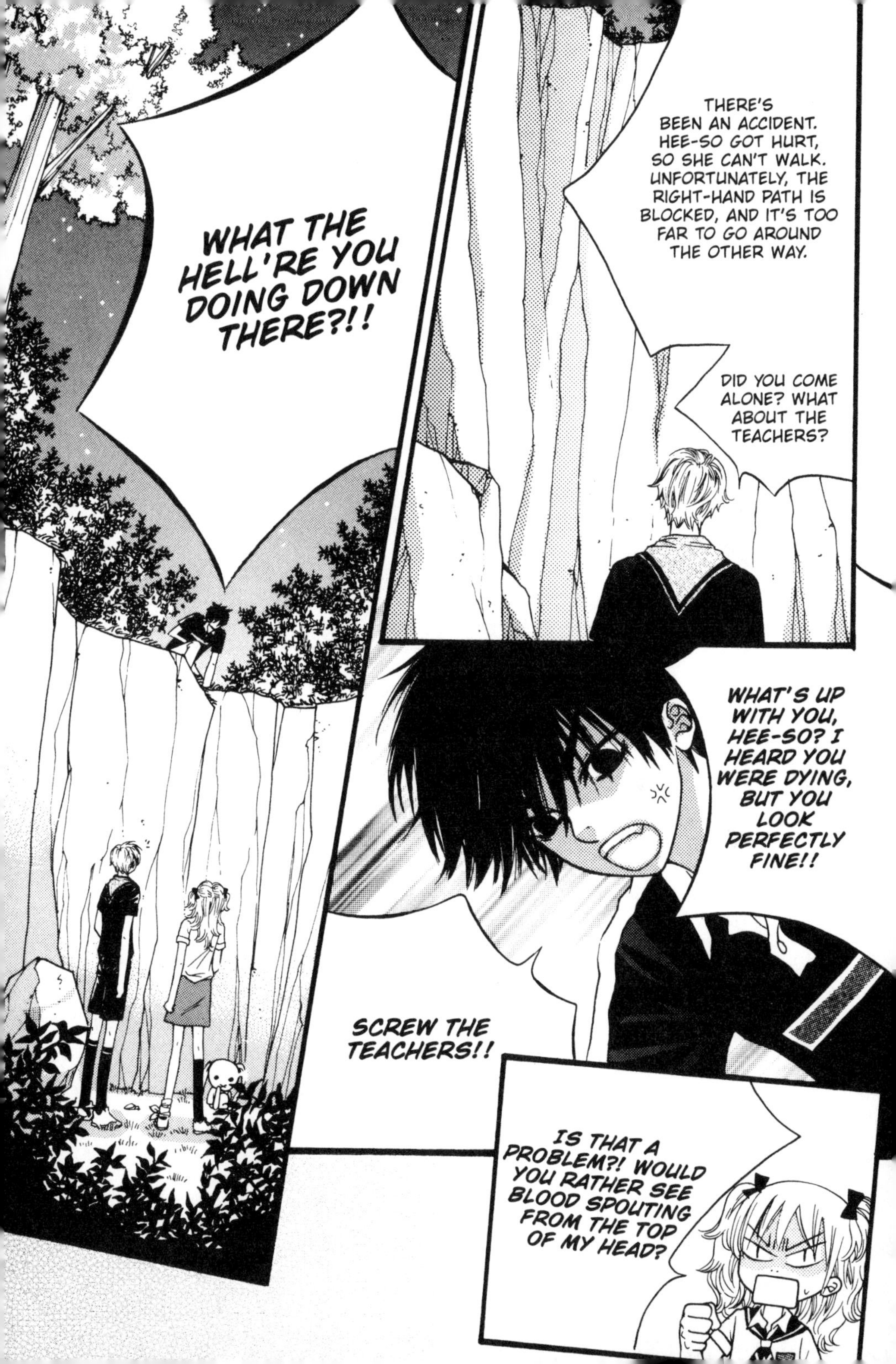
WHAT THE HELL'RE YOU DOING DOWN THERE?!!
THERE'S BEEN AN ACCIDENT. HEE-SO GOT HURT, SO SHE CAN'T WALK. UNFORTUNATELY, THE RIGHT-HAND PATH IS BLOCKED, AND IT'S TOO FAR TO GO AROUND THE OTHER WAY.
DID YOU COME ALONE? WHAT ABOUT THE TEACHERS?
WHAT'S UP WITH YOU, HEE-SO? I HEARD YOU WERE DYING, BUT YOU LOOK PERFECTLY FINE!!
SCREW THE TEACHERS!!
IS THAT A PROBLEM?! WOULD YOU RATHER SEE BLOOD SPOUTING FROM THE TOP OF MY HEAD?

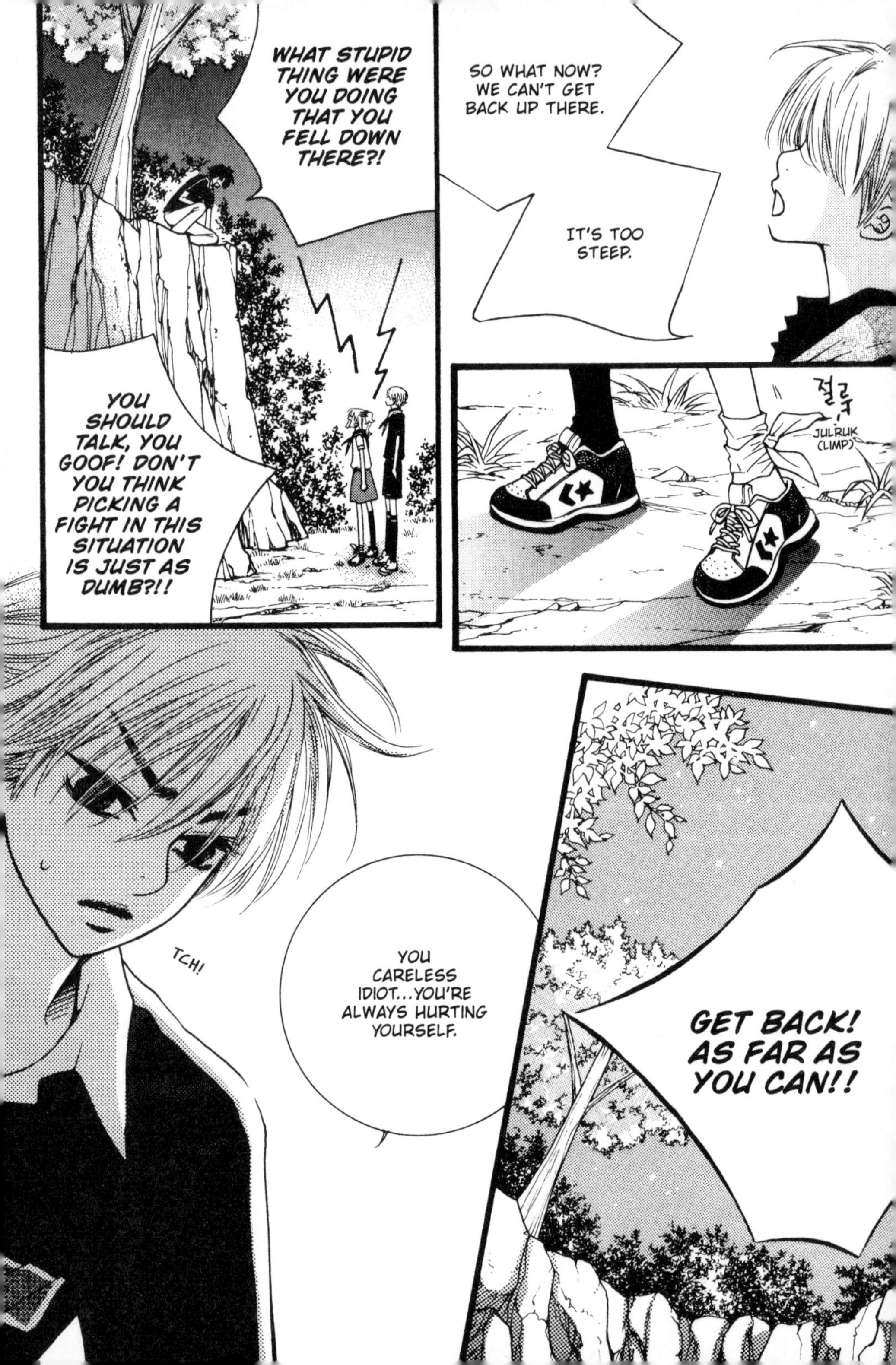
WHAT STUPID THING WERE YOU DOING THAT YOU FELL DOWN THERE?!
YOU SHOULD TALK, YOU GOOF! DON'T YOU THINK PICKING A FIGHT IN THIS SITUATION IS JUST AS DUMB?!!
SO WHAT NOW? WE CAN'T GET BACK UP THERE.
IT'S TOO STEEP.
절뚝
JULRUK (LIMP)
TCH!
YOU CARELESS IDIOT...YOU'RE ALWAYS HURTING YOURSELF.
GET BACK! AS FAR AS YOU CAN!!

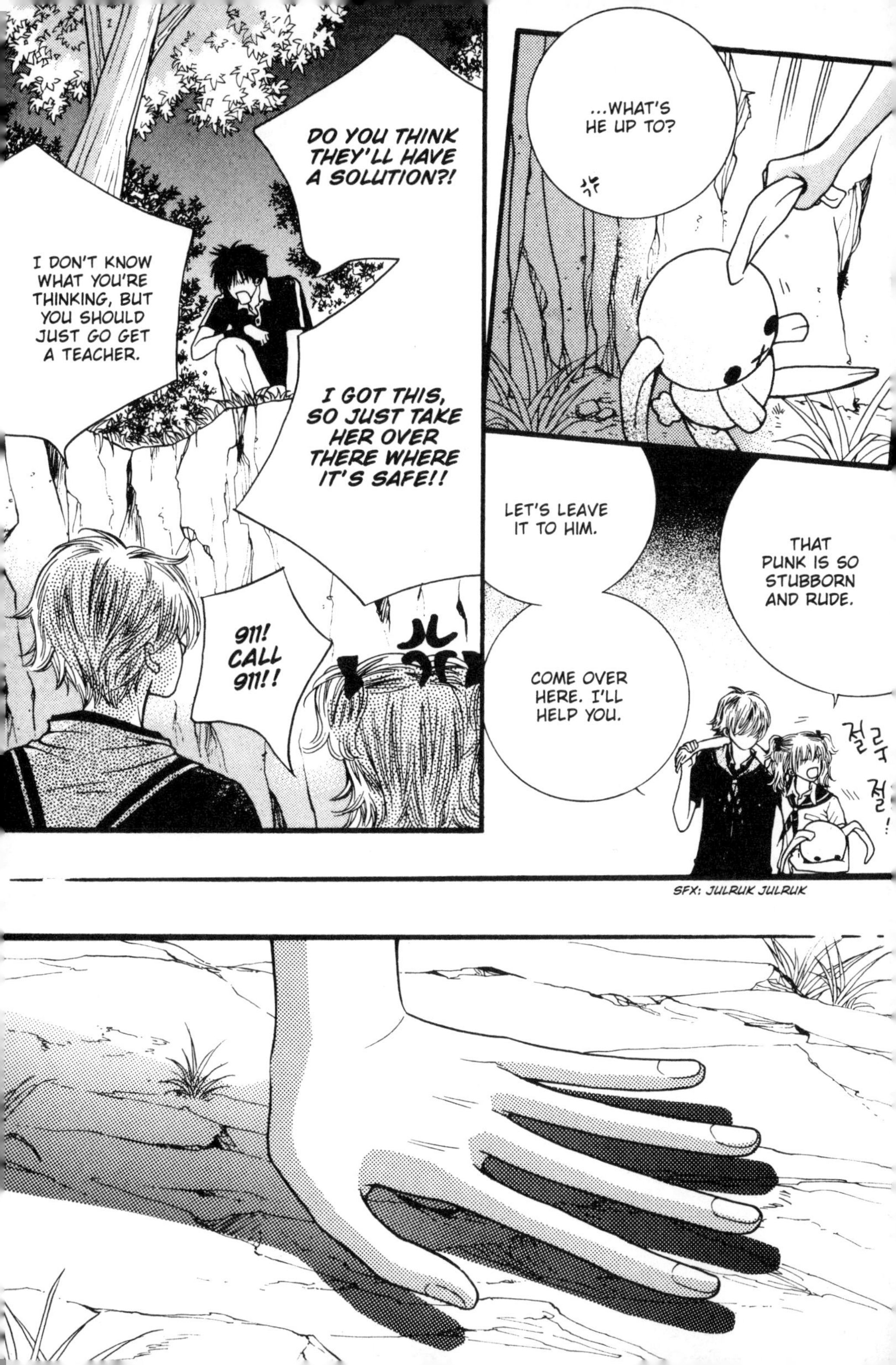
DO YOU THINK THEY'LL HAVE A SOLUTION?!
I DON'T KNOW WHAT YOU'RE THINKING, BUT YOU SHOULD JUST GO GET A TEACHER.
I GOT THIS, SO JUST TAKE HER OVER THERE WHERE IT'S SAFE!!
911! CALL 911!!
...WHAT'S HE UP TO?
LET'S LEAVE IT TO HIM.
THAT PUNK IS SO STUBBORN AND RUDE.
COME OVER HERE. I'LL HELP YOU.
절룩 절!
SFX: JULRUK JULRUK

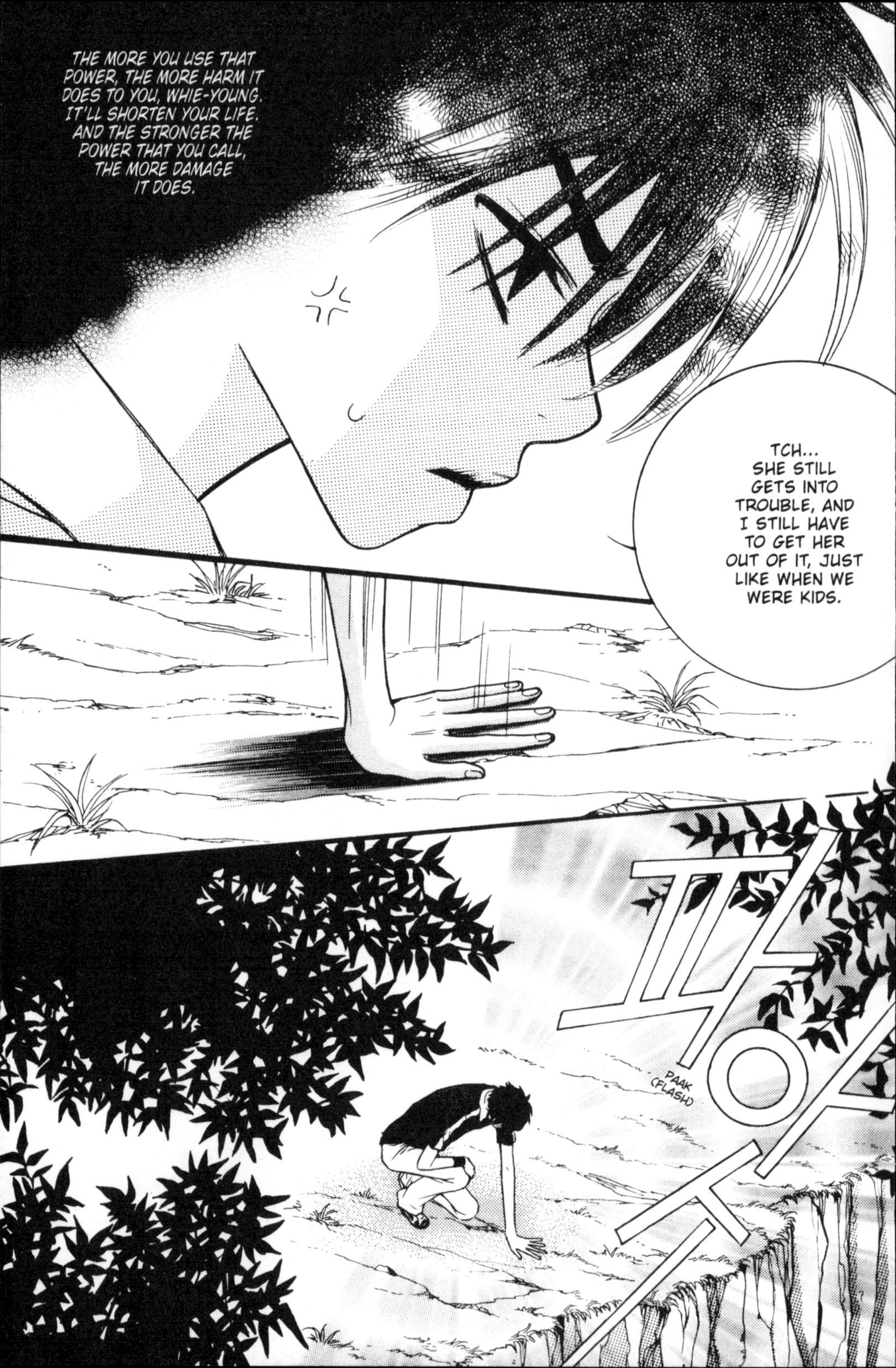
THE MORE YOU USE THAT POWER, THE MORE HARM IT DOES TO YOU, WHIE-YOUNG. IT'LL SHORTEN YOUR LIFE. AND THE STRONGER THE POWER THAT YOU CALL, THE MORE DAMAGE IT DOES.
TCH... SHE STILL GETS INTO TROUBLE, AND I STILL HAVE TO GET HER OUT OF IT, JUST LIKE WHEN WE WERE KIDS.
PAAK (FLASH)

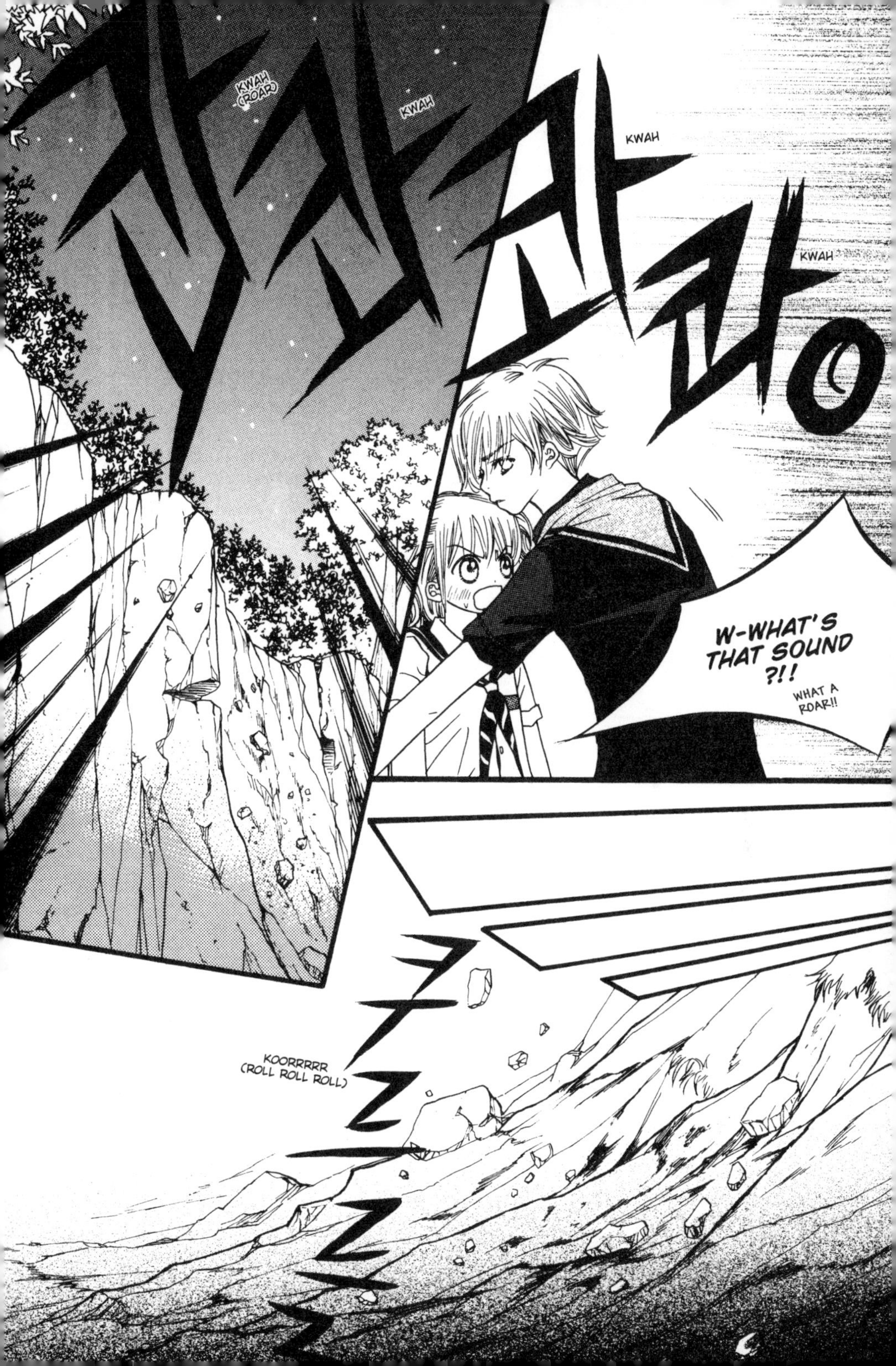
KWAH (ROAR)
KWAH
KWAH
KWAH
W-WHAT'S THAT SOUND ?!!
WHAT A ROAR!!
KOORRRRR (ROLL ROLL ROLL)

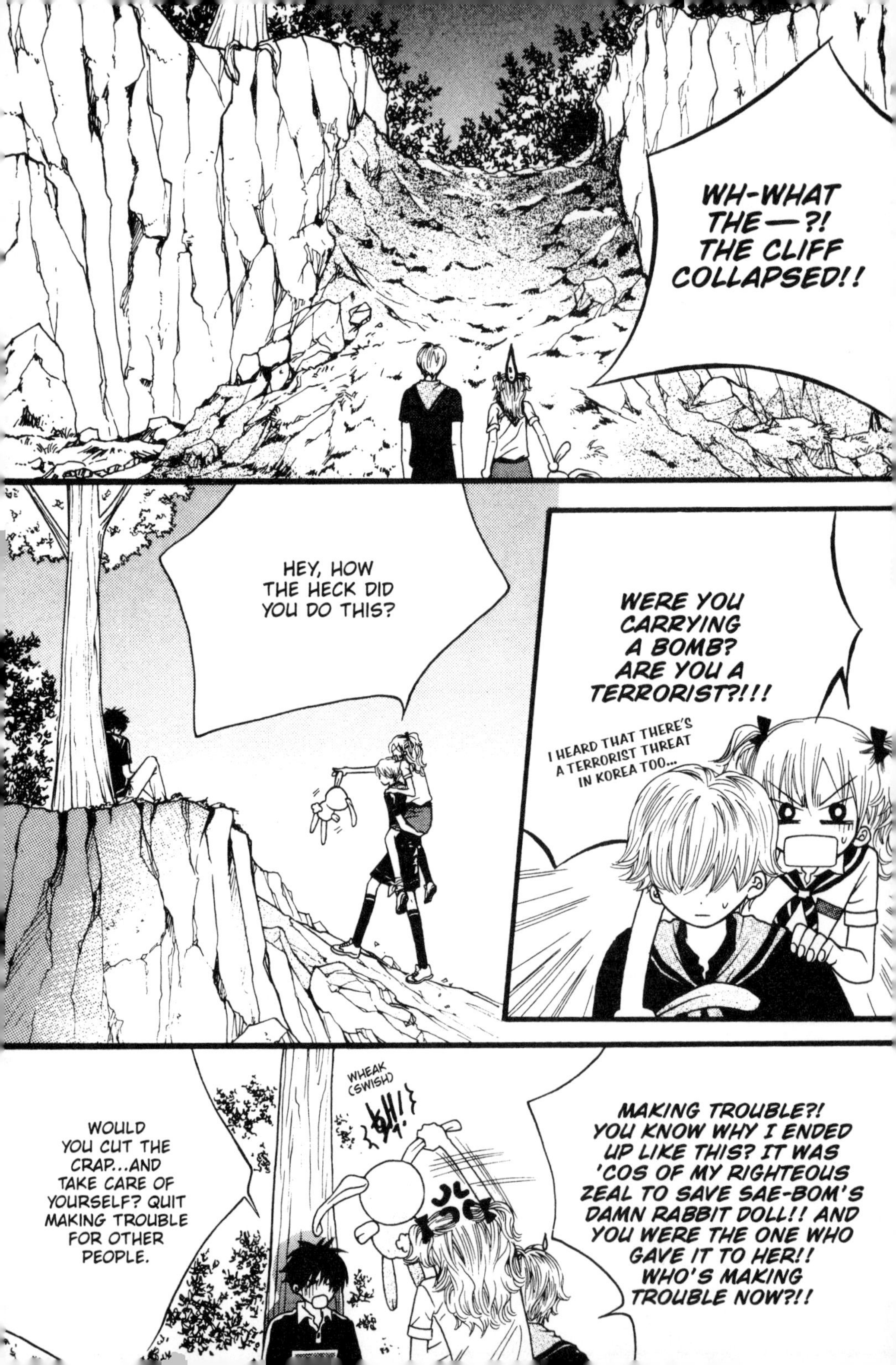
WH-WHAT THE—?! THE CLIFF COLLAPSED!!
HEY, HOW THE HECK DID YOU DO THIS?
WERE YOU CARRYING A BOMB? ARE YOU A TERRORIST?!!!
I HEARD THAT THERE'S A TERRORIST THREAT IN KOREA TOO...
WOULD YOU CUT THE CRAP...AND TAKE CARE OF YOURSELF? QUIT MAKING TROUBLE FOR OTHER PEOPLE.
WHEAK (SWISH)
MAKING TROUBLE?! YOU KNOW WHY I ENDED UP LIKE THIS? IT WAS 'COS OF MY RIGHTEOUS ZEAL TO SAVE SAE-BOM'S DAMN RABBIT DOLL!! AND YOU WERE THE ONE WHO GAVE IT TO HER!! WHO'S MAKING TROUBLE NOW?!!

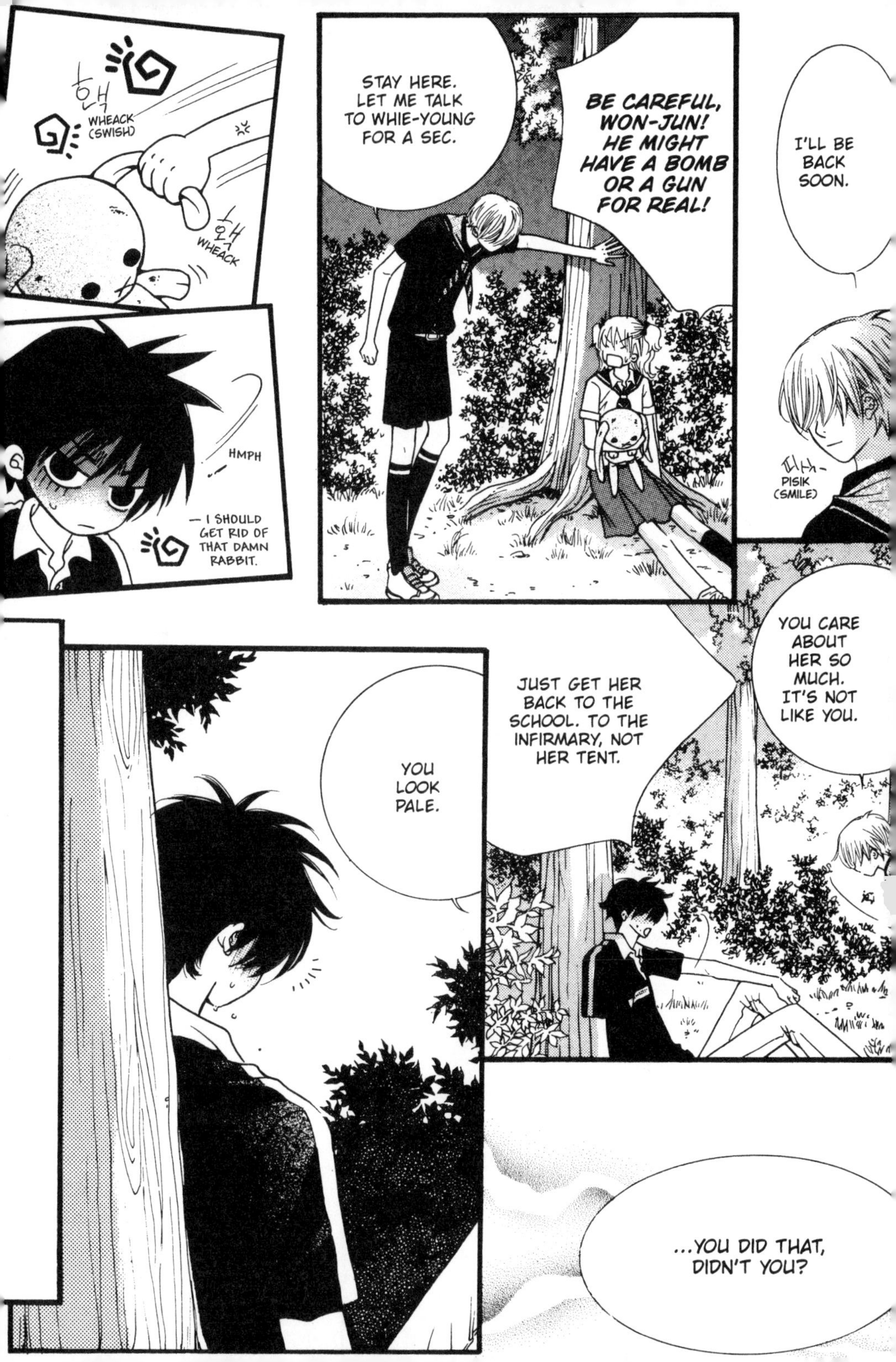
WHEACK (SWISH)
WHEACK
HMPH
— I SHOULD GET RID OF THAT DAMN RABBIT.
STAY HERE. LET ME TALK TO WHIE-YOUNG FOR A SEC.
BE CAREFUL, WON-JUN! HE MIGHT HAVE A BOMB OR A GUN FOR REAL!
I'LL BE BACK SOON.
PISIK (SMILE)
YOU LOOK PALE.
JUST GET HER BACK TO THE SCHOOL. TO THE INFIRMARY, NOT HER TENT.
YOU CARE ABOUT HER SO MUCH. IT'S NOT LIKE YOU.
...YOU DID THAT, DIDN'T YOU?

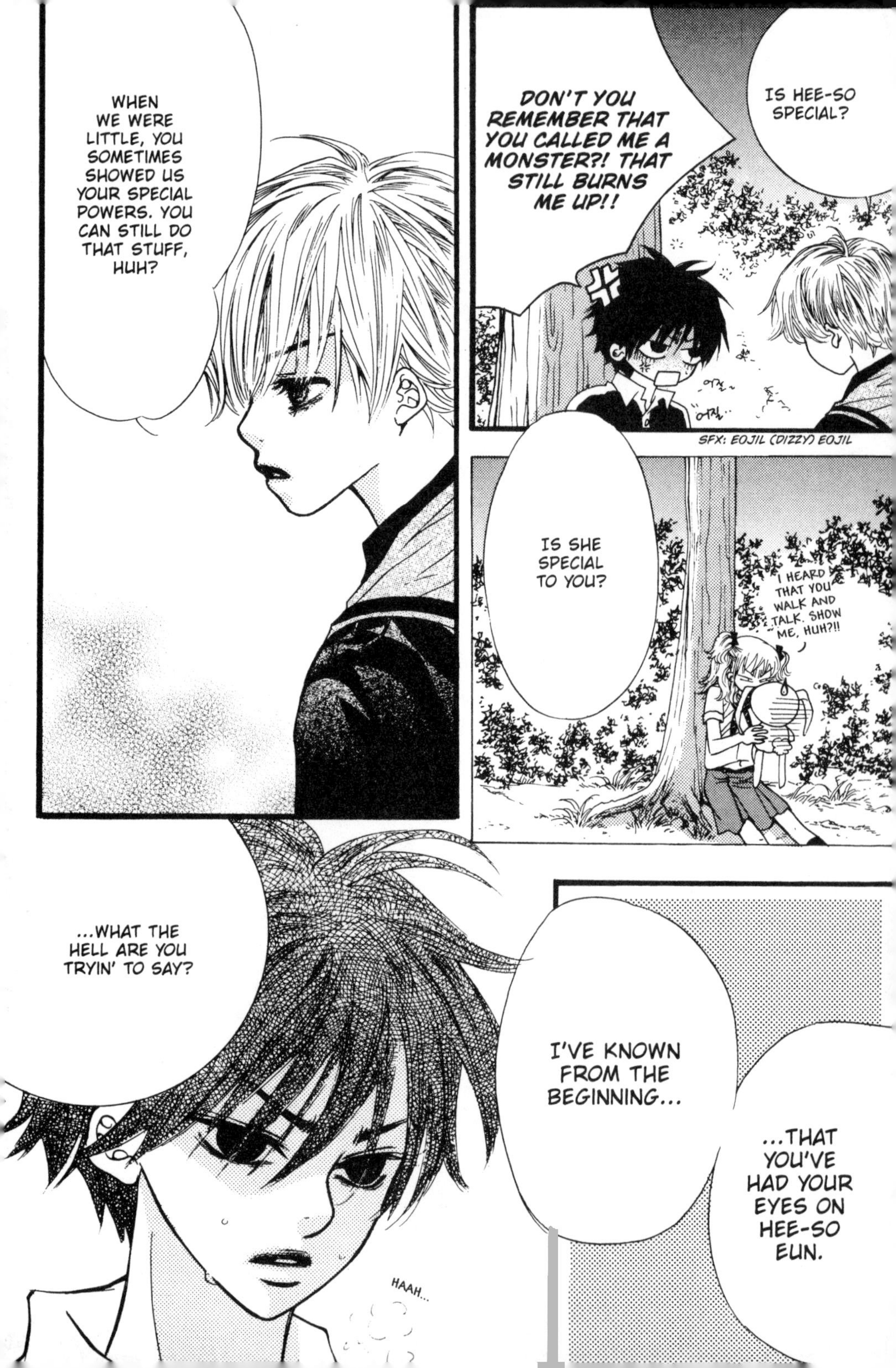
WHEN WE WERE LITTLE, YOU SOMETIMES SHOWED US YOUR SPECIAL POWERS. YOU CAN STILL DO THAT STUFF, HUH?
DON'T YOU REMEMBER THAT YOU CALLED ME A MONSTER?! THAT STILL BURNS ME UP!!
IS HEE-SO SPECIAL?
어질
어질..
SFX: EOJIL (DIZZY) EOJIL
IS SHE SPECIAL TO YOU?
I HEARD THAT YOU WALK AND TALK. SHOW ME, HUH?!!
...WHAT THE HELL ARE YOU TRYIN' TO SAY?
HAAH...
I'VE KNOWN FROM THE BEGINNING...
...THAT YOU'VE HAD YOUR EYES ON HEE-SO EUN.

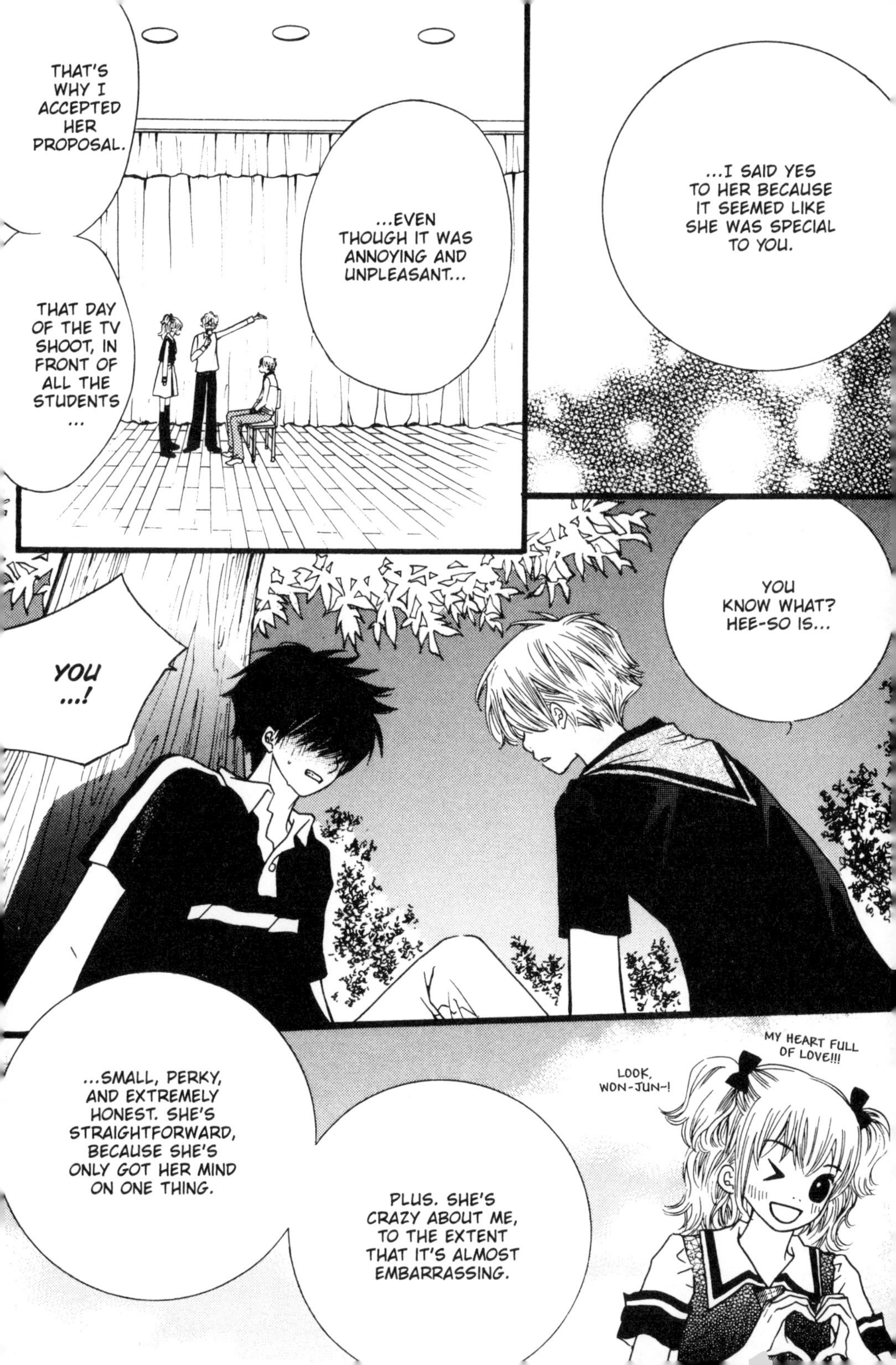
THAT'S WHY I ACCEPTED HER PROPOSAL.
THAT DAY OF THE TV SHOOT, IN FRONT OF ALL THE STUDENTS ...
...EVEN THOUGH IT WAS ANNOYING AND UNPLEASANT...
...I SAID YES TO HER BECAUSE IT SEEMED LIKE SHE WAS SPECIAL TO YOU.
YOU ...!
YOU KNOW WHAT? HEE-SO IS...
...SMALL, PERKY, AND EXTREMELY HONEST. SHE'S STRAIGHTFORWARD, BECAUSE SHE'S ONLY GOT HER MIND ON ONE THING.
PLUS. SHE'S CRAZY ABOUT ME, TO THE EXTENT THAT IT'S ALMOST EMBARRASSING.
LOOK, WON-JUN~!
MY HEART FULL OF LOVE!!!

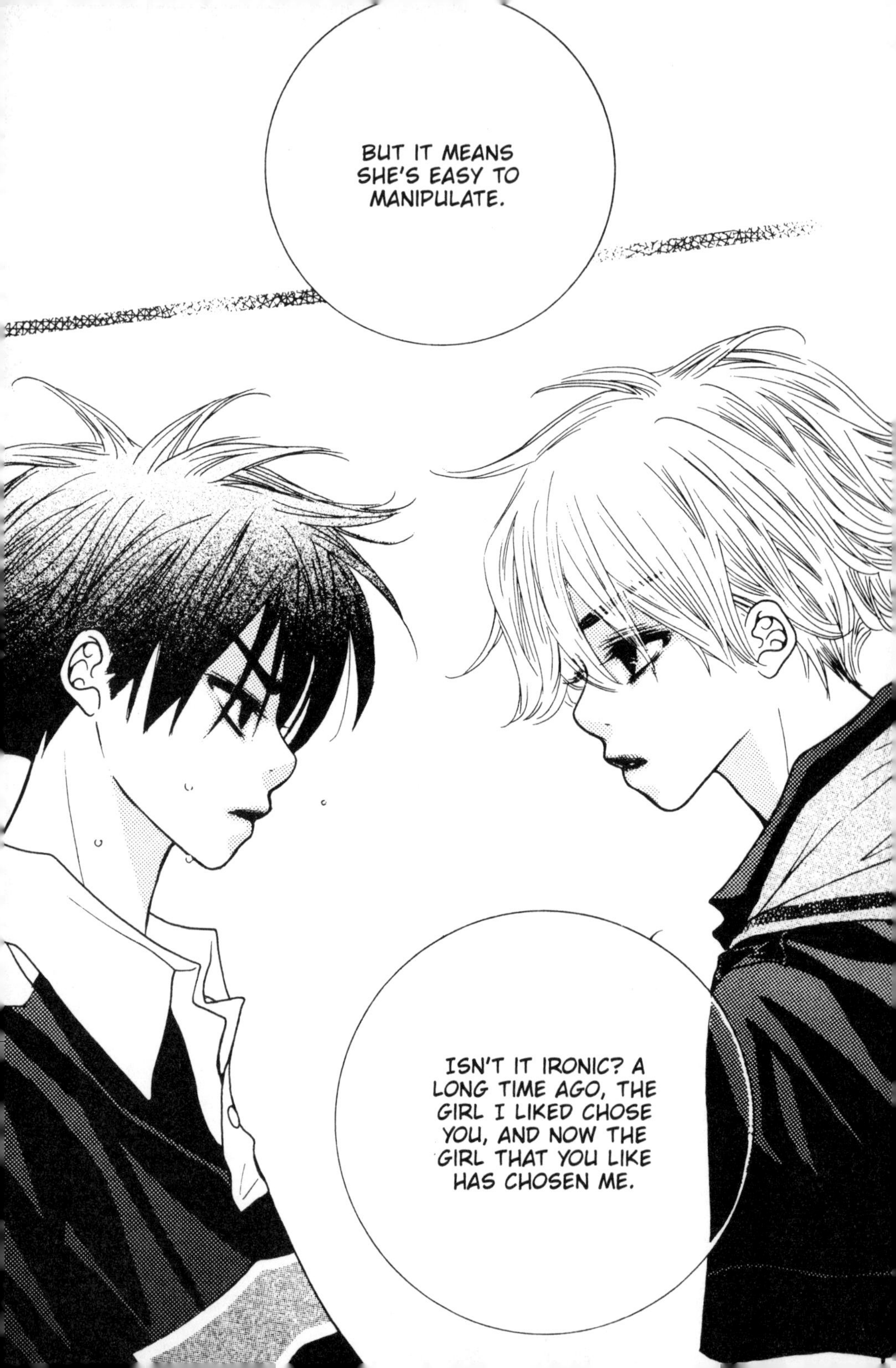
BUT IT MEANS SHE'S EASY TO MANIPULATE.
ISN'T IT IRONIC? A LONG TIME AGO, THE GIRL I LIKED CHOSE YOU, AND NOW THE GIRL THAT YOU LIKE HAS CHOSEN ME.

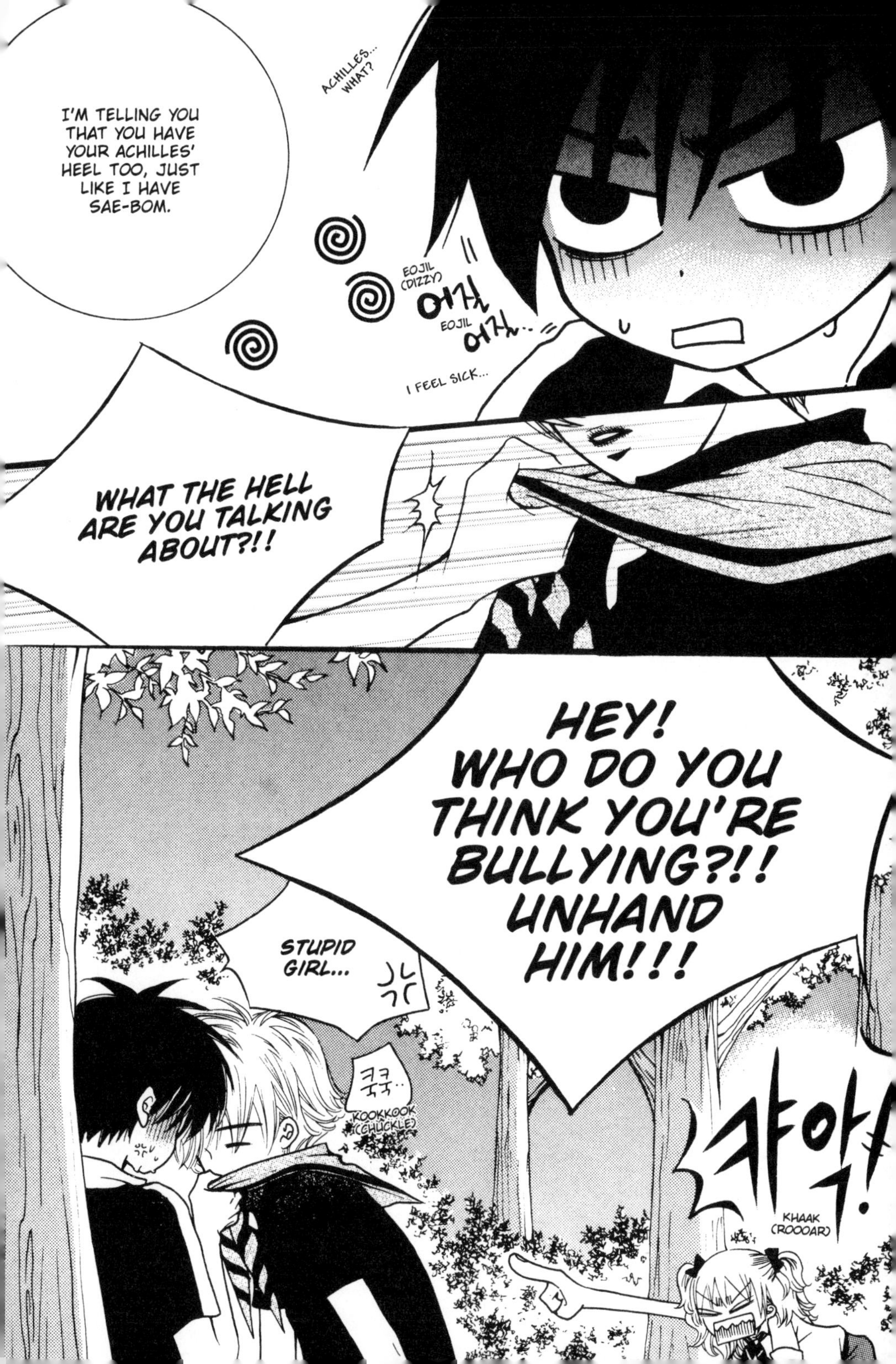
I'M TELLING YOU THAT YOU HAVE YOUR ACHILLES' HEEL TOO, JUST LIKE I HAVE SAE-BOM.
ACHILLES... WHAT?
EOJIL (DIZZY)
어질
EOJIL
어질...
I FEEL SICK...
WHAT THE HELL ARE YOU TALKING ABOUT?!!
HEY! WHO DO YOU THINK YOU'RE BULLYING?!! UNHAND HIM!!!
STUPID GIRL...
쿡쿡..
KOOKKOOK (CHUCKLE)
캬악!
KHAAK (ROOOAR)

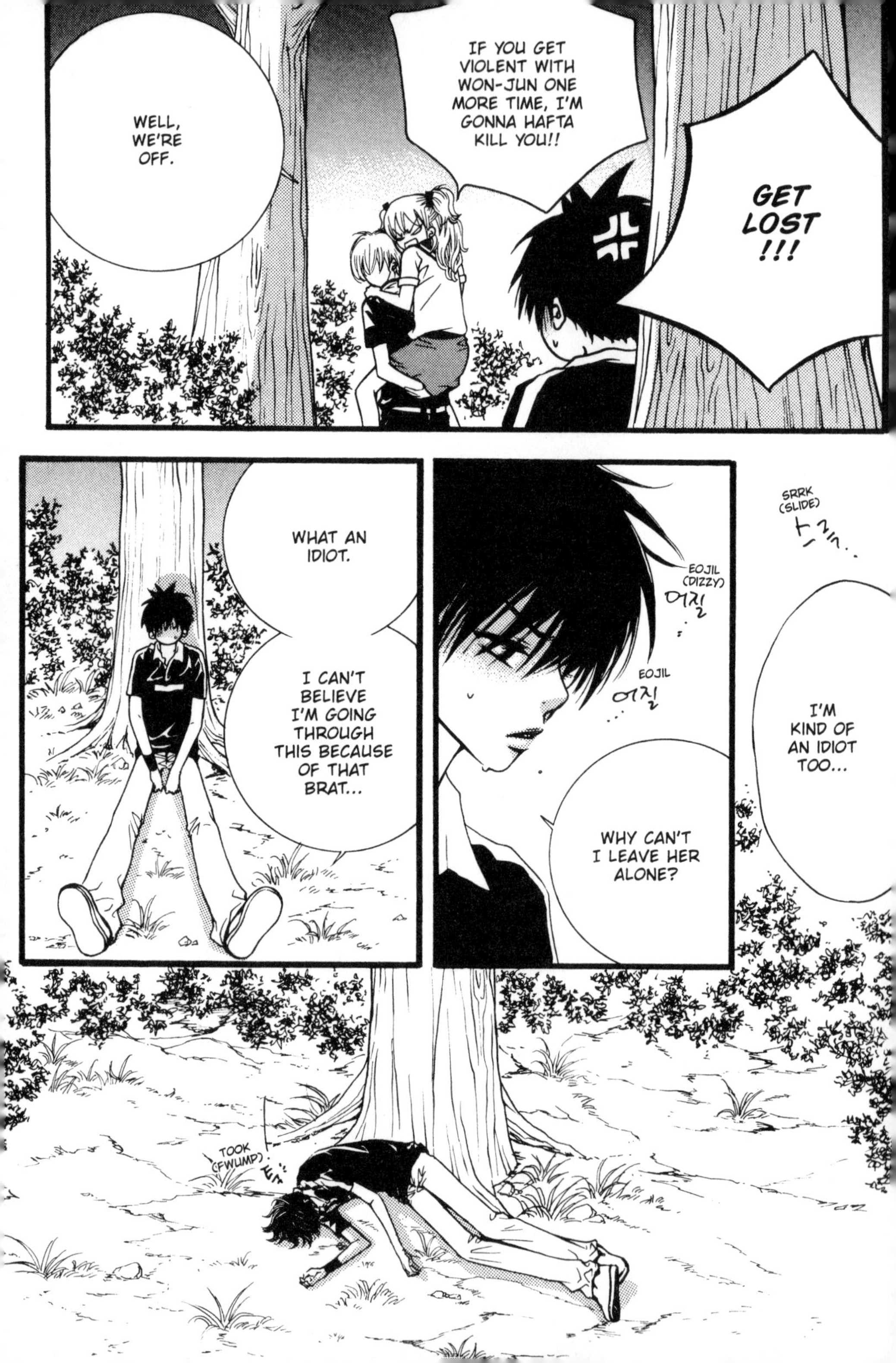
WELL, WE'RE OFF.
IF YOU GET VIOLENT WITH WON-JUN ONE MORE TIME, I'M GONNA HAFTA KILL YOU!!
GET LOST !!!
WHAT AN IDIOT.
I CAN'T BELIEVE I'M GOING THROUGH THIS BECAUSE OF THAT BRAT...
EOJIL (DIZZY)
어질
EOJIL
어질
WHY CAN'T I LEAVE HER ALONE?
SRRK (SLIDE)
I'M KIND OF AN IDIOT TOO...
TOOK (FWUMP)

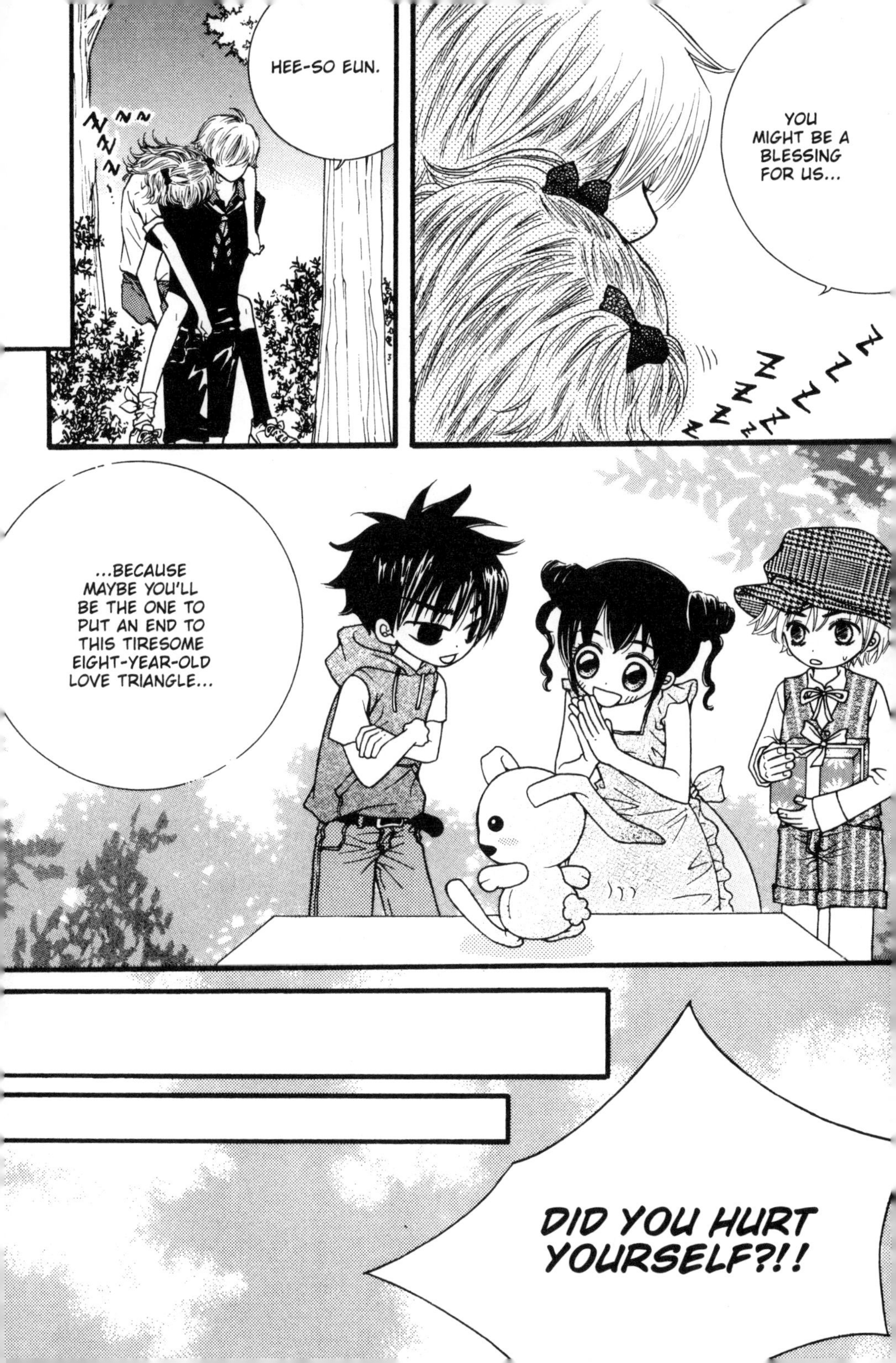
ZZZZ...
HEE-SO EUN.
YOU MIGHT BE A BLESSING FOR US...
ZZZZZZZZZZ
...BECAUSE MAYBE YOU'LL BE THE ONE TO PUT AN END TO THIS TIRESOME EIGHT-YEAR-OLD LOVE TRIANGLE...
DID YOU HURT YOURSELF?!!

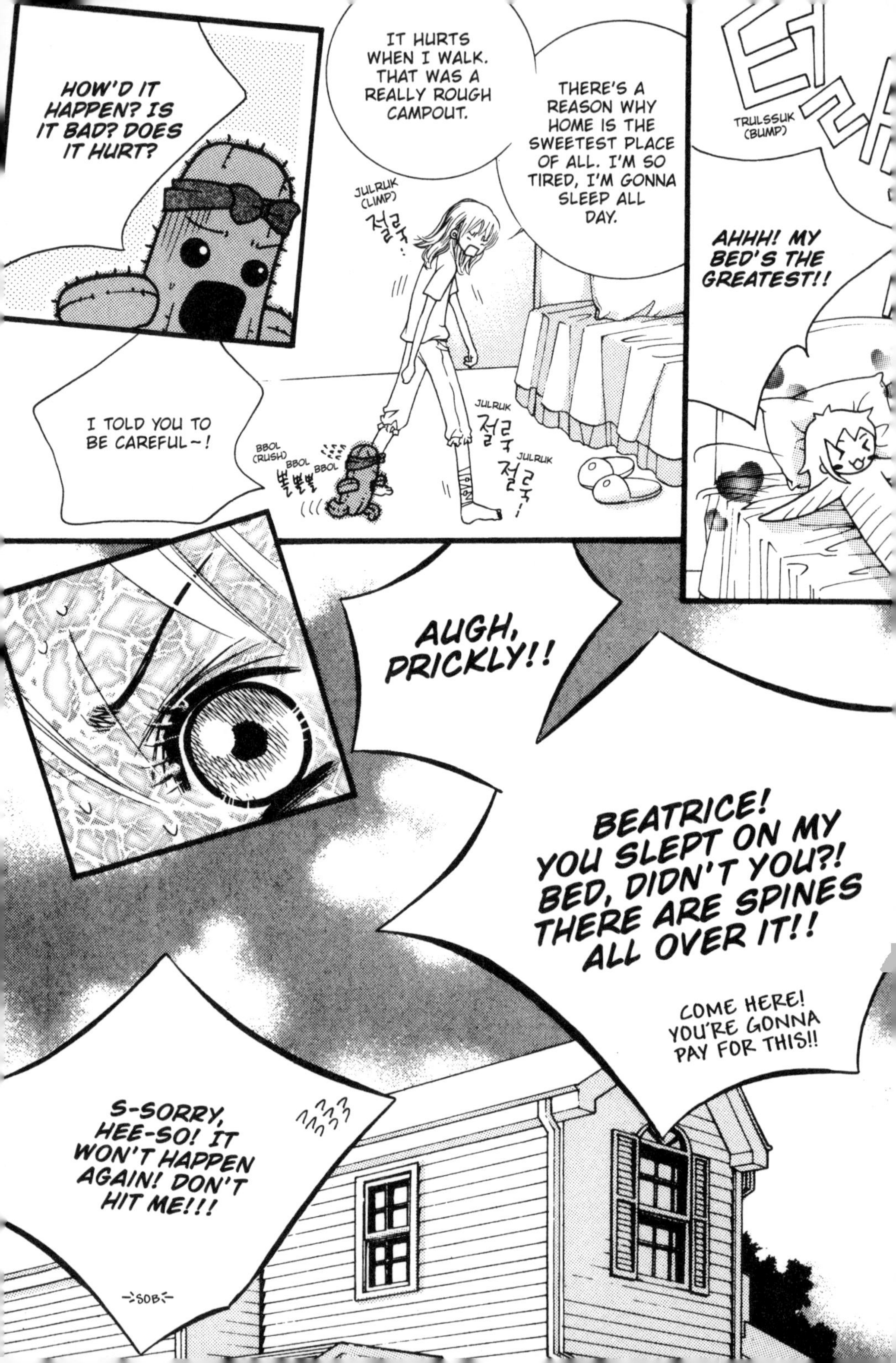
HOW'D IT HAPPEN? IS IT BAD? DOES IT HURT?
I TOLD YOU TO BE CAREFUL~!
IT HURTS WHEN I WALK. THAT WAS A REALLY ROUGH CAMPOUT.
THERE'S A REASON WHY HOME IS THE SWEETEST PLACE OF ALL. I'M SO TIRED, I'M GONNA SLEEP ALL DAY.
JULRUK (LIMP)
절룩
JULRUK
절룩
JULRUK
절룩
BBOL (RUSH) BBOL BBOL
뽈뽈뽈
TRULSSUK (BUMP)
털썩
AHHH! MY BED'S THE GREATEST!!
AUGH, PRICKLY!!
BEATRICE! YOU SLEPT ON MY BED, DIDN'T YOU?! THERE ARE SPINES ALL OVER IT!!
COME HERE! YOU'RE GONNA PAY FOR THIS!!
S-SORRY, HEE-SO! IT WON'T HAPPEN AGAIN! DON'T HIT ME!!!
SOB

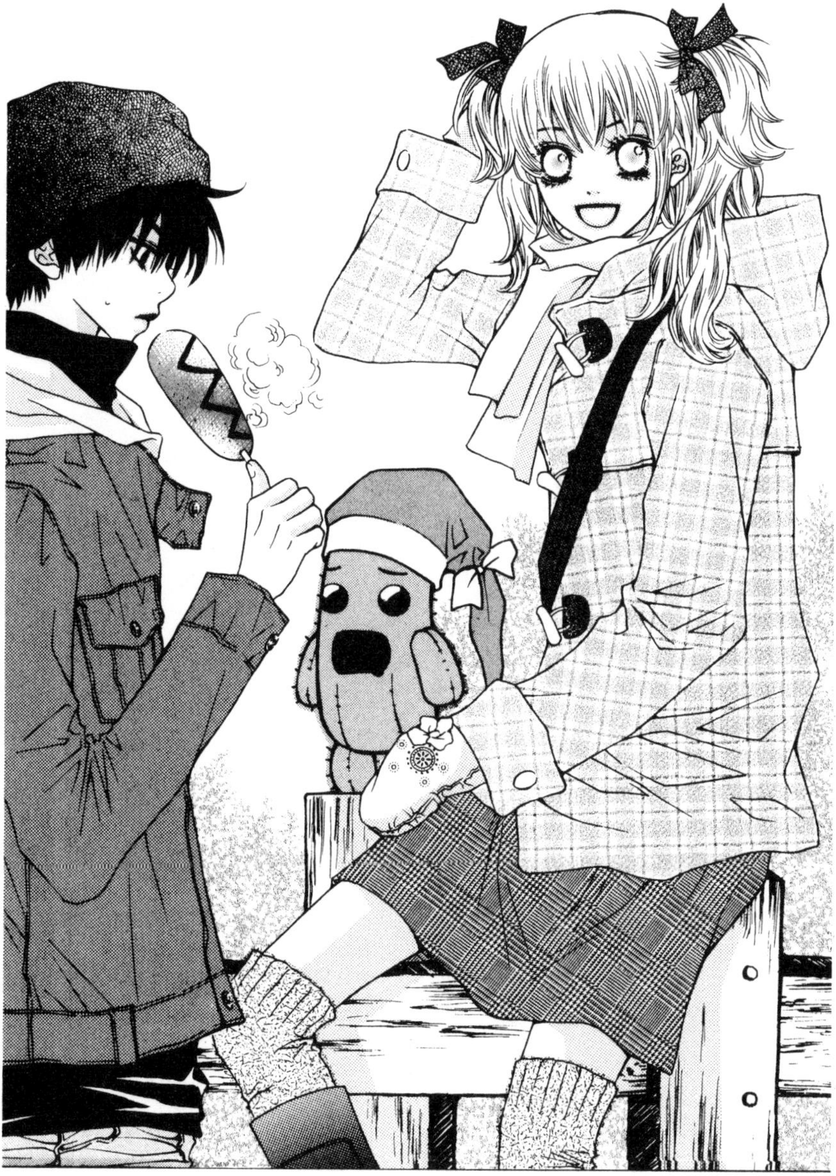

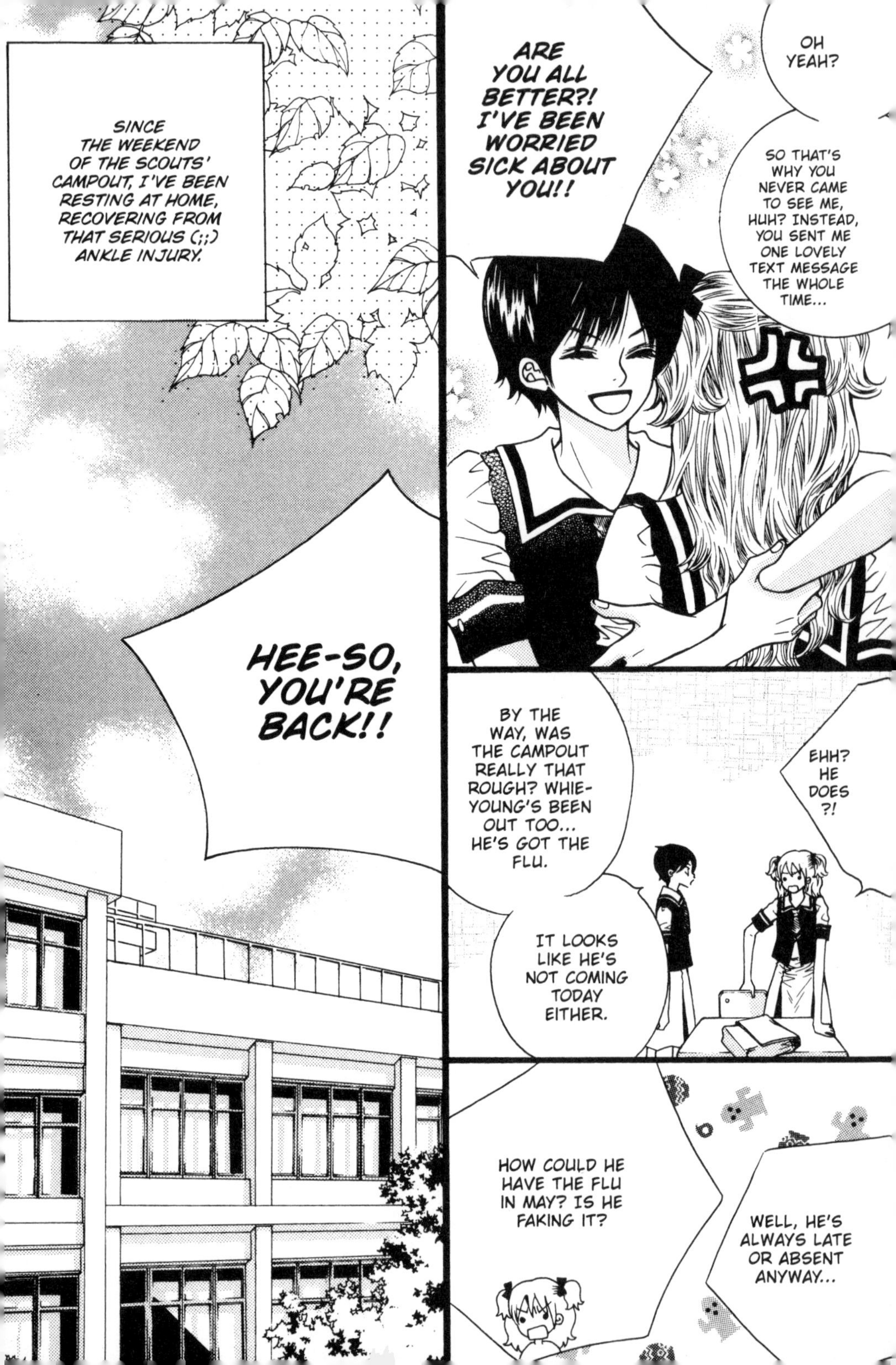
SINCE THE WEEKEND OF THE SCOUTS' CAMPOUT, I'VE BEEN RESTING AT HOME, RECOVERING FROM THAT SERIOUS (;;) ANKLE INJURY.
HEE-SO, YOU'RE BACK!!
ARE YOU ALL BETTER?! I'VE BEEN WORRIED SICK ABOUT YOU!!
OH YEAH?
SO THAT'S WHY YOU NEVER CAME TO SEE ME, HUH? INSTEAD, YOU SENT ME ONE LOVELY TEXT MESSAGE THE WHOLE TIME...
BY THE WAY, WAS THE CAMPOUT REALLY THAT ROUGH? WHIE-YOUNG'S BEEN OUT TOO... HE'S GOT THE FLU.
EHH? HE DOES?!
IT LOOKS LIKE HE'S NOT COMING TODAY EITHER.
HOW COULD HE HAVE THE FLU IN MAY? IS HE FAKING IT?
WELL, HE'S ALWAYS LATE OR ABSENT ANYWAY...

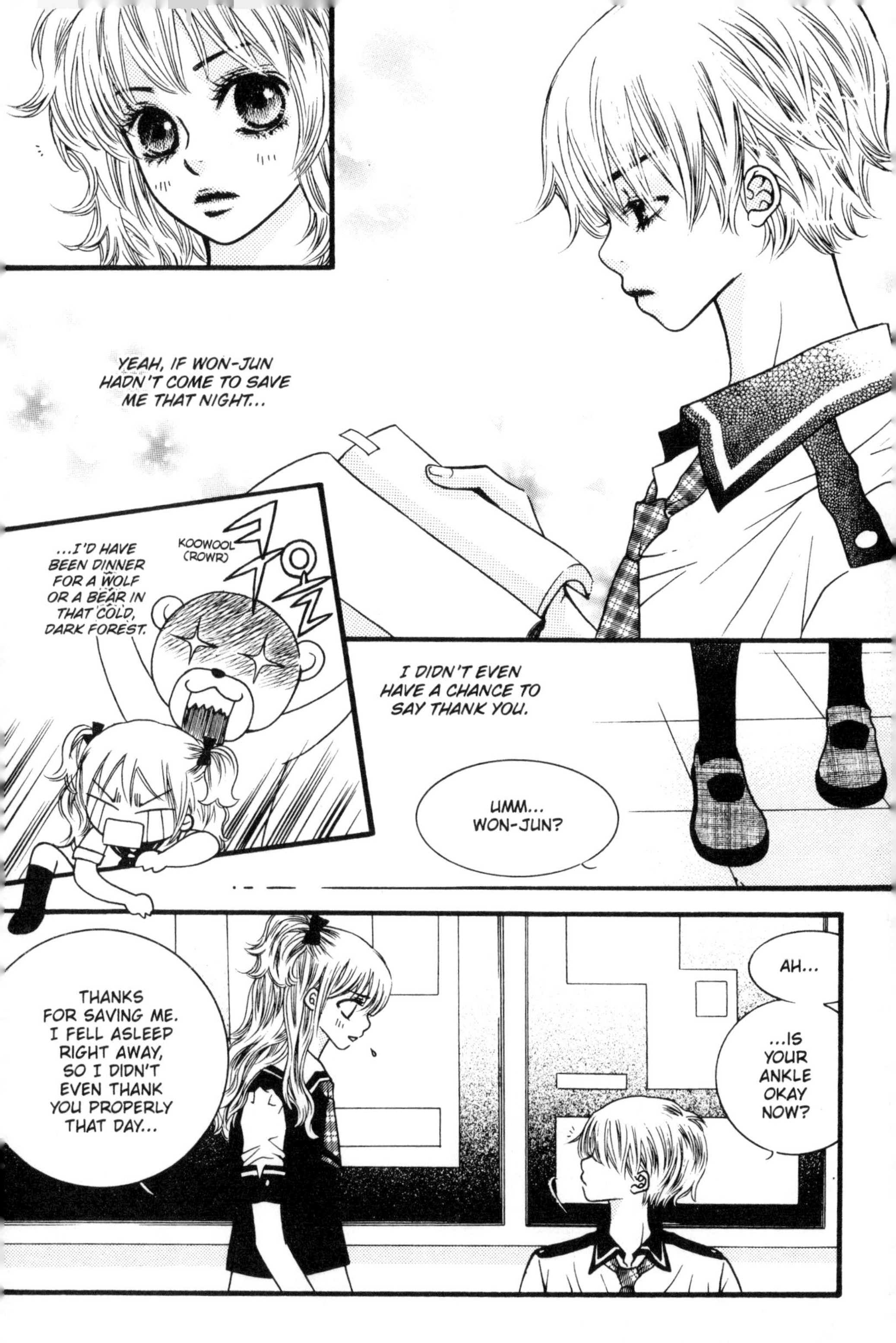
YEAH, IF WON-JUN HADN'T COME TO SAVE ME THAT NIGHT...
...I'D HAVE BEEN DINNER FOR A WOLF OR A BEAR IN THAT COLD, DARK FOREST.
KOOWOOL (ROWR)
I DIDN'T EVEN HAVE A CHANCE TO SAY THANK YOU.
UMM... WON-JUN?
THANKS FOR SAVING ME. I FELL ASLEEP RIGHT AWAY, SO I DIDN'T EVEN THANK YOU PROPERLY THAT DAY...
AH...
...IS YOUR ANKLE OKAY NOW?

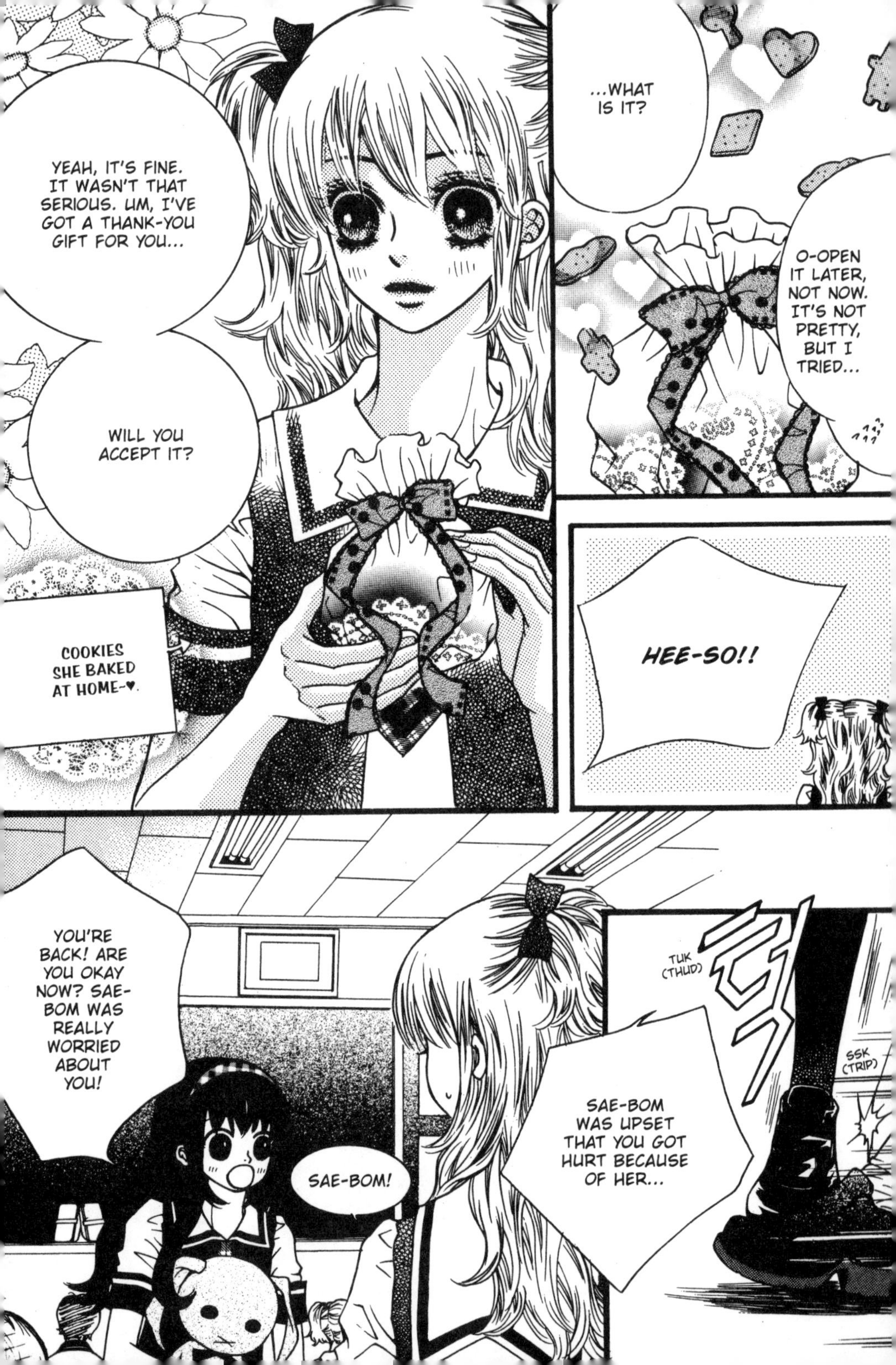
YEAH, IT'S FINE. IT WASN'T THAT SERIOUS. UM, I'VE GOT A THANK-YOU GIFT FOR YOU...
WILL YOU ACCEPT IT?
COOKIES SHE BAKED AT HOME-♥.
...WHAT IS IT?
O-OPEN IT LATER, NOT NOW. IT'S NOT PRETTY, BUT I TRIED...
HEE-SO!!
YOU'RE BACK! ARE YOU OKAY NOW? SAE-BOM WAS REALLY WORRIED ABOUT YOU!
SAE-BOM!
SAE-BOM WAS UPSET THAT YOU GOT HURT BECAUSE OF HER...
TUK (THUD)
SSK (TRIP)

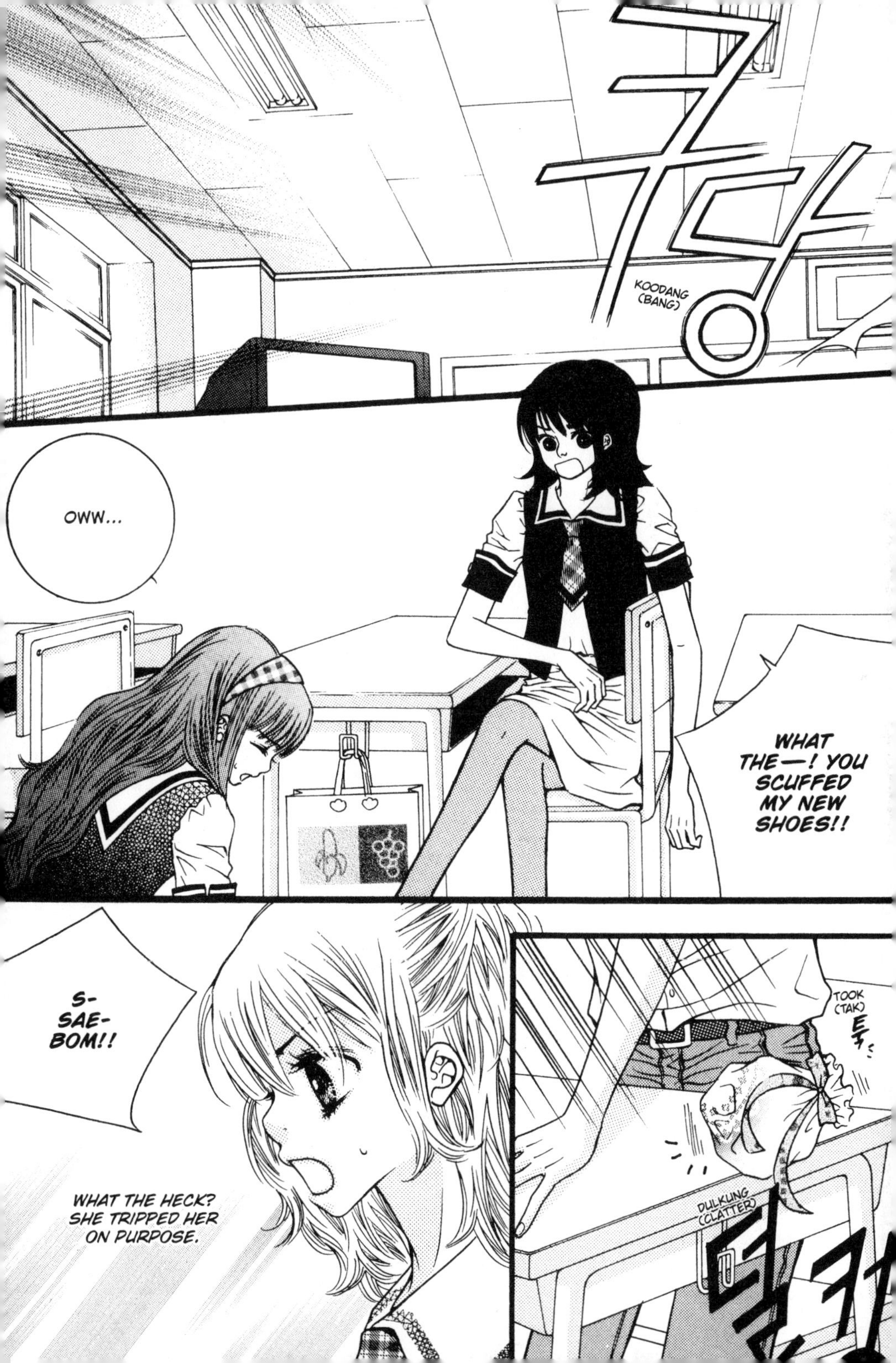
KOODANG
(BANG)
OWW...
WHAT THE—! YOU SCUFFED MY NEW SHOES!!
S-SAE-BOM!!
WHAT THE HECK? SHE TRIPPED HER ON PURPOSE.
TOOK
(TAK)
DULKUNG
(CLATTER)

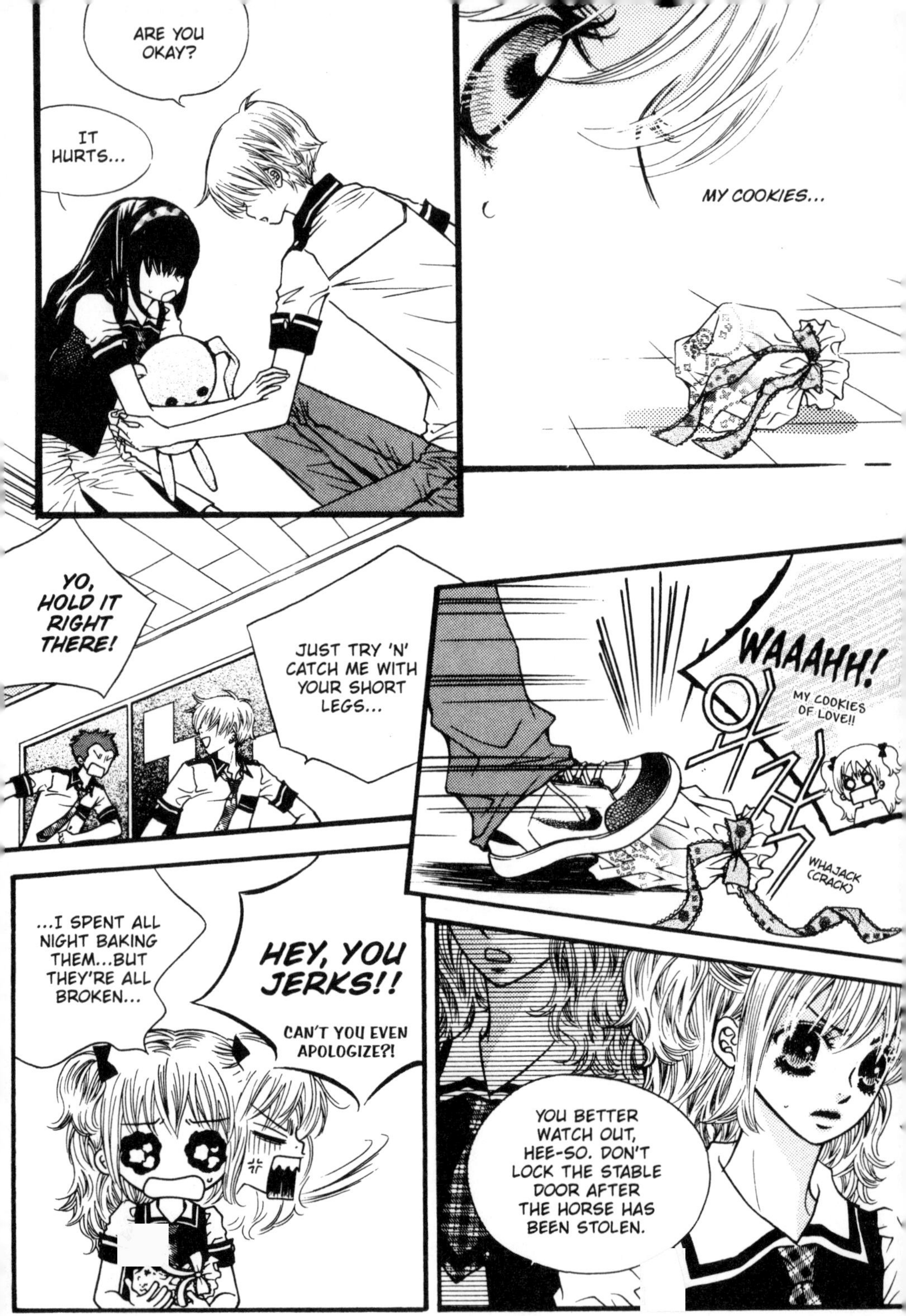
ARE YOU OKAY?
IT HURTS...
MY COOKIES...
YO, HOLD IT RIGHT THERE!
JUST TRY 'N' CATCH ME WITH YOUR SHORT LEGS...
WAAAHH!
MY COOKIES OF LOVE!!
WHAJACK (CRACK)
...I SPENT ALL NIGHT BAKING THEM...BUT THEY'RE ALL BROKEN...
HEY, YOU JERKS!!
CAN'T YOU EVEN APOLOGIZE?!
YOU BETTER WATCH OUT, HEE-SO. DON'T LOCK THE STABLE DOOR AFTER THE HORSE HAS BEEN STOLEN.

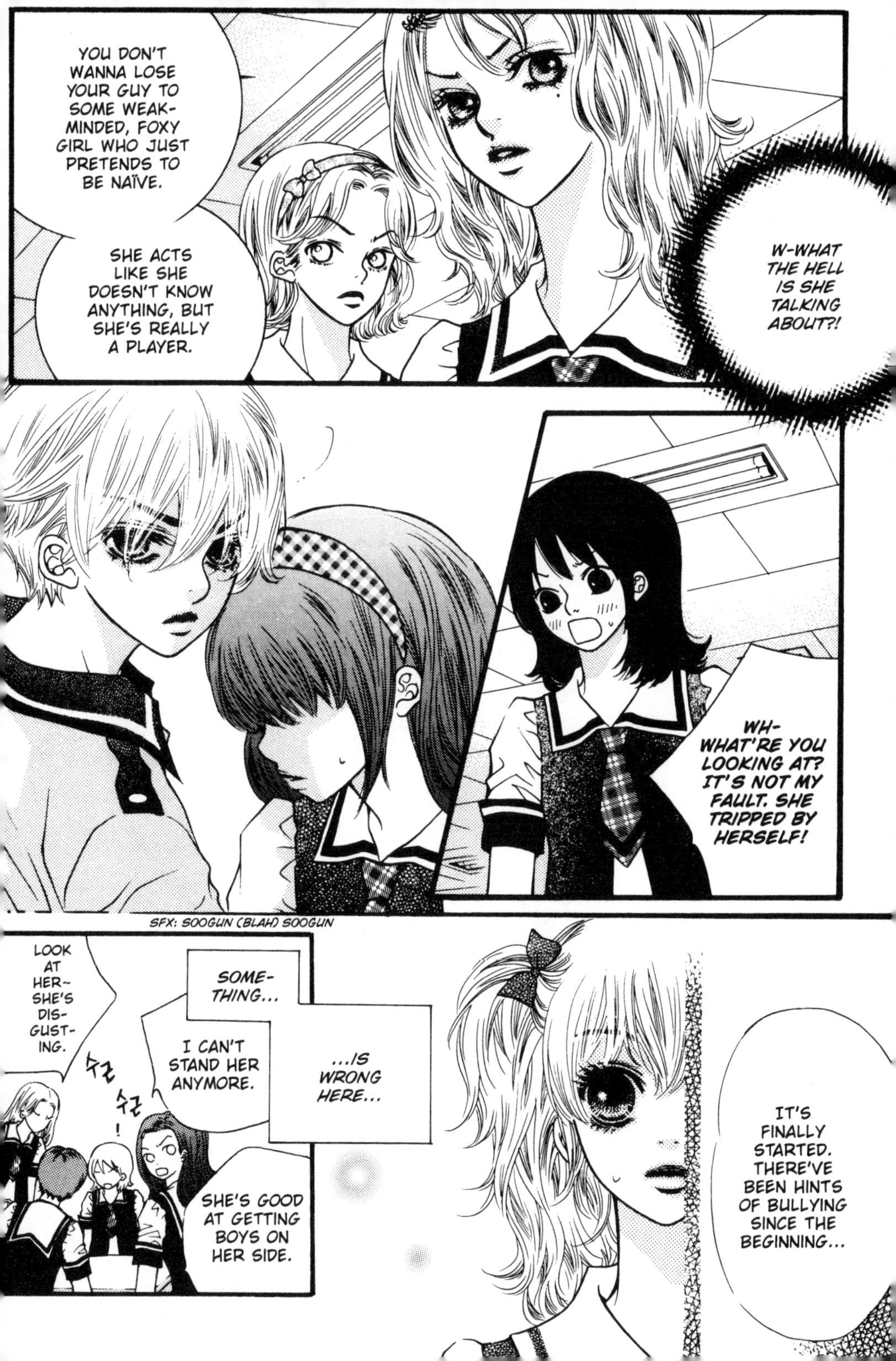
YOU DON'T WANNA LOSE YOUR GUY TO SOME WEAK-MINDED, FOXY GIRL WHO JUST PRETENDS TO BE NAÏVE.
SHE ACTS LIKE SHE DOESN'T KNOW ANYTHING, BUT SHE'S REALLY A PLAYER.
W-WHAT THE HELL IS SHE TALKING ABOUT?!
WH-WHAT'RE YOU LOOKING AT? IT'S NOT MY FAULT. SHE TRIPPED BY HERSELF!
SFX: SOOGUN (BLAH) SOOGUN
LOOK AT HER-SHE'S DIS-GUST-ING.
수군
수군
!
SOME-THING...
I CAN'T STAND HER ANYMORE.
...IS WRONG HERE...
SHE'S GOOD AT GETTING BOYS ON HER SIDE.
IT'S FINALLY STARTED. THERE'VE BEEN HINTS OF BULLYING SINCE THE BEGINNING...

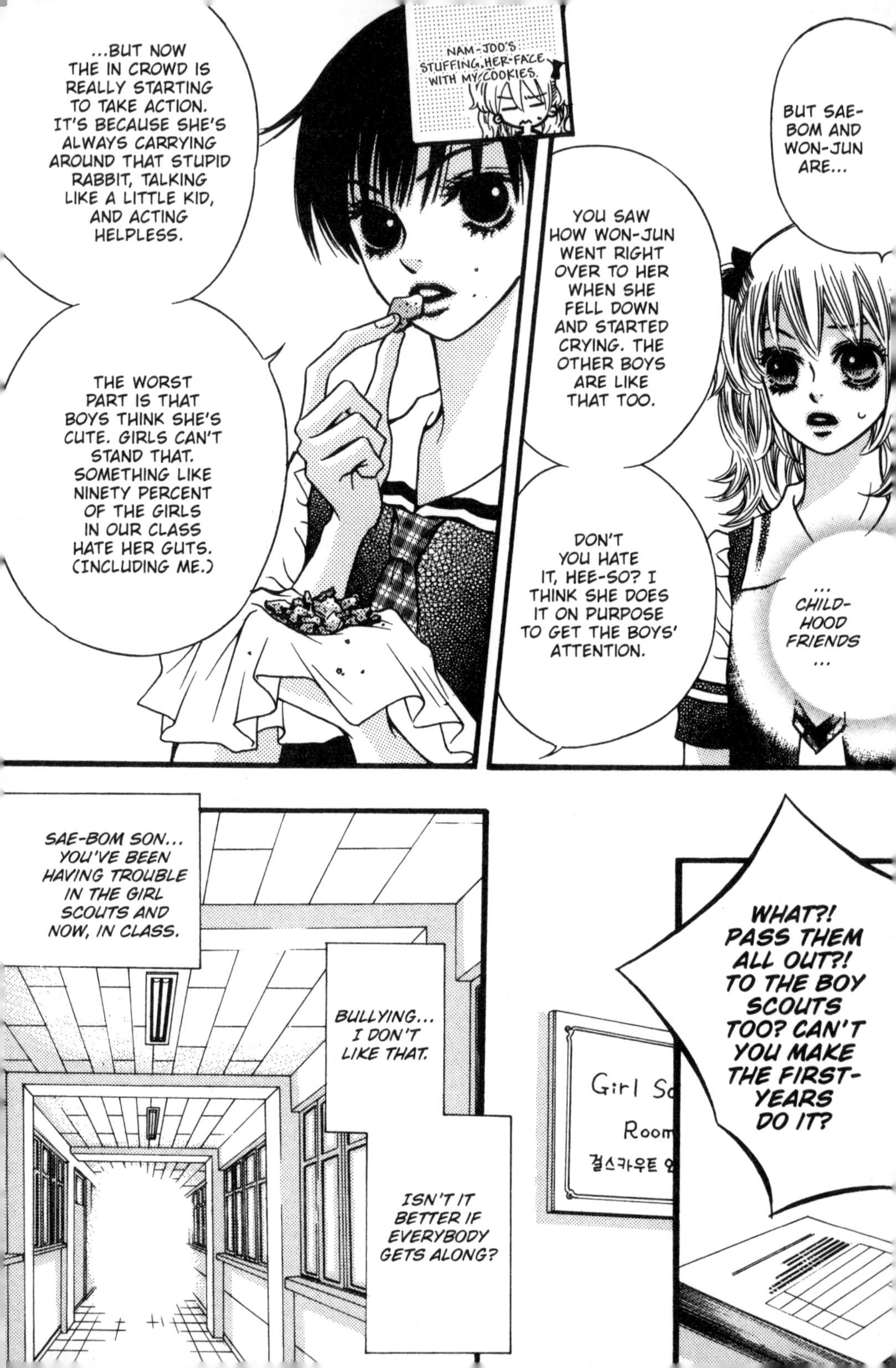
...BUT NOW THE IN CROWD IS REALLY STARTING TO TAKE ACTION. IT'S BECAUSE SHE'S ALWAYS CARRYING AROUND THAT STUPID RABBIT, TALKING LIKE A LITTLE KID, AND ACTING HELPLESS.
NAM-JOO'S STUFFING HER FACE WITH MY COOKIES.
THE WORST PART IS THAT BOYS THINK SHE'S CUTE. GIRLS CAN'T STAND THAT. SOMETHING LIKE NINETY PERCENT OF THE GIRLS IN OUR CLASS HATE HER GUTS. (INCLUDING ME.)
YOU SAW HOW WON-JUN WENT RIGHT OVER TO HER WHEN SHE FELL DOWN AND STARTED CRYING. THE OTHER BOYS ARE LIKE THAT TOO.
DON'T YOU HATE IT, HEE-SO? I THINK SHE DOES IT ON PURPOSE TO GET THE BOYS' ATTENTION.
BUT SAE-BOM AND WON-JUN ARE...
...CHILDHOOD FRIENDS...
SAE-BOM SON... YOU'VE BEEN HAVING TROUBLE IN THE GIRL SCOUTS AND NOW, IN CLASS.
BULLYING... I DON'T LIKE THAT.
ISN'T IT BETTER IF EVERYBODY GETS ALONG?
Girl Sc
Room
걸스카우트
WHAT?! PASS THEM ALL OUT?! TO THE BOY SCOUTS TOO? CAN'T YOU MAKE THE FIRST-YEARS DO IT?

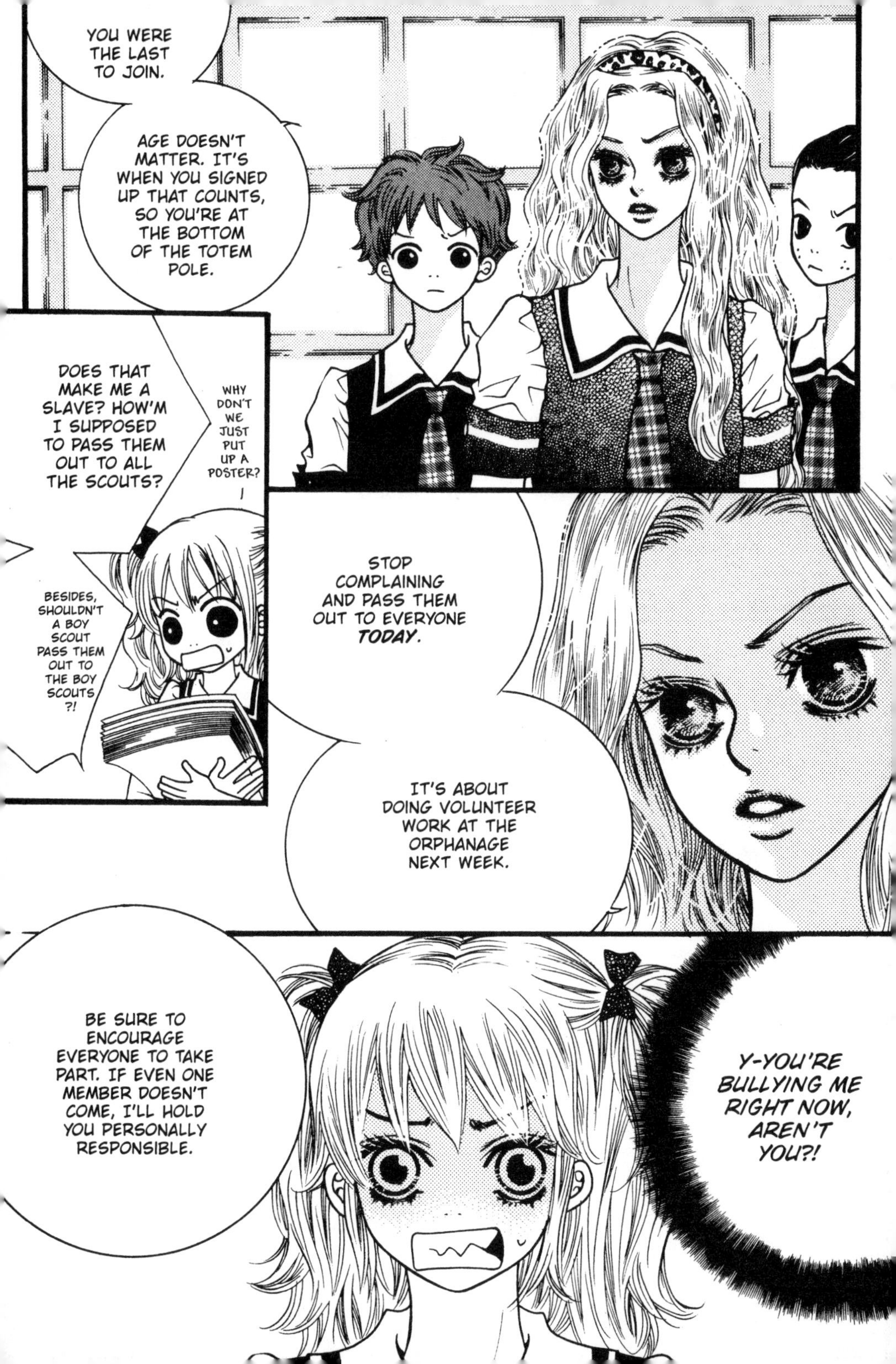
YOU WERE THE LAST TO JOIN.
AGE DOESN'T MATTER. IT'S WHEN YOU SIGNED UP THAT COUNTS, SO YOU'RE AT THE BOTTOM OF THE TOTEM POLE.
DOES THAT MAKE ME A SLAVE? HOW'M I SUPPOSED TO PASS THEM OUT TO ALL THE SCOUTS?
WHY DON'T WE JUST PUT UP A POSTER?
BESIDES, SHOULDN'T A BOY SCOUT PASS THEM OUT TO THE BOY SCOUTS ?!
STOP COMPLAINING AND PASS THEM OUT TO EVERYONE *TODAY*.
IT'S ABOUT DOING VOLUNTEER WORK AT THE ORPHANAGE NEXT WEEK.
BE SURE TO ENCOURAGE EVERYONE TO TAKE PART. IF EVEN ONE MEMBER DOESN'T COME, I'LL HOLD YOU PERSONALLY RESPONSIBLE.
Y-YOU'RE BULLYING ME RIGHT NOW, AREN'T YOU?!

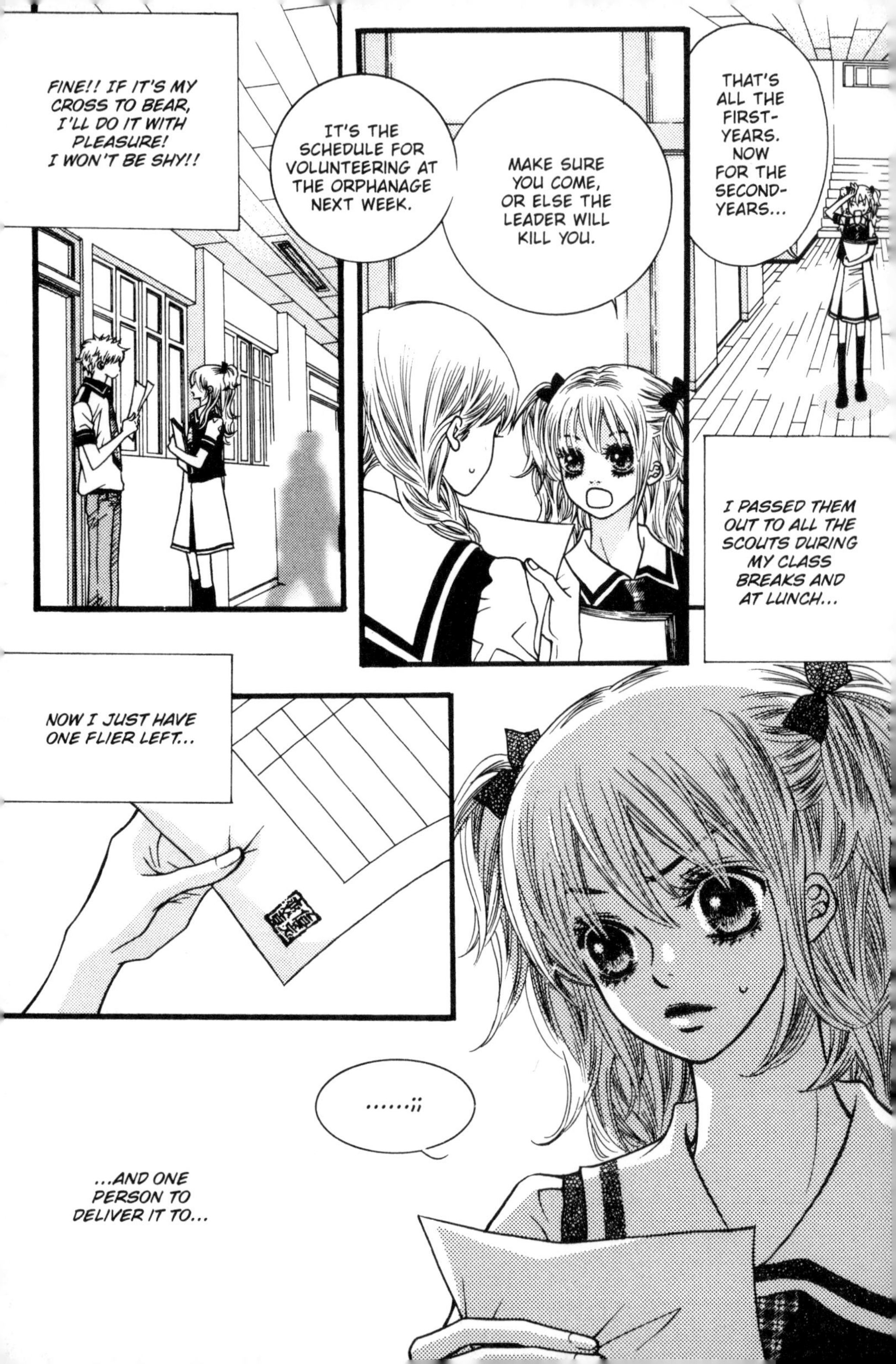
FINE!! IF IT'S MY CROSS TO BEAR, I'LL DO IT WITH PLEASURE! I WON'T BE SHY!!
IT'S THE SCHEDULE FOR VOLUNTEERING AT THE ORPHANAGE NEXT WEEK.
MAKE SURE YOU COME, OR ELSE THE LEADER WILL KILL YOU.
THAT'S ALL THE FIRST-YEARS. NOW FOR THE SECOND-YEARS...
I PASSED THEM OUT TO ALL THE SCOUTS DURING MY CLASS BREAKS AND AT LUNCH...
NOW I JUST HAVE ONE FLIER LEFT...
......;;
...AND ONE PERSON TO DELIVER IT TO...

STEP 8. WHIE-YOUNG JANG, YOU'RE SO MYSTERIOUS!

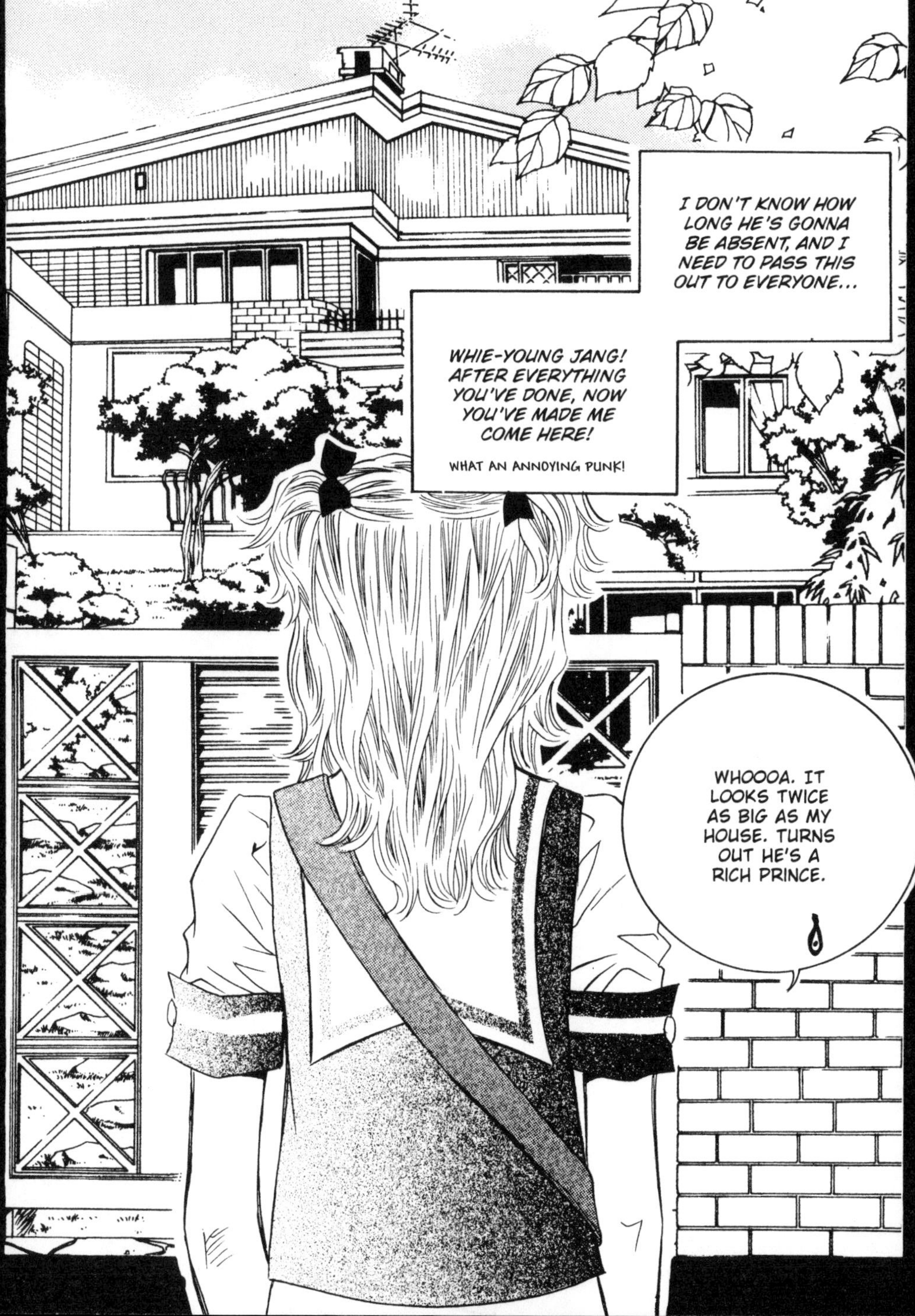
I DON'T KNOW HOW LONG HE'S GONNA BE ABSENT, AND I NEED TO PASS THIS OUT TO EVERYONE...
WHIE-YOUNG JANG! AFTER EVERYTHING YOU'VE DONE, NOW YOU'VE MADE ME COME HERE!
WHAT AN ANNOYING PUNK!
WHOOOA. IT LOOKS TWICE AS BIG AS MY HOUSE. TURNS OUT HE'S A RICH PRINCE.

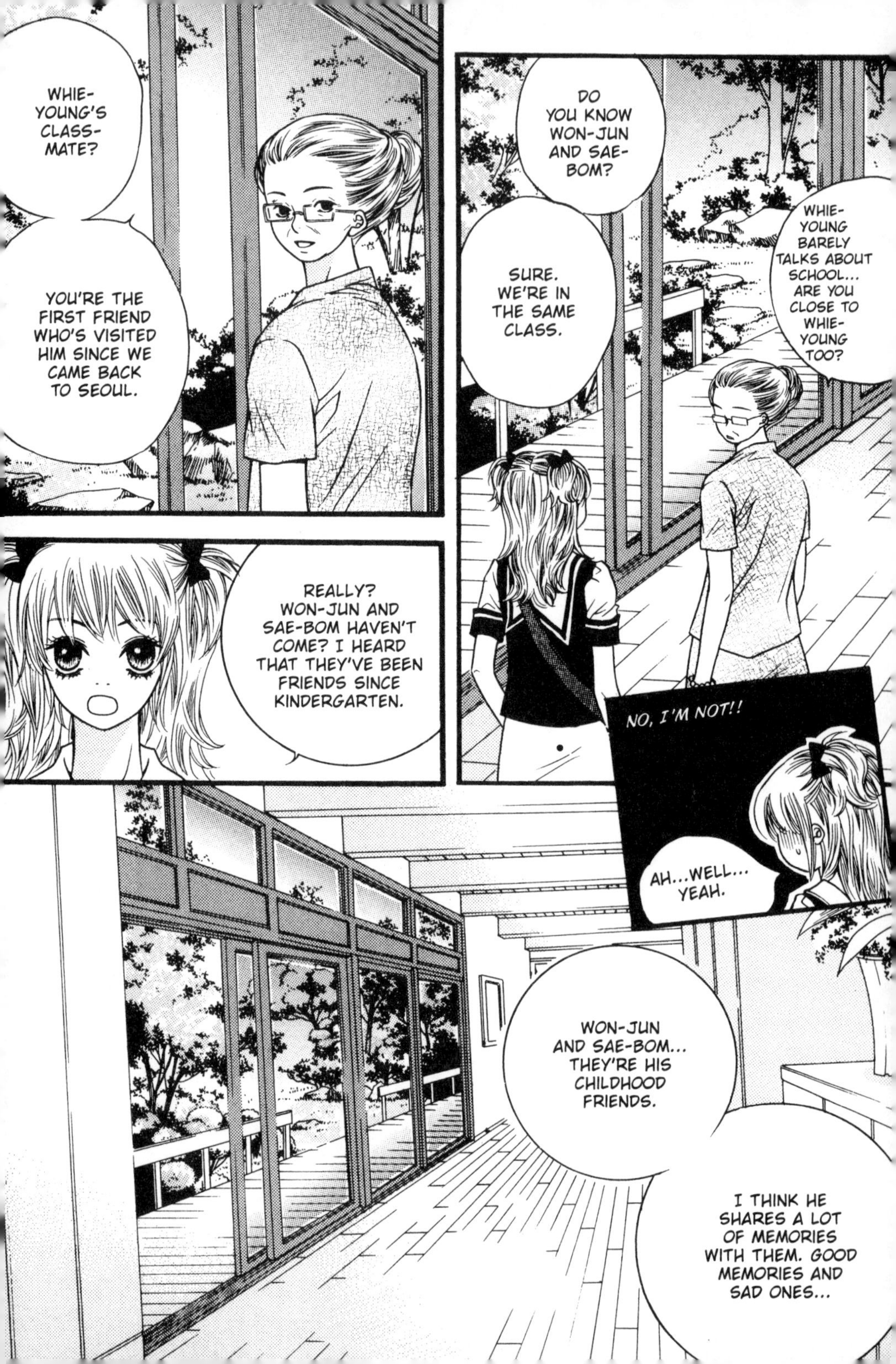
WHIE-YOUNG'S CLASS-MATE?
YOU'RE THE FIRST FRIEND WHO'S VISITED HIM SINCE WE CAME BACK TO SEOUL.
REALLY? WON-JUN AND SAE-BOM HAVEN'T COME? I HEARD THAT THEY'VE BEEN FRIENDS SINCE KINDERGARTEN.
DO YOU KNOW WON-JUN AND SAE-BOM?
SURE. WE'RE IN THE SAME CLASS.
WHIE-YOUNG BARELY TALKS ABOUT SCHOOL... ARE YOU CLOSE TO WHIE-YOUNG TOO?
NO, I'M NOT!!
AH...WELL... YEAH.
WON-JUN AND SAE-BOM... THEY'RE HIS CHILDHOOD FRIENDS.
I THINK HE SHARES A LOT OF MEMORIES WITH THEM. GOOD MEMORIES AND SAD ONES...

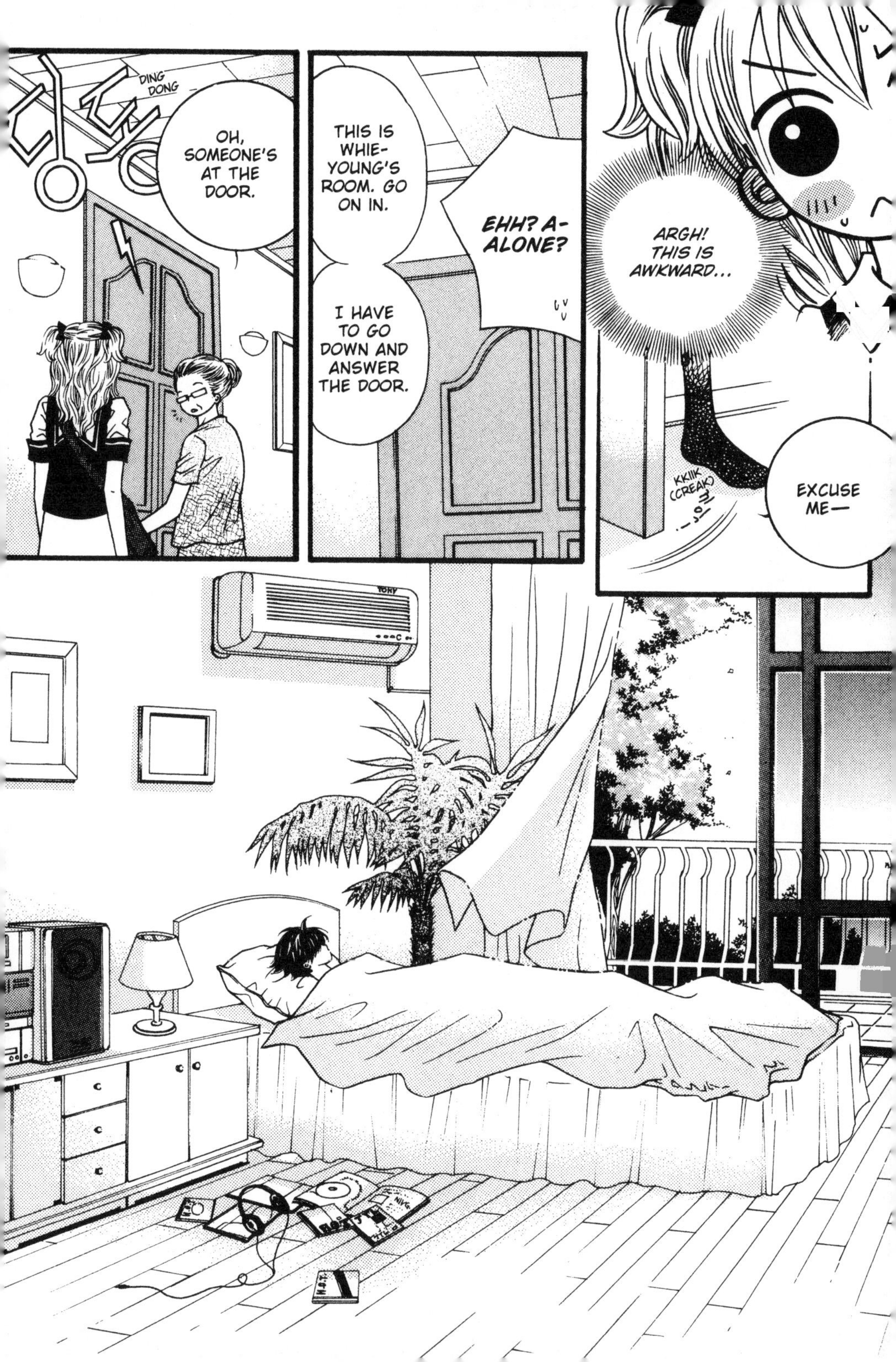
DING DONG
OH, SOMEONE'S AT THE DOOR.
THIS IS WHIE-YOUNG'S ROOM. GO ON IN.
I HAVE TO GO DOWN AND ANSWER THE DOOR.
EHH? A-ALONE?
ARGH! THIS IS AWKWARD...
KKIIK (CREAK)
EXCUSE ME—

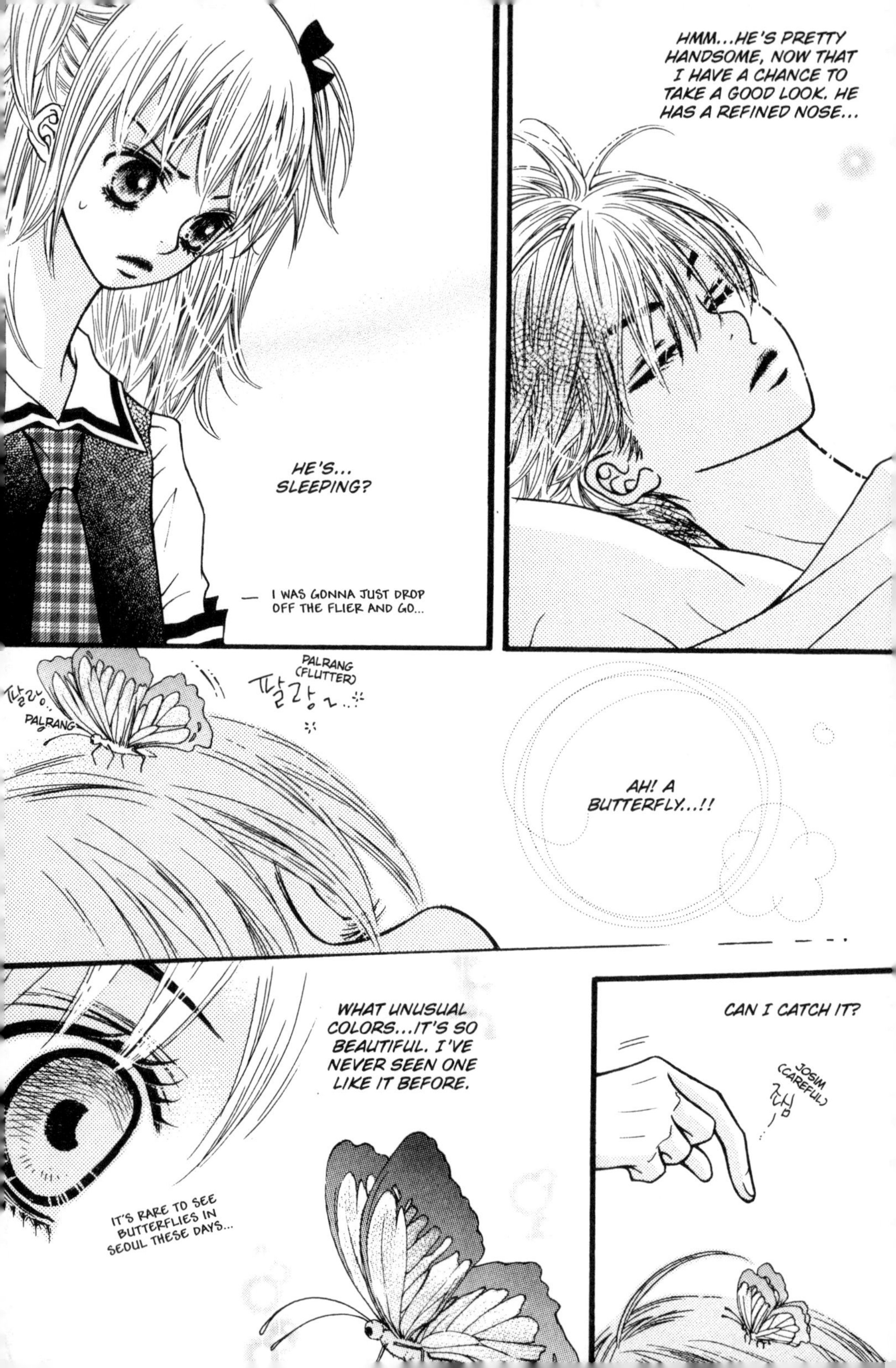
HE'S... SLEEPING?
I WAS GONNA JUST DROP OFF THE FLIER AND GO...
HMM...HE'S PRETTY HANDSOME, NOW THAT I HAVE A CHANCE TO TAKE A GOOD LOOK. HE HAS A REFINED NOSE...
팔랑.. PALRANG
PALRANG (FLUTTER)
팔랑~..
AH! A BUTTERFLY...!!
WHAT UNUSUAL COLORS...IT'S SO BEAUTIFUL. I'VE NEVER SEEN ONE LIKE IT BEFORE.
IT'S RARE TO SEE BUTTERFLIES IN SEOUL THESE DAYS...
CAN I CATCH IT?
JOSIM (CAREFUL)
조심

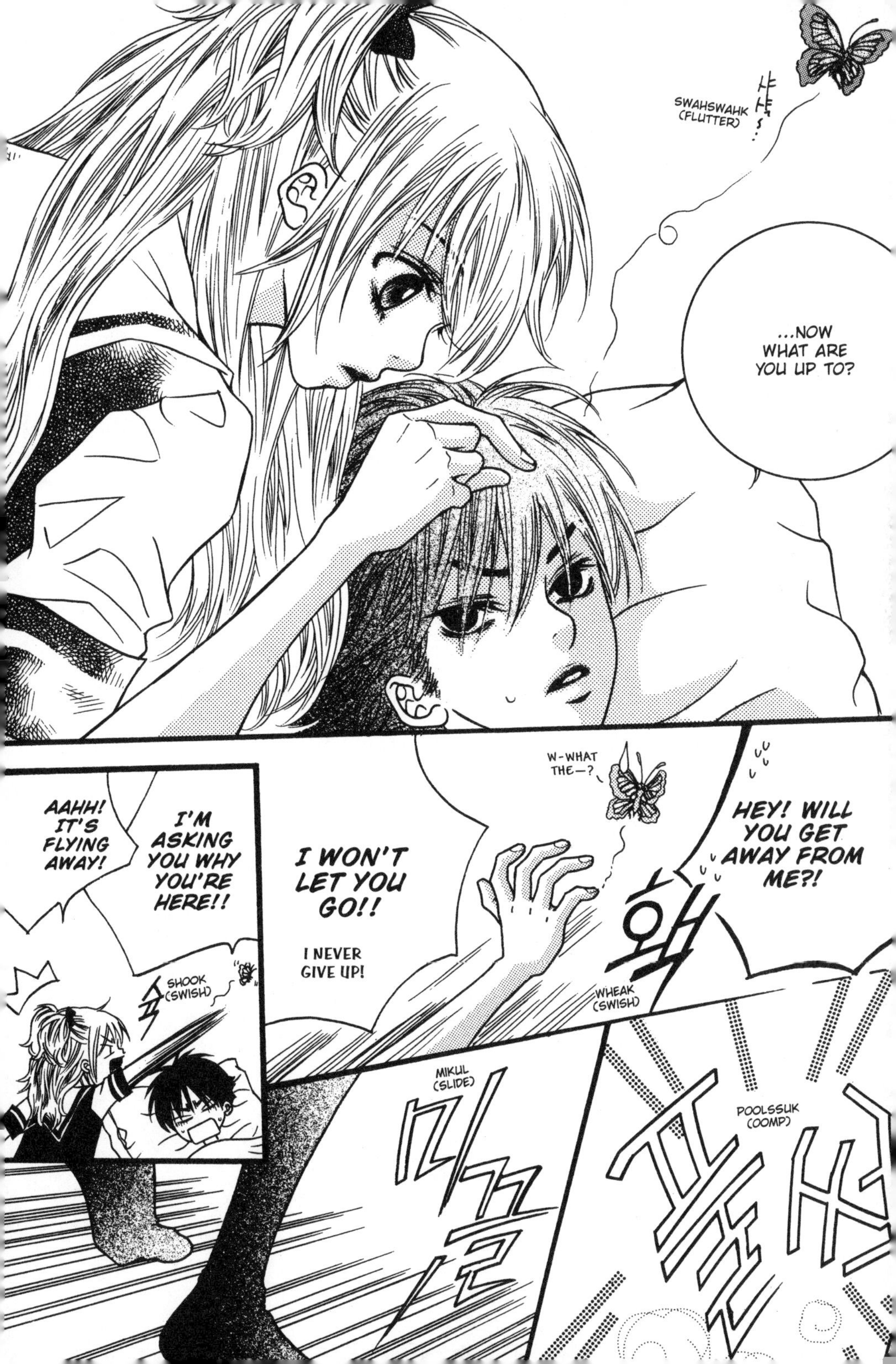
SWAHSWAHK (FLUTTER)
...NOW WHAT ARE YOU UP TO?
AAHH! IT'S FLYING AWAY!
I'M ASKING YOU WHY YOU'RE HERE!!
SHOOK (SWISH)
I WON'T LET YOU GO!!
I NEVER GIVE UP!
W-WHAT THE—?
HEY! WILL YOU GET AWAY FROM ME?!
휙
WHEAK (SWISH)
MIKUL (SLIDE)
미끌
POOLSSUK (OOMP)
풀썩

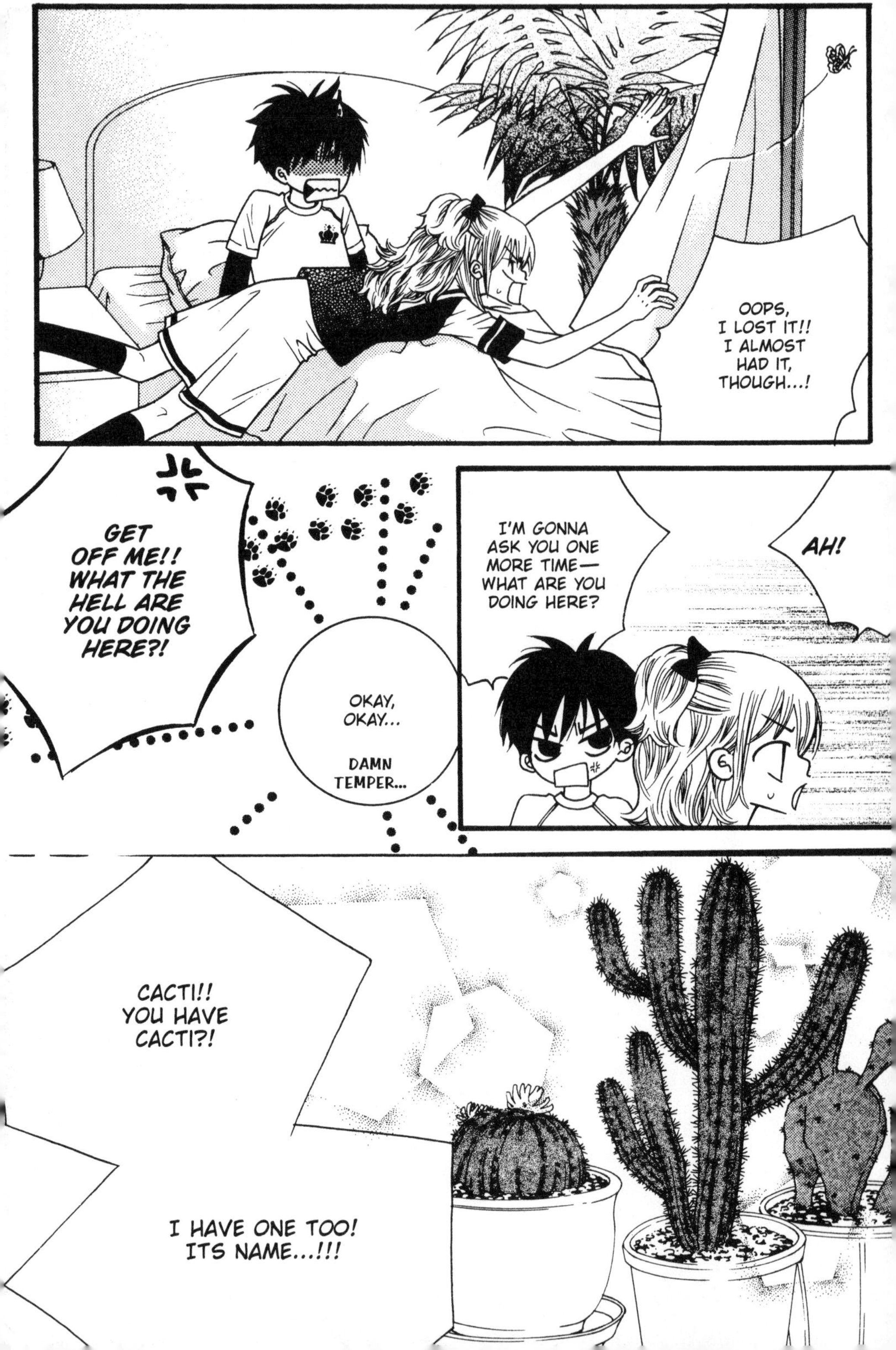
OOPS, I LOST IT!! I ALMOST HAD IT, THOUGH...!
GET OFF ME!! WHAT THE HELL ARE YOU DOING HERE?!
OKAY, OKAY...
DAMN TEMPER...
I'M GONNA ASK YOU ONE MORE TIME— WHAT ARE YOU DOING HERE?
AH!
CACTI!! YOU HAVE CACTI?!
I HAVE ONE TOO! ITS NAME...!!!

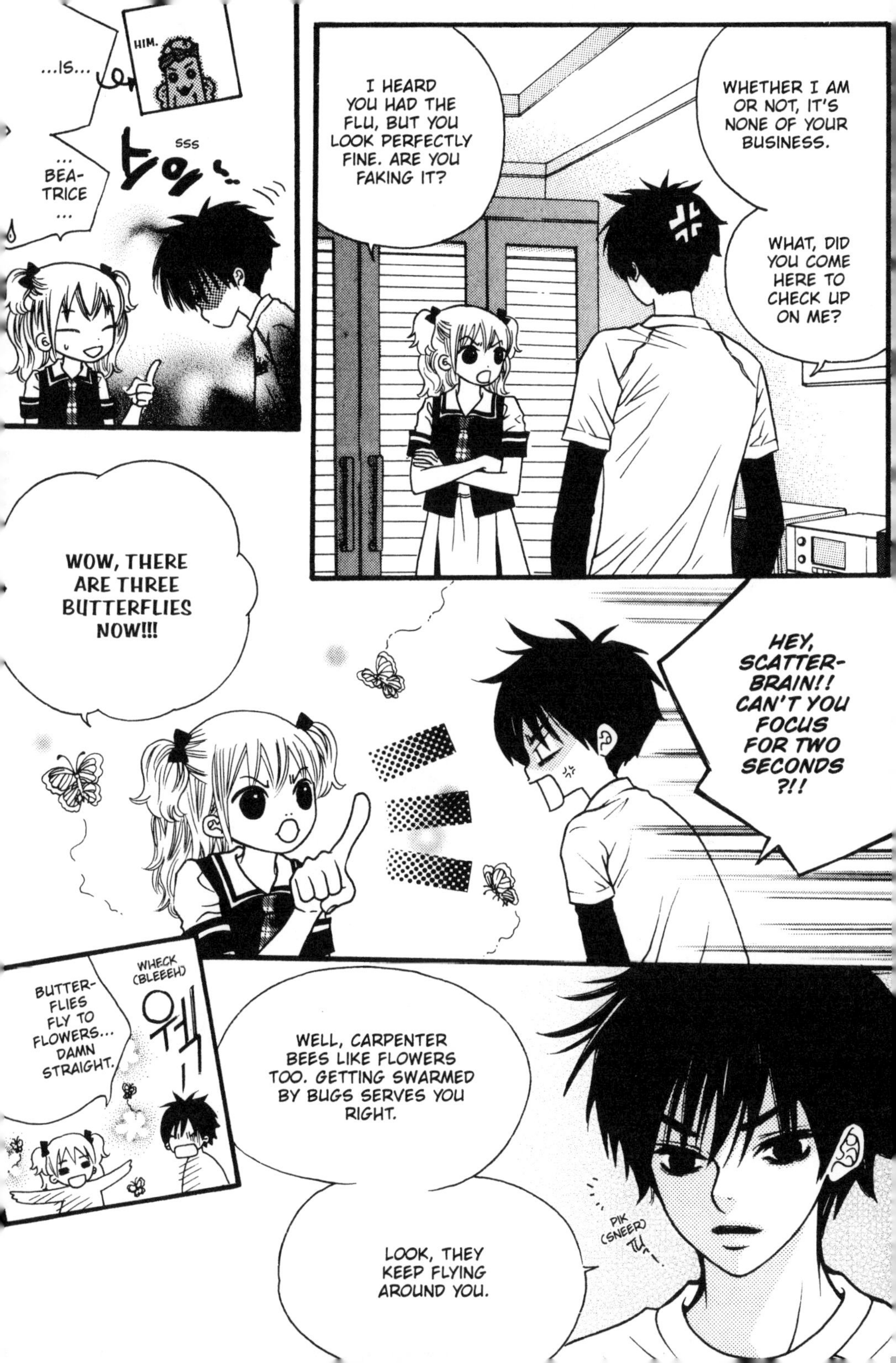

HIM.
...IS...
... BEA-TRICE ...
SSS
I HEARD YOU HAD THE FLU, BUT YOU LOOK PERFECTLY FINE. ARE YOU FAKING IT?
WHETHER I AM OR NOT, IT'S NONE OF YOUR BUSINESS.
WHAT, DID YOU COME HERE TO CHECK UP ON ME?
WOW, THERE ARE THREE BUTTERFLIES NOW!!!
HEY, SCATTER-BRAIN!! CAN'T YOU FOCUS FOR TWO SECONDS ?!!
BUTTER-FLIES FLY TO FLOWERS... DAMN STRAIGHT.
WHECK (BLEEEH)
WELL, CARPENTER BEES LIKE FLOWERS TOO. GETTING SWARMED BY BUGS SERVES YOU RIGHT.
LOOK, THEY KEEP FLYING AROUND YOU.
PIK (SNEER)

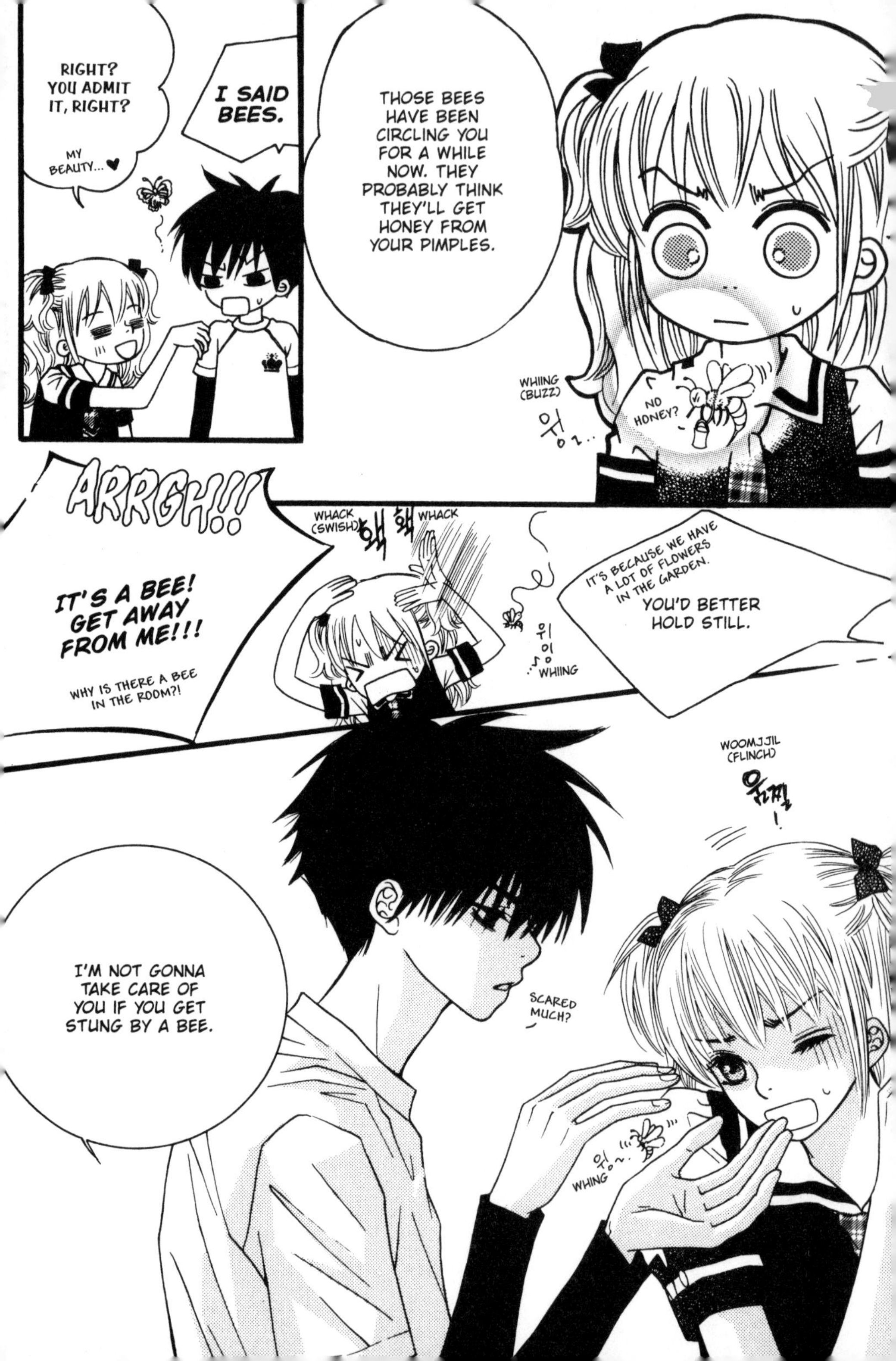
RIGHT? YOU ADMIT IT, RIGHT?
MY BEAUTY...♥
I SAID BEES.
THOSE BEES HAVE BEEN CIRCLING YOU FOR A WHILE NOW. THEY PROBABLY THINK THEY'LL GET HONEY FROM YOUR PIMPLES.
WHIING (BUZZ)
NO HONEY?
ARRGH!!!
IT'S A BEE! GET AWAY FROM ME!!!
WHY IS THERE A BEE IN THE ROOM?!
WHACK (SWISH)
WHACK
WHIING
IT'S BECAUSE WE HAVE A LOT OF FLOWERS IN THE GARDEN.
YOU'D BETTER HOLD STILL.
WOOMJJIL (FLINCH)
움찔
I'M NOT GONNA TAKE CARE OF YOU IF YOU GET STUNG BY A BEE.
SCARED MUCH?
WHING

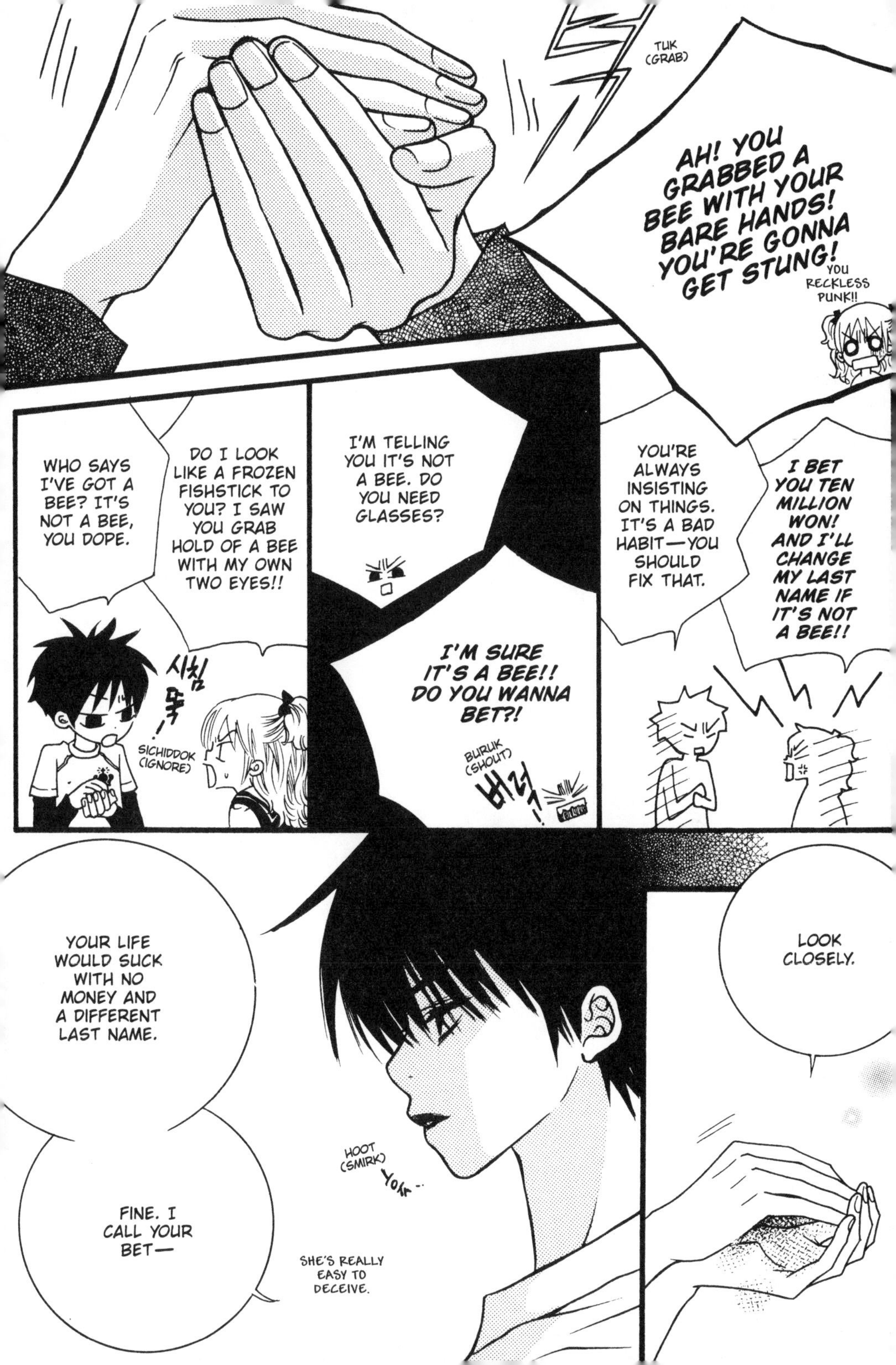
TUK (GRAB)
AH! YOU GRABBED A BEE WITH YOUR BARE HANDS! YOU'RE GONNA GET STUNG!
YOU RECKLESS PUNK!!
WHO SAYS I'VE GOT A BEE? IT'S NOT A BEE, YOU DOPE.
DO I LOOK LIKE A FROZEN FISHSTICK TO YOU? I SAW YOU GRAB HOLD OF A BEE WITH MY OWN TWO EYES!!
시침 뚝!
SICHIDDOK (IGNORE)
I'M TELLING YOU IT'S NOT A BEE. DO YOU NEED GLASSES?
I'M SURE IT'S A BEE!! DO YOU WANNA BET?!
BURUK (SHOUT)
버럭!
YOU'RE ALWAYS INSISTING ON THINGS. IT'S A BAD HABIT—YOU SHOULD FIX THAT.
I BET YOU TEN MILLION WON! AND I'LL CHANGE MY LAST NAME IF IT'S NOT A BEE!!
YOUR LIFE WOULD SUCK WITH NO MONEY AND A DIFFERENT LAST NAME.
FINE. I CALL YOUR BET—
HOOT (SMIRK)
SHE'S REALLY EASY TO DECEIVE.
LOOK CLOSELY.

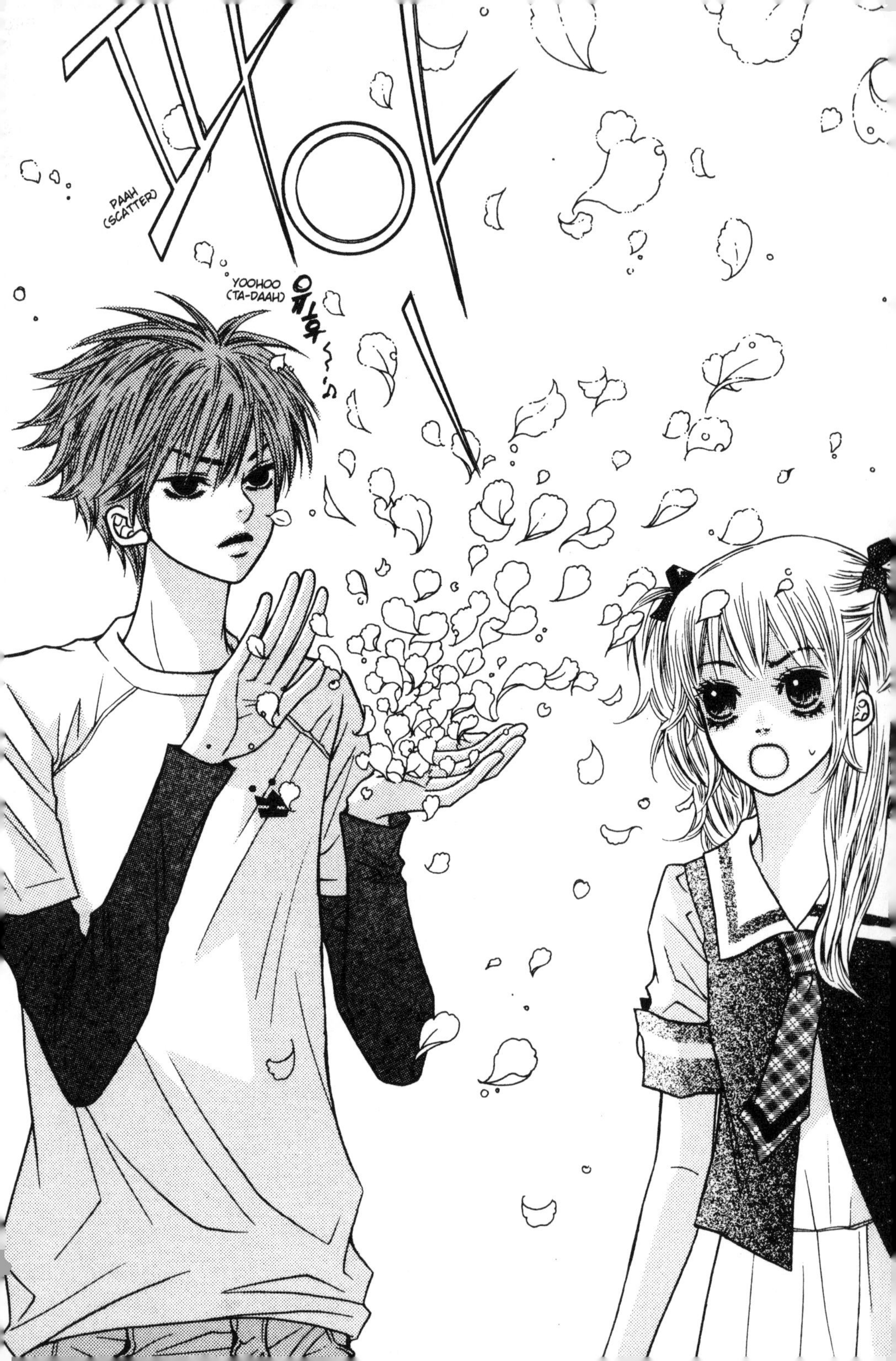
PAAH (SCATTER)
YOOHOO (TA-DAAH)

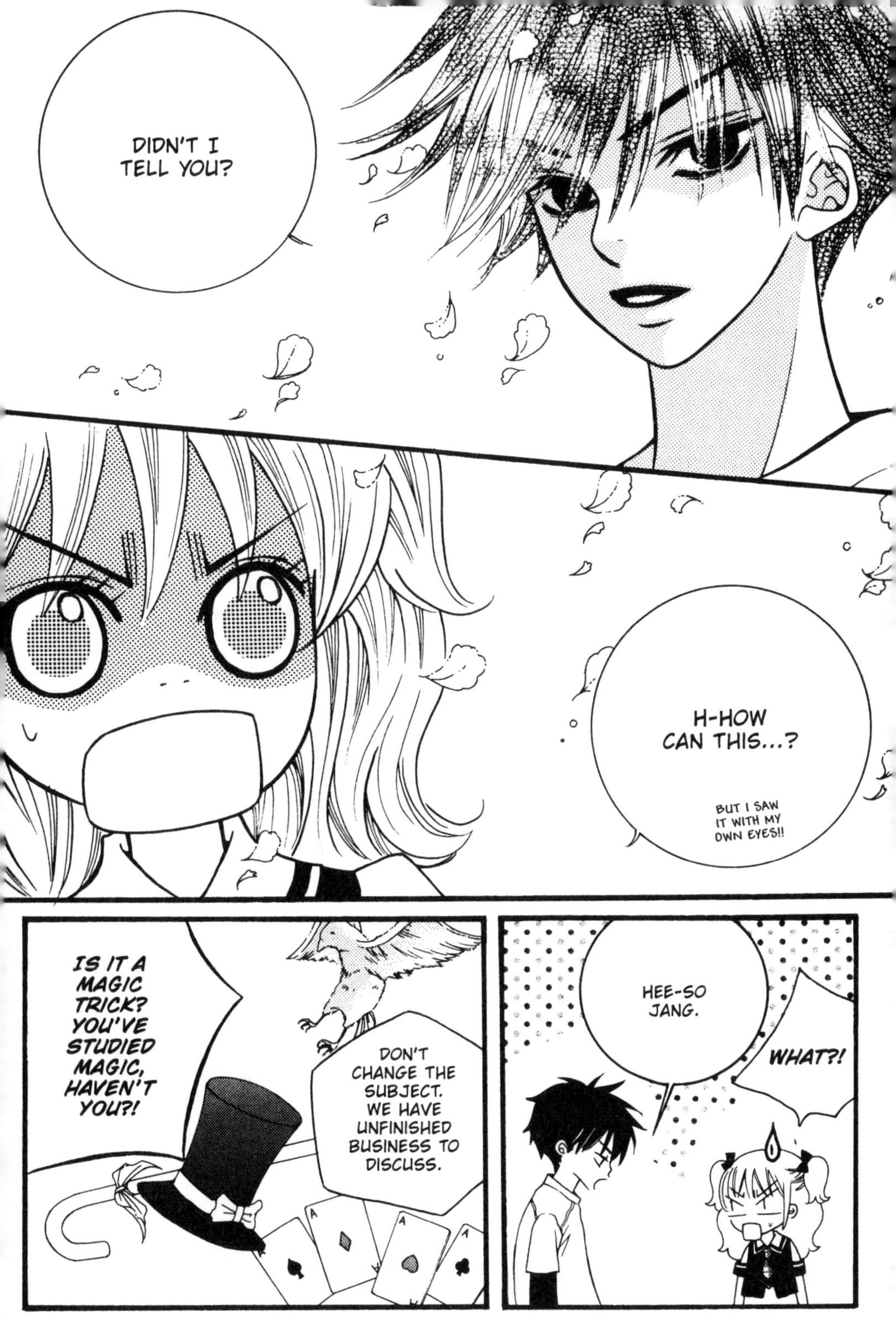
DIDN'T I TELL YOU?
H-HOW CAN THIS...?
BUT I SAW IT WITH MY OWN EYES!!
IS IT A MAGIC TRICK? YOU'VE STUDIED MAGIC, HAVEN'T YOU?!
DON'T CHANGE THE SUBJECT. WE HAVE UNFINISHED BUSINESS TO DISCUSS.
HEE-SO JANG.
WHAT?!

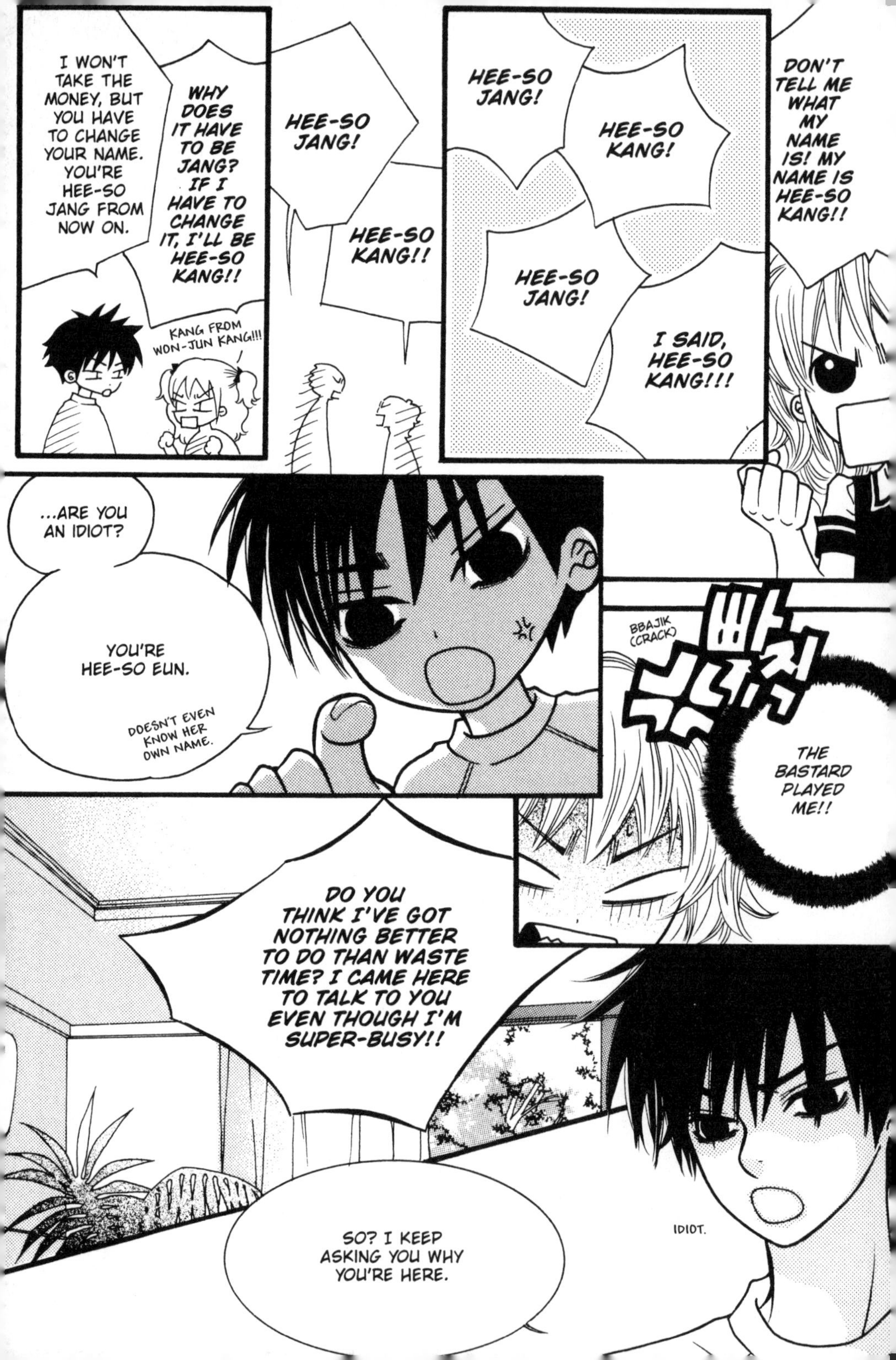
I WON'T TAKE THE MONEY, BUT YOU HAVE TO CHANGE YOUR NAME. YOU'RE HEE-SO JANG FROM NOW ON.
WHY DOES IT HAVE TO BE JANG? IF I HAVE TO CHANGE IT, I'LL BE HEE-SO KANG!!
KANG FROM WON-JUN KANG!!!
HEE-SO JANG!
HEE-SO KANG!!
HEE-SO JANG!
HEE-SO KANG!
HEE-SO JANG!
I SAID, HEE-SO KANG!!!
DON'T TELL ME WHAT MY NAME IS! MY NAME IS HEE-SO KANG!!
...ARE YOU AN IDIOT?
YOU'RE HEE-SO EUN.
DOESN'T EVEN KNOW HER OWN NAME.
빠직
BBAJIK (CRACK)
THE BASTARD PLAYED ME!!
DO YOU THINK I'VE GOT NOTHING BETTER TO DO THAN WASTE TIME? I CAME HERE TO TALK TO YOU EVEN THOUGH I'M SUPER-BUSY!!
SO? I KEEP ASKING YOU WHY YOU'RE HERE.
IDIOT.

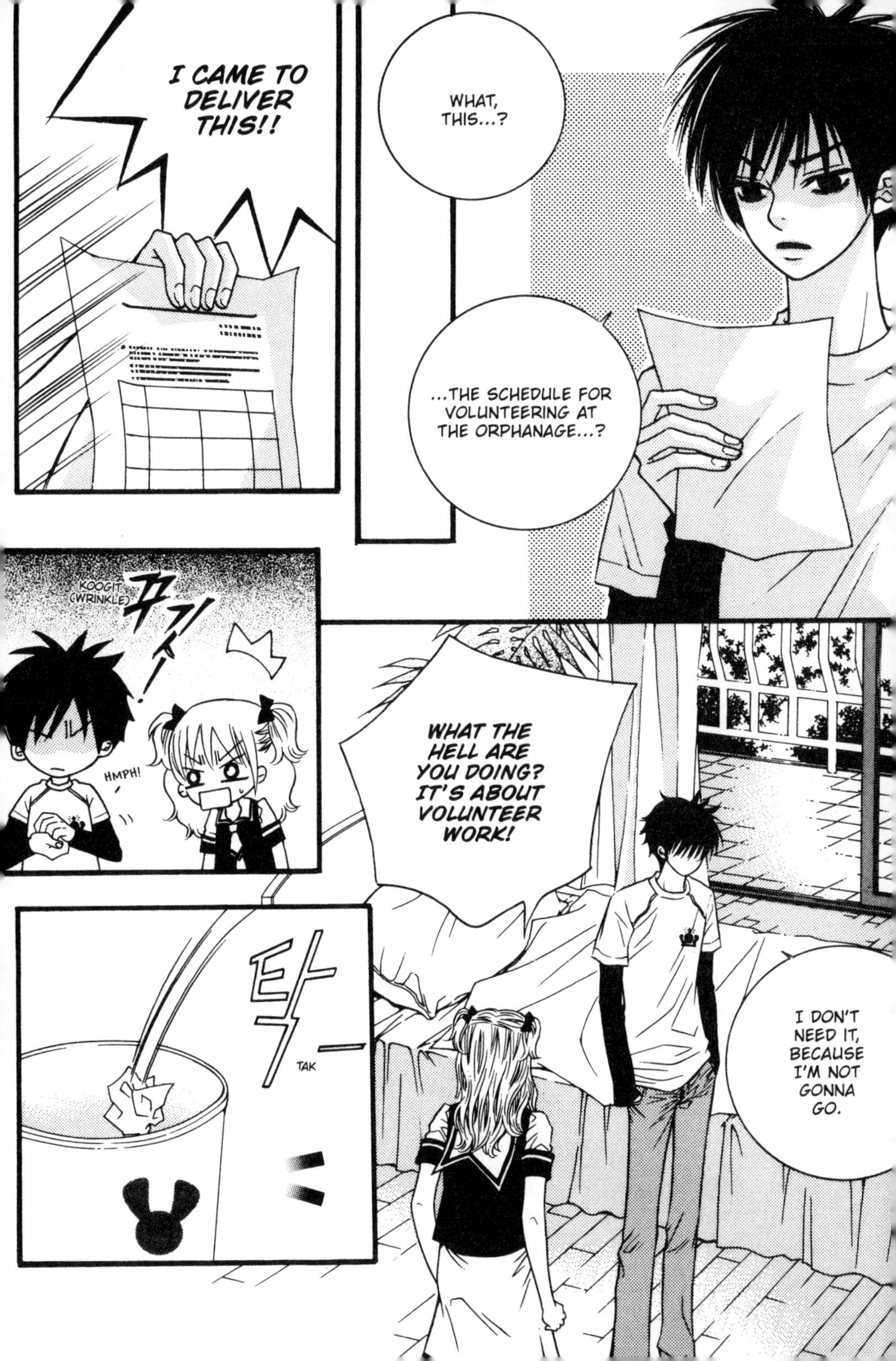
I CAME TO DELIVER THIS!!
WHAT, THIS...?
...THE SCHEDULE FOR VOLUNTEERING AT THE ORPHANAGE...?
KOOGIT (WRINKLE)
HMPH!
TAK
WHAT THE HELL ARE YOU DOING? IT'S ABOUT VOLUNTEER WORK!
I DON'T NEED IT, BECAUSE I'M NOT GONNA GO.

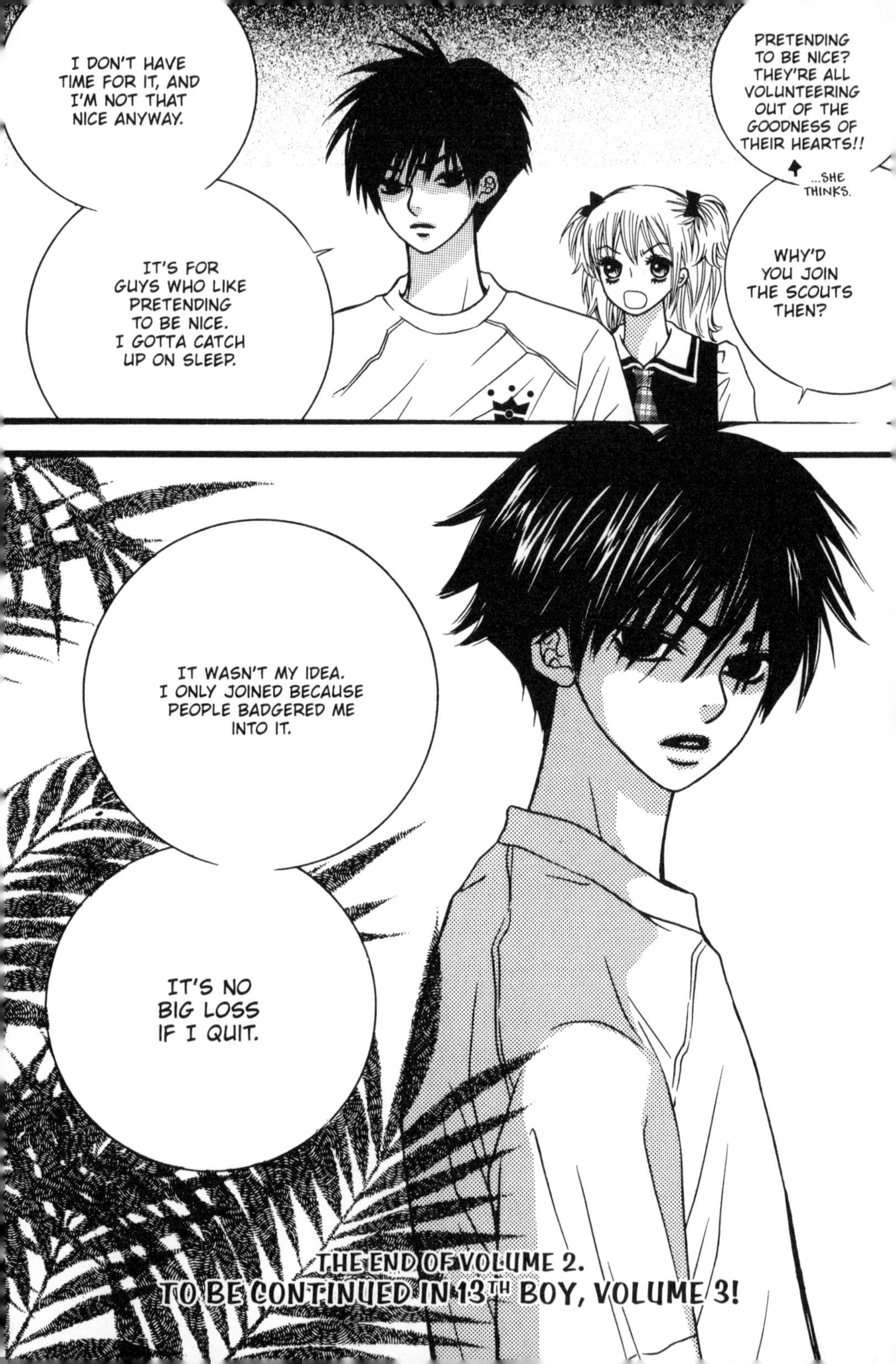
I DON'T HAVE TIME FOR IT, AND I'M NOT THAT NICE ANYWAY.
IT'S FOR GUYS WHO LIKE PRETENDING TO BE NICE. I GOTTA CATCH UP ON SLEEP.
PRETENDING TO BE NICE? THEY'RE ALL VOLUNTEERING OUT OF THE GOODNESS OF THEIR HEARTS!!
...SHE THINKS.
WHY'D YOU JOIN THE SCOUTS THEN?
IT WASN'T MY IDEA. I ONLY JOINED BECAUSE PEOPLE BADGERED ME INTO IT.
IT'S NO BIG LOSS IF I QUIT.
THE END OF VOLUME 2.
TO BE CONTINUED IN 13TH BOY, VOLUME 3!

13th Boy
Translation Notes

Page 05
Won: Korean monetary unit. A rough conversion rate is 1,000 won to $1 USD.

Page 130
Duk-bok-gi: A Korean dish of broiled and sliced rice cake, meat, eggs, vegetables, seasonings, etc.

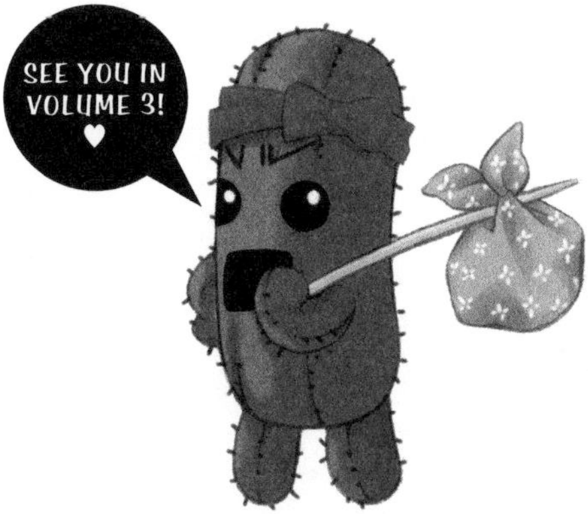
SEE YOU IN VOLUME 3! ♥

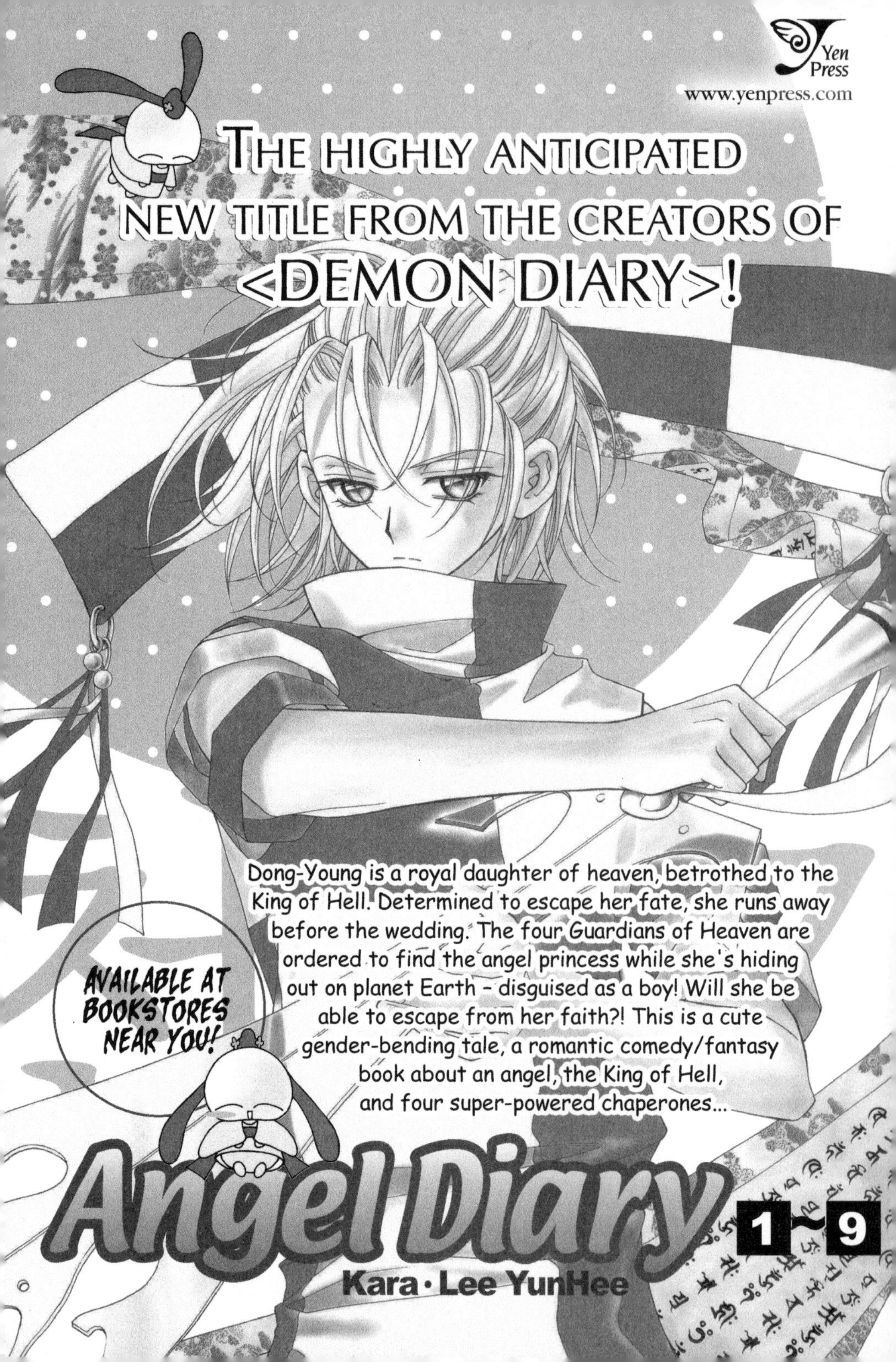
Yen Press
www.yenpress.com
THE HIGHLY ANTICIPATED
NEW TITLE FROM THE CREATORS OF
<DEMON DIARY>!
Dong-Young is a royal daughter of heaven, betrothed to the King of Hell. Determined to escape her fate, she runs away before the wedding. The four Guardians of Heaven are ordered to find the angel princess while she's hiding out on planet Earth - disguised as a boy! Will she be able to escape from her faith?! This is a cute gender-bending tale, a romantic comedy/fantasy book about an angel, the King of Hell, and four super-powered chaperones...
AVAILABLE AT BOOKSTORES NEAR YOU!
Angel Diary
1~9
Kara · Lee YunHee

Wonderfully illustrated
modern day crossover
fantasy, available at
your local bookstore
or comic shop!

Apart from the fact her
eyes turn red when the moon
rises, Myung-Ee is your average,
albeit boy-crazy, 5th grader. After
picking a fight with her classmate
Yu-Da Lee, she discovers a startling
secret: the two of them are "earth
rabbits" being hunted by the "fox
tribe" of the moon!
Five years pass and Myung-Ee
transfers to a new school in search of
pretty boys. There, she unexpectedly
reunites with Yu-Da. The problem is
he doesn't remember a thing about
her or their shared past!

Moon Boy 1~6

월요일 소년

Lee YoungYou

Yen Press
www.yenpress.com

Yen Press

www.yenpress.com

Becoming the princess... Isn't that every girl's dream?!

Monarchy rule ended long ago in Korea, but there are still other countries with kings, queens, princes and princesses. What if Korea had continued monarchism? What if all the beautiful palaces, which are now only historical relics, were actually filled with people? What if the glamorous royal family still maintained the palace customs? Welcome to a world where Korea still has the royal family living in their everyday lives! Only for this one high school girl, Chae-Kyung, is this a tragedy, since she has to marry the prince — who apparently is a total bastard!

THE ROYAL PALACE
Goong
vol. 1 ~ 6

Park SoHee

www.yenpress.com

THE MOST BEAUTIFUL FACE, THE PERFECT BODY,
AND A SINCERE PERSONALITY...THAT'S WHAT HYE-MIN HWANG HAS.
NATURALLY, SHE'S THE CENTER OF EVERYONE'S ATTENTION.
EVERY BOY IN SCHOOL LOVES HER, WHILE EVERY GIRL HATES HER OUT OF JEALOUSY.
EVERY SINGLE DAY, SHE HAS TO ENDURE TORTURES AND HARDSHIPS FROM THE GIRLS.

A PRETTY FACE COMES WITH A PRICE.

THERE IS NOTHING MORE SATISFYING THAN GETTING THEM BACK.
WELL, EXCEPT FOR ONE PROBLEM...HER SECRET CRUSH, JUNG-YUN.
BECAUSE OF HIM, SHE HAS TO HIDE HER CYNICAL AND DARK SIDE
AND DAILY PUT ON AN INNOCENT FACE. THEN ONE DAY, SHE FINDS OUT
THAT HE DISLIKES HER ANYWAY!! WHAT?! THAT'S IT! NO MORE NICE GIRL!
AND THE FIRST VICTIM OF HER RAGE IS A PLAYBOY SHE JUST MET, MA-HA.

vol.1~8

Cynical Orange

Yun JiUn

13th BOY ②

SANGEUN LEE

Translation: JiEun Park
English Adaptation: Natalie Baan

Lettering: Terri Delgado

13th Boy, Vol. 2 © 2004 SangEun Lee. All rights reserved. First published in Korea in 2004 by Haksan Publishing Co., Ltd. English translation rights in U.S.A., Canada, UK, and Republic of Ireland arranged with Haksan Publishing Co., Ltd.

English translation © 2009 Hachette Book Group, Inc.

Yen Press
Hachette Book Group
237 Park Avenue, New York, NY 10017

Visit our websites at www.HachetteBookGroup.com and www.YenPress.com.

Yen Press is an imprint of Hachette Book Group, Inc.
The Yen Press name and logo are trademarks of Hachette Book Group, Inc.

First Yen Press Edition: October 2009

ISBN: 978-0-7595-2995-3

10 9 8 7 6 5 4 3 2 1

BVG

Printed in the United States of America